WORLD GOVERNMENT, READY OR NOT!

Garry Davis

author of
My Country is the World

 THE JUNIPER LEDGE PUBLISHING CO.
Sorrento, Maine

Library of Congress Catalog Card Number 84-90504
Library of Congress Cataloguing in Publication Data

Garry Davis
World Government, Ready Or Not!
Bibliography
Includes Index
1. International Organizations—Addresses, essays,
   lectures, I Title
JX1954.D32 1984   341.2   84-23362
ISBN 0-931545-00-5

Manufactured in the United States of America
Printed by
Downeast Graphics and Printing, Inc.
Ellsworth, Maine

ACKNOWLEDGEMENTS

My first thanks to Denise Adeleine who paid the supreme price for her devotion and commitment to World Government. Without her total dedication to the functioning, virtually single-handedly, of the World Service Authority in its pioneer days in the 70's in France and then Switzerland, there might be no story to tell now; thanks to Jim Haynes, our first WSA agent in Paris, his apartment an ever open door to world citizens; to Will Reid, who literally crawled out of a Bangkok Immigration jail after nine months' incarceration, his WSA passport clutched in hand, and intrepidly made it to France on foot, testifying to an embarrassed French court in Mulhouse in 1974 when I was indicted for issuing it as to its efficacy. In this regard, my humble thanks to all those today carrying the World Passport in spite of the odds, exemplified by the few whose letters are included herein.

My thanks to Wiley Patterson Reis for her always available eagle eye in spotting non-sequitors, fuzziness and just plain mistakes in the manuscript over many months. My thanks to the WSA staff in Washington, Ingrid Dennison, Dorothy Meadows and Willie Lee, for their steadfastness, good humor and efficiency as "world officials" at extremely modest remuneration and without whom I could not have taken the time away from WSA finally to put this manuscript together. Thanks to Lorain Rothstein, Georgia Lloyd, Margaret Lloyd, Gerard Freed, and Jamie Babson for their financial aid and thanks to all those through the years too numerous to mention with whom I have discussed and refined the ideas herein. Special thanks to Joan Stadler for her indexing skill.

Then a heart-felt thanks to my children, Kristina, Troy, Tina and Kim, who have suffered an absent father for more days, months, alas, even years than I would have liked. My commitment to the larger "family" has I hope, at least in part, justified in their minds and hearts that mutually painful neglect.

A final thanks to my mother who knows and appreciates the agony of putting a book together who, from 1947 when I first conceived of my global role in life, to this day when I write these words from the back room of her home in Sorrento, Maine, has supported my mission with love and faith.

TABLE OF CONTENTS

APPENDIX

Foreword

by Edith Wynner

In 1984, two former American actors were campaigning for President: Ronald Reagan, seeking another four years in the White House; and Garry Davis (native-born American, World War II bombing pilot, stateless since 1948) who sought election as World President of the World Government of World Citizens.

WORLD GOVERNMENT, READY OR NOT is unlike any book we are likely to read this side of the year 2000. First, it is a Garry Davis Anthology and Documentary. Second, it is a record of Garry's walk-on encounters with humanity's longest running horror show, billed as THE INTERNATIONAL ANARCHY. Third, it is the most eloquent and moving. Fourth, it is a book to browse in, pause, and ponder. Ministers, strapped for a sermon topic, could hardly do better than fill several months of Sundays with readings from Garry's book. It's a must for the law schools, the courses on international law, international relations, the peace researchers, disarmers, and freezers.

How is it that this young American, with a privileged, chauffeur-driven childhood, starry-eyed with becoming a war hero, suddenly, amid all the pandemonium of war, began to listen to a different drummer? I once heard him tell a former pilot about the one experience out of all the horror that got him thinking. After each mission, bomber crews routinely released unused bombs as they flew back to their British base. Then one morning after such a mission, Garry learned that the bombs his plane had discarded, destroyed a Belgian village and its inhabitants. It was the realization that he was not only destroying the German enemy but also Allied people whom he was supposed to liberate that started the intricate process which transformed the bomber pilot into the future world citizen.

Thereafter Garry's life changed completely. Sometimes he reminds me of THE GOOD SOLDIER SCHWEIK, Jaroslav Hasek's classic satire on the World War I Austro-Hungarian Army. A good example is Garry's Chapter 12, describing his non-trip to Japan to campaign for World President. It has that subtle, sly Schweikian air of innocence. We see Garry tie all the petty functionaries into Gordian knots: the airline, the Japanese hotel staff, the bureaucrats, American Immigration, and especially the unlucky Judge Newton P. Jones who had to try to get everybody off the hook. Chapter 12 deserves to be read out loud for the fun in its splendid satire on the Sovereign Nations.

As a "name" person Garry is able to make the media help him publicize the plight of the millions of non-persons, the most wretched of the earth, the refugees, and stateless, Garry is their GLOBAL OMBUDSMAN. Their number is estimated at 16 million, but Garry thinks 20 million is more likely.

When Garry made his personal break with the war system by renouncing his American citizenship, he too entered the no-man's land of the stateless. I doubt he realized what he was getting into. But he quickly learned the facts of life of the undocumented for France wanted to deport him and when he sought asylum on United Nations' territory, he was driven off by United Nations' guards.

Garry is no theorist. Over the past 36 years he has learned by doing and being done to. Chapter 7, one of the most moving in the book, tells us what it's like to be a refugee. And once a refugee, the slide into statelessness is almost inevitable. Reading it brought tears to my eyes. Garry gives us a glimpse of some of the letters in his bulging World Service Authority files. They are a BAEDEKER GUIDE to the global misery circuit, pinpointing the latest stations of the Cross on the road to Calvary.

The letters come from those who managed to flee the land of their birth with little more than the clothes on their backs but they cannot remain in the country to which they fled, which refuses to grant them refugee status. Many have been imprisoned, tortured, released and re-arrested. And then by word of mouth they get to hear about Garry's WORLD SERVICE AUTHORITY documents and manage to send a cry for help. There is a plea from a Palestinian born in Gaza, who writes from Panama; a Burundian writes from Zaire; a South African sends his plea from Zambia; an Ethiopian writes from Iraq; a Ghanian from Lebanon; an appeal comes from an Iranian who fled to Turkey; a Kurd from Iraq sends his plea from West Germany; a Burmese finally reaches Saudi Arabia after crossing India, Pakistan, Iran and Iraq but the Saudis won't let him stay. There are letters from a Sri Lankan Tamil, a Namibian refugee in Zambia; and an Iraqi student from Yugoslavia.

These are Garry's people. Having made himself one of them, he has lived their lives in detention camps and prisons and knows the ordeals they face. Of all the global problems in desperate need of a functioning world government, Garry has taken as his domain that vast horde of refugees and stateless. No one rushed to bid against him. And he certainly has no competition from the UN High Commissioner for Refugees. Some 90,000 people have received his World Service Authority Passport, World Identity Card, World Citizen Certificate and even World Birth Certificate. Few are able to pay the fee for their "documents" or even refund the expensive postage. Many national governments accept Garry's World Passport. Ironically, a number of UN international civil servants prefer to use this passport instead of their own because of soured relationships between their nation and those to which they have to travel. Even some of the wealthy, unamused by confiscatory national taxation, like to have this Passport just in case...

During these thirty-six years, Garry bore witness to the desperate need for global government. Through large-scale practical experiments he has tried to put some reality into the eloquent but empty promises of the Universal Declaration of Human Rights. All the while he has had to wage his own struggle with apathy, poverty and rejection.

It is high time that the Nobel Peace Prize Committee, which has made so many outrageous awards, took a good look at Garry's work and gave him the Prize in 1985.

(As one of its pioneer founders in 1937, Edith Wynner and the world government movement have grown up together. Associated with Rosika Schwimmer, and Lola Maverick Lloyd, author of *World Federal Government In Maximum Terms,* Fedonat Press, NY, 1954, and co-author with Georgia Lloyd of *Searchlight On Peace Plans; Choose Your Road to World Government,* Dutton, 1944; 1949, lecturer, book reviewer of *World Peace News,* and social critic, Edith Wynner is presently Consultant to the Schwimmer-Lloyd Collection of the New York Public Library's Manuscripts and Archives Division.)

PROLOGUE

"Speak your latest conviction, and it shall be the
universal sense; for the inmost in due time becomes the
outmost, and our first thought is rendered back to us
by the trumpets of the last judgment---Nothing can bring
you peace but the triumph of principles."
                    Ralph Waldo Emerson, "Self-Reliance"

July 16, 1969: The moon--- When Buzz Aldrin, Jr., space traveler, planted his feet in the soft lunar cinders, looked toward the rising Earth through the viewfinder of his Minolta III, and activated the shutter, he took an ex-officio snapshot of the human race—or one-half of it—frenetically preparing its own nuclear destruction over questions of artificial national boundaries.

For those who have eyes to see, Adrin's phenomenal, space-visioned earthscape, exploding like a mystical yet brutally corporeal bombshell on the human psyche, revealed two of the unimpeachable yet most ignored realities of the 20th century: the global viewpoint and the incontrovertible unity of the human species.

Space-buddy and incidental United States citizen, Neil Armstrong could only bear prophetic witness, in that timeless moment of stepping off Apollo's ladder onto the moon's indifferent surface, to our universal and common destiny: "One small step for a man, a giant step for mankind."

Had he met up with any extra-terrestials at that moment, he would have had to introduce himself and co-human Aldrin as "citizens from that small planet just off the horizon."

Twenty-five years before Aldrin's and Armstrong's Space Age opener, the atomic bombs exploding over Hiroshima and Nagasaki had seemed to signal the final end to human warfare. The horror of 120,000 instantaneous deaths, lingering cancer, leukemia and disfigurement for tortuous years, seemed, when multiplied by national nuclear competition, to oblige that generation — my generation — to consider alternatives to humanicide.

"One world or none" was the christening ultimatum to the Nuclear Age.

My Country Is The World recounts in narrative form my personal and institutional response to the unprecedented challenge of nuclear war. It was my testament to Tom Paine's seemingly quixotic assertion that the world was his "country"...and mine

In the U.S. colonial era, a new nationalism was bursting into primitive and bloody bloom. Despite its initial success, one hundred, seventy-five years later — an "instant" in historical time — its flower had blossomed into a poisonous cancerous growth literally strangling our planetary turf like some mammoth diseased chrysalis, imprisoning a whole species ready for birth.

The United Nations, its ironic manifestation, was designed deliberately to prevent humankind's eventual "escape" into the free air of human sovereignty.

After becoming stateless in 1948, I had lived pragmatically the "one world" concept despite the often hazardous, sometimes humorous, and always utopian overtones. Readers will recall the unique circumstances that gave immaculate and imperative birth to the World Government, then to the World Service Authority, its administrative agency.

Today, twenty-four years and almost three trillion dollars worth of armaments after that first book, while the mortal seed of Hiroshima proliferates throughout the national world, while endemic poverty stalks one-half the human race like an avenging death-angel, while brave generals and military think-tank "specialists" calmly discuss nuclear "overkill" as workable options for resolving "conflicts" between opposing superpowers, while you and I live, nay, exist under a regime of "mutual assured destruction," this new book dedicates itself to the seemingly unmanageable proposition that *our true home, our native* land from which we draw our sustenance and well-being, *on* which we live and *from* which we will pass on, is Mother Earth herself, a pragmatic, unromantic, *legitimate* reality.

As such, it can only be protected by a functioning world government of declared world citizens.

The sun deck of the S.S. America, from where, on April 27, 1957, overlooking the Statue of Liberty, I issued a "Final Statement" as the symbolic "First World Citizen," no doubt had its counterpart on the good ship *Mary and John*, on which one of my ancestors, William Hodgkin I, arrived in the "new world" in 1632 from England. Like him, I arrived at the North American continent stateless. Would he not, I wonder, have subscribed, at least philosophically, to the notion that the individual was indeed capable of choosing his own government? For that matter, did not his descendents, indeed my ancestors, do that very thing in 1787?

This present book does not argue "for" the conceptual worldview from which derives our unitive Value framework. Humanity's wisdom heritage, hoary with

16

time yet refreshingly new, is already available now to one and all in drugstore paperbacks — a testament to the Aquarius Age of public enlightenment — in myriad "consciousness raising" movements from Arica to Zen, codified in churches, synagogues, temples, mosques and other spiritual "world territories," and taught by a plethora of gurus, swamis, yogis, and holy men and women throughout the world. This heritage needs neither defense nor affirmation here. If you still doubt the well springs of the Value world, hie thee quickly to these now myriad sources, which, if they be true, will only reflect your own good Inner Self.

No, just as Buzz Aldrin's uneering "family portrait" from neutral space is a simple, irrefutable and inescapable fact, we assert, with seeming dogmatism, the fundamental political legitimacy NOW of the human race as such, and that each human person has the right to a *bona fide* democratic political representation as a sovereign member of that legitimate race WITHOUT QUALIFICATI ONS.

In asserting that our species is already politically "legitimate," I will doubtless offend many of my fellow humans who may have a stake — however mistaken — in preserving the myth of national separativeness. But the hour is too late for such double-talk or double-think. The birth pangs of the new world order are already upon us and as necessity knows no law but its own, we are too busy attending to that long-heralded and momentous birth to still the shrill cries of infidelity.

Politically the world seems to have regressed since my original declaration of world citizenship over 30 years ago. Whereas in 1948 72 nations existed, today there are over 170 while innumerable ethnic groups claim the right of self-determination and eventual statehood. By the year 2,000, if the trend of political balkanization continues, our "global village" will be divided by over 200 "sovereign" nation-states, each imposing its absolute rule — as in feudal times — on you and me, wherever we happen to be born or reside.

As the nation-state increasingly exposes its impotence to resolve major problems facing its citizens, as national leaders daily reveal their blind drive for national power under the guise of defenders of the public trust, betraying the **global** public trust, as nuclear proliferation drives ever deeper the nails of humanity's coffin, the aware individual, facing the ultimate reality that he or she *has nothing more to lose* will turn desperately and hopefully to the only avenue left to earthly salvation: world citizenship and its sovereign institutions.

Already, there are millions of world citizens registered one way or another from virtually every corner of the world. This volume addresses itself particularly to them as a "How To Do It" manual to increase their effectiveness and political potency.

For dedicated one-worlders in allied organizations, this book is intended as absolutist "salt" to savor their relativist peace efforts. I confess I am doubly hard on them. Luke-warm commitment is not enough. Only those willing to live . . . or die **for humanity itself** are worthy of the name "peacemaker."

17

How many cry "Peace, peace," yet condone war?

Stretching beyond the "island" of this embryonically-organized world public is that vast sea of concerned, yet unmondialized citizens, fed up with the politics-as-usual, turned-off, cancelled-out, crying "a pox on all your houses," who know "the scoundrels are in power," but feel helpless and confused as to effective solutions to both their immediate and long-term problems.

For better or for worse, the world is their country too. The price of their survival is its protection and nurturing by democratic world institutions.

Then there are the sceptics, the pessimists, the prophets of doom of all ilks, the "sunshine patriots," the cop-outs. They will only be convinced by unassailable arguments and demonstrable truth. Like Arjuna of the Bhagavad-Gita, they may be closest to emancipation. . .and furthest from knowing it, just as the noon-day sun casts the deepest shadows. A converted sceptic risks becoming a sage.

Finally, there is the youth. . .the future. Since the writing of *My Country Is The World*, I have sired three new members of our species, Troy, Tina and Kim. While they accept with incredible and fearless nonchalance the proposition of one world and one human race, they have trouble understanding national frontiers and wars. The contrast of my 50 day imprisonment in 1975 in the Lucerne city jail for entering Switzerland "illegally," while Troy studied 80 km. away at *L'ecole de l'Humanite'* in the Swiss Alps, starkly revealed to him and his schoolmates the blatant and repressive duality exhibited daily by the world of separate states.

To you Troy, Tina and Kim and to all your generation, this book is primarily dedicated. By simple inheritance, the world is yours. Claim it. It is your absolute right. We, your parents, can do no more than build the bridge to one world. You must cross it to the Promised Land, the Millenium, on the other side.

"We hold these truths to be self-evident, that all men are created equal, that they are endowed by their Creator with certain inalienable Rights, that among these are Life, Liberty and the pursuit of Happiness. That to secure these rights, Governments are instituted among Men, deriving their just powers from the consent of the governed. That whenever any Form of Government becomes destructive of these ends, it is the Right of the People to alter or abolish it, and to institute new Government, laying its foundations on such principles and organizing its powers in such form, as to them shall seem most likely to effect their Safety and Happiness."

U.S. Declaration of Independence, 4 July, 1776

CHAPTER 1

"There is no first step to world government. World government is the first step."

Emery Reves *Anatomy of Peace*

THE ELLSWORTH DECLARATION
Garry Davis
4 September, 1953

"As long as there are sovereign nations possessing great power, war is inevitable. There is no salvation for civilization, or even the human race, other than the creation of a world government."

Albert Einstein

(Delivered at the City Hall, Ellsworth Maine, U.S,A,)

Good Evening, dear friends:

This meeting has its origin about five years ago in Paris when I walked out of the United States Embassy as a sort of political nonentity, or stateless person. My story, that is, what led to that action, what happened afterwards, and where I find myself today have become matters of public interest, if only because anyone who has the audacity to deal with nationstates directly as if he were equal or even superior in sovereignty, whether he is considered a fool or a sage, is at least an object of curiosity.

It is my experience however that much misunderstanding and even misrepresentation has occurred in the public mind concerning me. This is, to a great extent, my own fault. I have found myself unable many times to explain clearly and concisely the basic reasons for my actions. Perhaps I shouldn't have tried. Actions speak for themselves, and socalled reasons often confuse as much as clarify. But

21

also, the general press often print but half the story or sensationalize what is ordinarily quite a commonplace happening to entice the buying public. Flashy headlines replace objective and full coverage. This in turn gives rise to the cry of publicity seeker and the man stands condemned whatever his motives or sincerity. Mostly however I think that the subject itself is confusing and lacking in precedent, the subject being the wholeness of individual man, or his inherent total sovereignty with full authority and rights contrasted today against the seeming absolutism of the sovereign state expressed in nationalism. . .and his inherent cooperative urge as contrasted with a fiercely competitive economy. . .how he can reassert himself in modern terms, what techniques he can use, what philosophy he can call upon, what moral fibre he can evoke in the face of giant immoral pressures and fears, what historical precedents he has, and finally what human support he can command around him, both individually and institutionally. The subject in short is unlimited man's revolt against a limited society and demands full command of every ounce of an individual's spiritual, intellectual, and physical stature. In the light of this problem, my personal limitations become glaringly obvious.

But once more I find it necessary to speak in public knowing full well the dangers just mentioned. I may confuse as much as clarify; the press may mock or cry publicity-seekers, or merely ignore; and again I may reveal my limitations in not embracing the full subject. But it is necessary first of all because I find myself in my homeland, America, and in fact in the very seat of my birth, Hancock County, in very unusual circumstances, and I want those about me, my fellow Americans, to know what I am about; exactly what these circumstances are, and what I intend to do about them; and secondly, I feel a duty and responsibility to my many friends in Europe and throughout the world who have supported me in the past and shown me their hearts and minds with openness and deep conviction, a duty which I have not always fulfilled and a responsibility which I have not always accepted, but which tonight I will try to fulfill and accept to the full measure of my ability.

To introduce my subject, let me say that though you and I here are friends and from the same soil, we are separated by as wide a gulf as man has ever artificially created. I was a bomber pilot during the last war, and I first discovered this artificial gulf between men when flying over Germany bombing German civilians and cities. Till then I hadn't thought much about my fellowman, or myself as a member of a world community. I had been too busy growing up, having fun, and trying to earn a living. But in that starkly realistic situation, behind all the emotion and hysteria, I was literally forced to consider, for the first time I might add, the seeming foolishness of one group of human beings dropping bombs on another group, all members of the same human family. Certainly like them I had good reasons for my participation in the fight. Fascism was a public menace, a social disease, a cancerous scourge, and had to be wiped out at all costs. . .even

22

at the cost of **my** death and that of my buddies-in-arms. But even so, I had to wonder what was wrong with the organization of our human community when a social disease like Fascism was allowed to become so plague-like that only an opposing plague, no matter how justified, could halt its advance. I confess my political naivete while flying that engine of destruction, but I couldn't really understand why our leaders had let things get that far.

I wasn't alone in this wondering of course. Millions of young people were rudely shocked into the naked awareness that the social plague called war was a real part of their life. If nothing else, we were forced to start thinking about our responsibilities in this regard.

After the war I returned to my profession in the theatre. But the wondering continued underneath. Though we had a supranational organization called the United Nations supposedly to solve the problems of war and peace, poverty and plenty, the still absolute sovereign states, after a flurry of postwar disarmament, continued more hysterically than ever their superarmament race, especially my own and Russia, developing superbombs and super methods of killing off human beings. Taxes were increasing on individual citizens, relief budgets were cut as defense budgets were increased – though eminent scientists kept telling us that there was no defense against the absolute weapons now developed– more and more people went hungry, or were illclothed, or illhoused, refugees were dealt with apathetically or begrudgingly, the world's children were neglected, and general fear and insecurity were becoming commonplace.

Was it possible, I asked myself, that once again I was to be uprooted from my everyday life, this time to become a part of an even greater plague called World War III? Hadn't we learned anything from the last war, or the one before that, or the multitude of wars stretching back throughout man's bloody history? Does each generation have to go through this superfoolishness? Are we all so bankrupt of reason and moral fibre that we can't live in peace and cooperation with one another in one physical world? These questions and many more pounded at me with increasing urgency during the years of '46 and '47. What should I do? I kept asking myself. Where could the common man like me, the man-in-the-street, the fundamental integer without which there is no society, register his protest against this insanity? Where could I vote against war and poverty, and for peace and wellbeing? Who represented me, not only in the United States, but in the world community as well? In the U.S., there is law and order, government, a central control or brain, direct representatives of the people therein, if only in a political sense. Outside there is chaos and anarchy, a jungle world wherein raw force is the deciding factor, where individuals are helpless, and where only armies move in sinister and secret patterns. There is no World Parliament, no world constitution, no world law, or world economy, in short, no world brain or government. Instead on our one planet, there are about 80 separate and fully-sovereign political and economic units, all attempting to govern and provide securi-

23

ty for their individual citizens. Some are rich, some poor: some are large, some small. But all are absolute in their political power over their citizens, just as the original 13 American colonies or States were in 1780.

It's as if your body had 80 or so separate, and uncoordinated compartments, each with its individual command posts or brain, and each acting at crosspurposes and giving opposing orders to the various organs. What would be the result? Well obviously, we call such an uncoordinated man an idiot, and because we know he can't provide for himself, but eventually will either starve or be destroyed in some way, we put him into an institution for his and the public good.

But an objective observer on Mars, or indeed even on Earth, might very well apply the same idiocy to the organism we call humanity and of which we are all integral parts or cells whether we like it or not. He would see quite clearly that it lacks a unified coordinating center, or world brain. . .or government.

But what about the United Nations? Isn't that set up to do the coordinating job, to be the brain of humanity? The answer of course, divorced of sentiment and ideals, is implicit in the actions of the very nations which are members of the U.N. Behind the inspiring ideals, the noble convictions, and imposing facade, and discounting the paralyzed specialized agencies set up to deal with real human problems, or the educational aspects, the United Nations is merely a meeting-place for the representatives of some, not all of the nationstates to try to win world public opinion for their particular interests. As such, it is an effective smoke-screen behind which the most powerful nations carry on their absolute nationalistic policies. In short, it is neither united, nor is it inclusive.

I am aware in making these remarks of the high regard that the UN as such is held by many here in the US, but it is vitally necessary to divorce ourselves from false sentiment and vain idealism so that the naked reality of the world's condition can be faced if just and reasonable solutions to human problems are to be found. Certainly the United Nations is of immense value to me, the utterly neutral man, for by it I can see in startling clarity just what we lack and need. I might add that my experience indicates that there are few within the UN itself who are not being made increasingly aware of this lack and need.

After I became aware of the world's basic anarchic condition, which was certainly a spiritual as well as a political and economic anarchy, I like millions of others, was faced with the personal problem of what was **my** responsibility to the total world community? How could I relate myself directly and realistically with my fellowman, spiritually, socially and physically, not only as a protest, but as a practical way to fill in the vacuous area of world anarchy? I was truly an American, by birth, by upbringing, by forefathers, by conviction and by ideals, but I wanted no part of nationalism. But could the two be separated? And if so, what then was the position of the individual who managed such an unprecedented separation? In other words, how could he make an effective protest against a nationalism turned violent which thwarted and perverted humanitarian tendencies till men turned into mobs killing each other mercilessly and at the same time build his life on the constructive principle of social cooperation rather than on the jungle competition for bare necessities he saw all around him?

I wanted a corporate or federal or unitive world government to resolve the social organizational problem which in turn would resolve the economic problem with a world unitive economy; but first of all, I wanted a spiritual kinship, an awareness of a community of men derived from the same source, one human Organism, One Total Man, or more popularly, a world religion or universal church based on brotherhood, truth and love. From this, I knew and felt, would flow the other worldly institutions. Naive and oversimplified perhaps, but nonetheless sincere and heartfelt.

In personal revolt against nationalism to which I no longer wanted to contribute, and against raw competition with my fellowmen which I didn't understand and wasn't trained for, I went to Paris in May of 1948, and on the 25th of that month, before a U.S. Vice-Consul in the Embassy on the Champs Elysee, I took the formal oath of renunciation of my national citizenship, which is allowed by the Nationality Act of 1940. I did not deny being an American, which was an inherent part of me anyway, but I declared what I truly was in a larger worldly sense. . . .I claimed to a world citizen.

This of course was no new declaration, no original thought. Socrates made it, Tom Paine made it. Most philosophers, sages, and spiritual leaders have affirmed its principles of unity in one way or another. But there is no monopoly on such a universal truth. An so, now a common man had made it. To me, world citizenship expressed positively and clearly man's individual wholeness or completeness, his personal uniqueness and individuality, plus his fundamental unity with all other men, spiritully as well as physically.

The general press however, mockingly referred to me as "the self-styled world citizen". It is a fitting commentary on our present-day political institutions when an ordinary citizen must style himself that which they presume to represent, but cannot, and then be mocked for it in the nation's press.

Here in America, where national citizenship is idealized and sentimentalized beyond all reason, I was publicly ridiculed. Many called me simply a crackpot with a hairbrained idea; others thought I was merely one more publicity seeker of which America apparently had hundreds of thousands, though this was a pretty desperate way merely to get publicity. Others, less emotional and more objective, called me simply unrealistic, or impractical, or ahead of the times, though at the same time they usually were obliged to add that the world was in pretty much of a mess and **something** should be done. But generally, I was considered merely one more symbol of youthful confusion, and a sort of international orphan. . .or world waif. . .and very unAmerican.

I argued that to be an American meant infinitely more than just to be a United States citizen. Americans, I said, held fast to principles of liberty, democracy, public welfare, and world peace, principles for which my forefathers suffered persecution, worked and died and upon which the nation was founded. Who was the true American, I asked, the man who stood for the above principles, or the chauvinistic nationalistic or warprofiteer? But my voice was drowned out in derision.

I must add here that I did not ask others to follow or even not to follow my particular action. I merely said that it was my way, and that if others were concerned about the same problems, they must find their particular way of renouncing absolutist nationalism and extending their loyalty to the total world community since at that time there was no one central and neutral organization to which all could belong as universal as humanity itself.

But even so, my birthplace hadn't changed, nor my upbringing, nor my ancestors. Also when I dropped my hand no longer a US citizen, I was no wiser, no more industrious, no more patient. The sun still shone on me, and the rain still fell on me; I still had to eat, breathe and work; I still liked music and dancing and the theatre; I could still laugh and cry, or be serious or tell a joke; my friends were still my friends, and people who didn't like me anyway, still didn't like me anyway. In short, I was still very much me, despite my loss of national citizenship, and still very much a part of the total human community, and in fact, now a more direct part. In the real things, I hadn't changed a whit.

But like the pebble dropping on the surface of the water, I did make a ripple. . .on the surface. And to many people here in America especially, failing to dintinguish the surface from the actual body of water, or the illusion of reality from the Real Itself, here in this dualistic society, I had dared to call into question the fundamental, the essential, and so, the secure. To these, US citizenship was absolute security, despite A-bombs, and two world wars. Also I had renounced "the American way of life" meaning principally the security of physical comforts and even luxuries. And so I was considered an outcast and a heretic on two counts, politically and physically. Morally, few in America, questioned my motives or actions. Needless to say, I was a great trial to my family and friends during this period.

Well, what happens to a man who finds himself plumb in the middle of the world anarchy, where there are no political representatives at any level of government, where no authority is prepared to accept or identify you, where you have no stable home and no legal right to live, where you have no influence because you have no political status and so where friends are either afraid or reluctant to come to your aid, where human rights are laughed at, and one is mocked for presuming to affirm even that he or she is a human being, where every petty official becomes your master before whom you must bow and scrape if you find yourself obliged to ask for some meager necessity till you are screaming inside and ready either to kill, or ask God's help, torn between the two, where indignity is mixed with contempt and pity, where life is a series of waiting-in-line at a

26

window marked "alien" or "Stranger" behind which sits an indifferent clerk with only rubber stamps in front of him which determine your very existence, where the human spirit is crushed out of all shape and recognition until it withers of its own accord, where finally apathy and resignation nibble dumbly at the mind and heart till hope is gone.

Is this an exaggeration, coming purely from my imagination? Is the situation so bad? Ask the over 15,000,000 refugees in Germany, many living in made-over concentration camps. Ask the hundreds of thousands of stateless people in France and England who are allowed to live there but legally not allowed to work. Ask the North and South Koreans made homeless by a "foreign" power's war. Ask the stateless people of Africa and Asia whose very homes, miserable hovels that they are, are owned by colonial masters, and whose rights as human beings are ridiculed and scorned till they seethe in indignation and revolt and are ready to accept any tyrant who promises them freedom and more bread.

Ask me even.

Directly after my renunciation, my learning about these things began. The little clerk at the French police station had fifteen stamps in front of her, and nowhere to use them when I presented myself at her desk. She couldn't handle an ex-U.S. citizen who called himself a world citizen, born in America, yet residing in France, and without papers of any kind. **That** situation was in no lawbook or regulations manual she knew of. Legally I was outside the framework of the sovereign state of France. But physically I was inside. I had committed no crime or harmed anyone. My interests were purely humanitarian, positive, and outgoing, yet, being outside the law, I was considered a criminal for merely existing and suject to imprisonment. Such is the extraordinary position of a man caught in the lawless area outside of national sovereignty. Such also is the position that each powerful nation finds itself in in regard to other nations. It becomes suspect by another nation simply because there is no legal control of its actions by the other nation. By stepping outside the control of any nation-state, I discovered gradually that I had actually become sovereign in much the same way. And so I was suspect by that frustrated civil servant and by every government official I came up against thereafter. Finally in some desperation to keep me from jail, she stamped the back of a letter I had from the American Embassy in receipt of my passport. This gave me three pseudo-legal months to live in France. I asked her what I should do after three months. She shrugged and waved me out. After all, it wasn't her affair.

Just before the three months were up, the United Nations took over the Palais de Chaillot in Paris declaring that property international territory in a symbolic ceremony between Robert Shumann and Trygve Lie. Facing jail in France if I remained there, and jail in any other country I went to, I was literally forced to seek political sanctuary at the headquarters of this highest political authority in the world. It was the world organization after all; I would be privileged to present it with its first real citizen.

I remained on the steps of one of the U.N. Buildings for 6 days and nights. During this time, the curious but kind people of Paris supplied me with bread, cheese, fruit, and vin ordinaire. During that period I wrote a petition to the delegates through Mr. Lie asking for simple recognition of world citizenship. On the seventh day, I received my answer. I was expelled forcibly. The U.N. Secretariat, not having any police, requested the French Ministry of the Interior to please "invade" their so-called international territory and remove this piece of international flotsam. So on Sept. 17th about 50 French policemen wearing their sternest looks, came in, took me against my will and deposited me in France again, a distance of about 10 yards.

The U.N. could have done the job of course, but it might have looked a bit foolish for a squad of U.S. or Russian marines carring-out such a nonmilitary objective.

This somewhat ludicrous removal was the U.N.'s way of saying to me, "We don't represent you, so how can you expect us to recognize world citizenship? But further, we **can't** represent you because you're a stateless person, and we're composed only of states. As such, we, the United Nations, represent division and fear, and eventual war, whereas you, a neutral human being, obviously represent unity and peace. You have a sort of human sovereignty inherent in you, whereas we have only state sovereignty to link us ,but contrarily we have private or vested interests to protect at all costs; you don't, because you have nothing to lose. You are able to take our ideals, aspirations and hopes and apply them directly in human affairs. We are unable to do so because they conflict with our sovereign statehood. Now you can see why we must get rid of you even to calling in a national police force and facing ridicule for doing so. Your naive but natural request for recognition of world citizenship exposes our limitations, and that we can't afford."

This is the major lesson I have learned. The world's greatest statesmen, the ablest politicians, the national policy makers, the Presidents, Kings, Congressmen, Parliamentarians, and all lesser state servants, can only mark time until we, on the very bottom of the pile, the socalled man-in-the-street, the John and Jane Does of the world, the simple human being with nothing to lose but his fears, make a concerted, cooperative, and determined effort to move into world peace and prosperity. By "into" I mean we must actually declare freedom and security an inherent part of our essential humanity, and then apply it scientifically, technically and spiritually in our daily lives. Until that is done, the statesman remains trapped between principle and practice; he has nothing to lead or govern except that which exists, and we all remain chained to our insecurities, poverties, and fears.

That concerted and cooperative one world movement until now has been undefined and unorganized. But it has been generating in parts. Hundreds of nongovernmental international organizations reflecting every facet of man's interests

28

including innumerable peace and welfare organizations are ready for a coordinated, cooperative, corporate one world organization. Millions of ordinary people everywhere are certainly ready to recognize their essential kinship, to cooperate in harmony, share their labor and services, pool their resources, both intellectual and physical, and benefit each other individually and mutually. Many small nations even are ready to relinquish a part of their sovereignty to such a supranational authority having provisions in their constitutions for such.

I myself quite by circumstance became a focal point for such a common and neutral meeting-ground in Europe in 1948-49 and '50.

After my formal ejection from the U.N. territory, and from subsequent events such as an organized interruption from the U.N. balcony on Nov. 22nd wherein with friends I asked that humanity be given a representative in the affairs directly affecting us, and after two large meetings in Paris which were attended to overflowing, a spontaneous one world and world citizenship popular movement came into being which was genuinely planet-wide.

I was flooded with hundreds of thousands of letters from all corners of the globe, and from peoples of all nations, colors, sects, races, occupations, and origins. Only the Americans and Russians were cool to or skeptical of the idea, not because of the American or Russian people themselves, but because their leaders were too busy fearing, insulting and arming against each other to pay much attention to such an unrealistic third force as one world and world citizenship, especially if it began in the giant middle world between the two opposing forces. "Not economically practical," said the American businessman; "Not politically practical," said the Russian communist.

I was personally attacked from Pravda and the U.S. press alike, one with vitriol and personal character assassination, the other with patronizing spankings or veiled suggestions of mental derangement. Pravda called me a U.S. bought dupe, exporting American world government along with detective stories and powdered eggs. The U.S. press inferred that I was naively and unwittingly playing into the hands of the Communists by creating a giant peace movement in the West, and why didn't I go to Russia to begin my movement there, or if not, then come home and go into a defense plant...while I was being psychoanalyzed.

But to the rest of mankind, caught in the middle of this two-dimensional dialectic between two mighty physical forces, the reality of one world was overwhelming and the fact of world citizenship was grounded in truth.

But even if there were millions of one worlders and world citizens, very few agreed on general one world strategy and practically no one agreed on world citizenship tactics.

From the podium of the General Assembly of the United Nations on Dec. 10, 1948, came an appeal for help, which contained both one world strategy and world citizenship tactics. It came in the form of a document called *The Universal Declaration of Human Rights*. In effect, it was the greatest mandate to organize ourselves rationally ever given to mankind as a corporate body. On the other hand, it implied with uncompromising clarity that the United Nations as such is **not** that rational organization. The mandate was given to everyone on the planet. No one was excluded. When declared, it was hailed as a milestone in man's collective efforts to achieve freedom and security. But so far, five years later, it has not achieved freedom and security. So far, it's just another piece of paper with stirring words on it. Why is this? Why didn't men and women take this document, affirm the rights therein, and oblige their leaders to have them properly secured in a world organization? The reason is simple. But it may be a hard one to accept. Human rights apply only to humans, and until you and I throughout the world declare ourselves as such and organize that declaration so that wise and practical leaders can represent us as human beings, we can only expect less than human treatment in world affairs from our present leaders.

The very first article is a tool of mighty power cutting through prejudice, dogma, artificial beliefs, and general ignorance like a giant scythe cuts through weeds. For it is the expression of the Prime Law of Unity which binds all men as brothers both spiritually and naturally. All the other articles flow from it. It throws into bold relief all those who divide men artificially. It says: *All men are born free and equal in dignity and rights; they are endowed with reason and conscience and should act towards one another in a spirit of brotherhood.*

Here is no sectarianism, nor chauvinism. First of all here is the affirmation of the spiritual truth that all men are directly connected with their divine source or origin through individual conscience. This is the ontological approach to religion, that is, that each and every human being is immediately and intimately related to the Spirit or Deity, and can perceive that relationship intuitively without outside intervention. In other words, it reaffirms Christ's words, *The kingdom of God is within you,"* or Socrates' admonition to *"Know thyself,"* or the Hindu Bhagavad Gita's constant references to the All Self in every man.

Then this article affirms that all men are endowed with reason, or the ability to think and solve problems of physical survival and social relationships. What is this but a clear go-ahead to organize in a reasonable manner the affairs of our common social community? But how much reason is applied today in the political circles of the world? How reasonable is this foolish national pride, this organized manufacture of lies and half-truths and artificially created hates between tribes of humans in the world community, this hypocrisy called diplomacy which any child could expose, and which wouldn't last a minute in a town meeting? How much reason is there to areas of surplus food rotting on wharfs and railroad sidings and other areas of pitiful and unnecessary starvation, or periods when millions are unemployed, yet factories lay idle because it doesn't pay to produce? It is needless to go on. The facts are unlimited to demonstrate that not reason but utter foolishness actually governs our world community despite our most fervent aspirations and lip-service to ideals.

But if men are reasonable and guided by conscience, it is clear that men in general have no representatives in the world area. No one yet speaks for humanity in toto. We, as a world's people, are inarticulate, inchoate even, because we are unorganized. The *Universal Declaration of Human Rights* recognizes this for it gives us the green light to organize a world electorate to elect such world representatives from our midst. Article 21 (3) says; *The will of the people shall be the basis of the authority of government; this shall be expressed in periodic and genuine elections which shall be universal and equal suffrage and shall be held by secret vote or by equivalent free voting procedures.*

There is no mention of what people. . .just **the** people. That only means all the people there are. Do you begin to see, however, how this One People is denied in the very council chambers of this so-called world organization? That the reality of human community includes not only all those nations and peoples of the UN but also Germans, Italians, Africans, Ceylonese, Japanese, Chinese, Rumanians, Bulgarians, and of course all stateless people and those under colonial domination? In short, everybody?

We all belong to this One People whether we like it or not and despite our external differences. Though I am an American, technically I am a stateless person, so I fit into the World's People category directly, with no intervening citizenship. This is by no means a unique situation, but in fact quite common. And that, while it might seem to be a sign of utter chaos and despair, actually is a condition of great hope. In other words, there are millions like me **with nothing to lose.**

But what about our collective will. Is there such a thing? This is the most difficult thing I have experienced to make people believe. . .that in fact everyone wants just about the same things. These are expressed usually by slogans such as world peace, universal wellbeing, and personal freedom. But slogans like this have hidden other things. So people have become skeptical and cynical and bitter. It is the disease of our generaltion. But nonetheless, the collective will for such things exists and in greater quantity and power than any single man dreams.

If this is true, how then is it to be gathered, proclaimed, manifested, and secured? The Universal Declaration in Article 28 gives us a clue. It says that: *"Everyone is entitled to the* **social and international order** *in which the rights and freedoms set forth in this declaration can be fully realized."* In other words, social and international **order,** not anarchy, are conditions under which rights pertaining to all human beings alone can be secured. Order of course means law and government. International order means international law and government.

Obviously, there is no such thing today.

Human rights and freedoms apply only to a select few today. Yet Article 2 states that: *"***Everyone** *is entitled to the rights and freedoms set forth in this declaration, without distinctions of any kind, such as race, color, sex, language, religion, political or other opinion, national or social origin, property, birth or other status."* This only affirms what any reasonable man and every mother knows from time immem-

31

orial, that all men and women are indeed members of the same human community, and that subsequently there are no second-class world citizens.

No second-class world citizens! Do you realize what that means? It means that as well as being Greek, French, German, Russian, Indian, Chinese, Brazilian, Yugoslavian, Swedish, Italian, Malayan, Japanese, American or any other group, as well as being white, brown, black, red or yellow, as well as being an artisan or a craftsman, a merchant or a technician, a common worker or a king, a housewife or a queen, a national citizen or a stateless person, a man or a woman, a democrat or a republican, a Catholic or a Protestant, or Hindu, or Buddhist, or Moslem or Taoist or Jew, we are all united in world citizenship because we're all united in freedoms and human rights, as yet uncodified in world law.

There are other rights defined. But these few mentioned are enough to go ahead full steam with the actual organization of our one humanity.

If you agree with me up to this point— and I have really said nothing very extraordinary, nothing new certainly, perhaps even things which are so obvious and simple that they don't bear repeating— but if we are agreed at least in principle, let us be convinced as I am, from bitter and sometimes humiliating experience, that we must now help ourselves. No one will hand us freedom and security on a silver platter. No one can. Who can exercise your reason or conscience for you? Who can put them to work but you? Each man and woman here is abolutely and solely responsible for his or her thoughts and actions regarding his or her personal welfare. Let us first then secure ourselves deep within our own reason and conscience for only then will we be able to find a practical way to the wide glorious world of sovereign humanity.

In short, we must personally, each one of us, recognize ourselves as **individually sovereign,** that is, a world unto ourselves, an authority, sure, capable, self-motivated, self-contained, and self-governed, a full awareness of that part of us which is conscience and its servant reason. Let us realize fully that each one of us throughout the world, endowed with this very same conscience which links us all to the same Spirit or Origin, and reason, which links us all to each other, is in real fact then a **world** sovereign, and as such stands whole and free in the one community of men, above nations, sectional prides, narrow prejudices and jealousies, a World Patriot.

This is what I wish to affirm here tonight, world sovereignty. As human beings, we are all world sovereigns, the social and physical popular expression being world citizens, and no nation or power is able to deny that sovereignty or to deprive us of one iota of it.

This alone is democracy, for it includes all.

I have gone through five years of intense personal and public experience since my renunciation in Paris, and my affirmation of world sovereignty here tonight has been reached therefore after most careful and serious consideration. It is not a gesture of childish impulse or maudlin sentiment; it is not abstract idealism or fanatical necessity. It is a simple and obvious fact recognized now by peoples and governments alike. Further world sovereignty linked with world citizenship is at last that undefined concept which relates spiritual, social and physical fact together to make a totality of man.

I said that it is grounded on sound spiritual, social, and physical fact. What are these facts or Prime Laws which are recognized universally by peoples and institutions alike? Well, I have already stated them here in many ways, but in brief they may be expressed as follows:

1. There is but One Diety or Ideal, Goal, Vision, Absolute, Origin, Source, Mind, Spirit, Reality, Understanding, Wisdom, Truth, and so on, unitively conceived and intuitively, that is, by conscience, perceived, of which I am a living and integral part, as is all mankind; and

2. There is but one world, which is ideologically or intellectually understood, as my and mankind's natural home despite social groupings such as tribal, communal, regional, geographical, cultural, historical, ancestral, lingual, or professional and which constitutes my total social enviroment or community; and

3. There is but one physical human family, which is instinctively felt by common fundamental needs and wants, despite color, race, sex, birth, property, economic or other physical status, and thus one common citizenship.

Further, I am convinced that the full recognition of these three fundamental or Prime Laws constitute a spiritual, social, and physical trinity, in that the first represents personal or individual freedom, the second, social or communal justice or fairness, and the third, physical security and well-being, upon which the rational organization of human society must be based for the increased happiness of all.

It is on these three laws that you and I and the rest of our fellow men and women can move together out of the foolish, wasteful, chaotic, poverty-stricken circumstances we find ourselves in today into the prosperity and happiness of a new world of complete and joyous humanity.

I have said tonight that we must help ourselves to peace, security and well-being. I have said that our leaders were stuck and needed our help. I have affirmed world sovereignty and world citizenship as a spiritual, social, and physical fact; I have given the trinity of Prime Laws in confirmation of this fact. I have shown that people everywhere are ready for peace and prosperity, that the world is in dire need of these two. Then I have shown that only an international authority, a world brain, a supranational government can coordinate the immense diversity which is humanity, and make it live and breathe as it must if we, its coordinate parts, are to live and evolve. Further I have shown that the nations themselves,through the United Nations, have given We, the People, the mandate to create this world government through the *Universal Declaration of Human Rights* .

Here in this Town Hall in Ellsworth, Maine, in the sovereign United States of America, I, a world citizen, exist in a world anarchy. I am no longer able to tolerate such a condition. By the authority vested in me as a world sovereign, it is my duty and my responsibility to myself and to my humanity to hereby proclaim for myself a world government with full legal powers and prerogatives based on the 3 Prime Laws of One God, One World, and one Mankind. This government for the moment exists only in my person, but since all men are world citizens with full world sovereignty based on a full recognition of the 3 Prime Laws if they but affirm them, the proclamation of world government is everyman's right, privilege, and responsibility.

Presumptuous undertaking? Not at all, for nothing less will serve us, and we must risk being called presumptuous by narrow minds and closed hearts. I will answer that all new-borns are presumptuous in their demands for sustenance and attention and I am no exception. The world is certainly filled with wiser and better men, and I am the first to admit personal failings. But that confession doesn't alter my need. A world government is here born and if there are wiser and better men, let them come forward challenged by its obvious failings and helplessness. Let humanity have their services by all means. Let the spiritual leaders and Gurus, the World Teachers come from their ashrams, their meditative retreats and monastic centers in this grave hour of our common need, and give us their moral council and guidance. Let them breathe into this newly born government, given life by one insignificant man-in-the-street, the spiritual substance it must have if it is to prosper and serve men wisely.

It must have material sustenance as well if it is to grow in health, substantial physical nourishment. In fact, ideally, it must have all the resources of our common Mother Earth if it is to benefit all the citizens thereon, and a world government by definition excludes no one from its benefits. Materially speaking, our planet and our human community is like a giant factory supplying all the material needs to all who live at once on it and in it. And the sooner we short circuit the road that is travelled by millions daily to satisfy the world's material needs, the sooner we will all have more leisure and means for recreation, whether social, intellectual, artistic, or physical. Obviously the less effort we give to the means of life, the more time and energy we have to enjoy the ends of life, according to our individual interpretation. So our scientists and technicians carry the banner of progress for the human race, as they lighten the means and increase our opportunity to enjoy the ends.

Thus to solve the problem of managing our common factory for the mutual benefit of all, the most able scientists, technicians, managers, and administrators must come forward to give us their services.

Without this scientific management on the physical level of human activity, gross and criminal waste, inefficiency, giant unrests between workers leading to class struggles, bitter divisions between management and labour, and finally, when the national politicians can no longer govern the two opposed factions, the explosion of international war in the anarchic areas, leading to all the plagues of the uncoordinated or idiot man referred to earlier. In short, no sane business man would or could run his organization for a minute the way our world factory is run without going bankrupt.

Already many cooperative communities and industries exist, as well as large corporations in which complete coordination or cooperation plus scientific management is the guiding principle. The higher the degree of coordination by scientific management, the more successful the business. These understand fully the tremendous benefits which accrue to each member of a corporate or cooperative body. Full material protection within the corporate body is guaranteed. The largest corporate body of course, though still utterly uncoordinated, is the human species itself, and like the human body, only thrives in health and happiness when its various component parts are coordinated and working in harmony with its brain and spirit.

Therefore the third Prime Law of One physical human family must equate integrally with the first and second unitive laws. One for all and all for one must be the prime basis for a World Citizen's economy. This economy must evolve without disturbing one present law, but in fact utilizing certain economic laws now existent in every country for its prerogatives. Thus a World Citizen's Corporation must come into being which has as its purpose the complete integration and coordination of all the physical resources, means of production, and labor of the entire planet, for the direct benefit of all the consumers thereon, which excludes no one. Such a one world consumer's cooperative, linked to no politics or private interests because of its very inclusive nature, would allow each and every working world citizen to benefit directly from his or her labor and the labor of his or her neighbor throughout the total world community. But further, it would at last give complete material security to those who were unable to work due either to age or physical disability. It would eventually link up all existent cooperative and corporate endeavors, all specialized nongovernmental world agencies now paralyzed due to national and competitive tensions, to one scientifically but democratically-elected World Parliament or Corporate Congress whose sole duty would be to run our world factory efficiently and harmoniously for the benefit of all the producers and consumers therein.

The World Government here proclaimed and open to all, will undertake to initiate such a World Citizen's Corporation as its proper corollary on the physical or economic level of human activity.

For moral and physical support of this endeavor, it calls upon the mothers of the world, who are so intimately connected with the physical continuance and well-being of the human race. If men be in fact World Citizens, so every mother is a World Mother since her child is born first into the Family of Man itself. And so, they are the great heart of humanity, the well of infinite compassion, love and pity that nurtures us from our very birth. They are the breast of plenty, and without their blessing and heartfelt support, we will remain in the realm of idle words and vain idealism.

Then we call to the common citizenry from which we have come, to our brothers in the world community. We call them in all corners of the globe, in every marketplace, in every secluded retreat, and from all walks of life. We call to the reason and conscience which we know to be a part of every man. In the name of Humanity of which he is an integral and valuable unit, we ask him to identify himself, not only as a citizen of his own hearth, his local community, his region, and his nation, but also as a citizen of the entire world as his natural and fundamental right as well as duty. Until we do this and begin to work together, we will continue to deserve the slaveries, both spiritual and economic we today endure. In short, we dare to proclaim mankind's total existence as the highest allegiance and the most noble and elevating duty of its separate component parts or individuals.

And in Humanity's name, in which any reasonable man may speak without fear, I, a World Sovereign, hereby claim the territory of the entire earth as the proper home and the rightful possession of all mankind. As an actual symbol of that ownership, and for the now existent World Government, I claim here in the soil of my birth, the dot of land on which I now stand, as World Territory. Let it be henceforth known as World Citizen's Point, and marked only as 68 °25′30 ″ Longitude, 44 °32′30 ″Latitude.

Let all World Citizens accept this point as a territorial symbol of their highest allegiance, whereas this World Citizen claims it as the only legal territory within the continental limits of the United States of America whereon he can reside.

As I stand before you here, no national law covers my very existence. Since that day when I was brought back into France from the United Nations, I have lived in five fully sovereign nations, yet not one of those nations was able to represent me legally. But further, merely to handle me physically, they were all obliged to violate their own national laws. The most recent violation occurred when the U.S. Immigration authorities admitted me to this country last July 27th, frankly confessing to me at the time that no law covered my entry since I was not a U.S. citizen, not an immigrant, not a returning resident alien, and not a visitor, which four categories are the only lawful means of entering and residing in the United States.

According to the laws of this land, therefore, I am non-existent, a political and legal non-entity. Yet here I stand, in the City Hall of Ellsworth, a respectable community,in a conservative stronghold of the United States of America, the strongest power in the entire world, and though my very existence here calls into fundamental question that sovereign government, I remain untouched and unharmed. Just as the Immigration authorities were unable to refuse me though legally they were obliged to, so the law officer standing in the rear of this hall though legally obliged to arrest me because technically I am an illegal person, is unable

36

to do so because my authority as a sovereign entity unto myself is manifestly greater than his as a representative of the sovereign nation. This does not mean that I must not obey reasonable laws of conduct, and that if I disobey them, I will not be arrested by this same officer. It means only that the State as such is the servant of the sovereign individual, which is the basic principle of democracy, and when the individual, according to his reason and conscience, secedes from the State because he considers it no longer able to protect him and yet give him the freedom he requires, the State must follow him as his very shadow, because eventually his fellow human beings and neighbors, also individually sovereign and democractic, as well as the servants of the State itself, will recognize **him** as the fundamental integer upon which a greater and more inclusive State **must** be built if the whole community is to thrive.

Thus, as the territorial cornerstone of that Greater State, this dot I claim as the only piece of legal land on which I am now able to reside.

A point has no dimensions however, and therefore no physical existence, so neither can I actually live here, nor can the United States government claim it as national territory. Further, it having no physical existence, my claim needs no confirmation on the part of the national authorities as such, but only recognition from citizens throughout the world.

As a world sovereign, existing legally only in a worldly sense, I am able to give this point a legal existence based on the three Prime Laws of Mankind. So be it. Now every national citizen throughout the world is able to make a valid extension of his loyalty to the world community through this legal world territory without at the same time renouncing **any** humanitarian local or national responsibilites which are a part of the Whole. World citizenship is **not** incompatible with lower levels of citizenship so long as the duties and responsibilites of those citizenships reflect that of the greater.

At this moment, this is the only neutral but inclusive government in existence. It has no foreign policy, no political parties, indeed no politics even, no army, navy or air force, though civil armies, navies and air forces can perform many humanitarian duties once the threat of war is removed, no axes to grind, no special interests to protect, and no private profits to make. Its door is open to all and will be closed to none. With the firm guidance of a representative council of the World's Teachers and the World's Mothers, this government will be able to command the services of the most capable and farsighted men in order that humanity might be best served, and that positions of public responsibility not be usurped by lesser men. Methods of just selection can easily be incorporated into a World Constitution or Charter whereby humanity's real leaders may rise to the top without fear and without hindrance. Thus would evolve a World Parliament or Corporate Congress gradually to replace in the public mind the absolute nationalistic sovereignties of today. Through a World Citizen's Corporation, problems of food, shelter, clothing, health, education, labor, production, distribution, management and the like will be dealt with as a whole, scientifically and cooperatively. A unified world currency will evolve in due course based no doubt on a labor value rather than the unrealistic gathering and stockpiling of inert metal by separate nation-states.

The completing of mankind, so long talked about by philosophers and spiritual leaders, so long dreamed of by the persecuted down the ages, is at hand. It is started here tonight. A world government exists. . .if only in one common man and having but one dot of territory. No longer need we collectively hesitate. No longer need we argue about how long it will take, or whether the neighbor will come in. This neighbor **is** in, and it but remains for everyone to recognize and apply his own inness, or oneness.

The remaining task therefore is but a cleaning up one, a simple duplication. The main job is over, that of completing the microcosm. Each microcosm completed brings the macrocosm that much nearer completion. Borrow if you wish this global vision and determination. But do not be indifferent to your own survival and happiness. Examine these ideas and words with the searing blade of you own conscience and reason. They will stand even then. And do not hesitate for lack of experience. This work is unprecedented in these modern terms. Thus we are all youths in this task. But experience can only be gained by living our goal from the outset, by **being** members of the world community. And if we stumble, falter, even fall, there are others to carry on, for the reality of Man's Unity is a truth that cannot die.

I am a world sovereign. . .a forefather of the Human Race. Its government is here proclaimed.

Brothers and sisters, fellow World Citizens, join me in this glorious destiny.

CHAPTER 2

WORLD CITIZENSHIP REDEFINED

The world...universally outgoing, conceptually unbounded, the planet dynamically, synergistically and organically one with itself and the cosmos.

Citizenship...the restrictive rights and duties within a given social structure.

The two words together seem paradoxical. "You can educate either the citizen or the man," wrote Thoreau. Yet in their union lies the potential success of the human species; in their non-union lies the demise of a fatally-flawed creature which could not overcome its self-imposed global anarchy.

This is the perenniel mystery of the conceptual "joining" the perceptual. How and where does spirit dwell in the body?

World citizenship today implies the joining of the perenniel wisdom of humankind with up-to-the-minute geo-political and geo-technical reality.

"The term 'world citizen' can be better understood with a negative definition than with a positive one. If a citizen of a state with political frontiers is expected to pay allegiance to the government of the state to which he or she belongs and is expected to take arms against aliens who might invade the territory of the state, a world citizen recognizes the entire world as one's state and in principle does not recognize any member of one's own species as an alien to the world community to which oneself belongs. Such a person recognizes the earth as one's sustaining mother, the innate inviolable laws of nature as one's protecting father, all sentient beings as one's brothers, sisters and kin, and the world without frontiers as one's home. The world citizen's allegiance is to the foundation of truth, the universality of knowledge and the fundamental ground of all values."

Guru Nitya Chaitanya Yati, founder/head, East-West University

Before the industrial age and the electronic revolution, the identity and functioning boundary of social units was largely determined to the nation-state level by the mechanical barriers of geography. The working of government and the writing of history were from non-global perspectives. Loyalty to the feudal prince, or later, to the sovereign king was direct, one-dimensional and absolute. Society was aural, its extent determined largely by the human voice.

The development of the printing press, and in 1844, electronic informational transfer, established lines of communication from one relatively isolated social unit to another. A man's thoughts now could be known instantly from a distance. One did not have to know him personally. Indirect political representation was born. Inevitably the notion that the governed should have a voice in government became increasingly popular. Democracy, kindled in the context of rising expectations, inflamed revolution after revolution from east to west, north to south.

Yet here was born a tragic paradox: for the essence of democracy is universal participatory decision-making, whereas the essence of national sovereignty, a hangover from the feudalism and the absolute sovereignty of kings, is exclusivity and the non-participation of citizens outside the national boundary. Citizens "belonged" to the nation only while all humans outside that nation were "foreignors," or worse, "aliens."

This tragic contradition begins to be socially instilled almost at birth. One is not born a human, or politically, a world citizen, but "French," "English," "American," "Russian," "Chinese," or "Iranian." One could add that all labels at birth—"black, "white," "Arab," "Jew," "Catholic," etc.—are essentially false contrasted with the reality of the *human* emerging from a *human* womb *into* the world of humans.

Personal qualities are simplistically attached to national (and other) labels rendering violence and aggression easy to justify by their leaders. We are "good," "noble," "best," etc. because we are "British," or "American," or "Russian." Others are ipso facto "bad," "ignoble," "inferior." Unlike us, they are threats to be feared, even killed.

Those who identified directly with the world of humans were considered starry-eyed idealists, utopians, sentimental humanitarians, impractical moralists, or simply crackpots. The only empirical world "citizens" were the pirates sailing freely on the open seas. They were the forerunners of the multinational corporations, the world "citizens" of the industrial world. The practical world, the world of the 17th, 18th and 19th political power, was channeled into a framework based on unreality, the fiction of nationalism.

Then came the 20th century. Speed of transportation increased 100-fold in a few decades. Electricity and electronics linked the global surface eliminating time and distance implosively as barriers between humans leaving only divisive ideas, language...and politics, the surrogate of religion. A new "vertical" dimension was added, which, if translated, was the element of reciprocal support, or universality and wholeness.

The world became literally overnight, historically speaking, one community,

40

yet without overall management. The 17th, 18th, and 19th century sovereign state system, imposed by largely reactionary leaders, with notable exceptions, on the 20th century world of four major revolutions: technological, electronic, nuclear and space, proved and is proving daily to be totally inadequate to solve global human problems.

Indeed, the nation-centered way of "solving" problems *is the major problem*! The nation-state, by insisting on its absolute sovereignty, has become literally suicidal for the entire human species.

Today, with virtually no distance and no time between humans, each person is the focus of a global input. Everything happening in the world affects, sooner or later, each individual. With computers and satellites, the input to the individual has become fully supranational. Yet this irrefutable fact and its radical implications is popularly ignored.

A Middle East war raises the price of oil for everyone; an atomic bomb exploding in the South Pacific can mean leukemia for a baby born in Dayton, Ohio; dumping radio-active wastes off the coast of Florida can mean radio-active fish caught by fishermen off the coast of Iceland, Great Britain, France or Spain; a shortwave radio placed anywhere on the surface of the globe receives a babble of voices — and ideas — from all corners of the world community.

Everything is happening at once and everything is happening to everybody. This is the most revolutionary fact of *any* century.

Yet what of the individual's output? Here, the reciprocal truth is, if possible, even less realized. If everything is happening directly to everyone, then every individual should be outputting directly to everything. This means simply that every individual should have the capability of direct democratic effect on the world-at-large. The world's individuals should constitute for themselves a global governing body to represent each individual as an outputting co-trustee of the earth as a whole.

The apt analogy is the human body itself. Each cell is linked to the whole by a nervous system directly connected to the human "computer," the brain. For this almost unbelievable coordinating mechanism to order the necessary action required by a specific threatening situation, there is instant feedback from hurt cells. The "government" operates on the basis of both individual and common good; thus it is "global," not "national" or "local" in character.

Government itself can be likened to the brain or the management mechanism by which the entire organism and each individual cell or unit can be fulfilled in terms of the triad of self, local community and the entire human community. The evolution of the computer today promises instantaneous input and output potential to each human and to all humanity, thus for the first time in history permitting world government and global institutions to take their rightful place in human institutions.

World citizenship, then, is the only dynamic and imperative political identity capable of relinking the conceptual or moral value of the human being with the social and economic organization of his/her now planetary community. It expresses both the innate and inalienable sovereignty of each human as well as the overall sovereignty of the human species to which he/she belongs, also innately and inalienably. Thus it fulfils at once the criteria for ethical as well as ethnical politics. Also, it connotes a plan of ongoing political action at all levels of social activity, local to global.

If indeed the nation-state has lost its legitimacy as a two-dimensional, horizontal, we-and-they, zero (or negative) sum political entity in a three-dimensional, positive-sum, "We-the-people-of-the-planet-earth" world, then so also has personal commitment to exclusive national citizenship. Just as no one sovereignty or group of sovereignties can directly prevent any other from unleashing a third inter-national war, so also can no amount of commitment to merely national leaders bring the world situation under control.

But just as national citizenship had to be taught, learned and experienced in former centuries, not without great turmoil to the social norms of the period, so world citizenship must now be taught, learned and *experienced* in these final days of the 20th century.

To think, feel and act globally is almost without precedent in our recorded history. Only rare prophets have managed to do so, but without the aid of modern science and technology. And so they were vilified and put to death. But now, faced with Armageddon, we must all become as prophets, for, as Buckminster Fuller put it, "Either war is obsolete, or men are."

World citizenship is more than merely a political strategy. It "verticalizes" the individual raising him above the "left" and "right" of nationalistic politics, to meet and make functional the perenniel value systems which heretofore have been only the subject of religious credence. Thus it complements and fulfills all religious prophecies and integrates at the same time the synergistic worlds of instantaneous communications, energy and ecology with political power systems and institutions.

The "Promised Land" of the Hebrews, the "Peace on earth," and "Thy will be done on earth. . ." of the Christians, the benevolent social order of the Moslems, the world fraternal order of the Sikhs, the "Middle Way" of the Buddhists, the "universal world order" of the Bah'a'is, all are contained in and can grow out of the multidimensional, human, spiritual/political dispensation of universal world citizenship.

There is no other pathway to the future. . .and to the stars.

CHAPTER 3

WORLD GOVERNMENT COMMUNICATIONS

"Promote, then, as an object of primary importance, institutions for the general diffusion of knowledge. In proportion as the structure of a government gives force to public opinion, it is essential that public opinion should be enlightened."
George Washington's Farewell Address, 17 September, 1796

WORLD FUTURE SOCIETY 4TH GENERAL ASSEMBLY
Sheraton-Washington Hotel, Washington, D.C.
July 22, 1982

Panel 4202
Garry Davis, Chairman

This panel will address the subject of government as essentially a medium of communication. It true, then a world government would be a medium of world communication.

Government Defined

Since we're talking about government, we'd better start with some definitions. What exactly is government? It's defined by various dictionaries in various ways. Webster's claims it is "an exercise of administrative power" or "the established form of political administration." Another defines is as "the authoritative direction and restraint exercised over the actions of men in communities, societies and states..."

Whatever definition we accept, government cannot govern without first communicating its rules or laws to the citizenry concerning its functions.

But more basic even to governing is existing. At the risk of banality, for government to govern, it must first exist. I must therefore call the dictionaries to question. All have missed the essential point about government. Government just doesn't start all by itself. It is started by individuals. Citizens communicating with fellow citizens about a new social contract.

Thomas Paine explained the process in this way:

"It has been thought a considerable advance towards establishing the principle of freedom to say that government is a compact between those who govern and those who are governed; but this cannot be true, because it is putting the effect before the cause; for as men must have existed before governments existed, there once was a time when governments did not exist, and consequently there could originally exist no governors to form such a compact with. The fact therefore must be that the individuals themselves, each in his own personal and sovereign right, entered into a compact with each other to produce a government. . ."

This "entering into a compact with each other" is the essence of government. Therefore, it is basically communication. The thrust of this panel, therefore, will be to define government as essentially a medium of this civic communication process.

James Madison, credited with writing the U.S. Constitution, reminded us that
"A popular government without popular information or the means to acquire it, is but a prologue to a farce, or a tragedy, or perhaps both."

Breakdown of Communications Between Citizen and Government

This farce or tragedy foreseen by Madison is now being enacted on the world level where there is today an almost total breakdown in communication between national government and national citizen in terms of his or her inalienable rights to "life, liberty and the pursuit of happiness."

War itself is the most primitive example of this breakdown. A recent example of this total breakdown is nothing less than the United Nations Special Session on Disarmament. The travesty and betrayal by national leaders was expressed by the UN Secretary-General himself who warned the national delegates that "if we continue to temporize, there will be a massive disillusionment about the credibility of the professed allegiance of government to the aims of peace and progress around the globe."

To illustrate my thesis, I will use a few charts. The first is called "The Correlation of Speed of Communication with Social Organization In History." (P. 45)

Social Organization Equals Communication

Communication in turn depends on transport, whether physical, motorized, or electric. Therefore, if true that communication speed determines the extent of social organization, it becomes apparent that the speed of transport has had and is having a direct effect on our social, economic and political life.

Let us turn to our chart for a closer look at the correlation between speed and social organization. What is immediately striking is the dramatic contrast between speed of transport from the days of the Pharoahs—the horse—till literally the last century. A veritable quantum leap in transport speed beginning with the development of the engine in 1879 till today has revolutionized communications between fellow humans.

Physical speed is literally out of sight on our limited chart.

But another breakthrough of communication is equally startling. From Marconi's discovery of radio waves in 1895 to Kilby's microchips development in 1958, information has not only become instantaneous but ubiquitous. Radio and now modular frequency waves carrying television pictures now blanket the globe.

Over 4,000 communication satellites whirl over our heads as I talk.

Chart I

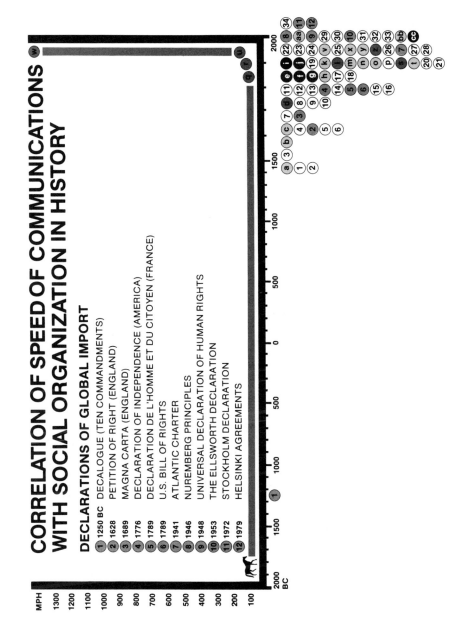

CORRELATION OF SPEED OF COMMUNICATIONS WITH SOCIAL ORGANIZATION IN HISTORY

DECLARATIONS OF GLOBAL IMPORT

1. 1250 BC DECALOGUE (TEN COMMANDMENTS)
2. 1628 PETITION OF RIGHT (ENGLAND)
3. 1689 MAGNA CARTA (ENGLAND)
4. 1776 DECLARATION OF INDEPENDENCE (AMERICA)
5. 1789 DECLARATION DE L'HOMME ET DU CITOYEN (FRANCE)
6. 1789 U.S. BILL OF RIGHTS
7. 1941 ATLANTIC CHARTER
8. 1946 NUREMBERG PRINCIPLES
9. 1948 UNIVERSAL DECLARATION OF HUMAN RIGHTS
10. 1953 THE ELLSWORTH DECLARATION
11. 1972 STOCKHOLM DECLARATION
12. 1979 HELSINKI AGREEMENTS

DATES OF GLOBAL IMPORT

#	YEAR	EVENT
1	1456	GUTENBERG BIBLE
2	1492	CHRISTOPHER COLUMBUS TO AMERICA
3	1509	ERASMUS "CITIZEN OF THE WORLD"
4	1620	PILGRIMS ARRIVE AT PLYMOUTH
5	1632	GALILEO CONFIRMS COPERNICUS THEORY
6	1648	PEACE TREATY OF WESTPHALIA
7	1684	NEWTON'S THEORY OF MOTION AND GRAVITY
8	1707	UNION OF ENGLAND AND SCOTLAND
9	1715	AGE OF ENLIGHTENMENT
10	1750	INDUSTRIAL REVOLUTION IN ENGLAND
11	1775	AMERICAN REVOLUTION BEGINS
12	1776	ADAM SMITH, WEALTH OF NATIONS
13	1776	SIGNING OF DECLARATION OF INDEPENDENCE
14	1787	UNITED STATES CONSTITUTION RATIFIED
15	1789	AMERICAN BILL OF RIGHTS
16	1791	THOMAS PAINE, RIGHTS OF MAN
17	1848	MARX, ENGELS, COMMUNIST MANIFESTO
18	1850	REVOLUTIONS IN FRANCE, GERMANY, AUSTRIA
19	1866	FIRST TRANSATLANTIC CABLE
20	1895	MARCONI SENDS FIRST WIRELESS MESSAGE
21	1899	1ST PEACE CONFERENCE AT HAGUE
22	1905	EINSTEIN'S THEORY OF RELATIVITY
23	1912	BEGINNING OF WORLD WARS - BALKANS
24	1920	LEAGUE OF NATIONS FORMED
25	1929	STOCK MARKET COLLAPSES
26	1939	WORLD WAR II
27	1945	ATOMIC AGE BEGINS OVER HIROSHIMA
28	1945	UNITED NATIONS FORMED
29	1948	UNIVERSAL DECLARATION OF HUMAN RIGHTS
30	1949	INT'L REGISTRY OF WORLD CITIZENS
31	1953	WORLD GOVERNMENT OF WORLD CITIZENS
32	1954	WORLD SERVICE AUTHORITY
33	1957	USSR LAUNCHES "SPUTNIK"
34	1969	FIRST MOON LANDING

Chart II

INVENTIONS OF GLOBAL IMPORT

	YEAR	INVENTION	INVENTOR
a	1450	PRINTING PRESS	GUTENBERG
b	1590	MICROSCOPE	JANSSEN
c	1608	TELESCOPE	LIPPERSHEY
d	1705	STEAM ENGINE	NEWCOMEN
e	1800	ELECTRIC BATTERY	VOLTA
f	1822	ELECTRIC MOTOR	FARADAY
g	1832	ELECTRIC GENERATOR	PIXII
h	1837	TELEGRAPH	MORSE
i	1856	STEEL	BESSEMER
j	1859	INT. COMBUSTION ENGINE	LENOIR
k	1872	MOTION PICTURES	MUYBRIDGE/ISAACS
l	1876	GAS ENGINE	OTTO
m	1876	TELEPHONE	BELL
n	1877	MICROPHONE	EDISON
o	1878	CATHODE RAY TUBE	CROOKES
p	1879	INCANDESCENT LAMP	EDISON
q	1881	ELECTRIC RAILWAY	VON SIEMENS
r	1887	AUTOMOBILE	DAIMLER
s	1892	DIESEL ENGINE	DIESEL
t	1895	RADIO	MARCONI
u	1903	AIRPLANE	WRIGHT
v	1926	TELEVISION	BAIRD
w	1929	ROCKET ENGINE	GODDARD
x	1933	FREQUENCY MODULATION	ARMSTRONG
y	1935	RADAR	WATSON-WATT
z	1937	JET ENGINE	WHITTLE
aa	1946	ELECTRONIC COMPUTER	ECKERT
bb	1958	MICROCHIP	KILBY
cc	1960	LASER	NAIMAN

● COMMUNICATIONS ● SPEED ● MOTOR ● OTHER

Nation-State Remains In Past Centuries

Let us note, however, a deadly contradition in political terms.

Despite the numerous inventions of global importance during the 18th, 19th and 20th centuries – and I have noted only the most important on the chart – the fundamental governing unit – the nation-state – remains unchanged.

It was born and evolved in the age of the horse, hand tools and outhouses yet carried over unchanged into a century of micro-wave technology, satellite communication and alas, nuclear power.

Our actual world is happening to all of us at once. In other words, a quantum leap has occurred in terms of reality rendering the fictions of the pre-industrial/electronic/nuclear/space world not only obsolete but suicidal. Thus while the ordinary human being enjoys worldwide data input simply by owning a transistor radio, he is bound politically to an essentially feudalistic institution totally bypassed by every human endeavor. Yet it is claiming his absolute and often dying allegiance in the name of "national sovereignty," a synonym for mass suicide.

In other words, while a totality of world events directly affects each individual, his or her civic or political output is not only indirect but almost negligible. From this contradiction arises the general feeling of impotence and apathy towards one's own possibilities of survival.

Growth of Nation-State

Let us now examine our next chart which reveals the exponential growth of this violent and cancerous political institution in the latter 20th century. (P. 48)

From 1790 when there were but 9 sovereign states, we note a gradual addition as revolutions of common people threw off the yoke of feudal princes and kings. Though democratic notions were taking hold of peoples' minds through the visual medium – in contrast to the aural society of feudal times – transport was still primitive and horse-bound. The nation was still a vast geographical territory eliminating lesser conflicts which till then plagued humanity.

But it is not until 1948 when colonial empires finally collapsed and the principle of self-determination of peoples took hold that the nation-state leaped in numbers throughout the planet. A simple extraplolation of that curve reveals that, if continued, by the year 2,000, over 200 exclusive nation-states will exist, each claiming a portion of the planet's turf and each with the right to wage war thus ironically legalizing the very decimation of the planet itself.

What is Sovereignty?

Let us turn to our fourth illustration which will serve partly to reveal the irrationality of national sovereignty. (P. 49)

As the title suggests, if population alone determined national sovereignty, New York City, Greater London, Tokyo, Mexico City, Los Angeles, and Shanghai would dominate 93 nation-states. A total of 62 cities, according to the 1981 World Almanac have populations exceeding 2 million, three hundred thousand, which is more people than 53 nation-states can count.

Evidently population does not determine national sovereignty.

EVOLUTION OF NATION-STATE SYSTEM

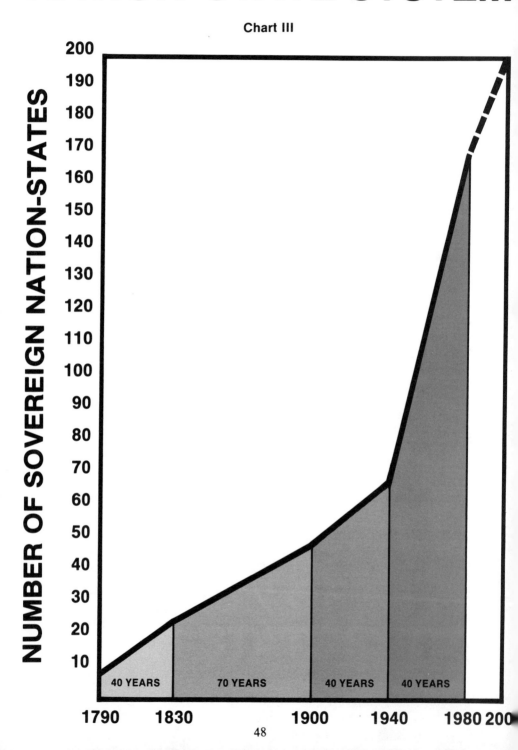

Chart III

NUMBER OF SOVEREIGN NATION-STATES

| 40 YEARS | 70 YEARS | 40 YEARS | 40 YEARS |

1790 1830 1900 1940 1980 200

Chart IV

92 NATION-STATES WITH POPULATIONS LESS THAN NEW YORK CITY

MICRO-STATES WITH POPULATION UNDER 300,000 - 16

BAHAMAS • BAHRAIN •BARBADOS • CAPE VERDE ISLANDS • COMORO ISLANDS •DJIBOUTI•EQUATORIAL GUINEA • GRENADA • ICELAND • MALDIVES • QATAR • SAO TOME AND PRINCIPE • SEYCHELLES •TONGO • UNITED ARAB EMIRATES • WESTERN SAMOA

NATION-STATES WITH LESS THAN 1,000,000 - 14

BOTSWANA • CYPRUS • FIJI • GABON • GAMBIA • GUINEA-BISSAU • GUYANA • KUWAIT •LUXEMBOURG • MALTA • MAURITIUS • OMAN • SURINAM • SWAZILAND

NATION-STATES WITH BETWEEN 1 AND 5 MILLION - 40

ALBANIA • BENIN • BHUTAN • BURUNDI • CHAD •CONGO • COSTA RICA • DEM. YEMEN • DOMINICAN REPULIC • EL SALVADOR • FINLAND • HAITI • HONDURAS • IRELAND • ISRAEL• IVORY COAST • JAMAICA • JORDAN • LAOS • LEBANON • LESOTHO • LIBERIA• LIBYAN ARAB R. • MAURITANIA • NEW ZEALAND • NICARAGUA • NIGER • NORWAY • PANAMA•PAPUA NEW GUINEA • PARAGUAY • RWANDA • SENEGAL • SIERRA LEONE • SINGA-PORE • SOMALIA • TOGO • TRINIDAD • TOBAGO • URUGUAY • ZAMBIA

NATION-STATES WITH BETWEEN 5 AND 10 MILLION - 22

AUSTRIA • BELGIUM • BOLIVIA • BULGARIA • CUBA • DENMARK • ECUADOR • GHANA • GREECE • GUATEMALA • MADAGASCAR • MALAWI • MALI • MOZAMBIQUE • PORTUGAL •SAUDI ARABIA • SWEDEN • SYRIAN ARAB R. • TUNISIA • CAMEROUN • UPPER VOLTA •YEMEN

- ALMOST 1 OUT OF 2 (42%) HAVE POPULATIONS LESS THAN PHILADELPHIA
- 60% OF STATES ARE AFRICAN, ASIAN, MIDEAST & OCEANIA
- 125 STATES IN DEVELOPING STAGE, 2/3 GAINED INDE-PENDENCE SINCE WORLD WAR II
- ONLY 20% RECOGNIZE HUMAN RIGHTS VIA DUE PROCESS

Every nation which has a constitution claims its sovereignty is derived directly from the people.

If indeed sovereignty ultimately derives from the people, then the only true sovereign on planet earth is the aggregate of human beings residing thereon.

That means humanity itself. It also means each human being, the fundamental unit of humanity. And herein lies the vital geo-dialectical key to world peace.

How Do Humans Communicate Or Identify?

To illustrate, let us now turn to our fifth and last chart in order to reveal both the breakdown in communication between citizen and national government and to support our basic thesis that only a world government can reestablish and in fact is reestablishing that dynamic communication process. (P. 51)

This chart reveals a total human communication process. For purposes of simplicity, I have indicated only four levels though there are no doubt many intermediate levels.

These four levels of communication are "dynamic" in character since each involves continual feedback to the individual. For purposes of explanation I call them "Dynamic Identifications."

If at first they appear obvious, so much the better because then my thesis that government is essentially communication will likewise appear obvious.

The first dynamic identification is 1 to 1, the most intimate relationship we have with our spiritual nature. Call it God, call it the Higher Self, Truth or whatever, still it is personal, subjective and the source of our entire conceptual value system. Our whole life is spent identifying with and identifying this first dynamic.

The 2nd dynamic identification is with the family, the first social and even political unit. As we pass through life, the family takes various forms: biological, legal, social and spiritual. But it is always the most intimate group identification where we first apply our value system outwardly, first test our strength and expose our weaknesses.

The 3rd dynamic identification is that with which we personally identify or accept beyond the family. Here there is immense variety. Here we have major and minor identifications. Two of the major ones are political and religious.

Being personal, this dynamic is still partial or relative. Its institutions are exclusive and competitive. While it stimulates internal cooperation and sharing, it breeds fear, aggressiveness and distrust outside its closed circle. Often, its philosophy and attitudes totally contradict the 1st and 2nd dynamic identifications. It pits human against fellow human. Economically, it promotes scarcity thinking and unjust patterns of ownership of property. Being essentially divisive, it leads finally to warlike attitudes and to war itself.

From 3rd dynamic political identification comes alliances, treaties, charters between equally "sovereign" states and the accumulated debris of wartime history.

"Global Village" Verus Nation-State

Here we find the mortal contradiction partially exposed by our first chart. For, as we saw before in our first chart, in terms of communication of information,

Chart V

DYNAMIC IDENTIFICATION FOR HUMANS

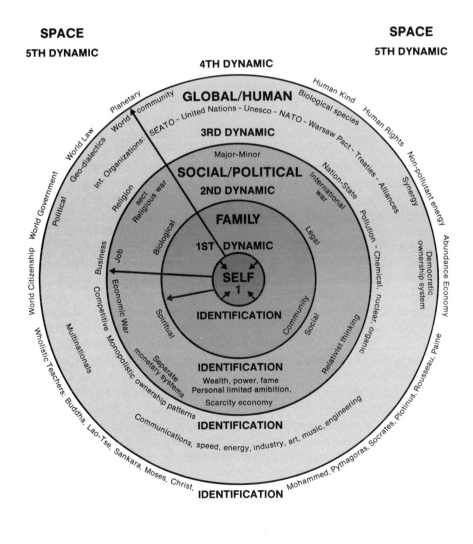

we live in a "global village." Yet, in political terms, we live in exclusive "villages" called nation-states. Here precisely is where communication between citizen and government has broken down, each government—and especially the two largest—expressing its paranoia or fear of "the enemy"—in a suicidal arms race. In legal terms, this is known as "Inter armes, silent legis" or "Between armed states, the law is silent." (See Chapters 11 and 13.)

In other words, when the head of government speaks or acts for the nation itself, the citizen is deprived of any individual civic power in the sacred name of "national security." Where the law is silent, the citizen status is obviously nullified, humans becoming mere subjects of dictatorships, overt or covert.

Today in Geneva, two men, Edward L. Rowny and Viktor P. Karpov, are talking about your fate and mine. And the rest of the human race. The sheer lunacy of this discussion wherein neither you nor I nor indeed humankind itself has anything to say is symptomatic of this catastrophic gap in communications.

In short, in a world of 170 odd-nation-states, the very essence of communication has broken down between government and governed. The nation-state itself has become part of a totally dictatorial system of government.

Let us face it squarely, no exclusive national citizen has any say in his or her very survival.

Exclusive Nationality Illegitimate

The legitimacy of national exclusivity was denounced at Nuremberg after World War II where German government officials were accused of crimes against humanity and of war crimes which allegedly transcended their national allegiance.

But does it not follow that all national leaders, under these same Nuremberg Principles, are likewise war criminals in that they are wilfully and deliberately preparing for World War III?

A glance at today's headlines of wars escalating and military budgets growing monstrously while humans suffer and die, only underlines the criminality of this exclusivity.

We must ask, however, if national government officials can be war criminals, how are national citizens innocent if they allow such crimes in the name of "national security," the Golden Calf of the 20th century? Are not exclusive national citizens who wilfully maintain that archaic and suicidal allegiance equally guilty as war criminals?

For a possible answer let us look at the last dynamic identification.

Before the ages of technological and electronic breakthrough, 4th dynamic identification was left to the sages, prophets, poets, philosophers, artists or pirates who were perhaps the first empiricists of the 4th dynamic—though a good case could be made for the desert caravans criss-crossing from East to West along established trade axes.

All the inventions mentioned are 4th dynamic in character.

Inalienable Rights Key To Reestablishing Communication

The notion of inalienable rights, always taught and exemplified by humanity's sages from time immemorial, finally codified in later-day constitutions, are the key to re-establishing communications between citizen and government.

Throughout human history from the Decalogue to the Helsinki Accords, men have defined wholistic or 4th dynamic identification values. Invariably, they relate the individual to his or her humanity or humane values put under pressure by exclusive or 3rd dynamic regimes.

Here on this dynamic, world law, human rights, world citizenship find their natural place.

A recent mandate for these global concepts is the *Universal Declaration of Human Rights.* Article 28 reads that *"Everyone is entitled to a social and international order in which the rights and freedom set forth in this Declaration can be fully realized."*

World Citizenship

Since 1948, when this Declaration was first proclaimed, millions of individuals throughout the world community have declared themselves world citizens.

They were giving evidence of the rise of a new and primal sovereignty, one which promised not only hope for survival but for success, both individual and communal . . . a sovereignty, in other words, which recognized both humanity as such and its fundamental unit, the individual human being.

The declaration of world citizenship is the first step toward realization of human rights for all.

It is the realistic path to world peace.

Because it is world humans communicating with fellow humans about their common survival.

We come then naturally to the role model for this vital process of relating a 4th dynamic human world with its appropriate 4th dynamic government.

To appreciate the process, as I already said, men become citizens and citizens begin governments. Or else inalienable rights are meaningless. For it is only to protect these that individuals establish a social and political order, carefully defined, and always at the consent of the governed.

The aware individual, therefore, faced with a worldly disorder, has first to declare his or her 4th dynamic political identification with his human community.

In declaring ourselves citizens of the world community in which we currently live, we are saying that essentially we are our own governors. We are reestablishing our innate sovereignty as humans in charge of our own destiny. This is the essence of the democratic principle and precisely where true sovereignty lies.

World Government Declared

In 1953, on September 4th to be exact, a government was declared based directly on this world citizenship identification.

From the beginning, it was a legitimate government if inalienable rights are sovereign. For it was founded by sovereign individuals who had no other government to represent them.

Its first act, that of communicating its existence publicly and calling for recognition from other citizens and government alike, supports the thesis of this panel, that government is essentially a communication medium.

Since that day, this world government of declared world citizens, using the *Universal Declaration of Human Rights* as its continuing mandate, has gained over 90,000 citizens.

Though small in present population, still it outranks 12 nation-states.

Global Identification

Each of its citizens is identified by the government. These identifications — world passports, world citizen registration cards, world birth certificates — are further communication devices designed particularly for national officials. While properly identifying the individual citizen, they confront head-on the claim of exclusivity of each and every nation-state. Being global by definition, they meet the requirements of 4th dynamic identification. They are thus empowered with a political and legal "clout" far beyond their innocuous appearance. In brief, they are powerful tools of global governmental communications. (See Appendix)

The World Political Network

Today, behind the nationalistic scare headlines, a new human sharing process is taking place called "networking." It is being aided and abetted by the computer age of which this general assembly is a dominant symbol.

This networking process is happening on the spiritual, political, social, educational, environmental and economic levels.

Networking is essentially communication between sovereign individuals.

The World Government of World Citizens is the political human network without which no further communication will be possible between humans. For it is the only world peace network, the only global communication strategy which can eliminate war — which may be described as the total breakdown of rational communication between humans — in the planetary community.

It is appropriate I feel to end this paper with a quote from World Citizen Buckminster Fuller who has honored this Assembly with his genius:

"Essence of the world's working will be to make every man able to become a world citizen and able to enjoy the whole earth going wherever he wants at any time, able to take care of all the needs of all his forward days without any interference with any other man and never at the cost of another man's equal freedom and advantage."

"Each human is a whole universe and there are now over three billion of them around the world."

Thank you.

CHAPTER 4

WHAT IS WORLD LAW?

"Since the sixteenth century there has been a rooted belief that organized force of a politically organized society was a necessary prerequisite for a regime of justice. Hence plans for a universal regime of justice have taken the form of plans for world-wide political organization—a universal super-state."
Roscoe Pound, "A World Legal Order," Fletcher School of Law and Diplomacy, 10/27/59

"The contemporary world, ever growing with continued exploration of outer space, angrily suggests that any hesitancy in creating a world rule of law is fraught with the peril of human extinction."
Dr. Luis Kutner, *World Habeus Corpus*, p. 206

Let's try to demystify the notion of world law.

Must it be legislated by a world parliament operating under a democratic world constitution, or be decreed by a world dictator, or proclaimed by a world guru, or, strange thought, is it already at work, independent of human ingenuity or malice?

All human beings are born from a female womb. Natural "law." Why not natural "world law" since it applies generally to everyone?

All human beings born within the continental limits of the United States of America shall be ipso facto considered United States citizens. Natural "law"? No, because humans born in France, Rumania or Thailand are not ipso facto U.S. citizens. Natural law—birth—has been converted into "positive law." The first is global, the second, national.

"All human beings born within the territorial limits of the home planet Earth shall be ipso facto World Government citizens."

Natural or positive law? Theoretically both since, for this historical moment, our human species lives only on Earth, (we think), and only a world government sanctions a planetary citizenship. If and when human beings are born on Mars,

55

according to the above theoretical law, they might not be considered World Government citizens but might enjoy a colonial status vis-a-vis the "home" government.

Examples of natural world law are limited by nature itself. You sneeze according to common world natural laws: "Inequality of bodily temperatures causing a rapid adjustment by driving air forcibly and audibly out of the mouth and nose by a spasmodic involuntary action." Russians, Eritreans, Jehovah Witnesses, Buddhists, blacks, Jews, Kurds, women, poets, garbage collectors, billionaires, Scots and the rest of our clan sneeze.

Sap rising in a tree, hospitality to the guest, sympathy for the underdog, love in all its forms, sharing food, keeping clean, municipal aid for the aged, young and infirm, fathers equitably distributing ice cream portions to their children, ships on the high seas passing on the right, collecting garbage, seeking truth, all are evidence of operative "world laws": of one kind or another, natural, social and conceptual.

These common "world laws" are taken for granted for the most part operating concurrently with local and national laws.

They give rise to the notion and actuality of a common world citizenship.

The purpose of the present chapter is to expose to you your pragmatic world citizenship *as a given fact* which you practice daily without knowing it.

Even more presumptuous is my intention to expose world law as the only genuine, legitimate, scientific and justifiable law both theoretically and actually operative! Only to the extent that local and national law conform to it is the lesser law justified. After almost a half a century reading learned treatises on world law by famous jurists and listening to eminent statesmen and politicians expound on it, after absorbing the Sabbath preachements of holy men from a dozen popular religions, I have yet to experience one serious leader either understanding or personifying it.

> *"Statesmen and legislators, standing so completely within the institution never distinctly and nakedly behold it. They speak of moving society, but have no resting-place without it."*
>
> Emery Reves, *Anatomy of Peace*, 1945

World law is too important a subject to be left to either the politicians or the lawyers. Neither is it a fit subject for religion or moralists. Since time immemorial, exclusive religions have strewn the battlefields of the world with human bodies and they do so today.

World law is the proper subject for declared world citizens.

Nation-state conditioning—the we-and-they syndrome—operating morally, politically and even biologically—competition for the necessities of life—force us to consider "world law" as "beyond" the nation-state, *thus beyond us*. It thus becomes the legitimate concern only of a millenial world parliament, peopled by super lawyers, statesmen and jurists, matchless in wisdom, goodness and efficiency. Since, in looking around at the human material available, and discovering only mediocrity clothed in an eloquence which panics at every crisis, we relegate superman to the movies and the Boob Tube and up the national armament budget in the name of conventional wisdom.

Complicating our problem is the relentless data phenomenon. With the proliferation of TV antennas on roofs worldwide – with cable and satellite input infiltrating more and more homes – suddenly we are bombarded with information from everywhere at once with no manual for classifying it as to survival importance.

While, on the one hand, this steady stream of undifferentiated datum invading our living-room fortifies our emotional and psychological reliance on "our" nation since this screened "reality" obviously revolves around "our" world, it exposes inexorably the narrowness of the political vision and impotence of our national leaders to cope with "outside" problems. The result is political frustration and schizophrenia leading in turn to anger, revolt and a proliferation of organizations "for" a future world government to legislate "world law."

World law is as close as your next breath not "beyond" your nation in the never-never Alice-in-Wonderland of world politics. It is you now, today, being human, decent, civilized, aware, loving and all that translated positively into normal civic behavior. And because it is the same the world over, the "laws" determining this conduct are "common world laws."

That makes you now a "common law world citizen," like it or not, black or white, left or right, queen or coolie, man or women, rich or poor.

I discovered the intimacy of the trilogy of world laws – conceptual, social and natural – only after divorcing myself from the mythical nation-state. But it wasn't until my 16th imprisonment – for daring to be "outside" the framework of their positive laws – that I finally understood the difficulty so many have in recognizing and accepting them. For the individual to accept world law as acting directly on him or her is to accept oneself as a sort of world sovereign responsive to such laws. When then of the vaunted sovereignty of the nation-state to which one is likewise affiliated? How can one equate both, seemingly mutually inconsistent? If I accept the relativism of nation-state sovereignty, I cannot at the same time consider myself as "beyond" it responsive to actual world laws.

Here is a new dilemma combining morality, sociology, politics and biology incorporated into one single person. There are no university courses on "World Law As Incorporated In And By The Human Being." There would no doubt be students for it but where are the professors?

The phenomenon of creating government however is not new to humankind. The personal confirmation of "common world laws" – preceeded on a national scale decades or even hundreds of years before – is an overt act of pledging allegiance to the only government extant declared precisely to give the common world citizenship legitimacy and ongoing function: the World Government of World Citizens.

This sovereign act of choosing a new government is not to be confused with joining an organization for a world-government-of-the-future. That would be tantamount to founding an organization in prison called "Freedom After Prisons Are Abolished"

The immediate and direct recognition of the sovereign individual of the already existant world laws transforms him into a world-government-in-microcosm! And that is the seminal and imperative act for world government to begin its external institutionalization. The aggregate of such transformed individuals' translates into a new social contract external to and essentially independent of all lower echelon contracts uniting smaller groups of humans.

By what right can we perform such a revolutionary act as pledging sovereign allegiance to a government which exists only in our person? Thomas Paine, that uncompromising fomentor of revolution for justice and human rights, put the matter succinctly:

> "It has been through a considerable advance towards establishing the principle of freedom to say that government is a compact between those who govern and those who are governed; but this cannot be true, because it is putting the effect before the cause; or as man must have existed before governments existed, and consequently there could originally exist no government to form such a compact with. The fact therefore must be that the individuals themselves **each** in his own personal and sovereign **right** entered into a compact with each other to produce a government; and this is the only mode in which governments have a right to exist, and the only principle on which they have a right to exist."

Thomas Paine, *The Rights of Man*

Such sovereign decision-making power of the individual in legal fact is confirmed in many national constitutions (See Chapter 13) as well as in all human rights declarations. Article 15(2), *Universal Declaration of Human Rights*, confirms the right of the individual to choose his government in the following words: *"No one shall be arbitrarily deprived of his nationality nor denied the right to change his nationality."*

The changing of nationality is not only the changing of government but, more important, the choosing of government. Here again, individual sovereignty is confirmed. Further, if I have the right to change my nationality, I also have the reciprocal right to renounce my nationality unilaterally, the nation being merely the external vessel into which I pour my portion of sovereignty as long as it serves my purpose. A refugee fleeing a repressive regime may not only have the desire but for sheer survival have to renounce his nationality. The United States has recognized the right of expatriation officially since July 27, 1868 by a special Act of Congress. (See Chapter 11, Section III-A)

The essence of democracy is, after all, individual free choice. Realpolitik begins always with what is actual, self-evident.

As of 1945, when both the nuclear age and the proliferation of TV antennas began, your actual citizenship extended horizontally to encircle the globe and vertically to meet hoary-with-age universal ethical standards.

Common world law—conceptual, social and biological—is operating today.

A common world government therefore is simply the individual and group recognition of these operative laws.

The only remaining task is to translate them into "positive" or institutional form.

CHAPTER 5

WORLD GOVERNMENT WILL BECOME VISIBLE IN 1980'S
A New Year's Message
December 31, 1979
Garry Davis

World events in the waning days of 1979 dramatically evidenced once again what the socially and biologically cancerous mushroom bursting over Hiroshima and Nagasaki 34 years ago exposed to humankind: "One world or none" is the christening ultimatum of our century.

As nation states plunge blindly toward a nuclear confrontation, their deadly we-they philosophy pitting fellow humans as exclusive national citizens against one another, concerned individuals arrive belatedly at the conclusion, in the words of James Reston in the New York Times of December 23, 1979, that "The world of divided states...is out of control."

But was the world of nation states ever "in control"? Are not nation states, vis-a-vis one another, by definition uncontrolled by any external law? And do not the largest and most powerful, the United States and the Soviet Union, insist on remaining uncontrolled by any higher authority?

When war became total—the primal lesson of the nuclear age—humankind, if indeed it sought and merited sheer survival, could no longer remain artifically divided behind national frontiers. It had to achieve its own legal identity. The industrial, electronic, then nuclear revolutions collapsed time and distance both constructively and destructively between humans until planet Earth literally become a global village. Exclusive national citizenship in such a pragmatic world became a worldwide suicide pact.

Despite eloquent warnings by moral leaders, scientists, educators, even enlightened statesmen, the national political world has remained essentially unchanged, continuing its mad arms race.

Though the United Nations General Assembly proclaimed in 1948 that human rights were universal, requiring sanction and protection by a "social and international order," it betrayed its own prescriptions by categorically refusing even to consider its transformation into a just and democratic world government. Instead, it institutionalized world anarchy. Extremists, whether political or religious, have with impunity used and use the nation state as a power base for their repressive policies, therefore degrading the citizens to mere serfdom. Today's headlines illustrate this deadly hypocrisy. (Editor's note: the Iranian hostage crisis.)

Pivotal historic events are often hid by surface concerns. They are gradually revealed with increasing clarity as consequent events whirl around them in ever larger circles. The declaration of World Government, September 4, 1953, from the City Hall of Ellsworth, Maine, was such an event.

It resulted both from the United Nations' human rights proclamation in Paris five years prior and the over 800,000 individuals from over 150 countries registering as World Citizens from January, 1949 till that auspicious date.

The declaratory act signalled the conclusion of the first stage of a new era of global politics designed to meet the strict requirements of human survival and well-being. From that significant date, citizens of world government have exercised, in direct affirmation of the Universal Declaration of Human Rights, their human sovereignty of direct and primary political choice, not without periodic repression from state officialdom.

If indeed the world of states is "out of control," then the world of humans is slowly giving concrete evidence of its innate and inalienable "control" through the legitimacy of world citizenship allied directly to its empirical political counterpart, the World Government.

The 1980s will see this vital tranferral of primal allegiance process accelerate exponentially as the nation state system continues to break down in the face of global problems facing the average citizen and as the World Government becomes increasingly visible to the desperate public.

While ethnic groups increasingly demand and exercise political self-determination, leaders of such groups will be forced to acknowledge the rationale of democratic world government as the only viable protection of their fundamental human rights already advocated by the United Nations' General Assmebly.

The various embryonic institutions of the World Government, particularly the World Court of Human Rights, founded June 12, 1974, will evolve as necessity and means permit. Judicial processes are desperately sought in the present Iranian-USA conflict by both parties. In the name of the world citizenry, the author has advised both the Iranian foreign minister and the U.S. president, on December 20, 1979, of the availability of the remedy of the World Court of Human Rights, as the sole judicial body extant independent of all national considerations thus guaranteeing impartiality.

A significant juridical signpost of this positive direction was contained in a recent opinion of U.S. District Court Judge Thomas A. Flannery, who endorsed the work for "...world peace through the vehicle of world citizenship and world government" in his memorandum opinion of December 19, 1979 in the case, Garry Davis v. the Director, U.S. Immigration and Naturalization Service.

The 1980's will witness as well the inevitable evolution of the World Citizen Party, the political arm of the embryonic World Government. The only truly world peace, human rights, and general affluence party transcending national frontiers, the World Citizen Party is designed to become the grassroots political vehicle permitting world citizens everywhere to enter local, national, and global elections with candidates standing on a platform of one world and one humanity under just and beneficient world law.

Though the time for nation states is fast running out, the era of humanity's fulfillment, long prophesied, is begun. To paraphrase a former, beloved U.S. president, "As not what your world can do for you, but what you can do for your world."

CHAPTER 6

HOW WORLD GOVERNMENT WORKS

Introduction

Opening Statement Of Garry Davis
World Government Seminar
May 10, 1980, New York, NY

You are aware, more than most, of the mortal crisis that confronts all life on this planet in today's nuclear-triggered world. As our president, Dr. Max Habicht has written, "Mankind simply cannot have peace and national sovereignty...The abolition of war," he notes, "requires the formation of new institutions."

Such institutions must obviously be sovereign. Such sovereignty must in turn have a two-fold character: that of the individual and of humanity as a whole. Herein lies the problem for peace-seekers everywhere. For whereas the individual is recognized in human rights declarations, the human species remains unprotected by world laws. "Who speaks for Man?" Norman Cousin asks.

World Government must derive both from your sovereignty and mine as world citizens and from the recognition of and commitment to humanity's inalienable right to protection and survival. For world government is both an extension of the individual and the political expression of humanity's very existence as a species.

If this is true, it follows that world government cannot be derived from the nation-state system, the very antithesis of peace and order.

I declared my allegiance to humankind as well as to myself as a world citizen over 30 years ago. As a stateless person, unrepresented by any national political process, I founded and head a new institution grounded in the sovereignty of the individual cast despite himself or herself in a world role as well as that of humankind.

That organization strives for the ultimate protection of humanity as a whole. It is not a think-tank nor a discussion group where good thoughts about human rights and one world are tossed back and forth.

It is a functioning world government.

Just as a germinating seed, no taller than a blade of grass, may contain the genetic code that will in time transform the struggling seedling into a giant redwood, so the World Government of World Citizens is *functioning* today to serve the interests both of humanity and of individuals. It is small—only 90,000 registered world citizens. It is weak as is every new-born creature. It is alternately ridiculed, ignored and persecuted by national authorities. But it is functioning. And it is growing. Its potential is all-embracing.

Historically, the institution is a spin-off of the world citizenship movement which arose spontaneously in 1948 in Paris, triggered by my renunciation of exclusive national allegiance and declaration of world citizenship against the background of the impotent United Nations.

The acid test of the validity of any revolution is its workability. How does this new institution, this World Government of World Citizens, work?

First, it works in the microcosm of each registered world citizen exercising the common world laws already incorporated in his or her person. It works in identifying persons from all corners of our planetary community who pledge it their prime allegiance, the first prerequisite for exercising the right of self-determination. It works in the growing recognition of its official documents by duly constituted governments. It works through its judicial arm, the World Court of Human Rights, which has issued writs of world habeus corpus on behalf of individuals facing capital punishment only for exercising their basic human rights—writs that have been observed by heads of state. It works finally because it is grounded in Absolute Necessity and the age-old morality of unity and universality.

In summation, the global input forced upon each individual by 20th century communications can only be met by a global output, not only of a technical, cultural, scientific or religious character, but of a civism already sanctioned and mandated by the *Universal Declaration of Human Rights* and the principle of law itself. The framework for that global civism can only be found in world government. One cannot exist without the other.

The day of the sovereign nation-state is ending. The era of humanity's fulfillment, the millenium of peace, prosperity and security, is at hand. The only remaining question is whether individual humans will recognize their obligations to humanity as a species before a final holocaust consumes all thought.

The answer may well lie in the convictions, energies, and the actions of those gathered here today.

I
The Case of Fred Haas, Conscientious Objector

On April 5, 1957, three years, seven months and one day after I declared the World Government from Ellsworth, Maine, Fred Haas walked into its office, opposite the United Nations Secretariat on 1st Avenue in New York.

Fred, age 19, had been "invited" to appear before the Selective Service Board #59 in his hometown of Forest Hills, N.Y. to serve in the armed forces of the U.S.A. He had filed for a status of conscientious objection on the basis of his philosophical and political beliefs. In a letter of April 3, 1957, signed by Meyer H. Goldenkauf, chairman of his local draft board, his request had been rejected.

"I'm a C.O.," he told me, "but not on religious grounds. And these are the only ones allowed by U.S. law."

"What are your grounds?" I asked him.

"Philosophical and political," he replied. "I just don't think national armies in today's world serve any useful purpose or conform to any valid philosophical concept. I've studied philosophers like Thoreau, Emerson, Plato and some of the Eastern prophets like Lao-Tse and Confucius. There was no room for violence in their ways of thinking. When I got this notice to go into the army, I just couldn't do it. I mean, if you want peace, you should first of all be peaceful yourself. That's only common-sense. Then why join an army? It's irrational. Then I heard about you. I like the idea of being a world citizen. Only I don't know exactly what it means."

In 1948 Edgar Ansel Mowrer, the well-known columnist, had suggested to me in Paris to recruit a "world police force" which Trygve Lie, the United Nations' Secretary-General, kept asking for.

"Just get a bunch of young C.O.'s from a lot of different countries," he told me as we sat at a sidewalk cafe on the Place de Trocadero where, across the street, at the Palais de Chaillot, the 3rd session of the General Assembly was being held, "and present yourselves on the balcony over there as the first de facto world police force."

Many members of the War Resisters International, the Fellowship of Reconciliation, the Mennonites, the Bahai's and other pacifist organizations rejected war on various grounds. The founding of the "World Peace Brigade" in Tanzania by well-known pacifists and its unfortunate break-up was a familiar story. I was a student of Mahatma Gandhi's Satyagraha campaigns having myself engaged in many one-man, non-violent campaigns, mostly on frontier lines between nations. But here, for the first time since the founding of a world government, was a young man with a smattering of philosophy, who, facing the contradiction of national military service, was interested in world citizenship as an alternative.

The notion of conscientious objection is negative, predicated on a supreme and continued allegiance to one's own nation-state. National law then still prevails, providing either punishment for those who refuse obedience or alternative service, yet still national. Since the concept of involuntary servitude was recognized as a human rights violation in article 4 of the *Universal Declaration of Human Rights* and since the promulgation of the Nuremburg Principles by the WWII allies, the obligation of national military service has and is suffering severe legal as well as civic stress.

Contrarily, in nations of continual crisis, such as Israel, where a whole people are under military subjugation, the notion of conscientious objection to army service becomes, to many otherwise enlightened citizens, treasonable. Again, the sole justification of militarists is the "security of the state" itself. However, as Emery Reves had pointedly written,

> "The nation-state is impotent to prevent foreign aggression; it no longer serves as the supreme institution capable of protecting its people against war and all the miseries and misfortunes that war brings."
>
> *Anatomy of Peace, 1945*

Given the real problem, neither the pacifist nor the C.O.s, have done their homework. They have no effective counter to the rationale of "state security." They should be asking, why is the state insecure? Then, carried the next step, why are all states insecure? *Obviously, they are all insecure against each other.* Only by such extrapolation does the reason become self-evident: a condition of anarchy exists between them.

Positively stated, there exists no common law against killing – other than moral law – to which all humans *as citizens* in the world community are subject.

Since the nations themselves cannot promulgate such a law, being by definition exclusive political fictions, obviously only the citizens themselves, both personally and collectively, can.

Thus the first task of a would-be conscientious objector to *national* military service is to eliminate its cause, i.e. anarchy in the world community. For, as an exclusive national citizen, he is colluding with the international anarchic condition.

He can therefore no longer remain an *exclusive* national citizen.

He must choose a higher civic loyalty, one which is grounded in common world law and order against murder. At that moment, he has annulled the notion of conscientious objection itself, making it irrelevant by virtue of his new civic commitment. By making a conscientious *pro*jection, he has effectively deprived the state of its violent rationale which is grounded on the condition of international anarchy.

Morally, politically and actually, he has exposed the state as suicidal in its pretensions to "national security," a pseudonym for war, in his name.

In other words, if Fred Haas pledged his sovereign allegiance to World Government *as an addition* to his U.S. citizenship much as the citizens of Virginia, Connecticut, Massachusets, New York and the other nine sovereign states did in 1787, he would be making a sovereign commitment to world peace through law which, both in political theory and in law, international as well as national, was unattackable by the U.S. government. This was not the civil disobedience that Thoreau advocated when the citizen was confronted with an unjust law, but the acceptance of a higher civil "obedience" or duty which nullified the provisions of the unjust law on the lower level. The U.S. courts would first have to decide whether his commitment to World Government was valid before it treated the question of his refusal to enter the armed services.

If, at the same time, he became a member of the World Government's constabulary, he would be further exposing the contradiction of the national army as a "peace-maker."

"I can't help you personally," I told Fred Haas, "since I am not really in the United States legally. But if you become a citizen of World Government, I can then act as your governmental representative vis-a-vis the United States government."

"What do you mean, World Government?" he asked in surprise.

"As a world citizen, I declared a world government in 1953 based on fundamental human rights to deal with just such problems. "

"A world government! That's super! Count me in. How do I join?"

"Very simple. It's like any organization. You sign up. Here, read this pledge of allegiance. If you agree with it, sign it. Or better yet, say it out loud and you're in." He read the pledge and reached for a pen. (See Appendix)

"Just what I've been looking for," he said, signing his name on the bottom line.

"O.K., stand up, raise your right hand." I looked around for a book, my eyes alighting on Emery Reve's *Anatomy of Peace*. "Put your left hand on this book and repeat the pledge to me."

Outside at the United Nations, a flag-raising ceremony was taking place. Sixteen new nations were being admitted, their symbols of sovereignty, the national flag, slowly rising on the poles spread along the sidewalk inside the international conclave.

"If nations can join the United Nations," I told him, "we individuals can join a world government."

After solemnly reciting the simple pledge, he sat down and asked, "Now what?"

"Now we'll let everyone know about your new status beginning with Mr. Goldenkauf. In a letter, recount the facts, first about your initial request for C.O. status, his refusal, then state your reasons again. Say that you're interested in world peace not war and that peace is the result of law not militarism. Then tell him you have added a new citizenship on a global level as your personal effort to evolve world law. Include the pledge. Also, if you want, quote article one of the Universal Declaration of Human Rights. 'Everyone is born free and equal in dignity and rights, etc. . . . and should act towards one another in a spirit of brotherhood.' As a member of the United Nations, the U.S.A. is commited to observe these rights. Make at least four copies, one to Dag Hammarskjold, the top civil servant in the world, one to Eisenhower, now your local president since he's the chief executor of the laws under which Goldenkauf is operating, and one to me as the coordinator of your new government. Keep one for yourself. Note on the bottom of the letter the three names for copies. Of course, you can send it to the media and to any organizations you want. That's about all. Now, go home and draft it and we'll go over it together."

Fred returned in three days with his draft. We worked it over finally getting it into the mail that afternoon, April 8, to Mr. Goldenkauf, Mr. Hammarskjold, and President Eisenhower. We had decided that on the day he was ordered to report to his induction center, he should remain at home in case the selective service board wanted to invoke the penal code for desertion from national service which applied in such cases.

"If they want to come and get you," I told him, "let them. You must be prepared to face the consequences of this commitment."

"Yes, but suppose the consequences are that I go to jail?" he asked anxiously. I looked at him. "Tell me, Fred, when you go into an army, do you have to obey all orders?"

"Well, sure."

"Then you are giving up your independent judgment, aren't you?"

"I guess so."

"And you are obviously giving up your freedom?"

"That's for sure."

"So if you go into the army willingly, aren't you accepting both total servitude and a robot status?"

"What are you getting at?"

"You seemed concerned about going to prison. But isn't the worst prison a bad conscience? At least, if the government puts you in prison against your will, you'd maintain both your judgment and paradoxically, your freedom. You told me you had read Thoreau. Remember when he was in prison for non-payment of income tax and Emerson passed by and asked him what was he doing in there?"

"Yeah I know. 'What are you doing out there, Ralph?' "

"That's right."

"I see your point. But what about the charges of traitor or being unpatriotic? My old man already thinks I'm a pinko and a few buddies think I'm a cop-out."

"That's to be expected. You're not the only one who has been condemned for following his truth. But we can eliminate at least some of the criticism. As a citizen of world government of serviceable age, you are about to volunteer for the world police force."

"I am!" he exclaimed. "But there is no world police force."

"There will be when you sign up," I replied starting to make out an application for the "Sovereign Order of World Guards." "At least, nobody will be able to accuse you of either cowardice or laziness. As to the accusations of Communist, forget it. The last thing the Communists want is a world government based on human rights with a world police force. That's heresy to world communism mainly because it exposes their nationalistic power base."

"It's logical," he said happily. "Where do I sign?"

I handed him the finished application form which read that, as a citizen of World Government he was applying for entry into the Sovereign Order of World Guards to be trained as a peace-maker, mandated by the Universal Declaration of Human Rights, under a regime of world law.

"I didn't know peace-making was such fun," he said after signing the form.

"Don't be too sure," I told him. "You might find yourself between two armies with nothing going for you but a uniform, a badge and your own guts."

"I'll take my chances. I just hope that before you send me between those two armies, you'll let them know I'm coming."

"By that time," I assured him, "you won't be alone. In fact, we might outnumber the two armies. But just the existence of a people's world police force would have an influence on would-be antagonists. The threat of peace-making can be as powerful, if not more so, than the threat of war."

Mr. Goldenkauf's reply arrived several days later. It was brief and to the point. Report for induction or face charges for desertion.

"It didn't work!" Fred exclaimed, after I read the letter. "I gotta go to jail. This'll kill my mother!"

"Wait. Slow down. Nothing's happened yet. Just the standard threat. Goldenkauf can't deal with the issues you raised. And as he's low man on the national totem pole, he's simply getting off the hook. The main thing is we've got a fast response. That's only the first step. There's a saying among salesmen: 'The sale begins when the prospect says no.' Now for the second step. Acknowledge his letter, state that he did not address himself to the issues you raised, that, as far as you are concerned, your reasoning is still valid, add that you have signed up as a World Guard and that you are fully prepared to face all the consequences of your action. Mail it registered as usual and send the three copies as before."

"But what good will that do," he wailed. "They'll just come and pick me up."

"Don't be too sure. First, remember that we've involved Washington by sending a copy to Eisenhower. Goldenkauf knows it. Also, we've involved the United Nations by sending a copy to Hammarskjold. That raises the issue to the international level. So essentially, the ball is out of Goldenkauf's court. He's done his duty. Now he'll just forward your letter down to Selective Service at the Pentagon. Any decisions made will have to come from there anyway. Don't think what you've done has no power. Remember, you're the citizen, the ultimate power-broker. You've exercised your sovereignty. You haven't just refused military service; you've opted for world service. Just sit tight. I know this is all new to you. In fact, there's no education for this kind of action, just some vague precedents. But hell, nobody's had to make world peace before, so we're all amateurs."

The day of Fred's induction came and went. He remained home. Nothing happened. No. F.B.I. agents came to pick him up. No military police. Only his family gave him problems, his mother tearfully professing that she approved of what he was doing, though she didn't understand it, because he wanted to do it, while his father accused him of unpatriotism and being an unwitting tool of the Communists.

Two weeks later, he dropped into the office. "What do I do now? Nothing's happened."

"If you leave New York," I told him, "keep your new government posted as to your new address. I don't know when we're going to need a world policeman."

"You mean I beat the draft?"

"You didn't beat the draft. You eliminated it. You've become the microcosmic solution to what the draft is supposed to solve. You exposed the government's false rationale without opposing it. Therefore, you're a legal 'hot potato.' You're a real menace now. The ball is in the government's court. I suspect it doesn't know what to do. Just sit tight and keep in touch."

Several weeks later, toward the end of May, I had occasion to visit Washington. I called an old friend, a prominent lawyer, to whom I recounted the story of Fred Haas. "Can you find out what action, if any, the Selective Service is going to take?" I asked him. He promised to try as he knew several lawyers in the department.

The middle of June, he called asking me to meet him for lunch at his alumni headquarters of a prestiguous Ivy League university.

"When I started nosing around among some friends in the Selective Service legal office," he started after we had ordered, "and mentioned the name Fred Haas, they backed off as if I were talking about the latest secret weapon. Naturally, I didn't pursue the matter further at that moment. But that sparked my curiosity. I zeroed in on an old pal who works with the Pentagon. After a good deal of friendly libation, I brought around the conversation to the kinds of cases he was getting in the C.O. department. Fred's story came out eventually.

"It seems his letters got tossed onto the desk of one of their staff lawyers. The more he studied them, the more intrigued he became. At least this was something different. The usual stuff is the Christian pacifist, or the black refusing to fight a white man's war or the radical who won't fight for Exxon or General Motors, you know, that kind of thing. But nobody till then had tried to step out of the whole blooming legal framework. That was a kind of fun. Well, he called another staffer over to have a look. But the more they looked, the less fun it became. Others were consulted. Finally, they called a full staff meeting to discuss the implications. They were definitely troubled."

So two letters from an average citizen received the full attention of the legal department of the military establishment of the largest, most powerful nation in the world.

"As you no doubt planned, they decided the issue was not simple C.O. First, there was the question of the status of 'world government.' What the hell was it? They didn't want to get into that. It was political; not their bailiwick. But then they were stuck with the second question of whether a U.S. citizen could pledge his allegiance to this alleged 'world government,' whatever it was. And thirdly, if he did, was he still a U.S. citizen? They didn't want to get into that one either. In fact, the guy told me, the more they debated it, the worse they felt. If they prosecuted Haas as a deserter, he could come up with all kinds of international law to justify his actions like that quote from the U.D.H.R. Then they've already had some problems with the Nuremberg Principles. And no lawyer paid by the Selective Service wants to defend national soldiery against human rights. The whole area is too fuzzy. Besides, they are all afraid of publicity. They know there are tens of thousands of young pups who would try to take advantage of it. Then there are the international implications. You can't keep a story like that within national boundaries. In short, it's a real can of worms. And when you add to that all the guys already in jail who might latch onto world citizenship once they knew about it, you've put the last nail into the coffin."

From my first talks with Nataraja Guru on board the S.S. America in 1950, I had become aware of the power of the knowledge of pure dialectics. Its application to the overall political scene, which the guru called "geo-dialectics," was a potent strategy by which to neutralize the oppressive laws of the nation. Pledging "allegiance" to World Government was the first step in applying that strategy. When Fred Haas performed that sovereign act, he exposed how weak the nation actually was. In Thoreau's essay on civil disobedience, he likened the state to an old lady counting her spoons—so weak it could be bent to one man's will. The evidence among nation-states of this truth was manifest daily as single men dominated current events despite the vast majority being diametrically opposed to their repressive policies. Mahatma Gandhi had reiterated this assertion by declaring that one just man could be the regenerator of all the unjust empires in existence,

"What was the final determination?" I asked my friend impatiently.

"When the government doesn't know what to do, it doesn't do anything. The buck gets lost. It just hopes the problem will go away. That's tantamount to setting up a committee. But the clincher came when some smart constitutional lawyer claimed that, if they prosecuted Haas, he could use the 9th amendment as his defense."

"And what's the 9th amendment?" I asked.

"Rights retained by the people, but unenumerated," he replied. "Very little judicial history on it. Only two pages in two hundred years. It's so broad, nobody knows how to use it. Called 'the sleeping giant' among constitutional lawyers."

"But how could it be used by Fred?"

"Simple. He could claim that one of those rights was the right to claim a higher civic allegiance. After all, the Declaration of Independence did claim that governments were instituted among men, remember?"

"But that's incredible!" I said. "If the U.S. Constitution can be used to add citizenship to World Government, then it is justified on constitutional grounds."

"I always suspected that Tom Paine was behind that amendment," he mused as we finished our coffee. "After all, Jefferson was in France at the time and Madison, who wrote the first eight amendments, was having a battle royal with Hamilton over the whole bill. Paine, who was the real people's righter, must have been advising Madison at the time."

"But wait, there's nothing in the U.S. Constitution about delegating power to a world government."

"Yes, but there's nothing denying or prohibiting it either. A national constitution itself implies the constitutional process. And that's the antithesis of anarchy. So, if the U.S. Constitution eliminated anarchy between the several sovereign states, then a world constitution by simple definition would eliminate anarchy between nation-states. But what's the legal bridge between a national constitution and a would-be world constitution? An affirmation of the right of the citizen to exercise an inalienable right to choose a higher civic allegiance. Now, if we take the 9th amendment seriously, Fred Haas, as a U.S. citizen, would have the constitutional right to delegate part of his sovereignty as a U.S. citizen to a world government not only to eliminate world anarchy but, ironically, to preserve the U.S. Constitution itself.

"Anyway, this is what this guy came up with. In plain fact, it's a legal bomb. They don't want this in court. They'll do anything to keep it out of court which means, in practical terms, sit on it."

"So what happens if Fred walks into a district court and asks for a declaratory judgment?"

"The merde will hit the fan." he replied matter-of-factly.

"What would be your legal advice?"

He hesitated. Finally, he said, "Wait. Let it ripen. The ghost of McCarthy still rides in Washington. You've won this small skirmish. But the main battle is yet to come and you'll need a lot more soldiers than you've got at this point. Somewhere down the track this will all come out. When it does, the public will be much more recptive to your ideas. Now, you're just a crackpot or at best a naive idealist. But for the American public, idealism doesn't pay. It's a luxury only those funded by the Carnegie Foundation can afford. And you ain't there yet."

I took his advice till now, 27 years later.

1984.

II
The Dennis Cecil Hill Case

Dennis· Cecil Hill, the British author, residing in Uganda during Idi Amin's reign of terror, was scheduled to die by firing squad on June 26, 1975, as an "enemy of the state."

The British journalist boldly and somewhat inadvisedly – as long as he was living in Uganda at least – had written that the president had been a "village tyrant." Whether this appellation fit or not is not relevant to our story. Whether free speech allowed a working author to defame a head of state is also not at issue here. What concerns us specifially is the aspect of the punishment fitting the alleged crime. No one can argue, least of all a head of state, that criticism of him personally, and/or his regime, merits the death sentence. The "security of the state," however, has become a catch-all for arbitrary detention, torture and even death by state leaders and their minions throughout the world to silence criticism by frustrated and oppressed citizens.

The case of Cecil Hill, therefore, posits the arbitrary power enjoyed by state leaders and their subordinates – who remain largely anonymous yet wield vast arbitrary power – against the honest individual who, on the assumption that justice will triumph if the truth becomes generally known, acts innocently and openly in criticising his government and/or its leaders.

In defense of President Amin, however, and in fact all heads of state, given the nation-state system, we can see clearly that their position is totally contradictory: they are the executors of law and order within the legitimate framework of their particular state, yet lead their state in raw combat, diplomatic or actual, vis-a-vis their fellow states.

Thus they are responsible both for internal order and external anarchy. Political schizophrenia is thus the sorry lot of the present-day head of state. He is continually painting himself into a political or diplomatic corner, where, on the one hand, he must extol normal civilized conduct to his national citizenry while at the same time exhort them mainly by fear and threats to justify or even glorify mass murder, i.e. war, also in their name.

The most base and deceitful examples of such a double standard of morality is revealed by the so-called Christian, Moslem and Jewish leaders who, in worshipping the same God, profess to universal ethics of love, justice and peace while at the same time maintaining a position of nuclear and conventional capability as national citizens vis-a-vis their professed brothers and sisters in other lands.

In the specific case under review here, a personal letter from Queen Elizabeth, seeking Amin's indulgence for a fellow Britisher, had not been sufficient to appease the President's stung pride. He insisted on a visit from the then Home Secretary, Mr. Callahan, as the price for Cecil Hill's release.

The honor and dignity of the United Kingdom, however, was not to be sacrificed for the sake of one human being, despite his British nationality, and despite the weekly coffee runs from Kampala to Gatwick, especially at the behest of a tiny African state led by a former sergeant in the British army.

What or who could save Dennis Hill? President Amin was commited publicly before the Ugandan people, and particularly his own army and elite guards, to avenge this insult to his person as head of state. He would lose face if he did not keep his public word. On the other hand, the public pressure building up outside the state made him aware that he had perhaps overstepped the bounds of public decency, and outraged the sensibilities of his peers. The official opinions of Presidents Kenyatta, Kuanda, Nyerere, Senghor, Monuto, Gaafir Al-Namiri and Ngouabi are not publicly known. We can assume nonetheless that they expressed their dissatisfaction and even disgust at the decision of a fellow African leader which undoubtedly did not ease Amin's twisted mind.

The World Court of Human Rights, founded June 12, 1974 in Mulhouse, France, though Dr. Luis Kutner, its Chief Justice, with the aid of his Commission on international Due Process of Law, had written and published the court statute—had yet to be activated in an actual judicial situation. (See Appendix)

On Friday, June 23rd, three days before the scheduled execution, from my office in Basel, Switzerland, I sent the following telegram to Dr. Kutner in Chicago:

"IN THE NAME OF THE COORDINATING COMMITTEE OF WORLD GOVERNMENT, I HEREBY REQUEST WORLD

COURT OF HUMAN RIGHTS ISSUE WRIT WORLD HABEUS
CORPUS AGAINST IDI AMIN ON BEHALF OF CECIL HILL
STOP
GARRY DAVIS
WORLD COORDINATOR

Fortunately, Dr. Kutner went to his office that Saturday morning. His response was immediate. He sent the following cable to His Excellency Idi Amin at Kampala:

"AT THE REQUEST OF WORLD GOVERNMENT OF WORLD CITIZENS IN BASEL, SWITZERLAND, AND THE COMMISSION FOR INTERNATIONAL DUE PROCESS OF LAW AND THE WORLD COURT OF HUMAN RIGHTS, I AM INVOKING YOUR EXCELLENCY TO ACCEPT THE HEREIN TELEGRAPHED WRIT OF WORLD HABEUS CORPUS IN BEHALF OF YOUR DETAINEE CECIL HILL, CONSISTENT WITH UGANDA'S SOVEREIGN STATUS AS A MEMBER OF THE UNITED NATIONS VOLUNTARILY ASSUMING THE HUMAN RIGHTS OBLIGATIONS OF THE CHARTER, UNIVERSAL DECLARATION OF HUMAN RIGHTS, AND OTHER PROTOCOLS AND CONVENTIONS GUARANTEEING THE SANCTITY AND INTEGRITY OF HUMAN BEINGS IN GLOBAL SOCIETY OF CIVILIZED NATIONS DEDICATED TO HUMAN DIGNITY AND STANDARDS OF DUE PROCESS OF LAW, RESPECTFULLY,
LUIS KUTNER
WORLD CHAIRMAN
COMMISSION INTERNATIONAL
DUE PROCESS OF LAW
WORLD COURT OF HUMAN RIGHTS"

At precisely 9 a.m., Chicago time, Monday, June 26, approximately six hours after Cecil Hill was due to be shot, Luis Kutner received a telephone call from Mr. Sam Msubuga, legal advisor of the Charge d'Affaires of the Ugandan Embassy in Washington, D.C

The burden of Mr. Msubuga's message was to inform Dr. Kutner that His Excellency Idi Amin had indeed received the telegraphed writ, was willing to comply to it and wished to negotiate Dennis Hill's release via his Washington Embassy with the official spokesman of the World Court.

On his desk, Dr. Kutner had an inch-thick book of authenticated violations of human rights in Uganda which he had been studying.

"We appreciate and accept the President's response to the writ," he told the legal advisor, his voice cool, not betraying his indignation at the atrocities committed by Uganda's former president. "As to the question of negotiation, please inform His Excellency that this is not a diplomatic matter. It is strictly judicial. Therefore, there is no question of negotiation. If the defendant is not released forthwith, this Court will issue a Show Cause Order to which the President will have thirty days to reply."

There was a short silence. Then, "Allow me to thank the Chief Justice for this further elucidation which I shall immediately transmit to His Excellency, the President. As soon as I have received further instructions, I shall inform Your Honor."

Two further telephone conversations between the Washington Ugandan Embassy and Dr. Kutner took place that fateful Monday.

Around 5 p.m., Uganda time, Cecil Hill was released from detention.

A perusal of the world media of June 27, 1975 will reveal a remarkable lack of news about a story which theretofore had occupied a good deal of space. Herein is the first full accounting of the incident.

It posits the empirical world government and its world court – utilizing the legal principle of habeus corpus raised to the global level – against the head of a nation-state, notoriously reputed for violating all legality and civilized conduct in his tragic reign, imposing capital punishment on the citizen of another state. I wish to emphasize that neither Dr. Kutner nor I considered the fact that Cecil Hill was a British citizen; for the purposes of both the World Government of World Citizens and its World Court of Human Rights, Hill was a de facto world citizen.

A sceptical reader may dismiss the incident as a dubious linking of isolated facts to prove a theoretical point or simply choose to ignore the obvious on the grounds that it was a one-shot with unusual publicity, a media "spectacular" where a weak, impressionable head of state was hoodwinked into accepting an "illegitimate" writ from a non-existent court, "authorized" by a fictional government run by a would-be do-gooder.

Heads of state, however, Idi Amin included, must assume a semblance of civilized propriety, not to mention legality, in their official actions. No head of state today, for instance, justifies armament budgets on the basis of conquering his neighbor or becoming "victorious" over an alleged enemy. All armament budgets are justified in the name of "national defense" or "national security" not national "offense" or "victory" despite the fact there is neither defense nor security in armaments per se. But "national security" is considered legitimate, therefore "civilized." It becomes, by this twisted logic, acceptable to the citizenry who, after all, must pay the bills.

Only 29 states from almost 170 or about 17%, admit due process of law procedures. That is, only 29 nations admit trial by jury and the principle of habeus corpus itself. Nevertheless, those seeking positions of public responsibility, whether by violence or consent, must maintain a facade of legality and/or

76

legitimacy, since the opposite is lawlessness and despotism

The uproar in the United States when the American public learned that President Nixon was bombing Cambodians in an "undeclared" war, that is, an "illegitimate" war, unlike the Vietnam war, which was "legitimate," was telling evidence of the need for so-called legitimacy even when the action is mass killing of other humans beyond national frontiers.

The writer was a legitimate killer in World War II as a B-17 bomber pilot, for which he was paid and duly decorated. His brother was "legitimately" killed, that is, by "legitimate" Nazi pilots dropping "legitimate" bombs on his destroyer during the invasion of Salerno, although the Nuremberg Decisions, ex post facto, condemned the so-called legitimacy of the alleged perpetrators of this war.

The Moscow Purge Trials of the early '50s also are telling evidence of the need for legitimacy by the state in carrying out its repressive policies as well as torture practices.

In the particular case under review here, President Amin was using his dictatorial powers, in the name of state security, to violate rights specifically defined in the *Universal Declaration of Human Rights,* viz. articles 2, 3, 5, 6, 7, 9, 10, 11, 18 and 19. While not possessing the characteristics of positive law, nonetheless, this Declaration binds all 154 member-states of the United Nations—to which Uganda affiliated itself October 25, 1962—specifically through article 56 of the Organization's Charter.

The World Government in this case was simply the legitimate framework claimed by over 190,000 humans as the political object of their prime allegiance, enjoining its empirical "court of world law"—empowered by one man's cognizance of his own judicial sovereignty—to utilize standard juridical procedures raised to the global level in a case of direct violations, even by a head of state, of fundamental human rights.

While it can be argued that our combined action was unprecedented, nevertheless it worked while the rest of the world watched in fascinated horror as yet another tragedy was about to unfold in unhappy Uganda. President Amin himself was offered a "way out" descending from "above" legally and in terms acceptable to his presidential office with little or no loss of face or dignity.

Had Dr. Kutner not been dedicated to the proposition that the world citizenry was already a subject of international law, had the principle of world habeus corpus not had the support of leading judges and jurists, including former ambassadors of the United Nations as well as former judges of the International Court at the Hague, had not the World Government of World Citizens been available as a global political "tool" for me to invoke as sanction, and had not the world been linked by instantaneous communication facilities, no doubt Dennis Hill would have, by simple ommission, faced a firing squad in the bloody Kampala police compound where so many perished before and since.

III
The Case of Yusuf Kaya

Yusuf Kaya was a Turkish citizen who lived in Coronado, California. He owned a house and property, earning his living as a journalist and writer. Though he was a resident of the United States with a proper visa, he still retained his Turkish nationality which obliged him to renew his Turkish passport every five years. This was normally done through the Turkish consul in San Francisco, a routine matter.

In mid-1972, Mr. Kaya decided to take a trip throughout the Middle East and Western Europe to gather material for a book about the status of women in various countries as an index of the political and economic status of each country.

Passing through West Germany on his way home, he suffered a heart attack and was hospitalized at Saarbrucken near the Franco-German frontier. There, as chance would have it, his attendant nurse, a lovely Rumanian political refugee, was taken by this lonely, attractive man, so desperately ill, and her heart went out to him without reserve. She already had a suitor, however, though she had given him no encouragement, in the person of one of the hospital directors, a Syrian. The personal rivalry was heightened by an absurd nationalistic conditioning of traditional enmity between Syria and Turkey though Kaya himself was no longer subject to it.

Blinded by jealousy and nationalistic enmity, disregarding all professional ethics, the director dismissed Kaya from the hospital to the dismay of the nurse, who, in desperation, took him to her tiny, one-room apartment.

While convalescing at the apartment of his now-fiancee, Kaya discovered that the term of his Turkish passport, valid until November 15, 1972, would soon run out. Were he still in Coronado, California, this would have presented no problem. However, since the Turkish consul in Frankfurt, West Germany, where more than 25,000 Turks lived and worked, contributing substantially to the Turkish economy through their monthly payments to relatives back home, was not only a state official but controlled this "population" with an iron bureaucratic fist, the problem for Kaya became not only convoluted but threatening to his very life.

Thoroughly "Americanized" in his attitude toward bureaucracy, he was unaware of the danger of sending his passport directly to the Turkish consul for renewal. His fiancee, however, still traumatized by her experiences in Rumania, her escape, the refugee camp through which she had passed and the precariousness of her present life, begged Kaya to utilize at least the channel of a German social security agency to request the extension. He did so in October.

Unfamiliar with Kaya's identity, the consul did not act on his request. As the deadline approached, Kaya became increasingly anxious since his re-entry permit to the United States was affixed to his passport. Finally, on November 15, he asked the social security agency to find out why his passport had not been returned, updated for another five years. The answer confirmed his suspicions. The consul was holding it up pending further information on Kaya. He curtly demanded Kaya's national identity card; but having lived in the United States for over ten years, Kaya no longer possessed one. The implication was clear for the consul: Kaya was either a wanted criminal, a deserter from the Turkish army, or a political refugee. In short, guilty.

In the meantime, as a desperate hedge against catastrophe, Kaya wrote to the World Service Authority, Basel, requesting citizenship of World Government plus a World Service Authority passport. We received the letter November 11, 1972. As we were receiving more than 200 letters daily during this period, we treated his letter as a normal request, unaware of the details.

Yusuf Kaya thus received both his World Government Registration Card and his WSA passport toward the end of November.

On December 16th, I received a second letter from Kaya describing his now desperate situation vis-a-vis the West German authorities. After receiving his documents from us, he had written a biting and bitter letter to the Turkish consul, exposing his "pandering attitude", unilaterally renouncing his Turkish nationality and informing him that he could keep the Turkish passport as Kaya would have no more use for it. So indignant was he at being treated like a serf, he was not deterred by the lack in Turkish law permitting renunciation of nationality. He received no confirmation on the part of the Turkish consul that this unilateral renunciation was either received, approved or denied.

What Kaya did not know was that the autocratic Turkish consul, suspicious after Kaya refused to respond to his request for the ID card, informed the Saarbrucken Commissioner of Foreign Police, an ex-Nazi by the name of Renner, that a certain Mr. Kaya, a Turkish citizen, was residing in Saarbrucken without papers and that he was wanted by the Turkish government for questioning.

Renner immediately summoned Kaya by letter to report urgently for questioning. He did so on November 18th informing Renner that soon he would have valid papers. The Commissioner replied that failure to present such papers would oblige him to turn Kaya over to the Frankfurt consul to be disposed of as the Turkish government saw fit.

Directly upon receiving his World Government Registration Card and world passport, he reported to the Commissioner's office to present the documents. "These are totally invalid," Renner told him angrily after examining the documents thoroughly. "Furthermore, they are prejudicial to your case. You have until December 31st to arrange your affairs. If, after that, you are still in West Germany, you will be taken into custody."

Yusuf Kaya left the Commissioner's office dejected and hopeless. How could he leave? He had no passport other than that of the WSA. Besides, he was now engaged. He could not depart without his fiancee. Also, he was still convalescing. There was no question of travelling at this time. He decided to seek the counsel of a lawyer.

After explaining the situation, beginning with his heart attack to the last meeting with Renner, he showed the young lawyer, Herr Brunner, his World Government documents as proof that he was represented by the new government based on human rights.

"But these are fraudulent," the lawyer told him impatiently. "There is no world government. Everyone knows that. I hope you did not pay good money for these. Please, I have no time for such nonsense. Good-day, Mr. Kaya."

It was December 27th, after the holiday season, that I returned to my file with the queasy feeling that some vital action was necessary for someone in immediate danger. Reading quickly through the urgent mail, I came once again on Kaya's last desperate letter. The gravity of his situation returned to me in a flood of anxiety. A man recovering from a heart attack cannot escape like a thief in the night. His unilateral renunciation of Turkish citizenship would be considered at least an act motivated by guilt and possibly considered treasonable. The Turkish government would never allow such a dangerous precedent to stand unpunished, a precedent which attacked the fundamental sovereignty of the state itself.

Now, having been literally rejected by the nation-state system, represented by West Germany and Turkey, Yusuf Kaya was desperately seeking help from his new government in which he truly believed.

But how could his new government help him? It was little more than a political fiction to which he had given his allegiance, a letter-head, mail-order government of monumental ambition and no resources. Or was it? What, after all, were those threatening him? Were they not also political fictions, a collection of individuals agreeing to constitute themselves within the framework of "government," then providing the machinery to give that fiction the semblance of reality? A traffic light physically is merely a red and green bulb set up at an intersection and programmed automatically to switch back and forth every 30 seconds or so. But only when it *functions* does it become a *traffic* light — only when it represents the "government" of that intersection allowing equal access to all the citizen drivers to movement through the crossing. Let it stick for even 30 seconds and citizen/drivers become nervous. The light has become "unjust"; it no longer guides traffic equitably. It has become "bad" government. It is no longer sovereign, that is, the citizens, with their feet on the gas or brakes, no longer delegate *their* sovereignty to it. It has reverted to a mere red and green bulb, no longer the fiction of "traffic" light. The result is revolution. The driver, after carefully looking to right and left, "breaks" the law and continues on his interrupted way.

But the "law" broke first. Henry Thoreau put it this way:

> *"Unjust laws exist: shall we be content to obey them, or shall we endeavor to amend them, and obey them until we succeeded, or shall we transgress them at once?...If the injustice is part of the necessary friction of the machine of government, let it go, let it go...but if it is of such a nature that it requires you to be the agent of injustice to another, then, I say, break the law. Let your life be a counter friction to stop the machine."*
>
> *On The Duty Of Civil Disobedience*

The West German and Turkish governments had broken the law of simple human justice in the case under review here. Kaya had turned to a new "traffic light," a global green light to which he had given his sovereign human allegiance. That was the key. The World Government may have been a fiction, but Kaya was not. Nor was I.

> *"The state is but a myth which perpetuates itself daily."*
>
> *Renan, 19th century philosopher*

The World Government could now legitimately exercise a *contract* of world sovereignty, recognized by both Kaya and myself, to get him back on the "freeway."

Would it work? That remained to be seen. The main point was that for Kaya, all other doors were closed. All lights were red! He was trapped by a system closed in on itself. He had nothing to lose by breaking the national law before it broke him. West Germany and Turkey were equal partners in the crime since both refused to admit even that national law was broken.

I sat down at my typewriter the morning of the 27th, inserted a World Government letterhead, addressing it to Herr Renner, Auswerdiges Amt, Saarbrucken:

> "With reference to the expulsion order your office imposed on Mr. Yusuf Kaya, this Authority wishes to point out that it derives from an administrative decision and not a penal court judgment. Thus it is not a result of any criminal activity on the part of Mr. Kaya. It therefore violates article 13(1), Universal Declaration of Human Rights: 'Everyone has the right to freedom of movement and residence within the borders of each state.'

> "Secondly, should Mr. Kaya be deported to Turkey, it is quite possible, in fact probable that he would face 'unusual punishment,' a viola-

tion of article 5, UDHR, in which the West German government would have colluded. Finally, Mr. Kaya advised this Authority that you informed him his possession of a WSA passport prejudiced his case. Since the WSA passport derives from article 13(2), UDHR, not only is your allegation false but it is prejudicial to your authority itself since it renders a judgment without judicial sanction or confirmation from your superiors.

"In view of these fundamental human rights and in conformity with German law, we hereby request a reversal of your decision with a restoration of Mr. Kaya's full rights in accordance with the abovementioned Declaration."

Copies of this letter were addressed to Chancellor Willie Brandt, Dr. Kurt Waldheim, Secretary-General of the United Nations, and Kaya himself. All were registered with return receipt requested.

Willi Brandt had just won an important political victory with his "Ostpolitik," whereby West Germany concluded a treaty with East Germany, thereby recognizing it as a separate sovereign state. This in turn prepared the way for both Germanys to become members of the United Nations. Mr. Brandt — a Nobel Peace laureate — would not be willing to risk exposure, I reasoned, by participating in a flagrant human rights violation. Signing the UN Charter meant a positive commitment of "universal respect for, and observance of, human rights and fundamental freedoms..."

I had learned both from former travels and innumerable dealings with the national official world from border guards to prime ministers that the nationalistic hierarchy, while seemingly solid and unshakeable, is in reality a house of cards, ready to be knocked down at the next election.

In Buckminster Fuller's words:

> *"Each of the sovereign nations' 'top men' cannot but wish with all his heart to move in the direction of realization for peace, through abundance for all, by risking more than perfunctory disarmament. The leaders are deterred from doing so however, not by the intransigence or treachery of 'the enemy' as the propagandized public-enemy image would suppose, but by their own political party without whose support they would have no chance of ratification of their acts. Their own party is deterred from such support by the constant threat of unseating not by the 'enemy' but by the political-party adversaries within their own respective national political systems."*

> *Utopia Or Oblivion*, Overlook Press

As for the U.N. Secretary-General, though he had no authority to effect any changes whatsoever in the status of the nation-states, out of respect for his office, and to imply that the affair was of an international character, a copy of the letter to him was mandatory.

Renner, at least in theory, like Mr. Goldenkauf, in the Fred Haas case, would be neutralized, unable to act further in the fear of reprimand from higher authority. The affair still physically resided in his office, but no longer were arbitrary decisions possible since an "auslander" element had been introduced. World Government, whatever that was, was watching.

When Kaya received his copy on December 29th, he went immediately to the Foreign Police office to see Renner. The Commissioner blandly pleaded ignorance of the letter whereupon Kaya sought out Herr Brunner, the lawyer who had summarily rejected his case before.

As the lawyer read the letter, reported Kaya, his eyes grew wide. A letter from the "World Government" quoting human rights, copies to the Chancellor, the U.N. Secretary-General and God knows who else! What was behind this facade?

"You see, Herr Brunner," said Kaya, "I am truly represented by World Government, fraud or not. And you cannot deny the reason of its arguments."

"Very interesting," replied the lawyer. "Very well, I will take the case." He picked up the phone, called Renner, told him brusquely that he was representing Mr. Yusuf Kaya and would need an extension of 30 days to study the file. A German lawyer was now addressing a German official who was obliged by law to respect his request.

Kaya returned to his fiancee's apartment to spend an exhilarating New Year's Eve.

The Turkish consul, however, was less than happy over Renner's extension. When Kaya did not show up in custody on January 1, 1973, wires began to hum. Renner explained the delay. The consul asked for instructions from Ankara. The reply was formal. The government wanted Kaya or else. A diplomatic incident was brewing. What if some – or all – of the 25,000 Turks in West Germany decided to follow Kaya's example and become citizens of the World Government? What of national sovereignty?

When the subject has refused allegiance, and the officer has resigned his office, then the revolution is accomplished."

On The Duty Of Civil Disobediance, Henry Thoreau

Once again Kaya wrote explaining the new situation. His fiancee included an anguished plea as well. The danger was now greater than ever, she wrote. If Yusuf were returned to Ankara now, the least he would face would be life imprisonment. He could also face a firing squad.

Once again I sat down at my typewriter this time addressing a World Government letterhead to Chancellor Willi Brandt:

"Mr. Chancellor,

We refer to our letter of 27 December, 1972, addressed to Herr Renner...of the Auswerdiges Amt, Saarbrucken, concerning the residence of Mr. Yusuf Kaya in West Germany. A copy of this letter was addressed to you as well as to Dr. Kurt Waldheim, United Nations and to Mr. Kaya.

...We have been informed by Mr. Kaya, in a letter dated 10 January, 1973 that, despite our intervention, Mr. Renner has received no instructions to extend Mr. Kaya's residence permit despite (its) extension from 31 December to 31 January, and he will therefore be forcibly expelled as of this latter date despite the obvious physical hardship and even danger such an act will incur.

You especially can appreciate, Mr. Chancellor, the vital importance in today's world of gross and flagrant denial of human rights, which in the past led to such catastrophes as World Wars I and II, of joining principle with practice if we are not to have a recurrence of such horrors. Indeed the very Preamble of the Universal Declaration of Human Rights affirms that the 'recognition of the inherent dignity and of the equal and inalienable rights of all members of the human family is the foundation of freedom, justice and peace in the world...' while the U.N. Charter dedicates itself to 'fundamental human rights' in its Preamble.

In the face of arbitrary administrative decisions by subordinates which abrogate human rights, supported by callous indifference of state leaders paying lip service to the same human rights...we cannot but hold responsible not the subordinate government official but his superiors, and in fact he or she who constitutionally represents the welfare of the people and each individual, i.e., the head of government.

We have confidence, Mr. Chancellor, that once brought to your attention, appreciating the gravity of the situation both for Mr. Kaya and for all those whose rights are being daily denied by those in power, you will see that justice is done, in other words, that his rights of residence, security of person and consideration as a person before the law (articles 2, 3, 7, and 13, UDHR) be respected by Your Government.

In the event that we have no confirmation that is the case, either from Mr. Kaya or from the competent authorities in Your Government, we shall be obliged to take whatever measures we feel necessary to expose this situation for the public record, as of the 27th January 1973."

Copies were sent by registered mail to Kaya, Renner and Dr. Waldheim. On January 15, I received a letter from the Office of the Chancellor, Bonn, stating that my letter had been readdressed to the Secretary of State of the region where Kaya was residing

The days passed with no word from Kaya. Finally January 25 came and went. On the 26th, I sent Kaya by express mail a World Ballot, asking him to vote for me as his representative according to article 21(3) of the UDHR. This would

84

give me added leverage, I felt, if it came to a court case. (See Appendix)

But what more could I do? There was always the media, of course. Only there was no story as yet. Nothing had happened, only threats and letters. Besides, such personal situations are so common as to be unworthy of media attention unless the victim was a known personality. Even the angle of World Government citizenship to avert tragedy was not always strong enough to avert the tragedy. Once I had commited myself as the "World Coordinator" to Kaya's fate, I had to be prepared to share it whether it be the hangman's noose or retribution.

I had to go to Saarbrucken, therefore, on the 31st to cast my lot with Kaya's. Somehow I had to enter West Germany only on my WSA World Passport. Then I would be in the same position legally as he was. If the West German authorities arrested him, they would have to arrest me also. Alone, Kaya could not attract much media attention, but with me tagging along in handcuffs, and a statement outlining the episode already in the hands of the press if we were arrested, we would be assured of some public attention at least.

Once again I returned to my typewriter: *PRESS RELEASE, 1400 H., January 31, 1973*
Saarbrucken:

> *Garry Davis, World Citizen, entered West Germany today on his WSA passport no. 00001 to represent Mr. Yusuf Kaya, citizen of World Government and holder of WSA passport No. 04462. Formerly of Turkey, residing temporarily at 60 Dudweiler Str., Saarbrucken, c/o Mrs. Kalinova, Mr. Kaya is threatened with expulsion by the West German government today. No reasons have been given for this arbitrary action by the Foreign Police Office, 60 Mozart Str.*

> *The Turkish government, through its Consul General at Frankfurt, has demanded the "repatriation" of Mr. Kaya in order to stand trial for having renounced his Turkish nationality and pledging his allegiance to World Government. The Consul General has allegedly threatened Mr. Kaya with life imprisonment and possibly death for this action.*

> *Mr. Davis has been designated by Mr. Kaya to act as his representative in all matters pertaining to his rights according to the Universal Declaration of Human Rights. Thus, on January 18, 1973, Mr. Davis addressed a letter to Chancellor Willi Brandt exposing the situation as a flagrant denial of articles 3, 7 and 13(1) of this Declaration. A copy was addressed to Dr. Kurt Waldheim, Secretary-General, United Nations.*

> *Since no assurance to date has been given by the West German government that this threatened expulsion will not be carried out, the case must be pleaded before the bar of world public opinion.*

On January 30, I telephone Jim Haynes in Paris.

"What are you going to be doing between 2 and 2:30 tomorrow afternoon?" I asked him.

"At two-thirty, I have to leave for my course at the university."

"Good. Get a pencil and paper." After dictating the news release, I added, "If you don't hear from me between two and two-thirty, release it to the wire services with the addition that both Kaya and I have been taken into custody by the West German authorities. If I'm still free, I'll call you."

"Got it, but how will you get into Germany?"

"I'll let you know after I'm in."

The next morning, I rolled my little Renault out of the driveway, took the highway to Strasbourg, then up along the Rhine river and came finally to the Franco-German frontier on a lonely road, infrequently travelled. My heart pounding, I drove slowly through, waving at the sleepy West German guard who stared at me unmoving. So much for the fictional nation-state. Arriving at Saarbrucken around noon, I quickly found Mrs. Kalinova's apartment

They were amazed to see me. "What's happening?" I asked. "Any news?"

"No, not a word," Kaya replied. "I don't know what to think."

"What time does your lawyer get back from lunch?"

"Around 2."

"OK, let's have lunch first, then we'll pay him a visit at 2 sharp."

Herr Brunner was punctual. Kaya introduced me as a representative from World Government. The lawyer stared at me incredulously. I asked whether he had taken any further action. He said no.

"I am not surprised, Herr Bruner," told him coldly. I looked at my watch. It was now 2:10. "Most lawyers are interested in corporate law or divorce cases. They pay well. Few like human rights cases, maybe because there isn't much money in them. But this case is slightly different. First, a man is threatened maybe with the loss of his life. Secondly, he is affiliated with a new type government based on human rights. The issue is clear-cut: national law regarding so-called foreigners versus human rights protected by what we call world law. It is a breakthrough case. Perhaps you have not yet realized the profound legal implications. If Mr. Kaya is not competently represented by you, and as a citizen of our government, I will see to it that, as his counsel,you will bear the full brunt of reponsibility along with the West German government if his fundamental rights are violated."

He looked from me to Kaya and back. I returned his gaze without expression. He sighed.

"Very well. I am thoroughly satisfied as to the legitimacy of Mr. Kaya's claims, and indeed his present papers...uh...in the circumstances. I admit at first I was somewhat skeptical. They are...unusual, to say the least. But I can appreciate they have a certain...relevancy to his basic rights. I will do what is necessary.

Have no worry. There are a dozen ways we can prevent his deportation. I will see to it immediately."

"Thank you, Herr Bruner, and now, where is the nearest post-office?" It was 2:20.

"At the corner of the street."

"Let's go," I said to Kaya. We bolted out of the office much to the surprise of the lawyer. At 2:27 I had Jim on the telephone at Paris.. He had already put on his coat and hat.

"It's OK," I told him breathlessly. "He's saved. Hold the releases."

"Great! The World Citizen rides again!"

(Editor's note: So far as can be ascertained, Yusuf Kaya still lives and works in West Germany with full residence and working rights. The only document he required from the World Government was a marriage license. The West German government refused to marry a "stateless Turk" and a refugee Rumanian.) (See Appendix)

IV
The Case of the Twelve Deportees

In these early years of World Government's existence, while its numbers are slowly mounting, it "works" mainly by resisting encroachments by national governments on its claim to human rights protected by empirical world law.

It is like a resistance government or a government-in-exile. The nation-state world claims OUR territory at this historical moment, each particular nation asserting an absolute right to determine what is lawful or not within its particular portion of the planetary soil. Thus it shifts us back and forth at will using its absurd passport and visa control system across its obsolete and oppressive frontiers, a vast "refugee" population literally "in exile" on its own planet earth.

Perhaps the least understood and most precious characteristic of law is its concentricity. While it has a common center — the moral code based on righteousness — it can have layers of application, one within the other, without conflict. The individual, the family, the community, the nation and the world community or the species are the five distinct levels of primal identification. Each has its own set of "laws" or codes of behavior. But because the fifth level remains uncodified per se — the United Nations Charter, as all treaties between nations, is merely a fourth level document pretending to be fifth level — world laws, while both moral and natural, have not been recognized as positive except through the embryonic institution: the World Government. Inevitable conflict arises between the rigidly-enforced national law level and the small band of world citizens incorporating in and by themselves a new legitimacy based on species identification.

To illustrate, on the American continent in 1783, after the victory over the British, citizens of the individual states wanted peace "between" their then sovereign states. Virginia, Pennsylvania, New York, etc. were small nations. (Indeed many nations today are much smaller both in size and population than they were then). The territory, at least on the East coast, was totally apportioned by this new Balkan community. The state law, by definition, could not accomplish the task of peacemaking since each state had to retain its separate sovereignty for sheer existence. There was no "place" for peacemaking law "between" states since each had drawn its own legal circle to the exclusion of all the others. But a larger "circle" encompassing them all could be drawn with which the individual *could also identify.* No new territory was added. The same territory sufficed. A new layer of law was simply added which claimed sovereignty over the citizens of all the states combined. Now the territory was not only state territory but *also* 'American" or "United States" territory . . . legalized by a new constitutional framework to which all states finally agreed after the sovereign people had given their agreement through popularly-mandated conventions.

This is not federalism, an essentially mechanical process. The dynamic of law identification is essentially organic and spontaneous, immediate and direct. Trust is its essential component whereas federalism is grounded in mutual distrust. Trust in turn derives from a knowledge of first principles.

In the following example, the community of trust between fellow world citizens, one side acting as a threatened constituency, the other side, as its counterpart, the government, proved sufficient to nullify the exclusive "circle" of the nation-state which threatened the individuals concerned with death and/or torture and which twice in this century plunged the world into war while the threat of a final war pervades the entire national community.

Ten individuals in June, 1974, all detainees in the infamous city jail of Hamburg, West Germany, wrote to World Government for help. They all faced deportation back to their native countries. Most were students. They came from Cameroon, Ghana, Egypt, British Honduras, South Africa and Tunisia. Two others, whose WSA passports had been seized by the foreign police, were also threated with deportation to African states. Willie Brandt had been deposed by Helmut Schmidt as chancellor of West Germany.

Most of the students would face serious reprisals if returned to their respective countries. Imprisonment for not returning when their visas or passports expired would be the most moderate punishment. But the Cameroonians would face death. The government had changed since they had come for studies in Europe. Their families were deposed and many killed. Yet their Cameroonian passports had become invalid. Their very possession of these documents incriminated them in the eyes of the West German authorities who had recognized the new Cameroonian regime.

Our Basel office processed the twelve applications in early July. In view of the increasing number of black Africans living and studying in West Germany who wrote WSA for world citizenship and passports, and after the success of Yusuf Kaya to remain and work in that country, now, with these new applicants— ten had lived like animals for over 9 months in the sordid city prison— I felt the time had come to update for the Schmidt government the entire history of the WSA and its relationship to the Federal Republic while at the same time effecting the release of the twelve detainees. Specific mention could now be made of the newly- formed World Court of Human Rights the month before since copies of all official correspondence were now being sent to its chief justice, Dr. Luis Kutner, for the record.

One of the Cameroonians, Emmanuel Tchatat, was to have a final deportation proceeding on July 27, 1974. His father, uncle and two brothers had been killed by the then-Cameroon government, according to his first letter to us. There was no evidence that he would not meet the same fate if returned to Cameroon. But the West German authorities were deaf to his pleas. He possessed a Cameroon passport therefore he was Cameroonian. The national passport was the dominant symbol of the exclusive "circle" of nationalism, utilized by all states, large or small, Communist or capitalist, Jewish or Islamic, North or South, industrialized or underdeveloped, rich or poor. If you possessed one, you "belonged" to the nation that issued it. Period.

But now, Tchatat possessed a passport circumscribing the planet. Now he had someplace else to go. To the world community! In other words, the World Passport, no matter where he happened to be, placed him already in that larger community concretely symbolized by a bureaucratic device—a passport—officially accepted on the lower "circle" level by all duly constituted authority.

The possession of the global document by the individual under threat was actual not theoretical. In other words, the national authorities—like the French government—had to take a stand, negative or positive, on the validity of the document accepted by the threatened individual. The French government's continued confiscation of the WSA passport as "fraudulent" revealed the absurd and obsolete nation-state thinking. The Chinese people actually exist representing almost a quarter of the human race. For the United States government not to have "recognized" them for over a quarter of a century did nothing to make them fade away but only to expose the total irrationality of U.S. governmental thinking.

The non-recognition of the World Government and its passport by a particular nation-state would not make it fade away, disqualify the validity of its documents or deny its actual existence. On the contrary, such non-recognition would eventually be recognized for what it was: institutionalized myopia.

My letter then to Chancellor Helmut Schmidt was dated 19 July, 1974:

> Mr. Chancellor: We wish to call your attention respectfully to the activities of the above agency and specifically to the enclosed document (WSA passport) which has been issued to the general public on demand since 1954. A specimen copy of the original document was sent to the Diplomatic Mission of the Federal Republic of Germany in Washington, D.C. on 15 July, 1954 and I here enclose photocopy of the Mission's reply dated 26 August, 1954. You will note that the submitted passport was duly forwarded to the Federal Republic of Germany. Our circular letter of 15 July, 1954 to all Member-States of the United Nations as well as to the Diplomatic Mission of the Federal Republic of Germany read in part:
>
>> "Conceived originally as a neutral and global document of identity and potential travel document for stateless persons, refugees and victims of political, social and economic discrimination along the lines of the Nansen and IRO passports, the W.S.A. passport is now being issued generally, mandated by Article 13, (II), Universal Declaration of Human Rights, to which Your Government is a signatory.
>>
>> "In view therefore of Your Government's commitment in prin-

ciple to the articles of this Declaration as well as its support of progressive measures to secure their universal and effective recognition and observance, we acknowledge on behalf of present and future bearers of the W.S.A. passports the *de facto* recognition of Your Government without need of further advice.

"Further, we request respectfully the transmission of the enclosed specimen copy to the competent authorities of Your Government in view to obtain *de juris* recognition at the earliest opportunity principally to persons not possessing a nationality."

As a Member-State of the United Nations, the Federal Republic of Germany has assumed solemn obligations (Articles 55 and 56) to respect and observe fundamental human rights. It has recently come to our attention that certain individuals actually residing in West Germany whose identity and travel papers have for one reason or another become invalid have been detained arbitrarily by your Foreign Police. This agency has been solicited by these individuals for help.

Arbitrary detention is a direct violation of Article 9 of the *Universal Declaration of Human Rights* as well as Article 9(1) of the *International Covenant on Civil and Political Rights.* Certain persons facing deportation to their countries of origin face extreme hardship, even death, if so deported and have openly stated such to competent authorities of Your Government. Nonetheless, according to our information, such deportation orders stand. You can appreciate that in such circumstances, the Federal Republic itself becomes an accomplice in the violation of Article 5 of the U.D.H.R. as well as Article 7 of the *International Covenent on Civil and Political Rights.*

The individuals requesting our aid in terms of requesting to become citizens of World Government and bearers of World Service Authority passports are as follows: (Editors note: There followed the full list of detainees and the countries to which they were scheduled to be deported.)

In addition to these specific cases, we are delivering on demand the WSA passport to West German residents, mostly of African origin, who wish to be identified as world citizens since they find their national origins severely limiting.

You will appreciate, Mr. Chancellor, that Article I, Part I of the *International Covenant on Civil and Political Rights,* recognizing the right of self-determination of political status by individuals, affirms thus the inherent right of sovereign choice by the humans concerned. The right of the individual therefore to commit his or her civic and political allegiance to World Government is herein sanctioned. This personal commitment—which exemplifies the essence of the democratic principle—in turn obliges the state to recognize the limitations of its own sovereignty since the choice of government is determined by the *sovereign* individual.

As Heads of State are responsible for the collective as well as the individual welfare of the citizens within their constitutional mandate, they can but acquiesce in the decision exercised by these citizens in the logal extension of citizenship to the global level by means of World Government.

In the case of those individuals without any national allegiance or whose national allegiance has been compromised by circumstances beyond their control such as a change of regime to which they are not in accord, the World Government offers the only valid political protection for their innate rights. We add that this is not the first time we have been solicited for aid by residents of the Federal Republic facing deportation and detained arbitrarily by the Foreign Police. I refer to the case of Yusuf Kaya and you will find enclosed our letters of 27 December, 1972 to Herr Renner, Auswerdiges Amt, Saarbrucken and 18 January, 1973 to Chancellor Willie Brandt (Ref. 1813/14) outlining his situation and our position therein.

We wish also to bring to your attention the existence of the newly-declared and forming WORLD COURT OF HUMAN RIGHTS, brought into being by resolution of delegates of World Government assembled 12 June, 1974 at Novotel, Sausheim, Haut-Rhin, to afford judicial sanction for fundamental human rights and especially to implement the accepted legal instrument of habeus corpus on the global level. Dr. Luis Kutner, chairman of the Commission of World Habeus Corpus, has been appointed Chief Justice of the World Court of Human Rights.

We are confident that once this situation is brought to the competent authorities' attention, the individuals involved will receive justice both according to their fundamental rights as well as to corresponding Federal Republic law."

Copies of this letter were sent to Dr. Kutner in Chicago, Dr. Kurt Waldheim at the United Nations in New York, the Governor of the Hamburg prison and to the 12 World Citizens awaiting deportation. All letters were registered with return receipt requested.

The result was immediate. Either Helmut Schmidt himself or someone in the Bonn government had the foresight to recognize that a number of hot issues were involved: human rights violations v. national law, Africans v. Europeans, blacks v. whites, poor v. rich, and finally, the nation-state itself v. World Government. There was no need, the official who gave the release order felt, to risk opening such a "can of worms" simply for the sake of twelve aliens rotting away in the Hamburg city jail. Also, despite his being chancellor of West Germany, Helmut Schmidt was head of his party and as later events proved, was removed from office by the simple expedient of a national election. His political vulnerability was even more revealed by the alacrity of decision which accompanied my implied threats of public disclosure of flagrant human rights violations under his regime.

The detainees were released immediately. They were accorded residence rights as students. WSA received enthusiastic letters from Emmanuel Tchatat and a few others expressing their gratitude for WSA services.

The identification with world citizenship — the fifth level — once again bore witness to an actual "circle of law" which proved superior to that of the lower level national.

One of our major regrets is that the World Government staff is still pitifully inadequate to cope with the literally hundreds of thousands of individuals still in despicable jails and miserable camps due to the exclusive "circle" of national law.

CHAPTER 7

A STATEMENT SUBMITTED TO THE SUBCOMMITTEE ON AFRICA
of the
COMMITTEE ON FOREIGN AFFAIRS,
HOUSE OF REPRESENTATIVES
NINETY-SIXTH CONGRESS, FIRST SESSION
Economic and Military Assistance Programs in Africa
Congressman Solarz, Chairman
February 13/28; March 5/12, 1979
by Garry Davis
Founder/World Coordinator
World Service Authority

INTRODUCTION

This paper will address a refugee problem not generally considered by those
responsible for providing aid through national legislation.

That problem, put in simplest terms, is one of identity.

A refugee, "one who flees for safety," according to Webster, faces first and
foremost an identity crisis little realized and thus unresolved by good-willed aid
programs from affluent states.

In our world, divided by nation-states, each arrogating to itself, rich and poor
alike, the sovereign right to act without restraint both with regard to neighboring
states — despite lip-service to human rights — and to so-called dissidents within its
borders, the individual who "flees for safety" is the tragic symbol and the immediate victim of the ungoverned, i.e. anarchic world community.

Viewed as a global phenomenon, the refugee cannot but be considered in a
new light. As states, unable to relinquish their exclusive sovereign character —
the United Nations being merely the institutionalization of the anarchic world
community — undergo continual political convulsions, increasing millions of
humans are not only set adrift from their homes, their villages, their jobs, indeed
from the very infrastructure of social and economic linkages essential to a whole

life, but they are literally forced "outside" the nation-state system itself. Yet, ironically, rather than seeking true safety in a world order, they seek "horizontal" refuge within the very system which rejected them in the first place.

This viewpoint is reflected in a United Nations' High Commissioner for Refugees Supplement Report of 1 February, 1978 which states that refugees "belong to the 'nation of the nationless.' This nation has no president, no government, no ambassadors, no unions to speak for its people, many of whom have no real home, no passport to travel on, no place to go."

Seeking "safety" from persecution from one state, the refugee quickly becomes the unwilling victim of equally callous states, only now as an unwanted "alien," subject to the most degrading exploitation, harrassed by petty bureaucrats and unconcerned officials. He is considered an object of charity, a "basket-case" by organizations and states alike, either herded into primitive, makeshift, unsanitary camps or refused even the title "refugee," given a Laissez-Passer good for a month or so and told to move on, a "refugee-in-orbit."

The Report of the HCR for 1978 to the United Nations bears out the virtual impotence of the HC office to take action against states violating refugee rights. Section C(6), "Implementation of international instruments," para. 43, states: "While accession to the relevant international instruments, particularly the 1951 Convention and the 1967 Protocol, is of primary importance, it is not in itself sufficient to ensure effective implementation of internationally accepted standards for the treatment of refugees. In several instances, the necessary legislative and administrative measures of implementation have not been taken or remain incomplete."

Former High Commissioner for Refugees, Sadruddin Aga Khan, in a report of 3 October, 1977, stated that "I am obliged to report today that frequent and repeated infringements of the basic rights of refugees have continued in many countries. A large proportion of our time is taken up by representation to authorities in respect of the infringements of the basic rights of refugees and asylum-seekers which in certain cases have led to tragic consequences for the persons concerned." "Refugees," he continues, "have been victims of violence and subjected to torture, subjected to unduly long periods of unjustified detention and to measures of expulsion or return in disregard of the principle of non-refoulement."

According to the U.N.H.C.R., Poul Hartling, there are over 16,000,000 "official" refugees in the world today. However, neither the 1951 Convention for The Protection of Refugees nor the 1967 Protocol gave any indication as to the procedure to be followed for the determination of refugee status. Thus, the "official" refugee count in no way indicates the actual number of refugees in the world which is undoubtedly appreciably higher. Also, it must be noted that as of September, 1978, only 72 states out of 165 have ratified the 1951 Convention and only 67 of its Protocol, no Asian nation being among them.

We note in passing that, if the "population" of the refugee "nation" is 20,000,000, which is not unlikely, it surpasses that of 107 nations.

The individual refugee discards his national identity in his flight from persecution. From then on, the traditional view of the refugee "locks" him into the national system, but now on the very bottom of the social and economic ladder. Not only is he dispossessed of his tangible assets—land, home, business, personal belongings—but also the "invisible" or intangible property, including identity, linking him with the institutional tools by which alone he can acquire new property.

This loss of "ownership" status is more insidious and destructive than even the loss of tangible property for without these linkages, the refugee must remain a charity case, unproductive, draining on the resources of the productive world.

Clearly, the escalating problem of the refugee, a global phenomenon, requires total reevaluation by those seriously considering legislation designed for his aid.

The Problem of Identity

At the very moment when the individual becomes a refugee, that is, when presenting himself at the border of a neighboring state, he faces an almost insurmountable problem of identity.

The first inquiry of the border official does not concern itself with his physical needs, but with his identity, that is, what papers does he possess certifying that he is who he says he is; in other words, his "official" identity, not his real identity. Since he is dealing with the official of a state, he must produce ironically, a state document to "prove" who he is. Usually however, he arrived with only the clothes on his back after enduring unimaginable privations.

The UNHCR's 1978 Report points out that "The absence of adequate identification of a refugee can create practical difficulties in his relations with the authorities."

The attempt to resolve this problem by a Convention between states has produced a "Catch-22" situation with horrendous results. Article 27 of the 1951 Convention "provides that Contracting States," continues the above-mentioned Report, "shall issue identification papers to refugees lawfully staying in their territory who are not in possession of a valid travel document."

The refugee at the border, however, is not yet "lawfully" in the country of sought-for-refuge. As he does not possess a "valid travel document," the border official cannot issue him an entry visa. Not having an entry visa, he cannot enter "lawfully." If he is refused entry on the basis of no valid travel document, either he must return to his persecutors or enter "illegally." In the former case, he faces certain imprisonment and maybe death; in the latter case, arrest, detention and eventual deportation unless accorded "asylum."

This identification crisis affects the refugee's very existence, not to mention his livelihood. Of all people requiring freedom of movement in order to find new social and economic linkages, the refugee is obviously first. For without freedom of movement, he indeed becomes an object of exploitation and charity.

The UNHCR Travel Document, ironically, is not issued by the UNHCR but by the Contracting State, remaining the property of the issuing state. Establishing residence of the right to return, this "official" refugee document is refused to many bona fide refugees by the very state which granted them asylum in the first place.

What the Refugee Needs

To reply seriously to the question, what do refugees need? is to seek the root cause of this "nation of the nationless," now an escalating global phenomenen.

This basic identity crisis, especially among the children, is totally unrelieved by "aid programs" since they depend upon his "refugeeship" to function proper- ly. (This may explain the lack of advocacy on the part of appointed aid officials, to cope realistically with the *whole* refugee problem.)

The so-called refugee problem in global terms is everyone's problem, since, in plain words, the refugee is merely the most immediate victim—other than war wounded—of an ungoverned world.

The anomoly, therefore, of the position of a national legislator is that, in order to truly aid the refugee, he must first convert him into a "citizen" of *his* com- munity. In other words, his rights and responsibilities *in a civic sense* must be restored before any material aid can do its beneficial work. This is not to say that he must be returned to his country of origin since to do so often replaces one persecution for another, and often a deadly one at that, but to recognize and identify a citizenship *where he is*, "outside" the parameters of the state itself, i.e., in the world community.

In other terms, he must be identified and begin to function as a true "world citizen."

Aid to refugees, then, must be globalized, psychologically, civically and materially. In the discussion on multilateral aid at the hearings, which enjoyed a certain consensus at least among the committee members, the principle of this global context was accepted. The UNHCR, however, was considered the only conduit for funds when, by its own mandate, flawed at the outset by the absolute sovereignty of each state, it is institutionally unable to utilize in the above- mentioned manner, good-willed funds destined solely for refugee aid. It is not a government; it has no authority but that given to it by the very states which, in an anarchic world, create refugees in the first place. Thus it "locks" the in- dividual into the very system which rejected him but now as a non-person, a veritable affront to society, a "refugee."

What kind of agency therefore can aid the "refugee/world citizen"? Obviously, first and foremost, a global one, independent of any and all states politically. The ICRC and Red Crescent come to mind as do certain religious relief organiza- tions, operating worldwide in the field.

The World Service Authority is another, dealing principally in identity but founded to implement fundamental human rights in general.

So essential is this question of identity and travel documents and so overlooked by those considering aid to refugees that we refer, in conclusion, to the statement of a refugee representative from Lesotho, Mr. Ntsukunyane Mphanya, now residing in Botswana:

"Refugee movements are restricted because they cannot have Passports unless they convincingly show that they have good reasons to travel abroad. The time they are allowed to spend outside the country of political asylum is also strictly limited. Having no identity documents such as Passports, they live in fear of not being identified in case of accident or death. We therefore owe the World Service Authority a great deal of gratitude for providing, free of charge, the Passports which enabled our student refugees to travel to the countries which have offered them scholarships.. .

The WSA Passports also helped our students to study in countries other than those of their political asylum. The World Service Authority Passports remain valid for much longer time than that of UNHCR which are issued only for two years.

"A WSA Passport in the hands of a refugee from an independent State has one advantage over the UN Travel Document. The WSA Passport does not reveal the status of the refugee in question and thus protects him/her against prejudice, suspicion and inferior attitudes, as well as against follow-ups that may result in such things as kidnappings and blackmailing.

"In most cases, Immigration Officers do not understand why there should be refugees from what are popularly called Independent States such as Lesotho, and tend to suspect them as saboteurs.

"The WSA Passports also give confidence to our refugees as a means of identification in case of accidents. The UN Travel Document on the other hand is only issued on the production of written evidence that a refugee is to travel. The WSA Passports provide a sense of identity and confidence in the refugee. He feels that he is at least still a member of the world community. They are a welcome security against frustration, disillusionment, and identity crises which claim the lives of so many of our refugees whether they come from dependent or independent states of the world."

II

LETTERS TO THE WORLD SERVICE AUTHORITY

RIYADH, SAUDI ARABIA

I am Palestinian, born and grew up in Gaza. . . .I am not involved in politics, terrorism, societies, and liberation fronts and so forth.

I have heard that you provide a refugee passport under the world amnesty international laws — I don't have any passport at the moment. . . .

Ahmad-Mahmoud Abu Satte

BUKAVU, ZAIRE

I am of Burundi nationality refugeed to Zaire since 1975. At present I work as a bilingual secretary at the office of the Under-Delegation of UNHCR. (United Nations High Commissioner for Refugees.)

99

As I soon intend to undertake steps to enlarge my knowledge in the Middle East, I must have (the WSA passport). For actually the Travel Documents of the (Refugees') Convention (of 1951) are issued here in Zaire with great difficulty.

In order to have one, it takes one to two years running after the authorities (Foreign Ministry). Because out of 100 requests for the Travel Documents per year, 1 or 2 may be accepted.... As a refugee I am completely indigent with regard to the payment. I hope you will submit my case to the World Refugee Fund so that I can have (the WSA passport).

Siudayigaya S.A. Antoine

LISBON, PORTUGAL

I'm having a lot of problems with my actual passport that was issued by Democratic Republic of Sao Tome e Principe.

Anytime I want to get a visa or a permit in any country, I have problems with my passport. As I am a sailor and as I use to travel all over the world, needing by consequence to get in different countries, I get crazy with those problems of visas. So, I would like to have some information about how I can get an International Passport valid for all the countries...."

Jose Antonio da Conceicao Mota

DARUL NASAR, PAKISTAN

I have the honor to submit that I have come to know about your esteemed mission which in my opinion is the greatest step towards the unity and well-being of human race at large without discrimination as to the race, religion and creed.

It will definitely go a long way in the promotion of peace, security and close relations between the different nations of the world.

In view of these facts, I have the sincere desire to participate in your esteemed mission and beg the favour of supply of relevant documents to enable me to complete the formalities of passport etc. at my end.

Muhammed Rashid Akbar

TAIF, SAUDI ARABIA

I am from Afghanistan. About 2 years ago I came to Saudi Arabia. I am staying in Taif city with my family (wife and 4 children) but still we haven't got a stay visa for my family. You know we lost our country because USSR soldiers are in our country. My life and my family life danger to go back to Afghanistan. For that if possible we want to go to the U.S. My brother and his family is in the U.S....

Abdul Rasul

LUSAKA, ZAMBIA

Being a South African, I flee my own country in 1967 soon after the Soweto problems. I am not a party member, but a Refugee. But I am in Zambia, I have been in prison for the whole of 1978. RELEASED: For the second term, I was detained for 4 months. Here again I faced torture, humiliation—called a spy.... I wrote to the United Nations Hq. in Geneva—but no help.... For the last time

I am writing to you in this query and if there is no assistance, then I will go back to South Africa only to be shot dead by the Boers – if that is what the world body (UN) would like to read about next time. . . .

G.J. Mpingka

DAMASCUS SYRIA

I am a Syrian citizen, born in Damascus in 1955. I lost my father in 1967 war. So my life became so painful, and the life of my mother also. After 4 years, I lost my mother because of a painful disease as I could not obtain money for her treatment. I was at that time 15 years old. Therefore I travelled to Lebanon and worked for five years in building profession. After that I returned to Damascus to visit some of my friends. But the Syrian government caught me to serve the compulsory service. I finished this service after 4 years. Then I travelled to Greece and worked in Athens for 2 years. I learnt Greek and some English, but I could not stay in Greece beceause of the expiry of my passport. As a result of that, I returned to Damascus to have a new passport. I was saddened to be informed that I am prohibited to have a passport for reasons which I do not know. . . . In the name of humanity, please help me. . . .

Yassar Mohammad Horany

SALAHUDIN, IRAQ

After the war between Ethiopia and Somalia in 1977, I deserted Ethiopia and flee to Djibouti with my four children and wife. In Djibouti the Somali Embassy gave me a Somali passport.

On 8th August, 1977, I left Djibouti leaving the children and wife for Iraq where I am presently living and working for the last 4 years. But unfortunately the Somali Embassy in Iraq has refused renewing my old passport and took it back, saying that I am not a Somali citizen.

For almost 2 years I am living in Iraq without having any regular travel documents and no way of leaving Iraq for Djibouti where my wife and children are. Please and please help me and send me a World Refugee Passport which I am desperately in need of. I pray there will be no war!

Abukar Farah Jama

JEDDAH, SAUDI ARABIA

I was a national of Burma and during the crisis of Burma I crossed the borders of India, Pakistan, Iran, Iraq, and finally managed to enter into K.S.A.

That my entry and stay over here is illegal and that I would be caught by the police I would be sent to jail. On the other hand, I don't have work permit, I don't have a job, and I maintain my livelihood with great difficulty. That at present I am enjoying no national right and hence I want to be a World Citizen. . . .

Abdul Hussain

BEIRUT, LEBANON

I am a Ghanian soldier of 21 serving with the United Nations Interim Force in Lebanon. I will retire from the Ghana Army after six years active service for further studies. Prior to this, I would like to apply for World Service Authority Passport, Identity Card and a Birth Certificate. My Officer Commanding, Major Crabbe has agreed to act a referee.

Corporal Thomas Appiah

TUTICORIN, S.INDIA

...I wish to inform you that I have received my passport together with invoice and noted its contents, Your remarkable service rendered in time is admirable and honourable....

S. Thibursian Machado

ISTANBUL, TURKEY

I am an Iranian who has escaped from Iran to the free world to search some freedom which I hope to find by your help and you should know that all my future depends on your help.... I have lost my family, all my capital and whatever I had, and since only I was writing the truth and taking about the matter of the country, they discarded me and put me to the jail for some months but I got away by luck and help of couple of friends who are executed now God bless them. Now I am here with no money and nothing...and since I have no passport I am afraid of going out and finding some job so I could live with the money I earn. The police in here are very strict about those who are refugees or those who have escaped from Iran. That is why I am afraid of being return to Iran.... You do not understand how good it is to be free, to be able to go out from one cold room in Turkey.... I am sure that International Red Cross could help as well but the first step would be your help through your passport so I can be someone.... I will never forget your kindness all my life....

(Namewitheld for secuirity reasons)

VALENCIA, SPAIN

I am half South African and half Jamaican because my mother, she is from Durban, S. Africa and my father he is from Kingston, Jamiaca.... He was a seaman. So when I grow up I took a ship and the captain drop me in Spain and the Spanish police ask me my passport I don't have no passport. So they send me to the jail.... So lucky a man told me in the jail that I have to write the World Service Authority for World Passport.... All my past life I am suffering because I don't have no passport and no one to help me....

Ray Henry Irvaine

INDIANA, PA., U.S.A

I resolve differences of opinion by peaceful means, without resort to war. Therefore, a "world" passport, even if it would be a pure symbol, serves the important purpose of making people to think about the future, to consider alternatives to the established order of things...the "world" passport is, at least, a symbol of unity—an ingredient of peace that is an element of "perfection".

A. Michailo

TIDAHOLM, SWEDEN

I am in a Swedish jail at this time and will remain so until such time as I am in possession of valid travel documents. I have refused to divulge my name to any authorities which is my right.... The Swedish police are attempting to fabricate a false identity and nationality against me.... My only way of preventing this illegal action is for me to have some form of travel document...

Prisoner No. 253

RIYADH, SAUDI ARABIA

I am a student of Afghanistan and at present student at the University of Imam Mohammed Ibn Saud.

I finished my studies in 1978 at Kabul University, Afghanistan. After losing my elder brother, they wanted to imprison me as well, therefore I got refuge in Pakistan. I stayed there for a period of one year. Finally I got a chance of coming to Saudi Arabia by a passport which I can only use for going back to Pakistan.

In order not to be deprived of my property as an independent human, I am applying for an international passport which your office distributes for homeless people like us.

Azizullah Rafiqzad

DJIBOUTI

...Ironically we refugees in Djibouti (are) leading even the worst life human beings have ever tasted — their refuge in life. Our refugee status is stolen and died. We have (been) more (than) 3 years in Djibouti but I cannot get a card at all.

We aren't recognized as human beings but are treated as slaves.

I know your organization is on the service of all deprived people in the world. So I am badly in need of pity, your card and passport soon. Of course we cannot fulfil charge of the money.

Please for heaven sake try to give your motherly hands to me.

Mahamoud Abdulahi

DJIBOUTI

The day is longer than my life definitely.

I have served on different international ships for a period of 18 years. I have been using Ethiopian passport because my country is Eritrea. When one day I went to Ethiopia to see my family and renew my passport, the Ethiopian state took and refused to give my passport assuming that I might support the political activities of my country Eritrea.

Then I fled from Ethiopia to save my life here to Djibouti.... I am laying on your knees and begging you to send me WORLD SERVICE AUTHORITY PASSPORT.... Please send to me the passport and save my life.

Berhe Teklemariam

TEMA, GHANA

I'm the first born son of an ex-minister of state who was sentenced to death

103

which has now been commutted to life imprisonment.

My father suspected of his arrest as soon as he heard of Flight Lieutenant Jerry J. Rawlings's coup on 4 June, 1979. So he transferred all his assets to me for fear of being confiscated to government's chest.

Due to this I have been appearing very often before so many committees and commissions of inquiry for interrogation (never) without a torture.

Because of this brutal treatment, I have made up my mind to leave...and go somewhere in the world where I will have my freedom and right as a human being.

I have made every effort to secure passport locally but all my attempts have been spoiled.

Fortunately for me, a best friend of mine who has vowed to help me get out of Ghana brought me this address of yours as the only hope for me to escape any further torture....

(Name withheld for security reasons)

KHARTOUM, SUDAN

...I have been living in the refugee camp in Sudan since 1978...

Teclay Zeray Yahdodo

BEIRUT, LEBANON

...With due honesty and sincerity, I do greatly appreciate the outstanding activities of your Service, in defending, safeguarding and in coming to the rescue of those overlooked victims of the so-called "Human Civil Rights" all over the world.

Your continual efforts, and your serious positive task in assisting all suffering human beings, victims of international travel and communications' barriers, and trying to issue for them appropriate World Service Authority Passports, can only fill our hearts with gratitude, and render us thankful forever.

I, the undersigned, am one of those victims, suffering from the impossibility to travel anywhere, and this resulting from the circumstances in which my parents were living, and were unable to secure for me a sound and legal nationality.

Presently I am living in Lebanon, where nowadays the survival of any individual is a miracle, due to the unfortunate civil war in which the country is losing its human face.

Thus, my only hope remains your World Service Authority...

Vazken Moughalian

MOGADISHI, SOMALIA

I get some information...all about W.S.A. and its aid to the stateless people to which you are not connecting any conditions who want help from you, if he has nationality or not....

Ali Sh. Mahamud Kasim

COLON CITY, PANAMA

I left my homeland 7 years ago to continue my studies holding a passport issued by Israel's Government available for only 1 year. Now I cannot obtain a new passport from Israel's Immigration Office because I am Palestinian and I didn't renew it before the year it expired.

Now I am living in Panama City without a document valid to travel out of Panama...

Tawfik Ibrahim Musa Jebara

ILVESHEIM, W. GERMANY

I tried to prolong this passport by the Lebanese embassy in Germany. But they never sent me back my passport so that today I am without any passport or identity card. Then I heard of your organization, that you help people who have neither passport nor nationality. I urgently need a passport to lead a normal life as a foreignor in Germany....

Ghassan Ghazzawi

LUBECK, W. GERMANY

On 10 September, 1981 I went down with cargo ship m/s "Lucjan Szenwald" in Bremen, and I don't want life here. I have only Polish Seaman's Book but when I want emigrate I need any pass....

Witold Brylowski

BERLIN, W. GERMANY

I am Kurdish from Arbil, Iraq. I fled my country due to racial discrimination practiced by Iraq Baath regime towards Kurdish people....

I am writing to ask for help from your organization which is world known for its help for humanity...

Jartis Moaid Ismail

TEHRAN, IRAN

I am in receipt of your registered ltr. having W.S.A. Passport. I am highly obliged and grateful for your sincere cooperation, in real I have no words to pay you thanks.

I am trying to introduce this document to many peoples and also peoples showed much interest it. It is a valuable document for reasonable peoples....

M.S. Durrany

TEHRAN, IRAN

We have been apprised through a most reliable friend that your esteemed firm provides international passports for those who are stateless.

In April, 1980, we were expelled from Iraq, along with thousands of others, due to our Iranian ancestry. Everything we owned was left behind. Not only were we not allowed to take any of our possessions and belongings with us, we were not given our birth certificates, travel documents or passports to take along with us.

We entered Iran on April 10, 1980 and, at the present time, only have our "Laissez-Passees". So please be so kind to issue international passports to all the members of my family (10 from ages 9 to 28).

Many thanks, in advance, for your kind consideration and cooperation in this matter and thank you most appreciatingly for your understanding of the word

"HUMANITY".

Samireh Bakhtiar

PARIS, FRANCE

... I am a Sri Lankian Tamil by nationality born 4/1/55 at Jaffna. There is a struggle in Sri Lanka between the majority and the minority communities. The minority community fights for their freedom and their civil rights.

The Tamil United Liberation Front which represents the Tamil community...signed too many pacts with the governments to bring a settlement between two communities.... The Tamils lost their confidence and decided to live separately.

As a result of this, we the youths had been harrassed and attacked by the forces of the government for no reason. We were not allowed to move freely. Number of youths had been murdered and millions of millions worth of properties had been burnt to ashes

I was an owner of a business establishment with a fantastic capital. My establishment had been looted and burnt to ashes.... There was always danger for my life.

As I could not tolerate any further, I left my country and came to France with the intentional of seeking political asylum. But in France my application had been rejected on the count that I had not submitted any documentary proof in support of my persecution.

I spent numerous nights in the metro without proper facilities.... No proper guidance or assurance were given me by any individual or establishment. I lost my passport and my belongings while I was sleeping in an open place. I am helpless without a red cent. I have no correspondance with my parents in Sri Lanka who are living with fear and tears. I have no way of going to any country. I am dead sure that my life will be taken by the forces if I return to Sri Lanka. My brothers are in police custody (there) over suspicion of militant activities.

At these circumstances, I humbly beg of you to consider my pathetic situation....

(Name withheld for security reasons)

KARACHI, PAKISTAN

My father Abdul Rasool was a shopkeeper. His business became end and he is now Mujahid and fighting against Karmal/USSR forces.

My elder brother Noor Admad died in a camp SINZARI, 8 miles from Kandahar when air attacked by the USSR Air Force.

Leaving the dead body, we forced to migrate to Pakistan to take refuge along with my old aunt.

We are 4 brothers (with) ages 14, 8, 6, and 4 years. My old aunt cannot help to take the arrangements for education

In view of above, we cannot educate ourselves alone except help from other sources. Therefore, we beg to request that arrangements for our education may kindly be made....

Manzour Ahmad

JEDDAH, SAUDI ARABIA

Sometime I chance your service passports owned Turkish people. They said, if you get it World Service Authority Passport, you can catch job opportunity in a lot of countries.

Now I want own W.S.A. Passport. . . .

Ertugrul Cenber

KARACHI, PAKISTAN

We are five students between the ages of 15 to 19 years. We are Afghani residing in Kandhar. After the bombardment of Russian our houses demolished killing our entire family including mother, father, brother & sister, etc. We are now living hand to mouth as every essential of living is being looted by Russians and now we are all alone. After nothing is left we have migrated to Pakistan in camp but not yet settled. It will be highly appreciated if we are allowed to proceed to America to complete our education as we are losing our golden time for education. . . .

Nisar, Sheer, Khalil, Baseer, Manzoor

LA GUAIRA

As a political refugee from Ethiopia I had to leave the country in March 1981 on board this vessel. As I have no passport and only Ethiopian ID card and driver license I would like to acquire WORLD DONOR PASSPORT. Presently no Immigration Service of the ports this ship has been calling has given me permission to leave. . . .

Ghebre Bokurezion Zadik

LUSAKA, ZAMBIA

I am a Namibian refugee residing in Zambia under UNHCR and would like you to send me the forms for the WSA passport and identity documents. In addition to passport forms I will be glad if you send me those for registering as World Government citizen as well. Your service to world community is appreciated. I would also like to find out whether it is possible for the WORLD REFUGEE FUND INC to pay for my documents.

Elizabeth Niambari Nangolo

BELGRADE, YUGOSLAVIA

I am student from Iraq but I am study in Yugoslavia in the third year. I need help from your World Service to send me documents for passport. Because I know this is the first world office in the world they help every pupil in the world to live free.

Mohamed Abbas Rijab

PESHAWAR, PAKISTAN

I'm sending the application form of my mother. She recently came out of Afghanistan on pilgrimage pass, she urgently need World Service passport to obtain residential permit to be registered in her passport. . . . Thanking for your help and cooperation you are extending to most true cases of the people of Afghanistan.

107

CHAPTER 8

THE NATIONAL PASSPORT SWINDLE

"Swindle: To obtain money or property from one by fraud or deceit; to cheat or defraud." "Fraud:...4, Law. An intentional perversion of truth to induce another to part with some valuable thing belonging to him, so to surrender a legal right."

Webster's New Collegiate Dictionary, 1960

"Everyone has the right to leave any country, including his own, and to return to his country."

Article 13(2), Universal Declaration of Human Rights

A national passport represents arbitrary, exclusive, sovereign national frontiers. Its possession and use is imposed on the national citizenry by law. It can be and often is denied for arbitrary reasons. It belongs to the national government that issues it. It is essentially, therefore, a control device by a national government over its citizenry. By reciprocity, it also controls the entry and exit of citizens of other nations.

In the legal definition of fraud, the citizen has been induced "to part with some valuable thing belonging to him" i.e., his inalienable right to freedom of movement, by his forced acceptance of a bureaucratic device designed deliberately to control that movement.

The national passport system therefore swindles the individual of the inalienable right to freedom of movement.

Freedom of travel is a hollow mockery in the world of nation-states. All states from East to West, North to South, are in collusion with each other in perpetuating this fraud upon a docile public that is deceived by the very word "passport," as if it granted the right to travel. The exact opposite is true. Our right to travel is an inherent right and each state, in recognizing the sovereignty of the people, must recognize that right, either *de facto* or *de jure*.

108

The fraud is further compounded by the issuing fee for some passports. In Cameroon, for example, a "security deposit" of $3,000 is required before a passport is issued; in Ghana, the "up-front" price merely for the application form is 300 cedis, about $300. In Turkey, a passport can run as high as $1,500; in many other countries, particularly in Eastern Europe, it is virtually unobtainable.

To citizens of the so-called free and most powerful nations, the U.S.A., Great Britain, France, West Germany, the passport swindle only becomes apparent when a well-known person is refused a passport for political reasons or if a person is abroad being persecuted by another state. Citizens in legal or political trouble may have their passports revoked or even confiscated, leaving them at the mercy of the bureaucracy of a "foreign" state. Lack of a valid passport is a "crime of ommission." The author has been incarcerated thirty-two times for this "crime." A second-hand market in stolen national passports thrives on this modern dilemma.

The problem for the would-be traveler, however, does not lie only with whether he will be issued a passport, but also with where can he go with it. The mere possession of a national passport is not a "carte blanche" for world travel. The Rhodesian passport, for instance, during the Smith regime, was recognized only by South Africa and Switzerland, while the Hong Kong, Albanian and Cook Island passports, for example, enjoy recognition from a severely limited number of sister-states. Even the U.S. passport by itself does not guarantee worldwide travel. Seventy-two out of 162 states require visas before admitting U.S. citizens. As for the U.S. admitting citizens of other countries, a U.S. visa is mandatory. No "foreign" passport is recognized per se by the freedom-loving U.S.A.

In black African states, where passport issuance is concerned, the city-dwellers are often favored over bush dwellers. The rich, of course, are favored over the poor for two major reasons: they can afford the exorbitant issuing fees as well as the invidious "dash," and they can pay their way home in the event of trouble abroad. Because the national passport is the property of the issuing nation-state, that state assumes liability should a sister-state accuse the passport bearer of "undesireability." The accused may then find himself in arbitrary detention which the imprisoning state claims is only "protective custody," or he may be returned to his native country at the expense of his government where, more than likely, he will face trial and conviction for having behaved badly abroad.

If he has left his country to escape the army draft or because of political, economic or legal problems, he may prefer to remain in prison rather than risk being returned to his country to face certain imprisonment and, in some cases, execution.

With the rapid changes of government in certain parts of the world, being repatriated means certain death for those forced to flee for their lives in the first place. In such cases, to what avail is their national passport? It becomes a liability of dire consequence if retained for it connotes "propertyship" by the new government. Better to become stateless without any documents than to be linked to a state as "property" when return means certain imprisonment or worse. In such cases, the national passport is more than a deceit and a fraud. It is a death trap!

Viewed globally, all passports are absurd. The world community is indivisible by definition. Despite nationalistic prayers to the contrary, the Almighty did not create the sub-divisions called nations. At the risk of heresy, neither does He sanction or bless them.

The national passport and visa system, imprisoning millions in latter-day feudalistic serfdoms called nation-states, should amply confirm this unsuspected and for some, no doubt blasphemous fact. Nataraja Guru wrote in *The Memorandum On World Government*: "Poor men, who have to make a living wherever it is at present available to them, are kept from freely reaching out to their God-given opportunities by artificial manmade rules. These rules must be broken down. Travel becomes more and more difficult and rules are piled upon rules by nations big and small for no valid or justifiable reason except to retaliate in the name of national pride or exclusiveness. . . . One has to linger only a few minutes at passport or permit offices to be convinced of the large volume of suffering to which men and women are subject. . . ."

Rather than actively expose this shameful practice, the greatest intellectual and moral personages of our times, the religious leaders, the scientists, philosophers, sages, gurus, humanitarians, artists, leaders of vast industrial empires, directors of worldwide agencies aiding fellow humans in a hundred ways, all abjectly accept and utilize the potent symbol of their subjection to modern imperialistic bureaucracy: a national passport.

How did this debasing scheme evolve in the first place? Ramsey McDonald, Great Britain's Prime Minister in 1924 is credited with launching the modern passport system. National passports were considered for the most part a simple convenience issued at the request of the travelling citizen. The author's parents travelled yearly to Europe in the 1920's equipped only with a boat ticket and hotel chits. Since 1924, the system has grown gradually obligatory.

Today, most of us travel for personal reasons. In a survey conducted by the Passport Office of the U.S. Department of State in 1977, 69% of those requesting passports stated their reasons for travelling abroad were either "pleasure" or "personal." Six percent were on business, 2.5% for study purposes, and 5% on government business. Yet despite this overwhelming percentage travelling for non-political purposes, travellers are obliged to carry an essentially political identification.

What of the return to one's country? On returning to the United States, for example, the citizen is required to produce a passport. Otherwise he will be presented with a waiver form stating that to enter the U.S., he must produce a "valid passport" and not possessing such, he requests than an exception be made in his case. The "service fee" for issuing this form is $25.

The U.S. Supreme Court has specifically ruled that the Department of Justice cannot limit the travelling of its citizens. It follows that a U.S. citizen may re-enter his country without a government passport since such entry depends upon citizenship whether documented or not.

In a letter of November 25, 1975, however, to the Hon. Charles Percy, U.S. Senator, Robert J. McCloskey, Assistant Secretary for Congressional Relations, pointed out an ominous exception to the high court ruling: "The modern passport requirement was codified in the Immigration and Nationality Act of 1952, 8 USC sec. 1185a and b, under which it is unlawful for the United States citizen to enter or exit this country without a valid passport *during a time of national emergency.* Pursuant to this legislation, the President issued a proclamation on January 17, 1953 (proclamation no. 3004, 18fed. reg. 489) proclaiming a national emergency which is still effective today under which the Secretary of State was delegated the authority to issue passports and limit their validity to travel in certain geographical areas." (Emphasis added.)

We note first that no democratic process was involved here, only a presidential proclamation. Secondly, if we check the date of issuance of the "national emergency," January 17, 1953, we are struck by the astonishing fact that the White House resident was "lame duck" Harry Truman serving out his last three days! Eisenhower was inaugurated January 20, 1953. Thus the proclamation of a "national emergency" by an outgoing, no-responsibility president has justified till this writing giving all succeeding Secretaries of State an absolute dictatorship over 215 million humans as to whether they can exit or enter their own country without a governmental passport.

And the United States citizen considers his country the bastion of freedom, at least in comparison with other countries.

The contrast of the fraudulent, restrictive device called the national passport versus the need of the vast travelling public is nowhere more dramatically revealed than in the world of international civil servants whose primary political allegiance is, surprisingly enough, to their organizations rather than to their nations. Art. 100 of the United Nations Charter, for instance, reads: "In the performance of their duties, the Secretary-General and the staff shall not seek or receive instructions from any government or from any authority external to the Organization. They shall refrain from any action which might reflect on their position as international officials responsible only to the Organization.

Similar pledges of "allegiance" pertain for other international organizations such as NATO, UNESCO, the Council of Europe, and the like plus the myriad semi-official NGOs attached to the UN. There being no international government, however, to issue them a "valid" international passport, they make do with a national one supported by various and sundry ID cards to identity their international status.

Red Cross officials, other than Swiss officials whose national passport carries the Red Cross on its cover, often find their transnational work hampered by lack of a neutral travel document when their national passport is unrecognized by a sister-state paradoxically requiring their aid.

Seaman likewise, voyaging on the frontierless high seas, find the national passport ludicrously restricting. Forced to possess an exclusive territorial document while fulfilling a non-territorial task, the seaman is continually frustrated by expiring dates of validity, visa requirements, even changes of his domestic government which often render his national passport invalid. When his reasons for signing on a ship in the first place were to escape his native country, say, for avoiding military service, his first request at a consulate for extension of the validity of his passport indeed might result in his repatriation and imprisonment for desertion.

Other professionals, such as transatlantic pilots, stewards and stewardesses, travel agents, officers of multi-national corporations, journalists, and in fact all media personnel, scientists, artists of all kinds, engineers, students, migrant workers or any one engaged in activity of an apolitical and transnational character, find the current national passport system not only an affront to human dignity and commonsense, not only a colossal nuisance and perpetual harrassment from bureaucrats, but a manifest fraud to which they would never voluntarily consent if given the choice.

A word is in order about the origin of the first non-political or refugee passport. Fridtjof Nansen, the Norwegian Arctic explorer, zoologist and statesman, and Norway's delegate to the League of Nations, convinced his fellow delegates to establish an extra-territorial and anational passport for stateless persons and refugees, mostly White Russians, living in Europe in the aftermath of the first world war and the Russian Revolution of October, 1917. The "Nansen Passport" was the first truly international identification and travel document since it was issued to individuals of varying national origins. It thus fulfilled a vital need for those unfortunate persons totally deprived of any identification documents and therefore subject to continual bureaucratic persecution from national officials, often resulting in detainment in wretched camps for indefinite periods. For this humanitarian service, he was awarded the Nobel Peace Prize in 1922.

In 1938, the Nansen Office for Refugees, with its narrow mandate and meager funds, now officially mandated by the League of Nations, was trying desperately and heroically to cope with the growing problem of refugee identification for which efforts it was justly awarded the Nobel Peace Prize for that year. The official successor to the NOR was the United Nations High Commissioner for Refugees Office with an interim organization, the International Refugee Organization filling the gap from the collapse of the League to the founding of the UN in 1945. Passport, or rather, identity and travel document issuance, however, had passed from the refugee organization itself to the "High Contracting Parties" or nations which ratified a highly-circumscribed 1951 refugee convention. Nevertheless, the Norwegian judges conferred on this largely impotent HCR Office the 1954 Nobel Peace Prize.

The refugee is by definition the most immediate victim of the anarchic condition existing between equally sovereign states from which derives the absurd and oppressive national passport and visa system. The recognition by the Nobel judges that identification for refugees is an act of *world* peace is reciprocally to condemn the nation-state frontier world as antithetical to world peace, i.e., the cause of world conflict. But the above-cited organizations, devoted to the refugee "cause", do not and cannot consider the hapless refugee as a *de facto* world citizen, replete with innate and inalienable human rights like everyone else. Better to award the Nobel Peace Prize to those "refugees" who claim world citizenship than to those who help fortify that degrading status.

The individual the most exploited by the despised system is the bored and arrogant frontier guard who earns his living maintaining it with his daily presence. Low man on the totem pole, he must consider all who pass before him as "guilty" until they prove their innocence with the bits of paper his superiors have designated as "valid." The duality is as obvious as it is ludicrous permitting them to enter the modern fortress or not as its temporary rulers decree. A narrower, more morally and intellectually debilitating occupation could not be devised by the reasoning mind except perhaps that of diplomat who performs essentially the same ritualistic function but with the entire armed forces at his back, so to speak, and in more elegant if artificial surroundings with, of course, a substantial increase in emoulement. Both, however, are servitors of the almighty state . . . at the expense of their own humanity.

The ultimate exposé of the unmitigated fraud which is the national passport system orbit silently and mockingly above our collective heads by the thousands. The cosmonauts and astronauts circling the planet dozens of times daily could not but have wondered at Man's myopia in sectioning off his home planet in spite of its self-evident oneness. And upon returning to their arbitrary sections, after representing literally the sovereignty of the human race itself, did they present national passports at their respective frontiers? Ridiculous question? No doubt. But if so, how much more ridiculous when you and I cannot go about our own planet without bits of paper identifying us as being from a particular section of it.

No one, from Yuri Gagarin to Sally Ride, were issued national passports upon their departure from earth since they were not required upon their entry. Were they not then pragmatic world citizens, pioneers of all of our common destiny?

Neither the U.S. Secretary of State nor his counterpart in the Soviet Union is able to deny the legitimacy of this de facto world citizenship.

The dominating fact of space travel in our century logically updates the *Universal Declaration of Human Rights* article quoted at the beginning of this chapter, to wit: *"Everyone has the right to leave every planet, including his own, and to return to his planet."*

Further, the rightful complement to this already implemented article would be the following:

"Everyone has the right to freedom of movement and residence within the space borders of each planet."

It is only a matter of time before the human race claims the planet earth as its rightful home. The national passport will then be relegated to such quaint artifacts as the Iron Maiden, the boned corset and the whipping post.

CHAPTER 9

POSITION PAPER
1978

The United Nations vs. The World Government

Never before has it been so important to find a solution to the problem of substituting law for force in international affairs. It is almost a cliche to say that our very existence depends on finding a solution and finding it soon - but if this is a cliche it is also a frightening truth.

U Thant, *Secretary-General, United Nations, 1963*

1. Historical Background

The author fought with the Allies in World War II from the ruins and idealism of which came the present United Nations. His right to take an active role in the personal issue of world peace may be said to be categorical and sovereign. The same may be said of all combatants from whichever "side". To have been intimately involved with world war and not to play a dynamic part in world peace is to have fought in vain. Worse, it is a betrayal of one's brothers who died in battle and of the wives, mothers, sons and daughters whose deaths testify to the totality of 20th century war.

Two years after the atom bombings of Nagasaki and Hiroshima, the author came to realize that the United Nations, as originally and presently constituted, could not fulfill its avowed mission of world peace. Based on the principle of collective security of exclusive nation-states, which defect led to the collapse of the League of Nations and World War II, it lacked the sovereign legislative, administrative, judicial and enforcement ability, democratically controlled, to govern the world community wherein war would be outlawed.

The Dumbarton Oaks proposals of the Four Powers, the United States, Great Britain, France and the Soviet Union, condemned in advance the San Francisco Conference to a sterile exercise of national diplomacy which continues to this day. No nation proposed - in recognition of our being one world in time and space - to make us world citizens under a representative government dealing directly with people everywhere. Only China and Columbia expressed a willingness to delegate sovereignty to the organization while France and Venezuela paid passing tribute to a federal system. It must be added that a world legislature was proposed by Ecuador, the Philippines and Venezuela while more power for the General Assembly was proposed by Australia, Belgium, Canada, Chile, Costa Rica, Egypt, France, Greece, Guatemala, Liberia, Mexico, New Zealand, Norway and Uruguay.

· As to the veto of the Security Council, seventeen nations opposed it as completely contrary to the doctrine of the sovereign equality of states while Ecuador maintained flatly that it represented anarchy and the Australian delegate pointed out that if five states of the original United States had enjoyed a veto, the ten amendments to the Constitution would never have been adopted.

As one at least equally concerned with world peace as any United Nations delegate, in May, 1948, after becoming stateless by virtue of Section 401(f) of the U.S. Nationality Act of 1940, the author claimed the status of world citizenship. By so doing, he was fulfilling his international civic obligations implied by the Nurnberg Charter under Article 6(a)(b) and (c) which defines "crimes coming within the jurisdiction of the Tribunal for which there shall be individual responsibility."*

The right to assume individual civic responsibility in a given community is the essence of course of the democratic principle and the true meaning of sovereignty. This has been subsequently confirmed by Arts. 1, 2, 3, 6, 7, 15(2), 18, 19 and 29 of the *Universal Declaration of Human Rights.*

The author's direct relationship with the United Nations itself began on 11 September 1948 when he was ordered by ministerial decision to leave France. Repairing to the "international territory" of the U.N., about to hold its 3rd General Assembly at the Palais de Chaillot in Paris, he requested global political asylum as a World Citizen in a petition to then Secretary-General Trygve Lie. This petition specifically called for a review conference, according to Article 109 of the U.N. Charter to convoke a world constitutional convention to draft a world constitution for the governance of the world community. At the request of the Secretariat, he was summarily expelled from the "international territory" by the French police under orders from the Ministry of the Interior.

Once again he "petitioned" the General Assembly, this time from the balcony of the Palais de Chaillot the 22 November 1948, interrupting a session with the aid of friends and fellow World Citizens, calling for a world constitutional convention. Again, he was summarily ex-

---

*II. Jurisdiction and General Principles, Article 6, para. 2. The U.N. Secretary-General, in his Supplementary Report to the General Assembly of 24 October 1946 stated that "In the interest of peace, and in order to protect mankind against future wars, it will be of decisive significance to have the principles which were implied in the Nurnberg trials, and according to which the German war criminals were sentenced, made a permanent part of the body of international law as quickly as possible. From now on the instigators of new wars must know that there exist both law and punishment for their crimes. Here we have a high inspiration to go forward and begin the task of working toward a revitalized system of international law." On 15 November 1946, the U.S. delegation introduced a proposal to the U.N. "..to initiate studies and make recommendations for the purpose of encouraging the progressive development of international law and its codifications.." and reaffirmed "..the principle of international law recognized by the Charter of the Nurnberg Tribunal and the judgment of the tribunal." U.N. General Assembly Resolution 488 48(v) 1950, "Nuremburg Trials", entered the principles to international law.

pelled, this time by U.N. security guards. Increasing public support however coalesced into a worldwide movement for peace through world citizenship.

Dr. Herbert Evatt, then-President of the General Assembly, granted the author a personal hearing agreeing to distribute the petitions endorsed by a public meeting at the Salle Pleyel to all delegations.✶ On 3 December 1948, at a public meeting at the Velodrome d'Hiver, Dr. Evatt's personal response was read. In substance, he wrote that the United Nations was not constituted to make peace between the "Big Powers" but only "to maintain it once made."

From this public acknowledgment of its President that the United Nations was inherently unable to "make peace" between "Big Powers" - a situation which prevails today 30 years later - which required world law and its sovereign institutions, we, the people of the world, understood that world peace depended on each of us, not as exclusive nationals but as world citizens. We understood that we had to become identified as a "world people" before we could claim our right to determine our own political, economic, social and cultural destiny.

Coincident with these historical events, the General Assembly on 10 December 1948 proclaimed the *UNIVERSAL DECLARATION OF HUMAN RIGHTS* "..as a common standard of achievement for all peoples and all nations.." endorsing the principle of a world democratic legal order+.

Both the concept of world citizenship as well as the eventual world Government of World Citizens was thereby mandated by this United Nations document to which all Member-States became subject upon signing the Charter itself (Ref. arts. 55, 56).

Needless to say, despite article 109(3) which provides for a review conference after ten years of the U.N.'s existence, no such conference has yet been held, every member of the Security Council with veto power being on record as in opposition.✶

In the five years following the above events, literally millions of

---

+Preamble, para 4 and Article 28.

✶ U.N. General Assembly Resolution 375 (IV), 6 December 1949, "Declaration on Rights and Duties of States", Art. 14 states: "Every State has the duty to conduct its relations with other States in accordance with international law and with the principle that the sovereignty of each State is subject to the supremacy of international law."

ordinary citizens throughout the world actively endorsed world citizenship with more than 750,000 actually registering at the International Registry of World Citizens in Paris which the author founded with friends in January, 1949.

Given this popular mandate, and invoking both the highest moral principles and the imperative need of humankind in toto and each human being to survive, the author declared the World Government of World Citizens on 4 September, 1953 at Ellsworth, Maine, U.S.A.+

The administrative and executive agency of the new government was founded at New York City, January, 1954 under the name, World Service Authority.*

The first official World Government document, the World Passport, was printed and issued beginning in June, 1954. It was based on art. 13(2), *UNIVERSAL DECLARATION OF HUMAN RIGHTS.*

Sample copies were addressed to all national governments*, to the High Commissioner for Refugees, to the U.S. Federal Bureau of Investigation, to the Security Division, United Nations Secretariat, and to the International Federation of Travel Agents. Thirty-six governments acknowledged receipt of the sample passport, Ecuador, Laos, Cambodia, and Yemen accorded it *de facto* recognition and certain other governments indicated they would take advantage of the document when the occasion presented itself. No national government returned or rejected the document.

The 2nd edition of the World Passport was printed in November, 1971 and sample copies sent to all national governments.+ The third edition of the World Passport was printed in June, 1975 with samples again addressed to national governments.**

The World Service Authority central office is in Basel, Switzerland. It is organized as a non-profit association under Swiss Civil Code 60 ss. World Service Authority District II has offices in London and World Service Authority District III in Washington, D.C. The latter is organized as a non-profit corporation in the District of Columbia.

+ See ¨Ellsworth Declaration¨ (excerpted) appended.

**Purpose: 1) To realize fundamental human rights as outlined in *U.D.H.R.*; To promote technical, and global coordination of organizations, specialized agencies, etc. working for general good; 3) Provide documentation service for world citizenry corresponding to the articles of *U.D.H.R.*

* Accompanying letter appended

2. The United Nations - An Analysis vis-a-vis the World Government of World Citizens

The present U.N. Secretary-General, Dr. Kurt Waldheim, is not unaware of the Organization's defects. In his 1977 Annual Report, in noting "increasing frustration and disappointment at the failure to protect and promote human rights in various parts of the world.." he reminds us that "..it must be remembered that the existing machinery such as the Commission on Human Rights is intergovernmental and intergovernmental bodies of course reflect the position of Member-States."* Unfortunately his conclusions are vividly and tragically known to millions of victims of war, deprivation and torture: "Thus we continue to have a conflict between the individual asserted principles of national sovereignty and the broad commitment to human rights."**

His own concern for this lethal duality - reflected also by his predecessors - is apparent when he maintains that "For the work of the United Nations to be effective in the field of human rights, we need the active commitment, cooperation and political will of the international community."+

Exclusive nation-states however cannot exercise "political will" internationally which implies a political framework. What they can and do exercise is their "power will" backed either by economic clout or by armies. "Political will" outside the national constitutional framework presumes people acting civically in the world community. From this civic commitment evolves inevitably a corollary sovereign institution, divorced from nations, to which such individuals turn for help, giving it their primary loyalty, which becomes thereby capable of protecting human rights from violations by nations.

When the individual politically bypasses the nation-state in a unilateral exercise of his/her innate sovereignty, s/he is acting ipso facto as a citizen of the world. Further, s/he is incorporating the universal and unitive principles of world government just as the local and/or national citizen incorporates the principles of his/her locality and/or nation.

---

* Section V, para. 5
**Ibid
+ Section V, para. 7

The failure of the United Nations is nowhere more nakedly revealed than in the problem of disarmament. Since General Assembly Resolution 41(1) of 14 December 1946 to Resolution 31/72 of 10 December 1976, spanning 32 years of lip-service to the problem, general world disarmament has been grotesquely and disastrously mocked by 94 inter-national wars, over $6 trillion of the world's tax-payer's money spent on destruction, over 50 million killed and many more crippled, made homeless and refugeed, a 1977 global armament budget of over $300 billion - almost 8% of the world's gross national product when endemic poverty is the daily grim condition of hundreds of millions - and an overkill capacity hundreds of times over. "Stocks of nuclear weapons," writes Dr. Waldheim*, "have already been sufficient to destroy the world many times over, and yet the number of warheads has increased five-fold in the past eight years." Not only does the Secretary-General recognize the universality of the problem - "..In a period where a new form of world society symbolized by the United Nations, is emerging, (disarmament is) a problem which vitally affects them all (the majority of the medium and small Powers)" - but that all nations "should play an important part in a comprehensive approach to disarmament aimed at real disarmament **in the context of world order.**" (Emphasis added.)+

Though his appeal for "world order" is understandably addressed only to national powers - which inadvertently exposes the fundamental contradiction of the underlying premise of the United Nations itself - he can only mean the **political** reality of a world sovereign, i.e. legal power which can only derive from the true sovereigns, humankind and its fundamental integer, the human person.**

Since the nation-state is by definition incapable of extending itself politically beyond its own sovereignty, the aware individual must recognize his/her sovereignty as **already** directly allied to that of humankind itself on a *de facto* or actual as well as moral basis. The Founding Fathers of the United States of America, to take but one example, recognized both a *de facto* and morally-based common citizenship between 1778 and 1887 yet politically disunited. They remedied the situation with the U.S. Constitution. That common world citizenship is the dynamic conceptual and actual fact of the 20th

---

* Section IV. para. 3. 1977 Annual Report
- Section IV. para. 8   ''   ''   ''
**Appended are statements from Heads of State advocating the rule of law as indispensable to world peace.

121

century rendered by contrast startling apparent by the totality of nuclear war - paling into virtual insignificance all lesser problems - as well as by related global crises such as pollution, gross economic injustice, depletion of the planet's resources and the like.

The institutionalization of our common world citizenship, as we have pointed out, has already begun. Thus the complementing of the international penal code of the Nurnberg Decisions by the World Government of World Citizens removes the fundamental cause of war, i.e. the absolute sovereignty of nation-states. Only by so doing can nations disarm in security and world peace eventually ensue as trust and cooperation become reinforced by just world law.

In his Report, the U.N. Secretary-General overtly sanctions the extension of individual sovereignty - as already codified by the Nurnberg Decisions - beyond one's national allegiance. In discussing the administration of the U.N.*, he maintains that the Charter "..is very clear on the exclusive international loyalty of the Secretariat.."+

Moreover, every Member-State is obligated "to respect the exclusively international character of the responsibilities of the Secretary-General and the staff.."*

The primary **political** allegiance then of Dr. Kurt Waldheim and every member of his staff is to an organization - not a government to which an individual can affiliate civically - which he admits publicly as the highest civil servant of that organization is constitutionally powerless to sanction and protect fundamental human rights, the first of which is the right to live. This paradoxical political allegiance is duly sanctioned by the U.N. Charter, the binding international instrument of all Member-States. It follows that the sovereign right of all humans to identify themselves **politically** as world citizens allied to its governmental counterpart by a simple pledge is likewise condoned implicitly by the United Nations Charter. Not only Article 15(2), *UNIVERSAL DECLARATION OF HUMAN RIGHTS*, sanctions the right of the individual to choose his/her government, but the U.N. Charter itself as well as the *INTERNATIONAL COVENANTS*

---

*Section X, para. 2
+Article 100(1): "In the performance of their duties, the Secretary-General and the staff shall not seek or receive instructions from any government or from any authority external to the Organization."
* Article 100(2), U.N. Charter

ON HUMAN RIGHTS+ recognize the right of self-determination of peoples and that the States Parties to these Covenants "shall promote the realization of the right of self-determination and shall respect that right in conformity with the provisions of the Charter of the United Nations."

Furthermore, the United Nations by definition and by Article 20(1), *U.D.H.R.*, recognizes the right of association. Notwithstanding the first three words of its Charter: "We, the People...", it does not however admit membership by individuals. It cannot therefore disapprove the founding by individuals **unrepresented** democratically by its mandate of a governmental institution to which they can associate as sovereign citizens thereby fulfilling **their** determination "to save succeeding generations from the scourge of war...reaffirm faith in fundamental human rights, in the dignity and worth of the human person, etc..."*

Again, the Secretary-General condones this position in his remarks concerning the helplessness of the Commission on Human Rights+ when he writes,"..in the present circumstances of international affairs, I feel that my actions must be governed by one overriding criterion, namely, what approach will best serve the welfare of the individual concerned."**

This humane "approach" is clearly and unequivocally spelled out in the Preamble of the *UNIVERSAL DECLARATION OF HUMAN RIGHTS* itself: "Whereas it is essential, if man is not to be compelled to have recourse, as a last resort, to rebellion against tyranny and oppression, that human rights should be protected by a regime of law.." And Art. 28 confirms the character of this "regime of

---

+ *The International Covenant on Civil and Political Rights*, opened for signature on 19 December 1966, entered into force for the following States on 23 March 1976: Barbados, Bulgaria, Byelorussian SSR, Canada, Chile, Columbia, Costa Rica, Cyprus, Czechoslovakia, Denmark, Ecuador, Finland, German Democratic Republic, Federal Republic of Germany, Hungary, Iran, Iraq, Jamaica, Jordan, Kenya, Lebanon, Libyan Arab Republic, Madagascar, Mali, Mauritius, Mongolia, Norway, Romania, Rwanda, Surinam, Sweden, Syrian Arab Republic, Tunisia, Ukrainian SSR, U.S.S.R., United Kingdom, United Republic of Tanzania, Uruguay, Yugoslavia, Zaire, Spain, Panama, Poland.

**Part I, art. 1(3)

* Preamble, U.N. Charter
+ General Assembly Resolution 728 (XXVIII): "The Economic and Social Council approves the statement that the Commission on Human Rights recognizes that it has no power to take any action in regard to any complaints concerning human rights."
**Section V, para. 6, 1977 Annual Report

law": "Everyone is entitled to a social and international order in which the rights and freedoms set forth in this Declaration can be fully realized."

The oppressed individual must therefore avail himself of the most effective "approach" to secure protection of his fundamental rights and freedoms "in the context of world order."

The WORLD GOVERNMENT OF WORLD CITIZENS then represents the genuine political genesis of that world order which already has myriad other manifestations far advanced such as communications, technology, commerce, medicine, travel, etc. and represented in some measure by the specialized agencies.

The Secretary-General defined in his 1977 Report our very World Citizen allegiance: "The United Nations is also..the symbol of a higher and more ambitious **political** and social aim, the evolution of an international community with interests, aspiration and **loyalties** of a far more wide-ranging kind."* (Emphasis added.) He concedes that the U.N. "is in search of its identity and its true role.." which again is to say that it has not found either yet, and that "..It tends to react rather than to foresee, to deal with effects of a crisis rather than anticipate and forestall that crisis." As a result, he adds, "its problems sometimes seem insurmountable and its frustrations intolerable."+

The United Nations therefore, as presently constituted, based on exclusive national sovereignty, represents world **dis**order or, to put it boldly, international anarchy. It is thus per se an institution of discord and conflict. Its Secretary-General however tells us that "We are, I believe, beginning to see the birth of such a community (international)**

We World Citizens allied wilfully to World Government are in common accord with the Secretary-General of the United Nations on this point. But we would go further. Neither the world community nor humankind are abstractions. Both are dynamic facts of the 20th cen-

---

* Section I, para. 11, 1977 Annual Report
+ Section X, para. 6 ″ ″ ″ . His predecessor, U Thant, in discussing the obligations of the S.G. stated: "The Secretary-General operates under the Charter in a world of independent sovereign states, where national interests remain dominant despite ideological, technological and scientific changes, and despite the obvious dangers of unbridled nationalism... The truth is of course, that the United Nations, and the S.G., have none of the attributes of sovereignty, and no independent power..."
**Section I, para. 11, 1977 Annual Report

tury, of the Space Age. And to imagine that humankind and the world community can endure in an 18th century political system of separate, exclusive nation-states armed with nuclear weapons is not only utopic but suicidal.

In the light of the total crisis facing our human race, the exercise of individual world sovereignty becomes not only legitimate by virtue of the highest conceptual values taught by humanity's sages from time immemorial, by the total interdependence of each and all to a common eco-system as well as to common social needs, and by the entire plethora of "international instruments" aforementioned mandating and sanctioning the new planetary role of the individual, but it is the very price of human survival.

No less than Dr. Waldheim himself on 20 May 1974 admonished us to accept individual responsibility for world affairs with these words:

"The choice is in our hands. No nation and no individual can be a bystander at this critical moment in the history of the world. There are occasions when the magnitude and complexity of the tasks we face make a sensitive and responsible individual feel dispirited and helpless. But as the record of the last 30 years shows us, there is nothing beyond our capacity if we act collectively. That is why it is so important that every one of you recognize your responsibility not only as a citizen of your own country, but as a citizen of the world - and above all, an active one."

We, the WORLD CITIZENS of WORLD GOVERNMENT, have approved and acted upon the United Nations' Secretary-General's endorsement of that wilfull and legitimate civic role.

****

Appendix

(The following three letters were addressed to all nation-states either through their Washington, D.C. embassies, U.N. missions, Paris embassies or Berne embassies.)

UNITED WORLD SERVICE AUTHORITY

Suite C - 1315   270 Park Avenue   New York 17, N.Y.   Plaza 8-0574

July 15, 1954

Your Excellency:

We have the honor to invite your attention to the enclosed samples with reference to the operations of the United World Service Authority. In accordance with the aims of the United Nations, and with the sanction of the United States Government, the UWSA is a documentary and technical assistance agency to serve the needs of the stateless persons, refugees, and aliens throughout the world.

The documentary department of the UWSA is designed primarily to bring about in due course a uniformity in personal identification certificates, thereby facilitating technical procedures of all natures. The mere centralization of personal identity information for stateless people on a world-wide scale will give protection to the individual as well as to national governments.

As can be seen by the enclosed samples, the application form and passport require proper legalization, complying therefore with the requirements of national government with regard to the issuance of visas for valid travel purposes.

Such a legalized and standardized identity document is necessary not only for travel purposes, but also for movements within national borders and registrations of all kinds required by national and local law.

In order to assist local governmental institutions in providing proper identification for all persons lacking such, the UWSA is establishing agencies in major cities throughout the world, headed by local nationals. These agents will be in the employ of UWSA and charged with the responsibility and authority to act in behalf of the New York head office.

The World Passport is now being issued from the New York office. It is duly filed with the United Nations' Security Police and with the Department of Justice, Washington, D.C.

UWSA and its agencies is ready to co-operate fully with representatives of your Embassies and Consulates, thereby serving the needs of all persons concerned.

Yours very truly,

(Signed)

Garry Davis - Director

WORLD SERVICE AUTHORITY

4002 BASLE, SWITZERLAND

December 29, 1971

Your Excellency,

We have the honor to enclose herewith a specimen copy of the second edition of the World Service Authority passport for the attention of the competent authorities of your Government.

Conceived originally as a neutral and global document if identity and potential travel document for stateless persons, refugees and victims of political, social and economic discrimination along the lines of the Nansen and IRO passports, the WSA passport is now being issued generally, mandated by Article 13, Section II, *UNIVERSAL DECLA-RATION OF HUMAN RIGHTS.*

In consideration of Your Government's membership in the United Nations and com-mittment therefore in principle to Human Rights, as expressed in the Preamble to the Charter, we acknowledge on behalf of present and future bearers of the WSA passport its *de facto* recognition by Your Government without need of further advice.

Further, we request respectfully the transmission of the specimen copy to the compe-tent authorities of Your Government in view to obtain its *de jure* recognition principally for persons not possessing a nationality. We would appreciate your early advice on this point.

In the meantime, may we request respectfully that all bearers of the WSA passport be given every consideration when presenting his or her request for a travel visa at a given Consulate under Your Government's jurisdiction, or at a particular frontier post by responsible authorities.

This letter has been addressed to all national governments listed in reference as well as to the Human Rights Commission, United Nations and the Secretary-General.

Sincerely,

(Signed)

Garry Davis
Coordinating Director

127

WORLD SERVICE AUTHORITY

4002 BASLE, SWITZERLAND

July 15, 1975

Your Excellency,

With reference to our letters of 15 July, 1954 and 29 December, 1971, (copies enclosed), we have the honor respectfully to invite the attention of Your Government to the enclosed specimen of the third edition of the World Service Authority passport.

This document is issued since 1954 on public demand according to the principle of freedom of movement as defined by Article 13(2), *Universal Declaration of Human Rights*, and Article 12(2), *International Covenant on Civil and Political Rights*.

The Individual bearer of the document enclosed assumes full responsibility for its utilization in his or her recognition of the innate sovereignty of the human person, as recognized by Articles 1, 2, 3, 6, 7, 9, 12, 13, 15(2), 17(2), 28, 29, *Universal Declaration of Human Rights*; Preamble (Paragraph 2) and Chapter 1, Article 1(3), *Charter of the United Nations*; and Part 1, Article 1(1), *International Covenant on Civil and Political Rights*, and in excercise of the fundamental human rights recognized by all Member-States of the United Nations by virtue of the aforementioned and also, in particular, by virtue of Articles 55 and 56 of that association's Charter.

We would like to point out that innumerable individuals today are deprived of travel possibilities due simply to lack of valid identity documents withheld for one reason or another arbitrarily by the state in which they happen to live. With regard to exit permits sought for emigration purposes, the W.S.A. passport presents the unique advantage of conforming to the right to leave any country, including one's own, whereas the national passport connotes exclusive state control over the individual and thus also state liability with regard to said individual. Thus both the state and the individual benefit through the use of the former (W.S.A.) document, which places the responsibility of exit and comportment thereafter on the individual conerened, again in strict conformity with his or her fundamental human rights.

Special types of circumstances as well have come to our attention from the public demand for the W.S.A. passport:

— families separated because husband and wife possess passports of different nationalities and are expelled from a particular state for political reasons;

— new-borns unclaimed by the state wherein they are born, thereby depriving them of a birth certificate and thus passport, resulting in separation of mother and child;

— sick persons seeking vital treatment in a country abroad either unable to obtain travel documents from the resident state, or said documents for political reasons are not recognized by the state in which they seek treatment;

— students with scholarships from universities abroad unable to obtain either a passport or an exit permit from their country of origin;

— resident refugees unable or unwilling to obtain a passport of the country of residence and whose former passport is no longer valid;

— refugees and stateless persons not covered by the various Conventions for such;

128

— nationals of countries whose passport is not recognized by other states due to inter-governmental policies;

— individuals held in arbitrary detention for lack of valid identity and travel documents:

— national citizens travelling or studying abroad during which period their home government is replaced. thus placing them in a position of peril should they be returned or return willingly;

— individuals whose passports have been lost or stolen while travelling;

— individuals of particular religious persuasion (for instance, on pilgrimage) whose national passport is not recognized by states through which they must transit;

— young people travelling to broaden their understanding of their fellow humans and of themselves. often frustrated by state visa and border restrictions occasioned by the particular political prejudice of their national passport;

— individuals travelling for cultural. scientific, educational, economic, or other reasons outside the framework of state allegiance who seek a neutral identification in keeping with their humanitarian activity in concert with colleagues in other parts of the world:

— non-governmental international staff personnel whose duties necessitate travel yet whose national passports compromise and even contradict their pledged commitment to the international law mandating their organization (in this regard we have included in the 3rd edition of the W.S.A. passport a 6-page section for affiliate identifications for optional use by the bearer and/or his or her affiliation);

— media personnel whose profession necessitates world-wide travel often hampered or actually blocked by the political prejudice attached to many state passports;

— individuals who consider the national passport in general a contradiction to fundamental human rights.

With regard to personal liability, since the commission anywhere of civil crimes subjects the individual in question (excepting, of course, diplomatic personnel) to the laws locally in force. protection, if any, afforded by a national passport would not apply to the W.S.A. passport. Contrarily, the national passport, in these cases, proves inconvenient and embarrassing to the issuing state, which tends to accrue responsibility for the criminal act via the proprietary nature of its document.

Since travellers today are both legally obliged and indeed consciously willing to accept full responsibility for their civic actions no matter in what part of the world they may be. it is unnecessary for their identity and travel documents to be attached to national considerations for which they are not responsible. On the contrary, a neutral document conforming to needful personal identification sworn true and correct by the individual in question and locally certified performs a highly utilitarian service for both the individual and the state in general.

In that close to 10,000 W.S.A. passports are already in circulation—a list of state from which W.S.A. passport bearers derive is appended—and, according to our information from these bearers, innumerable Consulates are still unfamiliar with it or reject it *per se* through ignorance of its mandate or simply lack instructions from their Ministries, we would appreciate the position of Your Government with the least possible delay. This position will be communicated to all present and future W.S.A. passport bearers through our official News Bulletin and other channels. We would like to point out as well that while certain states have recognized the document on a *de jure* basis, others have taken contradicting positions in that while the Consulates may have issued visas to the W.S.A. passport, frontier control officials then annul them—we are aware, of course, that there are different Ministries involved. On the other hand, bearers have been frequently refused visas at Consulates while subsequently admitted at the frontiers of the same state.

This letter will be published in our official News Bulletin and has been addressed to all national governments—Switzerland excepted—either through Consulates or directly to the Foreign Ministries; to the Secretary-General, United Nations; to the U.N. High Commissioner for Refugees, Geneva; to the Chief Justice, World Court of Human Rights, Chicago; and to the President, European Court of Human Rights, Strasbourg.

Most respectfully,

(Signed)

Garry Davis
World Coordinator

Enclosures:
— Specimen, W.S.A. passport, 3rd edition
— Attestation of Understanding
— List of states from which individuals have requested W.S.A. passports
— Copies of letters, 15 July, 1954 and 29, December, 1971

STATEMENTS OF HEADS OF STATE CONCERNING WORLD ORDER/LAW

Sir Winston Churchill, *Prime Minister of the United Kingdom, 1945*

"The creation of an authoritative all-powerful world order is the ultimate end towards which we must strive. Unless some effective world super-government can be set up and brought quickly into action, the prospects for peace and human progress are dark and doubtful."

Sean F. Lemass, *Prime Minister, Irish Republic, 1963*

It is essential that the concept of world peace through the rule of law should be brought constantly before the minds of the people of the world.

Leopold Sedar Senghor, *President of the Republic of Senegal, 1965*

It is possible to speak of organized state-controlled society only when the rule of law has definitely replaced brute force and vengeance in the relations among men. The international society will be truly established only when the rule of law will reign supreme over the relations among states.

Palden Thondup Namgyal, *Chogyal of Sikkim, 1965*

The object of law is to achieve right conduct which alone ensures security, happiness and peace for all. This conforms to the teachings of The Buddha. Thus the rule of law has been the ideal in our country for centuries of our history...World peace can be attained only through one rule of law for the whole world.

Einar Gerhardsen, *Prime Minister of Norway, 1965*

The people of Norway firmly believe that international conflicts should be settled in a peaceful way through law, and that it is possible to realize this aim. We consider that this fundamental task, essential as it is to the safeguarding of human rights, require the joint efforts of all of us.

Lester B. Pearson, *Prime Minister of Canada, July 20, 1965*

The need to maintain peace in the world today is of vital concern to us all. Peace is necessary, not only for security, but for survival. It remains the goal for which we must strive unceasingly. I believe that it is through application of the concept of justice to international relations that world peace will ultimately be attained. Justice resting on the Rule of Law can alone ensure the fundamental freedoms of all people and provide for peaceful settlement of disputes to the end that war may be avoided.

Jens Otto Krag, *Prime Minister of Denmark, September, 1965*

The rule of law is essential to the maintenance of World Peace, and throughout centuries men of goodwill have worked toward the goal of letting a philosophy based on law decide actions of nations and establish institutions permitting law to be a decisive factor in the relations between countries.

Milton Margai, *Prime Minister of Sierra Leone, 1963*

We in this part of the world strongly feel that the time is ripe for international law and international legal institutions to be brought up to date to meet the challenge of these perilous times.

Hussein I, *His Majesty the King of the Hasmemite Kingdom of Jordan, Aug., 1965*

A foremost achievement of humanity in its painful evolution toward the modern world has been the sanctification of the rule of law to relationships among nations. The future of mankind is contingent upon the achievement of this goal. It is the more imperative and overriding when judged against the mortal peril of mutual annihilation which throws a dark shadow upon the whole globe. Needless to state that pious hopes to achieve world peace through law would not, even with the best of intentions, achieve it. It is the common task of us all to strive for its attainment through appropriate structures, functions and, above all, attitudes of mind and spirit which respect fundamental principles of justice, morality and equality before the law, in the relationships of individuals within each society, as well as in the relationship of societies in the community of nations.

Jomo Kenyatta, *President of Kenya, September 1965*

Man in an ordered society has discovered that the price of liberty is eternal vigilance, but this in no way conflicts with his innate desire for consensus and accord rather than contention and conflict. In such a society, it is mandatory that the law of "might is right" should be abandoned in favor of the impartial rule of law.

Zalman Shazar, *President of Israel, 1963*

It is the lesson of man's historical experience that there can be no peace without justice, no lasting peace between oppressor and oppressed. The expression of justice is law, and it is only through the rule of law that the sway of peace can be assured for our endangered, peace-craving world.

Abdulla As-Salim As-Sabah, *Emir of Kuwait, 1965*

Believing deeply in the principles of the United Nations Charter and the Convention of Human Rights and establishing her relations with other countries on the principles and foundations of international law, the State of Kuwait exerts every effort towards the promotion of the dictates of law for the realization of the cherished goal of establishing a world society living in peace and security.

Adbul Salam Mohamed Arif, *President of the Republic of Iraq, September, 1965*

Islamic law is based on a respect for justice. The Quoran, Sura 4, Verse 58, states "and if you are called to adjudicate between people, then justice should be your guide." Islam also abolished distinction between people and made them equal and did not recognize any distinction because of race, color or locality.... International cooperation cannot be secure unless the rule of law prevails and states follow the precepts of equitable laws. Under a law-observing international order, peace will prevail, nations and individuals shall be secure in their everyday life and civilization will prosper.

T. Kittikachoom, *Prime Minister of Thailand, 1965*

That law should prevail in the relations between men and nations is a posture, a proposition and even a problem toward which we have tirelessly turned our efforts. Indeed, the one fundamental belief, the intellectual staple that aptly expresses the aspirations of right-thinking men in this modern world is certainly to be found nowhere else than in the concept of the rule of law which stands out clearly as the most potent idea of our times.

Rachid Karame, *Prime Minister of the Republic of Lebanon, 1963*

..the liberty of the nations of the world can be fully assured only if governments can be certain in advance that, if disputes should arise between them on certain given points, there will be international jurisdiction competent to resolve the differences in question. These basic ideas will not be accepted internationally unless and until a general movement of public opinion imposes them...

Pierre Werner, *Prime Minister of Luxembourg, 1963*

Events show us daily that the consolidation of peace in the framework of justice is dependent on more and more people in positions of responsibility becoming aware of the necessity of subordinating selfish desires and interest to the rule of Law.

Gustavo Diaz Ordaz, *President of the United Mexican States, 1965*

...our international position is based on a principle of universal value and permanence, that the unquestionable force of our international policy rests on the unalterable foundation of the law, whose respect is our best contribution to the cause of peace.

Rainier the III, *Prince of Monaco, 1965*

The only form of true civilization shall be for all men as well as for all states a civilization where the law will be unimpeachable and will always take precedence over force.

Mahendra Bir Bikram Shah Deva, *King of Nepal, 1965*

Most of the ills of modern times can be remedied if the principles of law are universally applied and voluntarily accepted by all nations of the world. All human beings are aware of the growing danger to their very existence posed by the stockpiling of, and competitive race in, nuclear armaments. Peace being a prime and deep concern of mankind, it has never been more important than today for the world community to strive for an ordered society through the rule of law.

Keith Holyoake, *Prime Minister of New Zealand, 1965*

At no time has it been as vital as it is today that the rule of law should take the place of force as a means of settling international disputes. No lasting peace will be possible until we have a world order based on, and regulated by, law.

S. Radhakrishnan, *President of India, 1963*

Just as in the national field nations can only secure their progress and social welfare through the rule of law, so also the community of nations must strive to advance the cause of human welfare through obedience to the rules of law; for nations can prosper only when peace is established and violence is banished as an instrument of settling international disputes.

Diosdado Macapagal, *President of the Republic of the Philippines, 1965*

Man's centuries of struggles for the light in his search for peace, his art, his culture — all the accumulated wealth of the world's wisdom and his entire civilization — these are in danger of total annihilation. There seems to be no other alternative for mankind as it faces the reality of these dangers than to agree to settle international disputes through the rule of law.

F.T. Wahlen, *Federal Counsellor of Switzerland, 1963*

The Swiss Government and the people of Switzerland are convinced that the respectful observance of the rule of International Law by all governments constitutes the best possible way of guaranteeing world peace. Our regard for the authority of law in dealings between states is marked by the large number of eminent Swiss who, from Vattel to Max Huber, devoted themselves to the cause of international law, thus taking their place among thinkers of all nations, whose work may be of guidance to you today in the task confronting you.

Jules K. Nyerere, *President of Tanganyika, 1965*

Human society has developed as the rule of law has spread from the family to the village, from the village to the tribe and then to the nation. Only as just and enforceable law has been accepted in these different units of organization has it been possible for people to live in peace and security with one another. The present dangerous tensions between nations, which so frequently breaks out into violent conflict, is an indication of the absence of law in the international field. It must be a matter of great concern to all who value peace and progress that efforts should be made to establish law in this remaining sphere.

Same, *1963*

There exists a growing body of international law which is normally observed in the relations between nation states, although there can be no codification of this until there is an accepted World Government. There is not, however, a World Authority capable of enforcing International Law.

Jimmy Carter, *President of the United States, January 20, via Voice of America*

I want to assure you that the relations of the United States with other countries and peoples of the world will be guided during our administration by our desire to shape a world order that is more responsive to human aspirations.

Abubakar Tafawa Balewa, *Prime Minister of the Republic of Nigeria, 1965*

The whole world is passing now through one of the most disturbing phases of its history, and we are all witnessing the sad spectacle of nations divided against themselves in parts of Latin America, Asia, Africa, America, and even Europe.... (the) message of peace and good-will among men of all races and colours, based upon the solid foundation of the rule of law, should make us reflect upon the future of our world and at the same time appreciate that there is no other course left to us but that of a constant endeavor to achieve world peace through the rule of law.

Cemal Gursel, *President of the Republic of Turkey, 1963*

Turkey, as clearly indicated in the United Nations Charter, is convinced that the only way to peace is through the ''rule of law'' and for this reason she is strongly attached to the United Nations ideals. It has consistently been the policy of Turkey to protect freedom and justice, maintain world peace and contribute to the progress of human welfare. To realize these ideals, respect for democratic principles and fundamental human rights should be secured and all international disputes should be settled in accordance with the principle of the ''rule of law''.

Harold Wilson, *Prime Minister of the United Kingdom, 1965*

We are all aware of the vital peace-keeping role of the United Nations, but keeping the peace alone is not enough. It is also necessary, as the Charter proclaimed, "to establish conditions under which justice and respect for the obligations arising from treaties and other sources of international law can be maintained." Peace cannot exist without law and justice. Justice depends on the development of law and of fair and peaceful means for the settlement of disputes.

Petar Stambolic, *President of the Federal Executive Council of Yugoslavia, 1965*

Threats to peace are ever more numerous as there exist forces which do not hesitate to secure their political and economic interests even at the risk of war. Very little is needed for the sources of conflict to be transferred into real war. The activity of peace-loving forces is, therefore, of particular importance. They reject the use of force and war and demand that all disputes between peoples and states should be solved peacefully on the basis of respect for the principles of justice.... The general efforts for peace and a better future of mankind can hardly be conceived without respect for rights and obligations in international relations, whereas the rule of law in international life contributes in particular, toward this end.

John F. Kennedy, *President of the United States of America, 1963*

Supremacy of law within nations insures the freedom of men. Supremacy of law in the community of nations can free mankind from the dread of nuclear war. The rule of law must replace the rule by force if we are to look forward to a stable world — a world which is hospitable to economic and social progress.

Faysal, *King of Saudi Arabia, 1965*

We, as Muslims and the (people) responsible for the service of the Muslim holy places, believe in peace which is based on right and justice as an essential part of our creed. The words "al-Islam" and "as-Salam" (peace) are derived, in our Arabic language, from the same root, and God Almighty has named Himself as Alam (peace) so mankind may appreciate the importance of peace. Peace on earth will not be attained unless the grounds of right and justice have been firmly rooted in each state where citizens and non-citizens alike may enjoy them, so that all are assured of the authority of law to uphold their dignity, protect their possessions, and help them exercise their freedom.

Eric Williams, *Prime Minister of Trinidad and Tobago, 1965*

To a people like ours born in the wars and cradled in the lawlessness of the colonial regime, the reign of peace and the rule of law, the achievement of World Peace through Law are not abstractions. The smallest of the small in physical area, the least of the apostles in economic resources, lacking the power to make war, we join those who make peace; kept for so long outside the law, our spirit, passing in compassion and determination around the whole earth, salutes the world and looks for equals in all lands, some divine rapport equalizing us with them. Trinidad and Tobago, emerging from submerged colony into independent nationhood, represents yet another link in the long chain of mankind's repudiation of any contract in perpetuity to surrender its freedom — a freedom which has slowly been broadening from precedent to precedent in the development of humanity's dream of a world in which people of different races and colours dwell together in unity.

135

Lyndon B. Johnson, *President of the United States, September, 1965*

International law has been primarily concerned with relations between states. In pursuit of justice, it must now concern itself more than in the past with the welfare of people. So I look forward to the day when the relief of hunger and misery and ignorance in all parts of the world will be fixed in legal obligation as it now is in my own country. When our world law embodies the right of the despairing to hope, and the responsibility of the fortunate to help, then it will be strengthened a thousandfold in the cause of peace. There are those who say the rule of law is a fruitless and utopist dream. It is true, if it comes, it will come slowly. It will come through the practical and wise resolution of numberless problems. But to deny the possibility is to deny peace itself and to deny that flowering of the spirit which we must believe God meant for man.

Mohammad Ayub Khan, *President of Pakistan, 1963*

In Pakistan, as in most other countries, we are firmly wedded to the principle of the Rule of Law; but the extension of the Rule of Law from the national to the international sphere is the crying need of the hour. For, in a world tormented with mutual suspicions and menaced by nuclear warfare, there is no hope for mankind if peace and security are not established and maintained by the Rule of Law.

Tage Erlander, *Prime Minister of Sweden, 1965*

"Lands shall be built upon Law and not upon Deeds of Violence. For when Law rules, the Lands prosper." These words which are to be found in a Provincial Swedish Law Code of 1295 and which express a conviction shared by men of good will the world over through the centuries, have not lost their truth in today's world. More than ever, it is urgent that human relations within and across national boundaries be based on law and reason.

****

CHAPTER 10

THE POWER VOTE VS. THE SUICIDE VOTE

"The will of the people shall be the basis of the authority of government; this will shall be expressed in periodic and genuine elections which shall be by universal and equal suffrage and shall be held by secret vote or by equivalent free voting procedures.

Article 21(3), *Universal Declaration of Human Rights*

"The 'broad democratic principle,' as everyone will probably agree, presupposes two conditions – first, full publicity, and secondly, election to all offices. Democracy without full publicity – a publicity reaching beyond the organization's own members – is inconceivable ... an organization that is hidden from everyone but its members by a veil of secrecy cannot be called democratic.

".... The second criterion of democracy, the principle of election ... is taken for granted in politically free countries ... "

Lenin, *"What Is To Be Done,"* 1902

The national vote in general has lost its power to effect fundamental change in our affairs. The reason is fairly obvious. Contemporary problems beginning with war itself are in large part generated by the very institution, the sovereign-state, that controls the elective process.

Electing a national president in a world of anarchy between states is tantamount to prisoners choosing a prison warden whose primary task is to preserve the prison system itself. "I swear allegiance to the Constitution...etc."

A national election in an anarchic world, therefore, only confirms a latter-day system of collective national suicide. It is an act of collusion with international violence rather than a civic act of creative change.

Does the silkworm "vote" for the crysallis to break open or does a new-born "vote" to enter the world?

"Statesmen and legislators, standing so completely within the institution never distinctly and nakedly behold it. They speak of moving society, but have no resting-place without it."

Emery Reves, *Anatomy of Peace,* 1945

The exclusive national election admits and confirms the existence of the exclusive nation, thereby implicitly condoning lawlessness between nations. It is an "Alice-in-Wonderland" politics not only resolving nothing, but deluding the electorate by a farcical display of pyrotechnics into believing it is performing a useful and democratic social service for the general good.

The cows herded outside the slaughter houses of Chicago voting on which butcher should kill them would be performing as useful a service as national citizens voting for a national president today.

Why does not democratic representation, i.e., voting, take place on the global level where our common problems are? The above-quoted article from the *Universal Declaration of Human Rights* is mandate enough. Why is not the popular will represented in the council halls of the United Nations from which the UDHR originated instead of the one vote, one nation absurdity with the five "super-powers" enjoying a veto power in the Security Council? Even one of its own secretary-generals, Dr. Kurt Waldheim, in a press statement of May 20, 1974, endorsed in bold terms the concept and legitimacy of world citizenship:

"The choice is in our hands. No nation and no individual can be an innocent bystander at this critical moment in the history of the world. There are occasions when the magnitude and complexity of the tasks we face make a sensitive and responsible individual feel dispirited and helpless. But as the record of the last 30 years shows us, there is nothing beyond our capacity if we act collectively. That is why it is so important that every one of you recognize your responsibilities, not only as a citizen of your country, but as a citizen of the world–and above all, an active one."

The Secretary-General was confirming no less than a call for global *political* action as set forth by the above-quoted article. Raising the franchise to the global level is simply claiming our right as *world* citizens to be represented democratically on that level. By so doing, we complete the revolution begun in the early 18th century by such universal thinkers as Rousseau, Montesquieu, Locke, Thomas Paine, Jefferson, Thoreau, Emerson and others.

Shallow minds and faint-hearted spirits will reject "world revolution" as too grandiose and utopian. But, in the words of Jean-Louis Revel [*Neither Marx Nor Jesus*] "The expression 'world revolution' means, simply, revolution, for the revolution of the 20th century must, of its nature, be worldwide."

"The meaning of the term 'The revolution of the 20th Century' is equally clear: the revolution that will solve the problems of the 20th Century. Such problems are not hard to identify. We must eliminate the threat of atomic suicide; we must renounce armaments and put an end to war; we must stabilize the birth rate; we must equalize the standard of living; and we must protect and make use of the earth's resources with a unique plan of conservation and development. Even this preliminary list is sufficient to make clear that the problems involved can be solved only on a planetary level, and by a world government. World Government is the only possible goal of a revolution

today, as it is the only goal which can make a revolution feasible."

What then is the relevance of an exclusively national presidential election given the above-cited problems? Can a national president solve *world* problems? Obviously not.

Our political thinking, carried over from the 18th century, refuses to meet this question head-on. Since the electoral framework for world voting does not yet exist—though with computers/satellites the technology is ready—we assume that it should not exist. We conveniently forget the origins of the nations to which we now give our sovereign allegiance. The Australian Commonwealth of 1901 was established by an unofficial yet popularly-elected constitutional convention which literally replaced the standing government. The U.S. Declaration of Independence was signed by 55 men who boldly designated themselves as "the representatives of the United States of America in Congress assembled..." when the Constitution of the U.S.A. was ratified fully eleven years later. '.

Military coalitions such as NATO and its counterpart, the Warsaw Pact countries, represent military half-way houses, bloc-oriented, created transnationally, neither strictly national nor yet global but with a definite independent status. NATO headquarter's territory in Belgium enjoys "extra-territorial" status by treaty as does the United Nations "territory" on the East Side in New York city.

Both the Communist and Socialist Internationals, composed of national parties, at various periods determined by a confluence of world events, have attempted without success to create the illusion of global unity while maintaining the state as their primary power base. The success of Socialist and Communist parties, such as it is, reflects the popular dissatisfaction with the monopolistic capitalism of industrial nations combined with the promise of worker affluence, largely exposed in actual practice as mythical. (See Chapter 16, Who Owns The World?)

But the fundamental flaw in such a strategy is in thinking that political parties, only nationally based, can be dominated by one national party, no matter how powerful the state over which the party has control. The very divisive character of the nation-state system automatically precludes such domination. Socialism vitiates its pretensions to universality by likewise attaching its fundamental power base to the sovereign state.

Neither doctrinaire communists nor socialists have carried their thinking or their strategy to the world community level. World government is considered heretical nonsense to Marxists who, if pressed, will speak vaguely of the eventual "withering away of the state."

My personal experience with doctrinaire Communists in the late 40's, as briefly detailed in my first book, was revealing by their fanatical opposition to world citizenship or "cosmopolitanism," considered heretical to pure Marxism/Leninism. Elevating democracy to the global level was vilified as the crassest "bourgeois ideology" and, interestingly enough, the most dangerous menace to "world communism."

THE TRILLION DOLLAR RAT HOLE

Since 1958 the U.S. Government has spent over a trillion dollars on war budgets, not including the hundreds of billions for war-connected space flights, veterans' benefits, interest to the bankers on money borrowed for previous wars, etc.

A trillion dollars is a thousand billion, or a million million. It's quite a bit of money. And it's all gone, with not much to show for it except mutilated people and a lot of graves—a trillion dollars dropped down into a giant rat hole.

But just suppose that trillion had been spent for life instead of death, for people instead of profits. What would a thousand billion dollars have bought us?

$450 billion	Could supply a new $15,000 home or apartment for half the families in the U.S.
5 billion	Could build 2 new $30 million hospitals for each of the 16 biggest cities in the U.S., a $20 million hospital for each of 100 smaller cities, a $2 million clinic for 1,000 different small towns.
20 billion	Could be given to cancer research.
10 billion	Could be spent to cure 5 or 6 other major diseases.
20 billion	Could end the pollution in the Great Lakes.
10 billion	Could freshen up every river and stream on the continent.
20 billion	Could be used to plant a billion trees along highways, in cities, towns, and in the countryside.
20 billion	Could build 1,000 new colleges at $20 million apiece.
80 billion	Could fund 4,000,000 new scholarships a year at $2,000 per student.
10 billion	Could build 10,000 youth centers at $1 million each.
10 billion	Could revive the buffalo herds in the West and grow more grass in order to double the cattle herds and lower the price of milk and beef.
10 billion	Could make a dozen oases in the Sahara Desert.
50 billion	Could supply 50 million farm families in South America and Asia with gasoline-driven tractors.
Leaving: $285 billion	For defense and other expenses

TOTAL

— Based on material by Vince Copeland

$1,000,000,000,000

Seemingly opposed national parties unite at the national frontier to present a unified "foreign policy" vis-a-vis other nations. The "Trillion Dollar Rathole" (Opposite page) shockingly illustrates the choice open to us as taxpayers. Does any national party offer you that choice? Certainly not. The only "international platform" of a national party is an increase in the armament "rathole." Whether Democrats, Republicans, Social Democrats, Labor, Conservative, Radicals, Socialists, Communists, Christian Democratics, Progressive, Liberal, Congress Party, Libertarian, Farmer or what have you, advocates of social reforms from far right or far left, more or less government control, free market or planned market, balanced budget or deficit spending, profit-sharing or welfare state, etc., etc., no exclusive national party will promise the outlawing of war, the legalization of human rights on the world level, the elimination of inflation or poverty or the gap between the haves and have-nots, the elimination of world tension, and certainly not "life, liberty and the pursuit of happiness," or in fact the *solution* to any of the real problems facing you, the national voter.

So what is your national vote really worth? Does it really matter who is a national candidate when such world problems exist?

If war is possible between nations, national voting is irrelevant.

In other words, why vote nationally at all?

What then are we to think of the men and women who seek national power? Are they not mindful of the impotence of national office to effect change in our lives? And if they are, then are they not betraying the public trust they so avidly seek? To put it bluntly, the individuals who seeks "public power" knowing such power simply does not exist are merely ripping off the tax-payer. In any field other than politics, they could be indicted on criminal charges. On the other hand, if they are unaware of the impotence of the national politician, then they are only fools and will prove it if they achieve public office.

In today's nuclear world, let's face it, we must vote. But the seminal vote must be to ensure our survival at least. Otherwise, nothing else matters. If our present national vote only serves to seal our collective doom, is it not in reality a suicide vote? Are we not voting to die in a nuclear war or by radioactive pollution? What difference does it make how the furniture is arranged or if the occupants of certains rooms are "enemies" when the house itself is on fire? Arranging the deckchairs on the S.S. Titantic is an apt metaphor for national politics. With about 56% of the the human race undernourished or near starving, is it relevant that 4,000 satellites beam the results of a national presidential election on the 7 o'clock news to TV sets and radios throughout the world community?

If the political process does not address itself to the organization of earth society as such, what is its purpose then?

True, national political leaders make political hay by professing their support for "world peace through law." The phrase is now almost establishment writ. Former president Jimmy Carter, before the Foreign Policy Association in New

141

York, May, 1976, called vigorously for a "politics of world order":

> *"A central task of American foreign policy in the crucial next quarter of the twentieth century is the building of international institutions to manage critical world problems of vital importance to the American people and to all peoples and nations...A central element in the foreign policy of my Administration will be the building of effective international institutions to manage the critical world problems which now threaten our security as a free and prosperous society. The time has come, therefore, to supplement balance of power politics with world order politics."*

If Jimmy Carter meant to cede part of United States sovereignty to a world government, he did not spell it out in so many words. On the contrary, he was careful to point out in the same speech that "The maintenance of a global balance of power is obviously essential to the survival of the United States."

This is classical Orwellian doublethink and doublespeak.

Ronald Reagan continues the patent duplicity. As a former member of the World Federalists of California when he was governor—Senator Alan Cranston was president of that organization at the time—he is fully aware of the necessity of world government if world peace is to be attained. In fact, in his opening words to the General Assembly of the United Nations during its Special Session on Disarmament, June 17, 1982, he blithely told the astounded delegates that "I come to you not only as an American but as a citizen of the world..." and further on boldly enjoined "all members...(to) live together in peace under the rule of law forsaking armed force as a means of settling disputes among nations."

Reagan's fanatical devotion to "peace through strength" on the other hand needs no documentation here. The present U.S. deficit is mind-crushing evidence of his "fastest gun in the West" vision of the world. Other papers herein deal with this illusion fully and I hope conclusively. My intention here is to expose the deadly duality of national politics and national so-called leaders.

Former French President Giscard d'Estaing on October 25, 1975, declared publicly that only a "world politics can avert a world catastrophe." France is still the third largest exporter of armaments to developing countries.

Other national leaders have found it expedient from time to time to profess that the world *should* be governed by law and not ripped apart by anarchy, sentiments tending to placate the liberal side of their constituencies. They do nothing, however, to eliminate the vested war interests, including the vast industrial empires, management and labor, constituting "conservative" constituencies which often furnish a major part of their campaign funds.

The double standard of national political parties was superbly exemplified by the U.S. Democratic Party in 1968 which claimed that "it was only with member nations working together that (the United Nations) can make its full contribution to the growth of a world community of peace through law, rather than by threat or use of military force."

A "world community of peace through law" means world government, no more nor less. Fully sovereign "member nations working together" means continued anarchy. The political schizophrenia was unblushingly exposed. The 1984 Democratic platform plays the same treacherous tune for a seemingly apathetic public with its call for an increase in "national defense" while wistfully searching for a "peaceful solution to world problems.".

The Republicans slavishly follow suit. In the 1976 foreign policy plank, a final sop was thrown the United Nation's way, with allusions to "strengthening" it, while at the same time a strong statement on continued "national defense" totally neutralized the obvious palliative. Reagan, however, no longer talks about a "strengthened United Nations." On the contrary, his present U.N respresentative, Jeanne Kirkpatrick, is an obstinate and even zealous advocate of absolutely no changes in the present U.N. charter. Her Soviet counterpart, incidentally, mirrors her sentiments.

But like a compost pile, the political ferment is steaming, alive, with potentially fertile loam ready to burst into growth if properly seeded. And what is the catalystic seed from which such growth can emerge? What should be the battle-cry of today's oppressed national citizen? In other words, how are you being ripped-off? *You are paying for the national "suicide pact" without being directly represented.*

In plain words, whether you know it or not, you are not a "citizen" in the sense that you have control over your destiny; you are as enslaved as the serfs of old or the colonists of the 19th century. Taking a page from U.S. history again, the grievances of the American colonists in the 18th century crystalized into "No taxation without representation."

Beset with worldwide inflation, rising unemployment, a host of economic exploitations, horrendous cost of Big Government, you the national citizen, are being taxed for armaments for your own destruction, for the maintenance of anachronistic national frontiers, absurd spy systems, for the monstrously expensive diplomatic world, embassies, consulates and legations plus personnel engaged exclusively in maintaining the deadly farce, the roccoco bungling of the dis-United Nations with its sterile, eternal debates, in short for an 18th century political world hell-bent for destruction which will make the collapse of the Roman Empire seem in comparison like a garden party called on account of rain.

The rip-off is truly worldwide. We, The People Everywhere are the real victims. Because no one will survive Big Boom III. And we are all being taxed NOW to insure it!

Can you imagine an irony more tragic...and more stupid?

"No taxation without WORLD REPRESENTATION!" must become the battle-cry of the disillusioned, indignant and tyrannized citizen

A new world party must arise from our ranks to enfranchise our common will

143

for freedom, peace and well-being worldwide.

If the nations can join the United Nations with its proven record of total impotence to resolve basic human problems, the individual can extend his or her political affiliation to a world party overtly dedicated to world institutions for the elimination of problems affecting his or her very life.

A world citizen party can operate on the one level which national parties deny exists but where alone solutions can be found to world problems, i.e., the world level. A global candidate can stand for election to a world parliament much as Willi Brandt declared his candidacy for European Parliament fully five years before it was finally founded. Or he/she can run for world president. (Remember, a functioning world government has been operating for over 30 years). But it can operate just as well on the municipal, state and national levels. On all lower levels of politics, individuals can run on a world government ticket thus complementing the top level.

To the charge of impracticability, we reply in Emery Reve's words: "The persistent opposition to reason and logic in political matters from those who have no other argument but 'practicality' is the most vulgar manifestation of human mind and behavior. It would never be tolerated if the conduct of human affairs were based on principles and guided by reason."

Practically every known human activity is already operating on trans-national or global lines with media leading the parade. Multi-nationals, international NGOs, NATO, UNESCO, specialized agencies of the UN, over 2,000 international organizations including labor unions and banking syndicates, all with "world directors," "international Secretary-Generals" and staff, "world advisory boards," etc. command respect, function and provide goods and services to the general public.

Why not world politics?

The human race has never balked at utopia. Today's banal world was yesterday's utopia. Besides if humanity is clever enough to wipe itself out, it follows that it is clever enough to devise methods to survive.

A world citizen party would provide both a "horizontal" and "vertical" vote. It would be transnational in that all WCP candidates—like all Communist and Socialist party candidates at least claim—would stand on the same ideological platform: world peace through just law and its institutions to design, execute, legislate, adjudicate and enforce such law. (See Chapter 20, *Is The Individual A Subject Of International Law?*) Unlike the Communist and Socialist parties, however, a world citizen party—and this is the unique and revolutionary innovation—would be running world candidates, thus for the first time in political history, your vote would be "vertical" or global, a logical extension of democracy—as mandated by the above-quoted article in the UDHR.

This three-dimensional vote will be charged with real political power, the power of the sovereign individual at last regaining his/her rightful place in the political process. It would at once expose the strictly national political party vote as

WORLD BALLOT		世界投票用紙	

WORLD BALLOT #		世界投票用紙 #	
District ( )		地区 ( )	
Issued by		発行元	
World Election Commission		世界選挙委員会	
Suite 1101, 1012 14th St., N.W.		Suite 1101, 1012 14th St., N.W.	
Washington, D.C. 20005 USA		Washington, D.C. 20005 USA	
Issued to:		発行先：	
Name:_____		氏名：_____	
Address: _____		住所： _____	
_____ Zip Code		_____ 〒	
World Government Registration #:		世界政府登録番号	
_____		_____	

PARTISAN OFFICES		党事務局	
WORLD PRESIDENT		党首	
Garry Davis		Garry Davis	
WORLD PARLIAMENT		議会	

MEASURES SUBMITTED TO VOTE OF VOTERS		選挙人は次の提案に投票する事	
	For		賛成
	Aga		反対
	Yes		はい
	No		いいえ
	Yes		はい
	No		いいえ
	Yes		はい
	No		いいえ

World Government Document 1319A	世界政府文書1319A

A concrete symbol of world democracy in action.

unrealistic, exploitive, impotent and in truth, a betrayal of the voter's trust.

A world citizen party would open the way for democratic and non-violent political action for all seeking effective implementation of their one world advocacy, in particular the youth of the world whose idealism, energy and courage seek honest outlets heretofore lacking on the national political front.

Certain national parties already contain planks fitting into a valid global "ticket." A "bio-political" network—the spreading Green Parties for example—is evolving to challenge the statism of the isolated and stifling national party system. A world citizen party can serve as the coordinating center around which the "spokes" turn to pull humanity's wagon to safety.

The registered citizen of World Government may complement that global civic commitment with the franchise affirmed by the UDHR mandate in order to strengthen our embryonic world institution with democratic safeguards. (The author has already declared his candidacy for world president on September 4, 1983. See Chapter 23). This strategy brings the global and local viewpoint together, like visualizing our planet and human race from the astronaut's vantage point while yet being planted solidly on the terra firma of one's own back yard.

In sum, the "power vote" is YOUR vote. . .as a declared citizen of the world. It signifies world power to Us, the world's people. It means that we refuse to pay for our own suffering and eventual nuclear death. It means that the world is our "country", our homeland, and we intend to organize it rationally and peacefully. It serves as a powerful antidote to all dictators, tyrants, torturers, exploiters and oppressors, big and small.

It is a wisdom vote, a one world vote, a human rights vote, a freedom vote and a world peace vote.

It is the turned-on, right-on, outgoing, far-out, synergetic, fraternal, pursuit of happiness vote.

Finally, it is the indispensable fulfilment of democracy.

Let us claim it. It is our human right.

We have nothing to lose but our national chains.

CHAPTER 11

WORLD CITIZEN DAVIS TAKES CASE TO SUPREME COURT

1. Press Release

FOR IMMEDIATE RELEASE September 2, 1981

WASHINGTON, D.C. – Garry Davis, a World War II bomber pilot who dramatized the need for world peace through world citizenship by renouncing his nationality in 1948, is asking the Supreme Court to side with him in challenging the concepts of expatriation and statelessness in our century which Immigration and the lowers courts claim he represents.

Davis's petition for a writ of certiorari, filed Friday, August 28, 1981 under docket no. 81-427, seeks a review of lower court decisions unholding the Immigration and Naturalization Service (INS) position that Davis is an "excludable alien" and a "stateless person."

In the personally prepared petition, Davis counters the claim by stating that "the alleged expatriate who does not acquire an other nationality remains in a legal vacuum vis-a-vis all nations.

"As a stateless person," Davis said, "he has 'lost the right to have rights,' as former Chief Justice Warren put it."

In his petition, Davis also invoked the Ninth Amendment to the U.S. Constitution by saying that "it both limits national government and affirms natural rights 'of the people,' which have never before been used to justify a transcendent citizenship on the global level where all our major problems are, the most important being nuclear war."

For the past four years, Davis has been legally "excluded" from the United States while living in Washington and heading the World Service Authority (WSA) he founded in 1954 as the administrative agency of the World Government of World Citizens, which he declared in 1953 at Ellsworth, Maine.

As a "stateless person," Davis has been jailed more than 20 times in eight Western democracies for lack of identity papers considered valid by various bureaucracies. Since 1954, he has carried identity documents, including a world passport, issued by the WSA. WSA documents are now being held by more than 225,000 persons.

Davis claims in his petition that his world passport has already been recognized by the INS on three separate occasions, besides being officially approved by

147

a half-dozen national governments and accepted for entry by more than 60 other governments – including the United States – on a case-by-case basis.

"This is really a test case," Davis said, "exposing the anomoly of exclusive national citizenship in one physical and technological world. While all national leaders claim to want peace, world peace can only come as a result of a world public order based on a new civic compact between individuals. That's what world citizenship is all about. That's what protection of human rights means. And that's what the Ninth Amendment is really there for. Americans must realize there is a legitimate alternative to the arms race."

The case leading to Davis's petition to the U.S. Supreme Court began on May 13, 1977 when he arrived at Dulles International Airport identified only by a WSA passport. INS officials refused to accept the document or waive the visa requirements as before. They ordered him held in detention pending a hearing before an Immigration judge. At the hearing, May 17, 1977, Davis was declared "excludable." He appealed to the Board of Immigration Appeals and on September 27, 1977, the Board upheld the decision.

After waiting for over a year for the government to move, on July 17, 1979, Davis took the INS to court, seeking a habeus corpus writ from the United States District Court for the District of Columbia.

On December 9, 1980, Judge Thomas Flannery denied the writ. Davis appealed to the U.S. Court of Appeals and on March 29, 1981, that court upheld the lower court's decision.

In the present petition, Davis claims that neither the INS nor the lower courts considered his anomalous position of being considered both an "excludable alien" and a "stateless person." Neither did they consider the Ninth Amendment relevant to Davis's claim to world citizenship.

Davis's former counsel, David Carliner, had taken the somewhat obscure and misleading position that Davis was still a U.S. citizen in that an ambiguity at the time of renunciation arose because of Davis' intent as expressed in his statement at the time. The courts disagreed with that argument claiming the oath of renunciation along with Davis' statement admits of no ambiguity whatsoever.

"A vital point of law was never emphasized in counsel's argument," Davis said, "that the so-called right of expatriation is in effect nullified first if no other nationality is acquired, and second, if the alleged expatriate claims the right to live in his native land as I do. Besides, the U.S. Congress of 1940, when the present Act was passed, in considering the right of expatriation in the light of the centuries when the nation was building population, made a fundamental error of construction in the enabling legislation which I bring out in my petition. The plain fact is, no American since that Act has expatriated himself according to that statute. It simply can't be done legally. In other words, the whole question of expatriation for our time is in essential doubt."

Davis will argue the case himself if certiorari is granted by the Court. In the meantime, the INS has thirty days from date of filing to file a reply.

Case No. 81-427 thus awaits the Court when it convenes the first Monday in October.

II. Petition For Writ of Certiorari (August 28, 1981)

No. 81-427

IN THE
SUPREME COURT OF THE UNITED STATES
OCTOBER TERM 1981

GARRY DAVIS

Petitioner

v.

DISTRICT DIRECTOR
IMMIGRATION AND NATURALIZATION
SERVICE

Respondent

PETITION FOR WRIT OF CERTIORARI TO
THE UNITED STATES COURT OF APPEALS FOR
THE DISTRICT OF COLUMBIA CIRCUIT

Address of Petitioner: Garry Davis
3603 Ordway Street, N.W.   Petitioner Pro Se
Washington, D.C. 20016
(202) 364-0871

1. Whether 8 U.S.C. 1182(a)(20) is applicable to a native-born American who "expatriated" himself in accordance with 8 U.S.C. 1481(a)(5), thus becoming "stateless," who does not acquire another nationality and subsequently returns to the United States claiming it his permanent home.

2. Whether 8 U.S.C. 1481(a)(5), resulting in "statelessness", was the intent of Congress both in conception and adoption of the legislation and if so, whether such "expatriation" is constitutional in that it condones a condition of anarchy.

3. Whether the enabling statute of 8 U.S.C. 1481(a)(20) is validly constructed and, if not, can a United States citizen legally "expatriate" himself according to the construction.

4. Whether the Ninth Amendment of the United States Constitution can be construed as sanctioning the individual to exercise his natural and unalienable right to claim a citizenship transcending that of the nation in accordance with the concept of multiple citizenship enshrined in the Tenth Amendment.

TABLE OF CONTENTS

ii

APPENDIX:

TABLE OF AUTHORITIES

Cases:

iii

iv

United States Constitution, Statutes:

Other:

OPINIONS BELOW

The opinion for which review is sought here is the opinion of the United States Court of Appeals for the District of Columbia Circuit in Davis v. INS, Case No. 80-1071, decided on March 31, 1981, and is set forth in the attached Appendix (App.) B at page 1b. The opinion of the United States District Court for the District of Columbia in the same case (C.A. No. 79-1874, filed December 19, 1979), is set forth at App. C, p. 1c.

JURISDICTION

A timely petition for rehearing en banc filed in the U.S. Court of Appeals for the District of Columbia was denied August 5, 1981. The instant petition for certiorari is authorized to be filed on or before August 28, 1981 by No. 1254 of Title 28, U.S.C. and in accordance with an Order of July 1, 1981 granting an extension of time for filing.

The petitioner also claims the right of certiorari on the basis of:

1. "Three requisites for issuance of 'certiorari' are excess of jurisdiction, absence of appeal, and non-existence of another remedy." Mack v. District Court of 2nd Judicial in and for Washoe County, Dept. No. 2m 258 p. 289, 50 Nev. 318.

2. "Discretion of court on petition for writ of certiorari requires court to act according to its judgment and conscience, and it involves fair consideration of all peculiar features of particular questions involved." Axley v. Hammock, 50 S.W. (2nd) 608, 185, Ark. 939.

3. "Certiorari, to be justifiably granted, requires petition to raise issue of law of gravity and importance." Briesnick v. Dimond, 142 S.E. 118, 165 Ga 780 dismissing cert. 134 S.E. 350 35 Ga App. 668.

CONSTITUTIONAL PROVISIONS, STATUTES

The Ninth Amendment provides:
> "The enumeration in the Constitution of certain rights shall not be construed to deny or disparage other rights retained by the people."

The Tenth Amendment provides:
> "The powers not delegated to the United States by the Constitution, nor prohibited by it to the States, are reserved to the States respectively, or to the people."

Title 8 U.S.C. 1481(a)(5) provides:
> "From and after the effective date of this Act, a person who is a national of the United States, whether by birth or naturalization, shall lose his nationality by*******
>> (5) making a formal renunciation of nationality before a diplomatic or consular officer of the United States in a foreign state in such form as may be described by the Secretary of State."

1

Title 8 U.S.C. 1182(a)(20) provides:

". . . any immigrant who at the time of application for admission is not in possession of a valid unexpired immigrant visa, reentry permit, border crossing identification card, or other valid entry document required by this chapter, and a valid unexpired passport or other suitable travel document, or document of identity and nationality. . . (is excludable)."

Title 8 1101(30) provides:

"The term 'passport' means any travel document issued by a competent authority showing the bearer's origin, identity, and nationality, if any, which is valid for the entry of the bearer into a foreign country."

also

Title 28, U.S.C. 1254

Title 8, U.S.C. 1252

Title 8, U.S.C. 1101(g)

Title 22, U.S.C. 292

STATEMENT OF THE CASE

The petitioner, born in Bar Harbor, Maine, a World War II bomber pilot, became convinced in 1947 that exclusive nationality could no longer guarantee either himself, his native country or the world the fundamental rights of "Life, Liberty and the Pursuit of Happiness."[1]

A new social and political compact, he concluded, of a global character was essential in order to provide the institutions required to outlaw war between nations.[2]

In a worldly sense, he considered himself in a "state of nature" in relationship to his fellow humans which had to be transformed by a willful exercise of natural rights into positive world law.[3]

The only form available to him to divest himself of exclusive nationality was 8 U.S.C. 1841(a)(5) permitting willful and voluntary renunciation of nationality. Before a consular officer in the U.S. Embassy in Paris, he availed himself of this provision. Thus, in the terms implicitly defined by that Act, he became "stateless."[4]

1/Declaration of Independence.

2/"Wars between groups of men forming social units always take place when these units—tribes, dynasties, churches, cities, nations—exercise unrestricted sovereign power. Wars between these social units cease the moment sovereign power is transferred from them to a larger or higher unit." *Anatomy of Peace*, 38, Emery Reves, Harpers, 1945.

3/"Whereas it is essential if man is not compelled to have recourse as a last resort to rebellion against tyranny and oppression that human rights should be protected by the rule of law . . ." Preamble, Universal Declaration of Human Rights, U.N. Document.

"Everyone is entitled to a social and international order in which the rights and freedoms set forth in this Declaration can be fully realized." Art. 28, *ibid*.

4/"Being without a state or without nationality. . ." Webster's New Collegiate Dictionary, 1959.

2

At the same time, he set forth the reasons for this act of alleged renunciation. They were briefly, 1) to renounce national exclusiv,ity since its perpetuation colluded with inter-national anarchy, and 2) to identify himself as a partner with his fellow humans in a new compact he called "world citizenship."[5]

As an alleged stateless person, he has thenceforth been without or has had minimal rights or protection since 1948 from the various nations in which he found temporary residence. He has been incarcerated over 20 times in 8 Western democracies for the "crime" of not possessing "valid" identity papers. On two occasions, in 1950 and 1957, on seeking advice from U.S. consular officers abroad on how to return to his homeland, he was asked to "immigrate." On both occasions he noted his permanent address as the United States. The anomaly of "immigrating" to his home went unquestioned by either the consular officers, the State Department or the INS.

On July 27, 1953, he was forcibly brought into the United States against his will—while aboard the S.S. Queen Mary docked at New York—by Immigration officials.[6]

In order to protect his and other world citizens' rights against violation by national officials, on September 4, 1953 at Ellsworth, Maine, he declared a world government based on the Universal Declaration of Human Rights. In January, 1954, in New York, he founded the World Service Authority as the administrative agency of the new government.

On January 11, 1957, after his World Passport had been inspected by Immigration officials while he was still aboard a KLM plane at Kennedy Airport, he was permitted to enter the United States "without conditions."[7]

In June, 1975, petitioner entered the United States again identified only with the World Passport issued by the World Service Authority in Basel, Switzerland.[8] At Kennedy Airport, petitioner was granted a waiver of the visa requirements by Immigration officials.[9] He departed from the United States in September, 1975. He returned again in April, 1975 to attend his father's memorial service. Again, at Kennedy Airport, Immigration officials waived the visa requirements after inspecting his World Service Authority passport.[10]

On May 13, 1977, he again returned to the United States via Dulles Airport. As before, his only identification was the World Service Authority passport which stated that his home address was "1803 19th Street, N.W., Washington, D.C."

After two hearings, May 17, 1977 before Immigration Judge Emil M. Bobek, and Sept. 27, 1977 before the Board of Immigration Appeals, petitioner was declared 1) an "excludable alien, and 2) a "stateless person."

5/Full statement, Appendix 1a

"Whatever rights or attributes of sovereignty government may exercise are the free and revocable grants of the people..." *The Political Thought of the American Revolution*, 222, Clinton Rossiter, Harcourt, 1963.

6/See Transcript of Hearing, p. 14-15, A7 449 011, Exclusion Proceedings, May 17, 1977, INS.

7/See Transcript of Hearings, p. 11-12, Exclusion Proceedings, May 17, 1977, INS. (Immigration officials subsequently claimed petitioned was "paroled" into U.S.)

8/The passport states it represents Art. 13, Universal Declaration of Human Rights, that WSA is a global government administrative agency.

9/See Brief of Appellee, U.S. Court of Appeals, p. 6.

10/See Transcript of Hearings, p. 20, Exclusion Proceedings, May 17, 1977, INS.

3

Despite the determination, the INS took no appropriate action as provided for in Title 8 U.S.C. 1252, "Apprehension and deportation of aliens—Arrest and custody; review of determination by court," with regard to the petitioner.[11]

On July 17, 1979, petitioner petitioned the United States District Court for a writ of habeus corpus. (Civil Action No. 79-1874). In a Memorandum Opinion of December 19, 1979, Judge Thomas Flannery presiding, petition was denied. (App. B).

On May 17, 1980, petitioner appealed to the United States Court of Appeals for the District of Columbia Circuit. On March 31, 1981, appeal was denied in a Judgment with a Memorandum attached. (App. C).

On June 25, 1981 petitioner petitioned for Order Extending Time for Filing for a Rehearing En Banc, Time Having Expired to the United States Court of Appeals, District of Columbia Circuit.

The petition was denied on August 5, 1981. (App. D).

ARGUMENT

I

EXPATRIATION ALONE PRODUCES "STATELESSNESS", A CONDITION DEPRIVING THE INDIVIDUAL OF ALL POSITIVE RIGHTS. THIS IN TURN PRODUCES THE ANOMALY OF STATE SOVEREIGNTY VERSUS INDIVIDUAL SOVEREIGNTY, OR STATE LAWS/DECREES VS. HUMAN RIGHTS. THE INSTANT CASE REVEALS THE ANOMALY POSITING IMMIGRATION LAWS AGAINST THE RIGHT OF A NATIVE-BORN "EXPATRIATE" TO LIVE IN HIS NATIVE LAND.

Neither the District Court nor the Appeal Court considered this anomalous, thus intolerable for the individual concerned, situation.

a. The District Court Judgment defined the instant case as presenting "the issue whether a native born American may renounce primary allegiance to the United States and still retain rights to enter and remain in this country without a proper visa."[12]

The full weight of the judgment therefore rested upon the "fact" of expatriation rather than 1) whether rights were retained in spite of the alleged renunciation, 2) what anomalies pertained which became manifest only after the expatriating act as exposed in the instant case, 3) whether the Act itself permitting expatriation could be performed in view of the construction of the statute, and 4) whether the concept of multiple citizenship was relevant in view of petitioner's express declaration of world citizenship.

11/The last embarkation point from which petitioner arrived on May 13, 1977 was Heathrow Airport, UK. In that the British Home Office had already imprisoned petitioner for 12 weeks in 1953 as a "menace to the public good," arranging for his deportation in collusion with U.S. Immigration, he could not be returned to the U.K.

12/Memorandum Opinion and Order, 1st. p. (App. C)

4

The Court of Appeals, in upholding the lower court's finding, inferred that petitioner could acquire "lawful permanent resident status. . ." as an "alien," and further, that his "laudable military record could qualify him for naturalization."[13]

The "solutions" of "acquiring permanent resident status" as an "alien" or "naturalization" were not at issue either in petitioner's petition to the lower court or in his appeal petition.

In short, he does not, nor has he ever considered himself an "alien" to his native land. The incongruity of a natural-born American applying for naturalization did not bother the Appeal Court.

The respondent, in both trials, sought only to prove that petitioner did renounce his nationality, was therefore an "alien," and thus could only re-enter the United States with a "proper visa."

Thus, neither the District Court nor the Court of Appeals addressed directly the contradiction inherent in the statutes, 8 U.S.C. 1841(a)(5) and 8 U.S.C. 1182(a)(20) when allied together as in the instant case. Petitioner in brief cannot be removed from the United States despite the statute, as, for example, in *Jolley v. INS, 441 F. 2d 1245 (5 Cir.1971).*

b. The lower court Memorandum claimed that petitioner had "at various times entered the United States on a permanent resident alien. . .visa." (p. 2, para. 3). This is in error. The result of the "immigration" (See Statement of the Case, p. 7-8) was to be classified *by the INS* as a "permanent resident alien." The entries to the United States, with one exception, were permitted *by the INS* after waiving the visa requirements as outlined in the Statement of the Case herein.

c. The District Court Judgment further states that the Immigration Appeal Board "relying on 8 USC 1182(a)(20), found the petitioner excludable because he lacked a valid document of entry." (Page 3, para. 1).

In a subsequent section, (II, p. 9), Judge Flannery states that "An alien must possess a proper entry document upon entering the United States." Quoting 8 USC 1182(a)(20) as his authority, he concluded that 'The petitioner's World Service Authority Passport fails to qualify as one of the documents required by 8 USC 1182."

As previously noted, petitioner entered the United States on three separate occasions identified only with his World Service Authority Passport. Counsel for respondent in his appeal brief stated that "Davis has chosen to place himself above the law and seek entry into the United States with simply a document of his own creation—a World Service Authority passport." (Page 16, para. 1). Respondent failed to deny, however, petitioner's entries on "a document of his own creation" with full cognizance and approval of the Immigration and Naturalization Service.

13/See Memorandum, App. 2b

5

In accordance with the requirements of 8 USC 1101(30), petitioner herewith submits 1) photocopies of official national governmental letters in recognition of the World Service Authority Passport, and 2) various photostated entry visas of national governments—including that of the United States—affixed to WSA Passports as evidence that said passport "is valid for the entry of the bearer into a foreign country." (App. F and G).

d. Judge Flannery's final admonition (page 11) "that any person who desires to pursue this goal (to work for world peace through the vehicle of world citizenship and world government) while residing in the United States. . . must obey this nation's immigration and naturalization laws."

The INS, however, has no statutory authority to oblige petitioner to accept the status of a "permanent resident alien," or an "immigrant," or indeed any other status. It can either accept or exclude individuals in accordance with prescribed statutes.[14]

In conclusion, should an individual, as in the instant case, be a victim of mutually contradictory statutes, how can he "obey this nation's immigration and naturalization laws" when the INS itself finds itself unable to enforce them?

II

EXPATRIATION CANNOT BE EXECUTED THROUGH ENABLING LEGISLATION SINCE IT CANNOT LEGALLY BE PERFORMED "IN A FOREIGN STATE." YET 8 USC 1481(a)(5) MUST BE PERFORMED "BEFORE A DIPLOMATIC OR CONSULAR OFFICER IN A FOREIGN STATE." IF PERFORMED IN THE EXPATRIATING STATE, THE "EXPATRIATED" INDIVIDUAL COULD NOT LEAVE OR BE DEPORTED UNLESS HE HAD PERMISSION OF ENTRY FROM ANOTHER STATE.

The petitioner did not expatriate himself "in a foreign state."[15] He took the

---

14/The afore-mentioned forced entry—July 27, 1953—illustrates in an ominous way the frustrations of both the executive and judicial branches of the government in trying to reconcile the inconsistencies represented by the statutes here in question. For instance, should petitioner depart from the United States—"deporting" himself (See 8 USC 1101(g)) and return, will the INS take him into arbitrary custody (See Marcia-Mir v. Smith, C81-1084A, D.C. Atlanta), waive the visa requirements or as now again "exclude" him legally if not actually?

15/"A 'foreign state' with former section 17 of this title. . . providing for expatriation of American citizen who was naturalized under laws of foreign state was a country which was not the United States or its possessions or colony, an alien country, other than our own." Kletter v. Dulles, D.C. D.C. 1953, III F. Supp. 593. "In act providing for loss of United States nationality by participation in political election in 'foreign state' quoted words are not word of art, and in using them Congress did not have in mind fine distinctions as to sovereignty of occupied and unoccupied countries which authorities on international law may have formulated, but when Congress speaks of 'foreign state' it means a 'country' which is not the United States or its possession or colony', 'an alien country', 'other than our own',...." Hichino Uyeno v. Acheson, D.C. Wash. 96 F. Supp. 510, 515. (See also Bigley v. New York & P.R.S.S. Co., 1 05 F 74, 76; Brackett v. Norton, 4 Conn. 517, 521, 10 AM. Dec. 179; Cherokee Nation v. State of Georgia, 30 US 1, 15, 5 Pet. 1, 15, 88, Ed. 25; Cowell v. State, 16 Tex, App. 57, 61; Faber v. United States, 157 F. 140 141; Bezat v. Home Owners' Loan Corp., 98 P 2d 852, 855 55 Ariz; Kuniyuki v. Acheson, D.C. Wash., 94 F. Supp. 358, 360.)

6

Oath of Renunciation on United States territory or "soil." The embassy of any nation-state rests on territory belonging to the nation represented by the embassy.[16]

A diplomatic or consular officer, administering any oath to any national citizen, does so within the confines of that sovereign territory. He is not, consequently, "in a foreign state." The issue here is not superficial but substantive involving diplomatic relations between sovereign nations as well as the very existence of states themselves occupying specific sections of the planet.[16a] Only in the recognition of territorial sovereignty, of which the embassies are an integral part, can nations enjoy diplomatic relationships with each other or indeed even exist as such.[17]

This principle is recognized universally, and, as part of customary international law, is respected reciprocally by all nation-states.[18]

Therefore, for a United States citizen to "expatriate" himself, according to the statute, he must be both "before a diplomatic or consular officer..." *and* "...in a foreign state." This construction is not merely clumsy and irresponsible but deceptive and essentially inoperable.

The deception comes directly [when] the individual has become an alleged expatriate. He is *then* obliged to *enter* a foreign state. Theoretically and actually he should remain in the U.S. Embassy unless he already possesses another nationality and, therefore, presumably another passport. For to enter a "foreign state" without "valid" entry papers is as much a "crime" as to enter the United States illegally.

Yet, by permitting the Oath of Renunciation to be taken under the "cover" of an Embassy, away from the prying eyes of a "foreign state," the U.S. Congress is condoning and even abetting the post facto act of illegal entry.

The construction thus of the statute enabling expatriation is manifestly contradictory, unworkable and, in terms of "foreign" relations, inadmissible.[19]

16/22 USC 292 provides:

"Acquisition of sites and buildings for diplomatic and consular establishments:

(a) The Secretary of State is empowered to acquire...any building or grounds *of the United States* in foreign countries and *under the jurisdiction* and control *of the Secretary of State*...for the use of the diplomatic and consular establishments of the United States." (Emphasis added.)

"Jurisdiction is authority of law to act officially in particular matter in hand." *Frazier v. Moffatt,* 239 P 2d 123 108 CA 2d 379.

"Jurisdiction is controlling authority; the right of making and enforcing laws or regulations; the capacity of determining rules of action or use, and exacting penalties; the function or capacity of judging or governing in general; the inherent power of decision or control."

People v. Pierce. 41 N.Y. S. 858, 860, 18 Mis 83.

16a/During the recent takeover of the United States Embassy in Tehran with the capture of embassy personnel as "hostages" by the Iranian student militants with the acquiescence of the Iranian government, the Carter administration accused Iran of "abrogating international law" introducing a petition to the International Court at the Hague seeking judicial redress.

17/In the U.S. Embassy in Moscow, the Vaschenko and Chmykhalov families, Soviet citizens, have been living for 3 years, given "asylum" by the U.S. Government. Soviet authorities respect the *territorial* validity of the "foreign" embassy. A reciprocal respect by U.S. authorities would pertain if the situation were reversed in Washington, D.C.

18/"The law of nations is 'part of our law'." *Hilton v. Guyot, N.Y. 1895, 16 S. Ct. 139, 159, US 163, 40 L. Ed. 95.*

19/*"By what right (does one treat) a foreign state as a sort of sewer into which one is entitled to discharge his social detritus?" Expulsion des Heimatlos,* 60, Philonenko, Journal de Droit International, 1161, 117, 1933, quoted in Preuss.

7

The respondent claims, and both the District Court and the Court of Appeals concur, that the petitioner renounced his nationality "in a foreign state." (See p. 3, Brief of Appellee, Memorandum Opinion and Order, (1)(b) 3rd para., D.C. Memorandum, C. of A.) This judgment is in error. Petitioner, as stated, took the Oath of Renunciation before a consular officer *in* the United States, so recognized by the French State, that is, in the U.S. Embassy, situated on U.S. territory, in Paris.

Should the Court consider this argument specious, petitioner humbly suggests that the very concept then of "foreign state" is likewise specious, not to mention "foreign policy," "foreign affairs," and the like.

Your petitioner suggests that Congress recognized the anomaly of expatriation in our century if performed without acquiring another nationality or already possessing one (as do most emigres to the United States) in this mischievous construction. It has gone unchallenged till now for the obvious reason that an "expatriate" with intent to renounce all allegiance to the United States would have neither motive nor opportunity, as does your petitioner, to expose the inherent contradiction.

To consider this crucial issue another way, the construction of the statute should logically be:

...(5) making a formal renunciation of nationality before a diplomatic or consular officer in a United States Embassy in such form, etc.

However, such a construction at once exposes the basic fallacy of expatriation taken alone. For it implies that the "expatriate," being still on U.S. "soil" must then commit the act of illegal entry to a "foreign state," or else remain forever in the U.S. Embassy as a "stateless" person. This in turn exposes the "horizontal" character of "expatriation" where, when one state "loses" a human being, another state "gains" one.

If, however, the alleged expatriate chooses to remain "stateless," and does not wish to suffer the "punishment" which inevitably emanates from the state which he is forced to enter illegally, he must "verticalize" himself by claiming a transcendent civic status for the protection of his unalienable rights.[20]

Petitioner, in "entering" France after the alleged expatriation act by leaving the U.S. compound, broke the French law of entry, was subsequently declared "persona non grata" by French Immigration and given 48 hours to leave the country or face imprisonment.[21]

20/"...In consequence of many recent developments—the rising demands of people for human dignity values, the expanding identities for whom these values are being demanded, the increasingly realistic perception of the conditions of interdependence, and the growing insistence that a principal goal of global constitutive process is the protection of common interest—there would appear to be today a growing recognition and acceptance, even demand, that the protection and fulfillment of human rights be regarded as matters of international concern," for the employment of all constitutive functions, rather than as matters of "domestic jurisdiction." Indeed many of the policies about human rights would appear to be so intensely demanded that they are acquiring...not merely the status of "international concern," but in addition that of *jus cogens* or of a global bill of rights."

Human Rights and World Public Order, 135, McDougal, Lassell, Chen, *Yale University Press, 1980.*
21/Such incarceration would endure until petitioner obtained entry papers to another state or died.

"The powerlessness of the stateless person is most apparent in the limitation upon his freedom of movement, both of egress and return...Unable to enter the territory of a state lawfully, he is often compelled to do so clandestinely...." A Study of Statelessness, 139, UN document.

8

The original anomaly of "expatriation", i.e., becoming "stateless" in a world of states, began repeating itself till the present case.

While Judge Flannery acknowledged that "statelessness was the intended consequence of petitioner's May 24 (sic), 1948 actions at the United States Embassy..." (page 8, Memorandum and Opinion) and that "whatever harshness may attach to statelessness is therefore inapplicable to the instant case..." (page 9), he failed to note the anomaly resulting from the application of 8 U.S.C. 1841(a)(5) exposed in his Court by the petitioner's very presence.

In conclusion, since the Act of Renunciation can actually only be performed "...before a diplomatic or consular officer..." in a United States Embassy, those allegedly performing this Act do not do so in accordance with the enabling statute. This Court alone can determine if they, including your petitioner, have legally "expatriated" themselves.

III

BOTH THE NINTH AND TENTH AMENDMENTS TO THE CONSTITUTION ACKNOWLEDGE RIGHTS RETAINED "BY THE PEOPLE." IF THE EXPATRIATING INDIVIDUAL POSSESSES NO OTHER NATIONALITY NOR ACQUIRES ONE, GIVEN PRESENT STATUTES, THESE RIGHTS MUST BE EXERCISED BY INDIVIDUAL CONCERNED FOR THE PROTECTION OF HIS FUNDAMENTAL FREEDOMS AND SUBSEQUENT RIGHTS. THIS EXERCISE OF RIGHTS IS BOTH ANTERIOR TO AND INDEPENDENT OF NATIONAL CONSTITUTIONAL FRAMEWORK. ITS POLITICAL COROLLARY IS A NEW CITIZENSHIP OF A GLOBAL CHARACTER, HUMAN RIGHTS BEING UNIVERSAL, IDENTIFYING BOTH THE INCLUSIVE SOVEREIGNTY OF MANKIND AND THE UNALIENABLE SOVEREIGNTY OF THE INDIVIDUAL.

a. *The Dichotomy Between Expatriation and Statelessness*

Your petitioner personifies both the principle of expatriation and statelessness. Therefore this Court is faced with both latter-day political phenomena in the instant and novel case.

Congress has determined that expatriation is a basic human right. (Act of July 27, 1868, ch. 249, 15 Stat. 223). Then it applies equally to all human beings. Indeed, the history of expatriation reveals that it had to be considered reciprocally, that is, for incoming nationals of foreign states as well as for United States citizens.

In 1868, the United States Congress proclaimed:

"...the right of expatriation is a natural and inherent right *of all people*, indispensable to the enjoyment of life, liberty, and the pursuit of happiness;...any declaration, instruction, opinion, order, or decision of any officers of this government which denies, restricts, impairs, or questions the right of expatriation, is hereby declared inconsistent with the fundamental principles of this government." (Act of July 27, 1968) (Emphasis added.)

9

While the Act does not mention statelessness as such, the clear implication is that the result of expatriation is statelessness which by implication is "indispensable to the enjoyment...etc."[22]

At the 1930 Hague Conference for the Codification of International Law, the United States delegation made a strong plea for the incorporation of the principle of voluntary expatriation in these words:

> "For a century past, it has been the policy of my country that the right of expatriation is an inherent and natural right *of all persons.* It is true that allegiance is a duty, but it is not a chain that holds a person in bondage and that he carries with him to a new life in a new land...This principle is not a small matter. It is not a question of language or of formulae, or of phrases. It is a principle of *the rights of man* and of *the liberty of the human race.*" (Emphasis added).

The reference to "the rights of man" and "the liberty of the human race" vividly identifies the anomaly presented by the limitations of national law. For the rights of man and the liberty of the human race connote their protection by positive law transcending that of the exclusive nation, in other words, world law encompassing the human race as such.[23]

The collective nations, however, recognized that voluntary expatriation condones anarchy. For, in the Convention on the Reduction of Statelessness adopted August 30, 1961, Article 7(1)(a) states:

> "If the law of the Contracting State permits renunciation of nationality, such renunciation shall not result in loss of nationality unless the person concerned possesses or acquires another nationality."

With regard to the forcing of expatriated individuals upon another state, Sir John Fischer Williams, writing nearly half a century ago, (Denationalization, 8 Brit, Y.B., Int'l. L. 47, 1927) stated that:

> "...while positive interntional law does not forbid a state unilaterally to sever the relationship of nationality so far as the individual is concerned, even if the person affected possesses or acquires no other nationality, still a state cannot sever the ties of nationality in such a way as to release itself from the international duty, owed to other states, of receiving back a person denationalized who has acquired no other nationality, should he be expelled as an alien by the state where he happens to be."

Chief Justice Warren in *Trop v. Dulles,* 365 US 86, 102, described the stateless dilemma vividly:

22/"The status of statelessness entails a most severe and dramatic deprivation of the power of the individual. Just as, within the state, nationality is the 'right to have rights,' so also, on the transnational level, nationality is the right to have protection in rights. The stateless person has no state to 'protect' him and lacks even the freedom of movement to find a state that is willing to protect him... Statelessness often results in suffering and hardship shocking to conscience and the dignity of man."

3rd Report on the Elimination or Reduction of Statelessness, UN Document, 1953.

23/"Nationality is a concept created in the past to promote a minimum organization of the world under past conditions. The references and function of the concept cannot remain static: it must be as dynamic as the changing demands and identification of peoples and the changing configurations of the world and national constitutive process."

Human Rights and World Public Order, p. 957, McDougal, Lasswell, Chen, Yale U. Press, 1980.

10

"...There may be involved no physical mistreatment, no primitive torture. There is instead the total destruction of the individual's status in organized society. It is a form of punishment more primitive than torture, for it destroys for the individual the political existence that was centuries in the development. The punishment (of expatriation) strips the citizen of his status in the national and international community. His very existence is at the sufferance of the country in which he happens to find himself. While any one country may accord him some rights, and presumably as long as he remained in this country he would enjoy the limited rights of an alien, no country need do so because he is stateless. Furthermore, his enjoyment of even the limited rights of an alien might be subject to termination at any time by reason of deportation. In short, the expatriate *has lost the right to have rights.* This punishment is offensive to cardinal principles for which the Constitution stands..." (Emphasis added).

In brief, while the right of expatriation may be a human right and a basic freedom to an emigre nation such as the United States, it has become, in the political turmoil of the 20th century, ironically, a degrading deprivation of such rights as represented in the instant case.

In Afroyim v. Rusk, 387 U.S. 253, 268 (1968) this Court declared that "(i)n some instances loss of citizenship can mean that a man is left without the protection of citizenship in any country of the world—as a man without a country." But the very law permitting expatriation—8 U.S.C. 1841(a)(5)—in effect *condones* a state of anarchy for the individual who avails himself of this right. The stateless person, as the Court is aware, does not exist in a vacuum, legal or actual.[24] The very word "stateless", though, connotes the arrogant assumption that only the state enjoys legitimacy.[25] On the contrary, the right of expatriation is in reality the right to return to a "state of nature," that pristine state anterior to the organization of human societies into states or nations. It must be, therefore, the state where sovereignty begins.[26]

Your petitioner, while having allegedly expatriated himself from the exclusive national fiction, categorically denies that he "gave up" or could "give up" his native country. On the contrary, he renounced being exclusively national precisely in order to protect his country, part of the world community.

24/"...Everyman has a right to live somewhere on the earth." Thomas Jefferson, 1801 presidential address.
25/"The notion that states are the only appropriate 'subjects' of international law is belied by all the contemporary facts...about participation in the global processes of effective power and authoritative decision. This notion, unknown to the founding fathers and deriving from certain parochial misconceptions of the late nineteenth century, linger on to impede the protection of human rights merely because it sometimes serves the power purposes of the state elites... Historically, the greatest difficulty concerning participation in the world constitutive process has been this exaggeration of the role of the nation-state as the principal subject of international law. Because of the overwhelming emphasis of the 'sovereignty' of nation-states, there has been a great reluctance to recognize other participants in world social process as in fact active subjects of international law."
Human Rights and World Public Order, p. 178.
26/"Individuals themselves, each in his own personal and sovereign right, entered into a compact with each other to produce a government: and this is the only mode in which governments have a right to exist, and the only principle on which they have a right to exist." *The Rights of Man,* Thomas Paine.
"Everyman...possesses the right of self-government...individuals exercise it by their single will."
Thomas Jefferson, 1790
"The will of the people shall be the basis of the authority of government," Art. 21(3), U.D.H.R.

11

While this Court recognized in *Afroyim* that statelessness could result from expatriation, your petitioner suggests that the legislative body of the United States, bound by oath to uphold the constitutive process, cannot, in full knowledge and with willful intent, make laws which, in their exercise, condone lawlessness. If expatriation cannot be used as a punishment for crime as determined in *Trop*, the "punishment" being statelessness, then Congress cannot contrarily permit voluntary expatriation *without at the same time recognizing the inherent and unalienable rights of the expatriated individual,* or else the act becomes simply "the loss of the right to have rights," antithetical to the protection of the rights of "Life, Liberty and the Pursuit of Happiness."

The lower courts, in upholding respondent's irrational position, have imposed on the petitioner—and all other native-born Americans who may find themselves in the same position—what *Trop* considered a "penal punishment" but of a more insidious nature. Neither is he "in" or "outside" the United States but exists in a sort of legal vacuum continually under the threat of deportation or arbitrary detention.[27]

But how much more reprehensible—and ironic—do the U.S. exclusion statutes appear when the person excluded has "expatriated" himself for the generous reason of attempting to extend his sovereignty as an essential part of the constitutive process itself—on which both the several states and the federal union are founded—to the total world community for the promotion of world peace, a condition professed to be the No. 1 "foreign policy" of the present as well as past administrations?

One question before the Court therefore is, can the U.S. Congress, on the one hand, confirm the human right of "expatriation" as basic to freedom while at the same time deny the human exercising that right the corollary human right of freedom of travel and re-entry to his native country?[28]

To exclude him while admitting implicitly that he must live somewhere on the planet is to impose on other states the obligation of his protection, subjecting him to their tyranny as described by the former Chief Justice, or to maintain the continual threat of deportation or detention, though neither "solution" is justifiable.[29]

b. *The Ninth Amendment Implicitly Condones World Citizenship and World Government.*

The only Constitutional amendment referring specifically to "rights retained by the people" is of course the Ninth Amendment.

The expatriate is forced by the circumstances of his essentially unprotected legal situation immediately *to represent himself* in the exercise of these fundamental rights. In the words of McDougal, Lasswell and Chen:

27/"A person brought into the United States by the authorities and then released on bond is considered as having never entered the United States and as being in a position analogous to one who was stopped at the border and kept there." *Ling Yee Suey v. Spar,* CC A.N.Y. 1945 149 F 2d 881.

28/"Everyone has the right to leave any country, including his own, and to return to his country."
   Article 13(2), Universal Declaration of Human Rights.

29/"In my faith, the American concept of man's dignity does not comport with making even those we would punish completely 'stateless'—fair game for the despoiler at home and the oppressor abroad, if indeed there is any place which will tolerate them at all."
   Trop v. Dulles, Note 33, 643, E. Warren, CJ.

12

"...The substantive human rights prescriptions can never be made effective if the individual human being is not himself accorded competence to invoke them under appropriate conditions. The individual should be made a full subject of international law, with that access to all arenas, both international and national, which is necessary for him to protect himself." *Human Rights and World Public Order, p. 955.*

If it was not Congress's intent to 1) condemn the expatriate to a condition of perpetual "punishment", and 2) force a fellow state to undertake the obligation of residence under whatever conditions for the expatriate, then implicitly it expected said expatriate to exercise the "rights *retained* by the people."(Emphasis added).

Your petitioner, in his original statement at the time of his alleged renunciation, claimed to extend his sovereignty "as a member of the world community. . . ." to the "international vacuum of its government. . . ." a construction which emphasized the essential anarchic condition between nation-states. He claimed as well to be a "citizen of the world," both claims falling precisely within the concept and exercise of the Ninth Amendment as "rights retained by the people," as well as the concept of multiple citizenship recognized implicitly in the Tenth Amendment.

It goes without saying that these unalienable rights can neither be denied nor prohibited by this Court but contrarily, can only be affirmed by it.[30]

Petitioner claims therefore that statelessness is an inadmissible consequence of 8 U.S.C. 1841(a)(5) in that it condemns the "expatriate" to a condition of anarchy, and 2) that the new compact known as "world citizenship" with its corollary sanctioning institution, World Government, the aggregate of individual compacts, is the logical, inevitable and legitimate outcome of the application of the Ninth Amendment in the instant case.[31] (See *U.S. v. Cook,* D.C. Pa. 1970, 311 F. Supp. 618).

c.*United States District Court Memorandum Opinion Acknowledges Global Status of Petitioner.*

Judge Thomas Flannery stated in his Memorandum Opinion of December 19, 1979 in the instant case that:

"This opinion fails to prevent the petitioner or any other person from continuing to work for world peace through the vehicle of world citizenship and world government."

30/By elementary reasoning, if the people are sovereign, as inferred in both the Ninth and Tenth amendments, then they are sovereign not as "American" or national citizens, but as humans. It follows that the world's people, i.e., humankind, as such, represents the ultimate and largest sovereignty of which the "American" people are a part. As the national public order derived from the sovereignty of the people residing within the national community, so it must follow that a world public order can and must derive from the world's people residing in the world community. Then any social order which *excludes* the recognition of humankind itself as the ultimate sovereignty denies at the same time the essential sovereignty of the people from which itself derived. Thus a national constitution can neither deny, inhibit or in any way limit the sovereignty of humankind itself.

31/The Constitution of the state and the nation recognize unenumerated rights of natural endowment." *Colorado Anti-Discrimination Comm. v. Case,* 1902, 380, P 2d 34, 151 Colo. 230.

13

The definition of "vehicle," (*American College Dictionary*, 1950 Ed.) is "1, any receptacle, or means of transport, in which something is carried or conveyed or travels. . . . 3. a means of conveyance, transmission or communication, 4. a medium by which ideas or effects are communicated."

"Medium," according to the same source, is defined in part as "6, an agency, means or instrument."

The honorable Judge, in other words, did not consider either world citizenship and world government as mere concepts or ideals unrealizable in practical terms but on the contrary clearly acknowledged their pragmatic existence as valid "conveyers" or "instruments" or "mediums" for world peace.

Petitioner suggests that this acknowledgment represents an unprecedented construction to be viewed as within the purview of the Ninth Amendment, heretofore unutilized in any case in its broadest interpretation, i.e., the right to found government.

As the rights "retained by the people" can only be the natural rights referred to in the Declaration of Independence, the primordial one—the right to create government among consenting individuals where none existed before—merits full recognition by this Court.

Given the context of our desperate times in which nations continue their insane arming for a final test of force, yet the people of the world seek their legitimacy for their wholesale and individual protection against war itself and its dreadful consequences, this Court, oath-bound to adjudicate all constitutional issues, cannot refuse to consider this novel yet vital application of the Ninth Amendment which at once wisely defines the limitations of government and affirms appropriately the unalienable sovereignty of the people.

14

CONCLUSION

1. The lower courts' decision should be reversed because in the instant case, where petitioner is characterized as both an "excludable alien," and a "stateless person," the relevant statutes are clearly contradictory and, ipso facto, inoperable.

2. The construction of the statute enabling expatriation contains a fundamental error rendering the law unusable; said statute's constitutionality is questionable.

3. The Ninth Amendment, in recognition of rights "retained by the people," implicitly sanctions the natural rights of the individual to enter into a willful civic compact with others in accordance with their ongoing political and social needs and desires. The Court must subsequently recognize this new compact which, in the petitioner's case, is a world citizenship already subscribed to by hundreds of thousands of individuals throughout the human and world community.

Accordingly, for all the foregoing reasons, petitioner urges the Court to grant a writ of certiorari.

Respectfully submitted,

Garry Davis
3606 Ordway Street, N.W.
Washington, D.C. 20016
(202) 364-0871

15

APPENDIX

FULL STATEMENT OF PETITIONER, May 25, 1948

"In the absence of an international government, our world, political-ly, is a raw, naked anarchy. Two global wars have shown that as long as two or more powerful sovereign nation-states regard their own national law as supreme and sufficient to handle affairs between nations, there can be no order on a planetary level. This international anarchy is moving us swiftly toward a final war.

I no longer find it compatible with my inner convictions to contribute to this anarchy—and thus be a party to the inevitable suicide of our civilization—by remaining solely loyal to one of these sovereign nation-states. I must extend the little sovereignty I possess, as a member of the world community, to the whole community, and to the international vacuum of its government—a vacuum into which the rest of the world must be drawn if it would survive, for therein lies the only alternative to this final war.

I should like to consider myself a citizen of the world.

All history has shown—and especially American history—that peace is not merely the absence of war, but the presence of a superstructure of law and order, in short, government, over non-integrated political units of equal sovereignty. The world today is split by seventy to eighty of these sovereign units. Therefore, without the immediate creation of this superstructure of law and order, each unit must continue the idiotic, suicidal, unchristian and undemocratic anarthy of Nationalism, and the resulting atomic-biological war will then level all political, economic, religious, and personal differences by death.

The real question today seems to be: World Citizenship or World War?

One leads to peace. The other leads to oblivion.

And the choice is ours."

1a

NOT TO BE PUBLISHED—SEE LOCAL RULE 8 (r)
UNITED STATES COURT OF APPEAL
FOR THE DISTRICT OF COLUMBIA CIRCUIT

No. 80-1071   September Term, 1980

Garry Davis, Appellant   Civil Action No. 79-1874

v.   Filed March 31, 1981
                                               George A. Fisher
District Director, Immigration   Clerk
& Naturalization Service

Appeal from the United States District Court for the District of Columbia

Before: BAZELON, Senior Circuit Judge, ROBINSON and EDWARDS, Circuit Judges.

JUDGMENT

This cause came on to be heard on the record on appeal from the United States District Court for the District of Columbia, and was argued by counsel.

On consideration thereof, It is ordered and adjudged by this Court that the judgment—————of the District Court appealed from in this cause is hereby affirmed, in accordance with the attached memorandum.

Per Curiam
For the Court
/s/
George A. Fisher, Clerk

Bills of costs must be filed within 14 days after entry of judgment. The Court looks with disfavor upon motions to file Bills of Costs out of time.

1b

No. 80-1071—Davis v. District Director, INS

MEMORANDUM

For substantially the reasons set forth in the District Court's opinion, we agree that appellant effectively renounced his citizenship, *see* 8 U.S.C. 1841(a)(5) (1976). As the Immigration and Naturalization Service (INS) recognizes, this action should not foreclose appellant from reacquiring lawful permanent resident status. The INS Board of Immigrantion and Appeals expressly noted that appellant's immediate family members are United States citizens who could secure appellant a permanent resident visa, *see* 8 U.S.C. 1151(a), 1153(a)(1,5) (1976). Moreover, counsel for the INS advised this Court at argument that appellant's laudable military record could qualify him for naturalization, *see* 8 U.S.C. 1440 (1976).

UNITED STATES DISTRICT COURT
FOR THE DISTRICT OF COLUMBIA

GARRY DAVIS,

      Plaintiff,

v.

DISTRICT DIRECTOR Civil Action No. 79-1874
IMMIGRATION & NATURAL-
IZATION SERVICE

      Defendant.

MEMORANDUM OPINION & ORDER

This case presents the issue whether a native—born American may renounce primary allegiance to the United States and still retain rights to enter and remain in this country without a proper visa. Petitioner Garry Davis brings this suit in the form of a writ of habeas corpus. The petitioner seeks the writ to relieve him of the restraint and custody imposed by the Immigration and Naturalization Service ("INS"). The Board of Immigration Appeals on May 24, 1978 voted to exclude and deport the petitioner.

The petitioner is a native of the United States and served as a bomber pilot during World War II. On May 25, 1948, he voluntarily signed an oath of renunciation of United States nationality at the American Embassy in Paris, France.

The petitioner executed the oath in conformity with then Section 401(f) of the Nationality Act. Now codified at 8 U.S.C. par. 1481(a)(5), this section allows a native born American to voluntarily renounce United States citizenship. The statute reads the same today as in 1948:

(a). . . a person who is a national of the United States whether by birth or naturalization, shall lose his nationality by—

> (5) making a formal renunciation of nationality before a diplomatic or consular officer of the United States in a foreign state, in such form as may be prescribed by the Secretary of State. . .

The petitioner signed the oath of renunciation before the United States Consul. The oath of renunciation included the statement:

I desire to make a formal renunciation of my American nationality, as provided by Section 401(f) of the Nationality Act of 1940, and pursuant thereto I hereby absolutely and entirely renounce my nationality in the United States, and all rights and privileges thereunder pertaining and abjure all allegiance and fidelity to the United States of America.

1c

The petitioner, on May 25, 1948, also filed a statement of his beliefs with the United States Consul in Paris. The relevant portion of this statement, which forms the basis of one of petitioner's legal arguments, reads as follows:

> I no longer find it compatible with my inner convictions. . . by remaining solely loyal to one of these sovereign nation states. I must extend the little sovereignty I possess, as a member of the world community, to the whole community, and to the international vacuum of its government. . . I should like to consider myself a citizen of the world.

The United States Consul issued the petitioner a Certificate of Loss of Nationality of the United States on May 25, 1948. Petitioner henceforth devoted his time and energy toward the establishment of world government and the furtherance of world citizenship. He frequently travels abroad to promote these principles and goals. He has at various times entered the United States on a permanent resident alien or on a visitor's visa.

On May 13, 1977, the petitioner attempted to enter the United States on a passport issued by the "World Service Authority", an organization formed to promote world citizenship. The Immigration and Naturalization Service conducted an exclusion hearing four days later, on May 17, 1977. The petitioner stated at the hearing that "I am the president and the chairman of the Board of an organization called the World Service Authority." The administrative law judge found the petitioner deportable. The Board of Immigration Appeals affirmed this decision on May 24, 1978. The Board, relying on 8 U.S.C. par. 1182(a)(20), found the petitioner excludable because he lacked a valid document of entry. The petitioner filed the instant writ of habeas corpus on July 19, 1979.

The petitioner contends that he never expatriated himself. He alleges that the statement of beliefs he filed with the United States Embassy creates sufficient ambiguity to preclude renunciation of citizenship. The petitioner secondly argues that renunciation of citizenship requires the acquisition of another nationality. Finally, the petitioner alleges that Article 13 (2) of the Universal Declaration of Human Rights, providing that "everyone has the right. . .to return to his country," requires the INS to allow the petitioner to enter and remain in the United States without any immigration papers.

The Immigration and Naturalization Service argues that the petitioner is neither a citizen nor a national of the United States. He therefore qualifies only as an alien who must be excluded under 8 U.S.C. par.1182(a)(20). This statute requires exclusion if a person does not possess a "valid unexpired immigration visa." The Court agrees with the INS and will order the dismissal of the habeas petition.

I. PETITIONER LACKS THE STATUS OF A UNITED STATES CITIZEN

8 U.S.C. par.1481(a) codifies a long standing though little recognized principle of the United States: the right of expatriation. This principle establishes the libertarian concept that a citizen may voluntarily surrender his citizenship along with the panoply of rights and obligations that attach thereto. Federal statutory

2c

with the panoply of rights and obligations that attach thereto. Federal statutory law sets forth numerous avenues by which a United States citizen may voluntarily expatriate himself.[1] Federal Courts require only voluntariness and sometimes intent to uphold the validity of the expatriating act.

A. Petitioner's Intent was Unambiguous.

The petitioner alleges that his statement of beliefs, submitted on the same day he signed his oath of renunciation, creates ambiguity whether expatriation occurred. If factually correct, then the intent of the petitioner is open to question.

Whether subjective intent is a prerequisite to expatriation is an unresolved issue. Until the decision of *Afroyim v. Rusk,* 387 U.S. 253 (1976), the Supreme Court consistently held that objective proof of the voluntary act was enough to surrender citizenship.[2] The voluntariness concept espoused in *Afroyim* may be read, however, to encompass an inquiry into subjective intent.[3] Such an inquiry could be determinative of the validity of the expatriating act. For example, it is conceivable that a person may not intend to relinquish United States citizenship yet objectively perform an expatriating act enumerated in 8 U.S.C. par. 1481(a).

A voluntary oath of renunciation is a clear statement of desire to relinquish United States citizenship; therefore, the question of intent would normally not arise under 8 U.S.C. par. 1481(a)(5). *See* 3 C. Gordon & H. Rosenfield, *Immigration Law Procedure* par. 201.10b at 20-62, 73 (1979 ed.) (subjective intent, though perhaps relevant to some methods of expatriation, "irrelevant" to formal renunciation of American citizenship). In the instant case, however, the petitioner has raised the issue of intent by suggesting his statement of beliefs creates ambiguity over whether expatriation occurred. The Court would be reluctant to affirm the expatriation of a person who did not intend to relinquish citizenship. We therefore address the question of intent.

Contrary to the petitioner's allegation, the Court recognizes no ambiguity in the May 25, 1948 statement of beliefs the petitioner filed with the United States Consul. That statement leaves little doubt that the petitioner sought to relinquish his rights as a United States citizen. According to the petitioner's statement, he could no longer remain "solely loyal" to the United States; instead, "I must extend the little sovereignty I possess, as a member of the world community, to the whole community. . . ."

1/Each subdivision under 8 U.S.C. par. 1481(a) represents a separate and independent process that leads to expatriation. These subdivisions are independently self-executing; a citizen satisfying the provisions of one subsection may be expatriated pursuant to that provision.

2/*See, e.g., Nishiwaka v. Dulles,* 356 U.S. 129, 136 (1958) ("Unless voluntariness is put in issue, the Government makes its case simply by proving the objective expatriating act."); *Perez v. Brownell,* 356 U.S. 44, 61 (1958) ("Congress can attach loss of citizenship only as a consequence of conduct engaged in voluntarily"); *Savorgnan v. United States,* 338 U.S. 491, 502 (1950) (voluntariness, despite contrary intent, sufficient to uphold expatriation).

3/*See United States v. Matheson,* 532 F. 2d 809, 814 (2d Cir.) (interpret *Afroyim* to require subjective intent), *cert. denied,* 429 U.S. 823 (1976); 42 Op. Att'y Gen. 397 (1969) (*Afroyim* leaves open to individual petitioner whether to raise issue of intent).

3c

The statement of beliefs was devoid of any language recognizing a continued primary allegiance to the United States. Rather, the petitioner renounced his claim of sovereignty to any specific nation. His primary loyalty, according to his own language, belongs to "the world community." The Court finds that language renouncing primary loyalty to the United States and affirming primary allegiance to a world community complements, rather than conflicts with, a formal oath of renunciation of citizenship. The statement of beliefs therefore creates no ambiguity; it supplements the petitioner's clear intent to renounce United States citizenship.

B. Petitioner's Renunciation Was Voluntary

Voluntariness is uniformly recognized as a requirement toward upholding the validity of an expatriating act. The Supreme Court accordingly has reversed the expatriation of an American involuntarily conscripted into the Japanese Army, *Nishiwaka v. Dulles,* 356 U.S. 129, 138 (1958), reversed expatriation based solely on a conviction for military desertion absent a voluntary desire to renounce citizenship, *Trop v. Dulles,* 356 U.S. 86, 92-93 (1958), and reversed the expatriation of a person who voted in a foreign election but who did not voluntarily relinquish citizenship. *Afroyim v. Rusk,* 387 U.S. 253, 268 (1967). The Court recognized in *Afroyim* "that the only way the citizenship it (Congress) conferred could be lost was by the voluntary renunciation or abandonment by the citizen himself." *Id.* at 266.

Voluntariness was never at issue in the instant case. The petitioner independently and without duress renounced his citizenship by signing an oath of renunciation on May 25, 1948. The Court therefore finds that the petitioner's voluntary and unambiguous renunciation meets the strictures of 8 U.S.C. par. 1481(a)(5).

This finding necessitates a ruling that the petitioner expatriated himself. In many circumstances, a finding of voluntariness alone would be sufficient to uphold the act of expatriation.[4] In the instant case, as explained above, it was also incumbent upon the Court to examine intent. Having scrutinized these elements of expatriation, and having found that the petition's intent was unambiguous and the petitioner's renunciation was voluntary, the Court rules the petitioner no longer qualifies as a United States citizen.

C. Renunciation of Citizenship Does Not Require Acquisition of Another Nationality.

---

[4]/These circumstances occur when intent is not at issue. The question of intent will seldom be raised in adjudicating several types of expatriation. *See* 3 C. Gordon & H. Rosenfield, *Immigration Law & Procedure* 20.8b at 20-61-62 (1979 ed.) (*subjective intent normally irrelevant to expatriation based on acquisition of another nationality and voluntary renunciation of citizenship). In these cases, the court need only examine voluntariness. However, where, as here, the question of intent is raised by the petitioner, we believe it is appropriate to examine intent.*

4c

The oath of Renunciation recited by the petitioner, as applied to the applicable federal law, revoked the petitioner's citizenship. 8 U.S.C. 1481(a)(5) does not require allegiance to another nation; it only requires renunciation of United States nationality.

The framework of 8 U.S.C. 1481(a) reinforces the plain meaning of the statute. 8 U.S.C. 1481(a)(1) provides that an American national can lose his nationality by declaring allegiance to a foreign state, whereas 8 U.S.C. 1481(a)(5) provides a separate category for those who renounce United States nationality. By creating two separate categories—one for the acquisition of a foreign nationality and one for the renunciation of United States nationality—Congress could only have intended that each statutory section represents a separate method of expatriation.

The imposition of statelessness upon the petitioner cannot deter this Court from the requirements of the federal nationality law.[5] The Supreme Court recognized that expatriation may result in statelessness in *Afroyim v. Rusk, supra.* In *Afroyim* the Court declared that ''(i)n some instances loss of citizenship can mean that a man is left without the protection of citizenship in any country in the world—as a man without a country.'' 387 U.S. at 268.

Expatriation previously resulted in statelessness in *Jolley v. Immigration and Naturalization Service,* 441 F.2d 1245 (5th Cir.), *cert. denied,* 404 U.S. 946 (1971). In *Jolley,* the petitioner executed a formal renunciation of citizenship before a United States Consul in Canada. *Id.* at 1249. The petitioner subsequently returned to the United States without a visa. In affirming in INS's deportation order, the Fifth Circuit recognized that Jolley's oath of renunciation alone was enough to deprive him of citizenship:

> Recognizing that a citizen has a right to renounce his citizenship, Congress has provided in 8 U.S.C. 1481(a)(6) (now (5)) formal procedures for doing so. Jolley's renunciation satisfied these procedures.

Id. at 1249 n. 6; *see also id.* at 1259 (Rives, J. dissenting) (dissents becomes unclear if petitioner intended to become stateless person). *Jolley* thus demonstrates that expatriation, effectuated pursuant to 8 U.S.C. 1481(a)(5), requires only the renunciation of United States citizenship, and not the acquisition of a foreign nationality.

Finally, the Court must remain cognizant that statelessness was the intended consequence of the petitioner's May 24, 1948 actions at the United States Embassy.[6] The petitioner's statement of beliefs explicated that rather than remaining solely loyal to one sovereign state, ''I would like to consider myself a

---

5/''(T)he citizen's voluntary abandonment of his citizenship apparently will be effectuated if accomplished in compliance with law, even though statelessness may result.'' Gordon, The Citizen and the State, 53 Geo. L.J. 315, 360-61 (1965).

6/This finding answers the objection raised in the *Jolley* dissent. Judge Rives dissented there because, *inter alia,* he was unsure whether the petitioner intended statelessness. Herein, statelessness was the calculated result of the petitioner's actions.

5c

citizen of the world." In an interview with INS officials on May 13, 1977, the petitioner affirmed that "I have no nationality. I renounced my nationality 1948 in Paris, France...I am a World Citizen." The petitioner affirmatively sought his stateless existence. Whatever harshness may attach to statelessness is therefore inapplicable to the instant case.[7]

II. PETITIONER IS AN ALIEN AND THUS REQUIRES PROPER IMMIGRATION PAPERS TO ENTER AND REMAIN IN THE UNITED STATES.

Any person not a United States citizen or national is classified as an alien. 8 U.S.C. 1101(a)(3); *see* C. Gordon & H. Rosenfield, 1 *Immigration Law and Procedure* 2.3d at 2-22 (1979) ed.). The petitioner's voluntary expatriation deprived him of citizenship. He also lacks the status of a United States national.

The section of the expatriation statute that allowed the petitioner to voluntarily relinquish citizenship, 8 U.S.C. 1481(a)(5), speaks in terms of "making a formal renunciation of *nationality* before a diplomatic or consular officer..." (emphasis added). Moreover, 8 U.S.C. 1101(a)(22) defines a national as either a citizen or a person who owes permanent allegiance to the United States. The petitioner's expatriation deprives him of citizenship; his oath of renunciation stated that "I...abjure all allegiance and fidelity to the United States of America." The petitioner is therefore an alien by virtue of lacking the status of a citizen or national.

An alien must possess a proper entry document upon entering the United States. 8 U.S.C. 1182(a)(20) provides:

> ...any immigrant who at the time of application for admission is not in possession of a valid unexpired immigrant visa, reentry permit, border crossing identification card, or other valid entry document required by this chapter (is excludable).

7/The petitioner's contention that Article 15 of the Universal Declaration of Human Rights requires the acquisition of another nationality to uphold expatriation is without merit. The Universal Declaration of Human Rights is a United Nations Document. 3 U.N. Doc. a/810 (1948). It is well established that the United Nations Charter does not supersede United States law. *See, e.g., Haiti v. Immigration and Naturalization Service,* 343 F.2d 466, 468 (2d Cir.), *cert. denied,* 382 U.S. 816 (1965); *Vlissidis v. Anadell,* 262 F2d 398, 400 (7th Cir. 1959).

The petitioner's argument based on Article 13(2) of the Universal Declaration of Human Rights fails for the same reason.

6c

The petitioner's World Service Authority Passport fails to qualify as one of the documents required by 8 U.S.C. 1182. The Board of Immigration Appeals thus properly found the petitioner excludable. We therefore affirm that ruling and order the dismissal of this habeas petition. Because the petitioner has close relations in the United States who may apply on his behalf for a visa, the petitioner may remain in this country by merely assenting to permanent resident alien status.

The Court in no way wishes to deprecate the honesty of belief or depth of conviction that the petitioner feels for the cause of world citizenship. This opinion fails to prevent the petitioner or any other person from continuing to work for world peace through the vehicle of world citizenship and world government. (emphasis added) Any person who desires to pursue this goal while residing in the United States, however, must obey this nation's immigration and naturalization laws. We therefore only hold that if a person intentionally and voluntarily renounces United States citizenship, then such person must obtain proper visa certification to enter and remain in the United States.

An appropriate Order accompanies this Memorandum Opinion.

(signed: Thomas A. Flannery)
UNITED STATES DISTRICT JUDGE

Dated: 12-19-79

8/The petitioner raised for the first time at oral argument the theory that the Privileges and Immunities Clause of the Constitution, Article IV, Section 2, allows the petitioner to enter and remain in the United States by virtue of being a citizen of Maine. This argument, though novel, fails to take account of Congressional power to establish nationality laws.

The Privileges and Immunities Clause of Article IV, Section 2, serves to prevent one state from discriminating against another state. Article I, Section 8 of the Constitution establishes that "Congress shall have power... To establish an uniform Rule of Naturalization." This Constitutional mandate empowers Congress to define "the process through which citizenship is acquired or lost," to determine "the criteria by which citizenship is judged," and to fix "the consequences citizenship or noncitizenship entail." L. Tribe, *American Constitutional Law* 277 (1978).

These two constitutional provisions are not in conflict: a state may not discriminate against a citizen of another state, by, for example, restricting travel or access, but Congress has the power to determine the standards by which a person lacking the status of United States citizen shall enter and remain in the United States. Because Congress has determined that an alien must possess a proper document of entry to enter and remain in this country, the petitioner must either obtain a proper visa or be subjected to deportation.

7c

UNITED STATES COURT OF APPEALS
For the District of Columbia Circuit

No. 80-1071   September Term, 1980

Garry Davis,   Civil Action No. 79-1874
      Appellant

v.

District Director,
Immigration and Naturalization
Service   ARGUED 3-11-81

BEFORE: Robinson, Chief Judge; Bazelon, Senior Circuit Judge and Edwards, Circuit Judge

O R D E R

On consideration of appellant's petition for an order extending time for filing for a rehearing *en banc,* time having expired, it is
    ORDERED by the Court that the aforesaid petition is denied.

Per Curiam

United States Court of Appeals   FOR THE COURT:
for the District of Columbia

                                        George A. Fisher
Filed Aug. 5, 1981   Clerk
                                    BY:
George A. Fisher   /s/ Robert A. Bonner
     Clerk   Chief Deputy Clerk

Chief judge Robinson would grant the petition for extension of time to file for a rehearing *en banc* to and including August 31, 1981 only.

1d

OFFICE OF THE CLERK
SUPREME COURT OF THE UNITED STATES
WASHINGTON, D.C. 20543

July 2, 1981

Mr. Garry Davis
3606 Ordway Street, N.W.
Washington, D.C. 20016

Re: Garry Davis v. Immigration Director,
Immigration and Naturalization Service
A-1089

Dear Mr. Davis:

Your application for an extension of time in which to file a petition for a writ of certiorari in the above-entitled case has been presented to the Chief Justice who, on July 1, 1981, signed an order extending your time to and including August 28, 1981.

A copy of the Chief Justice's order is enclosed.

Very truly yours,

By

/s/ Katherine Downs
Assistant Clerk

sd
Enc.
cc (letter only):

Honorable Lawrence G. Wallace
Acting Solicitor General
George A. Fisher, Esq., Clerk
U.S. Court of Appeals, D.C. Circuit
(Your No. 80-1071)

1e

lf

CONSULAT
DE LA
ÉPUBLIQUE ISLAMIQUE DE MAURITANIE
POUR LA SUISSE
GENÈVE

World Service
Authority

4002 <u>Basel</u>

(Suisse)

Genève, le 28 juil. 1975

Dear Sirs,

In reply to your recent documentation in respect of W.S.A.
passports I wish to specify that its recognition will be
granted in the framework of Mauritanian laws. If Mauritanian laws and prescriptions are respected those passports may come into profit of visas for entry in
Mauritania.

The allowance of a Mauritanian visa will however remain
under the competence of the respective Mauritanian Representation of the circumscription, in my case for
Switzerland.

Yours faithfully,

P. Büttler, Consul

2f

MISSION PERMANENTE DE HAUTE VOLTA
AUPRES DES NATIONS UNIES

666 SECOND AVENUE
NEW YORK, N. Y. 10017
756-1595

No. 180/MPHV/72

     Le Représentant Permanent de la République de Haute-Volta auprès des Nations Unies présente ses compliments au "World Service Authority" et porte à sa connaissance ce qui suit :

     " Le Ministère de l'Intérieur et de la Sécurité accepte l'entrée en Haute-Volta de détenteurs du passeport neutre émis par la "World Service Authority".
     Toutefois, il est nécessaire de porter à la connaissance de cet organisme, à l'intention des détenteurs de ce document de voyage, que les titulaires éventuels devront se conformer à la Convention des Nations Unies et de l'Organisation de l'Unité Africaine sur le régime des réfugiés."

     Le Représentant Permanent de la République de Haute-Volta auprès des Nations Unies saisit cette occasion pour renouveler à la "World Service Authority" les assurances de sa haute considération.

New York, le 24 Octobre 1972

185

3f

REF: NY/UN/6 - 641

PERMANENT MISSION OF THE
REPUBLIC OF ZAMBIA
TO THE UNITED NATIONS
150 EAST 58 STREET
NEW YORK, N. Y. 10022

April 19, 1973

The Coordinating Director
World Service Authority
4002
Switzerland

Dear Sir,

I have the honour to refer to your recent letter under cover
of which you forwarded a specimen copy of the second edition of
the WSA Passport for approval by competent authorities of my
Government.

I am pleased to inform you that my Government has
recognised and accepted the Passport as a genuine and valid travel
document of identity.

Yours faithfully

T.C. Kapoma

For:Charge d'Affaires a.i.

TCK:jg

4f

EMBAJADA DEL ECUADOR

WASHINGTON

August 5, 1954.

United World Service Authority
270 Park Avenue, Suite C-1315
New York 17, N. Y.

<u>Mr. Garry Davis, Director</u>

Gentlemen,

Further to your letter of July 15,
regarding passports to be used by refugees and stateless
persons, we are now in receipt of the views of my Government
on your ideas about the use of the proposed document for
international identification.

Ecuador has always given cooperation and
assistance to refugees and stateless persons, by giving
them special travel documents which have been accepted by
other countries. My Government believes that your idea
is interesting and, providing all requirements are
complied with and security maintained, Ecuador would accept
such documents for purposes of being used instead of a
passport.

Furthermore, my Government believes that
if your office decides to open an office in Ecuador for
legal and security reasons, you must include among the
Directors of said office a Representative of the Ecuadorean
Government from the Ministry of Foreign Affairs.

In summary, Ecuador accepts your world
passport as travel document for personal identification.

Yours very sincerely,

Dr. José R. Chiriboga V.
Ambassador of Ecuador.

187

13

Visas / Visas / Vis\tos buenos / Внзы / التأشيرات
Reisovormork / Vizoj]

...AL DE HONDURAS
... AL. CALIFORNIA, E. U. A ..

No. 354

Visas y válidas por Noventa dias,
a partir de la fecha de su ingreso al país.

Bueno para dirigirse a Honduras.

Clase de Visa TURISTA

Derechos en timbres cancelados $ —

9 de Mayo de 1979

VISA PARA MULTIPLE APLICACION
DE ENTRADA HASTA POR EL TERMINO
DE (12) MESES

CONSULATE GENERAL OF HONDURAS
SAN FRANCISCO, CALIFORNIA
CANCILLER
CARLOS R. CALLEJAS

12

Visas / Visas / Vistos buenos / Внзы / التأشيرات
Reisovormork / Vizoj]

CONSULADO GENERAL DE COSTA RICA
SAN FRANCISCO, CALIFORNIA
VISA DE TURISTA

Buena para ingresar a Costa Rica por
vía Aérea debiendo llenar el portador
los requisitos que las regulaciones exigen.

Visa No. 015 Derechos 5

de MAY 9 1979 de 196

Cónsul General de Costa Rica

Se entiende que la persona a la cual se le extiende
la presente visa es portadora del llaveto de salida
de Costa Rica.
Esta visa es válida para permanecer en Costa Rica
por 3 mesi min.

COSTA RICA
Juan Santamaría

2 -1 JUN 1979 2

ENTRADA
Migración

188

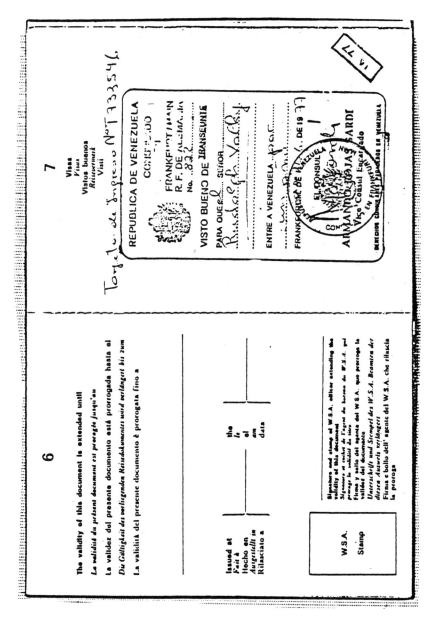

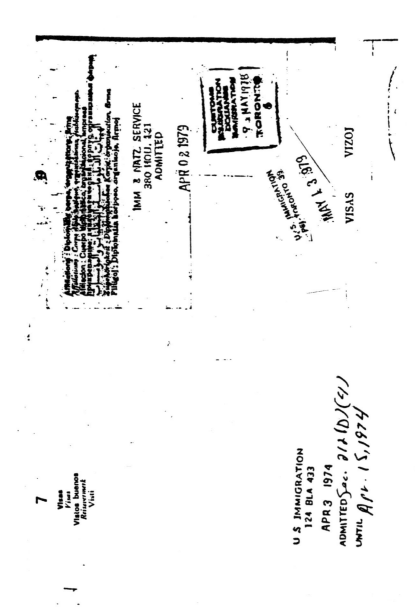

10g

190

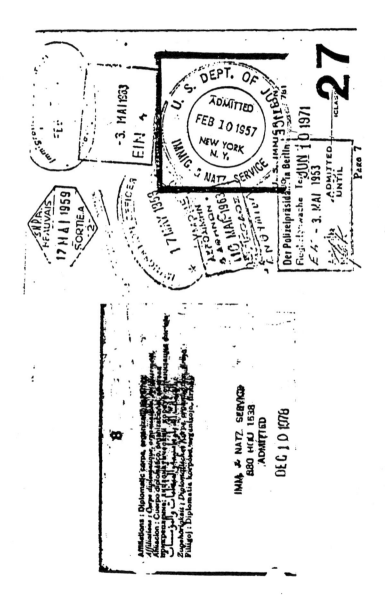

N° 047819

Name / Nom / Apellido / Name / Nomo: **PICHARDO ROJAS**

Fore names / Prénoms / Nombre / Имя (имена) / Vorname / Antaŭnomoj: *Freddy De Jesus*

Born at / Né á / Lugar de nacimiento / Место рождения / Geboren in / Naskiĝloko: *Santo Domingo, Dominican Republic*

Occupation / Profession / Profesión / Профессия / Beruf / Profesio: *Estudiante*

The / Le / El / Дата / Am / Je la: *16.05.56*

Home address / Domicile / Domicilio particular / Местожительство / Anschrift / Domicilio: *Calle G. N°35 Barrio Maria Aux-iliadora, Santo Domin-go, Dominican Rep.*

СССР ВИЗА М
у070680 № 362624
Шереметьево

п. Без гражданства /док-т ООН/
фамилия Пичардо Рохас Фредди
Имя, отчество из Хесус
Дата рождения 1955
с детьми до 16 лет
Цель поездки студент, на каникулы
Из учреждения МИН-ВО с/х, ТПИ
В визах Доминиканская Республика
Действительна для выезда из СССР с 25.05.19.80
и въезда в СССР до
через легитимные пункты СССР,
открытые для вассожирского движения

21 05 19 80
О.Р.ПЕИ

В Ъ Е З Д

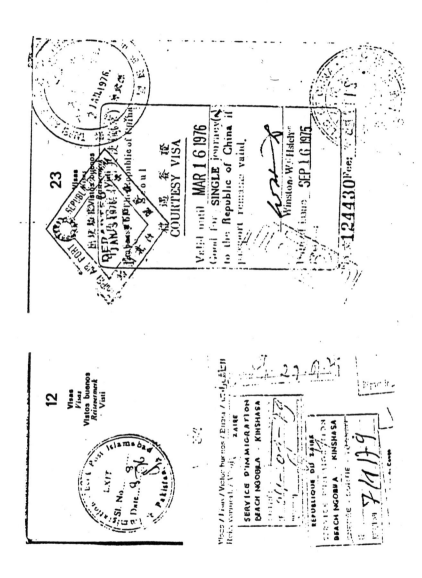

23

Visas
Visa
Vistos buenos
Reisevermerk
Visti

護 照 簽 證
COURTESY VISA

Valid until MAR 16 1976
Good for SINGLE journey
to the Republic of China if
passport remains valid.

Winston W. Hsieh
SEP 16 1975

124430 Fee:

12

Visas
Visa
Vistos buenos
Reisevermerk
Visti

EXIT
Sl. No. 9
Date 9

SERVICE D'IMMIGRATION
BEACH NGOBILA - KINSHASA
ZAIRE

REPUBLIQUE DU ZAIRE
BEACH NGOBILA - KINSHASA
ENTREE - SORTIE

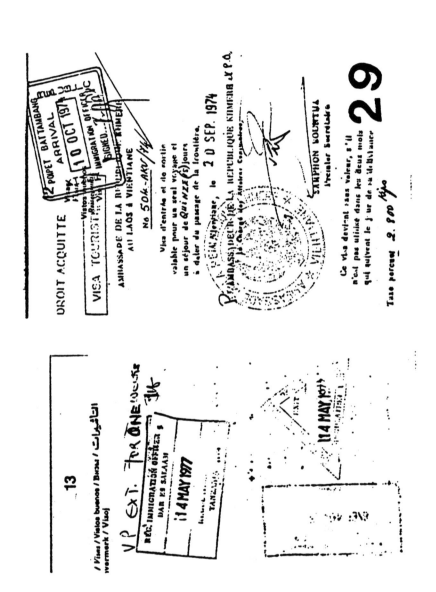

DROIT ACQUITTE

VISA TOURIST

AMBASSADE DE LA RÉPUBLIQUE KHMÈRE
AU LAOS à VIENTIANE

No 504-AKV/74

Visa d'entrée et de sortie
valable pour un seul voyage et
un séjour de QUINZE (15) jours
à dater du passage de la frontière.

Vientiane, le 20 SEP. 1974

AMBASSADE DE LA RÉPUBLIQUE KHMÈRE
Le Chargé des Affaires Consulaires

SAMPHON KOUNTUL
Premier Secrétaire

29

Ce visa devient sans valeur, s'il
n'est pas utilisé dans les deux mois
qui suivent le jour de sa délivrance

Taxe perçue 2.800 kip

2 POIPET BATTAMBANG
ARRIVAL
10 OCT 1974
IMMIGRATION OFFICER
SIGNED

13

/ Visa / Visos buenos / Basu /
vermerk / Viso/

VP EXT. FOR ONE MONTH

REG. IMMIGRATION OFFICER
DAR ES SALAAM
14 MAY 1977
TANZANIA

14 MAY 1977

12g

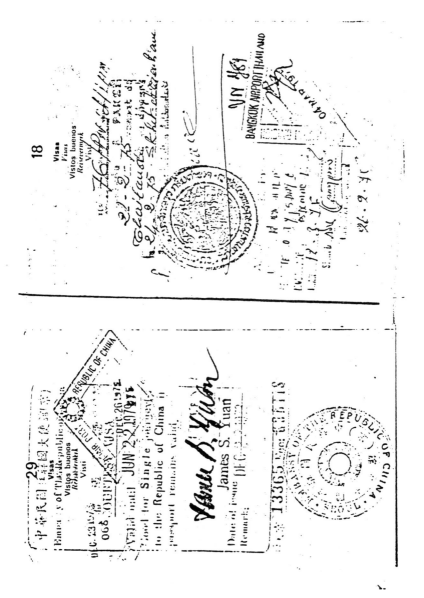

195

18g

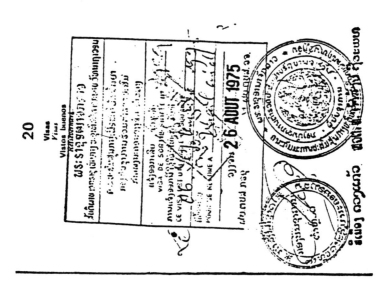

196

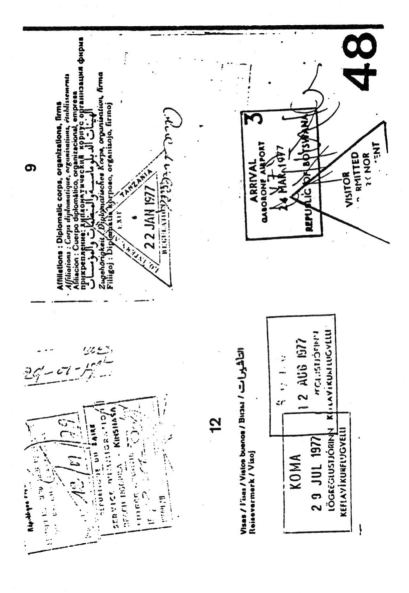

7g

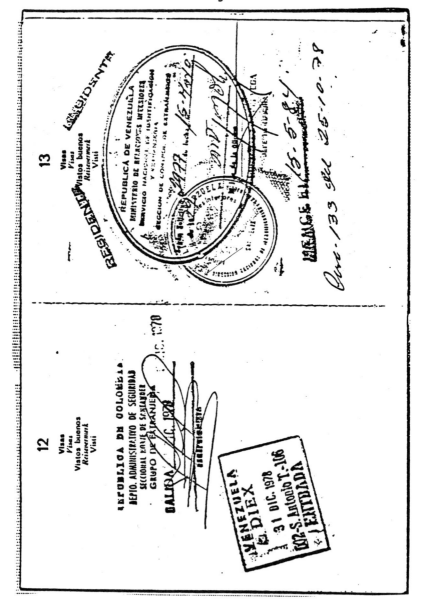

198

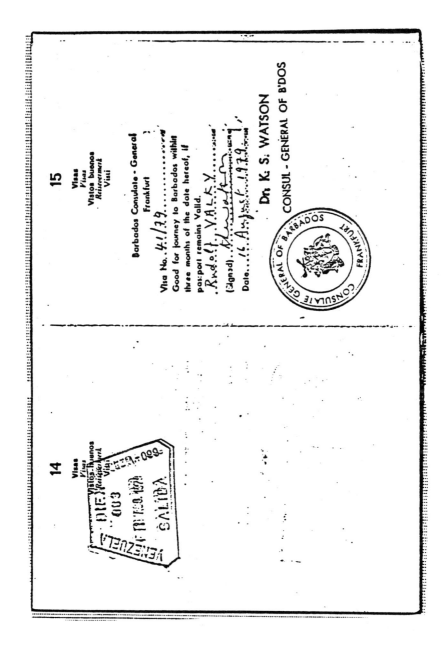

15

Visas
Visa
Vistos buenos
Reisevermerk
Visti

Barbados Consulate - General
Frankfurt

Visa No. 41/79 ....

Good for journey to Barbados within
three months of the date hereof, if
passport remains valid.

Rudolf VALKY ....

(Signed) ....

Date ... 16 August 1979 ......

Dr. K. S. WATSON
CONSUL - GENERAL OF B'DOS

14

Visas
Visa
Vistos-Buenos
Reisevermerk
Visti

VENEZUELA
SALIDA

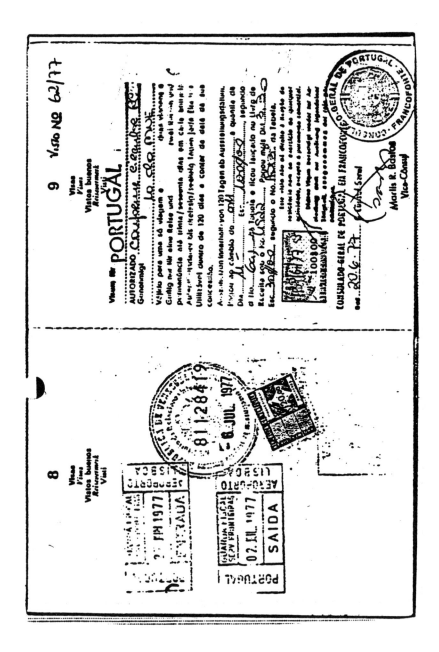

14g

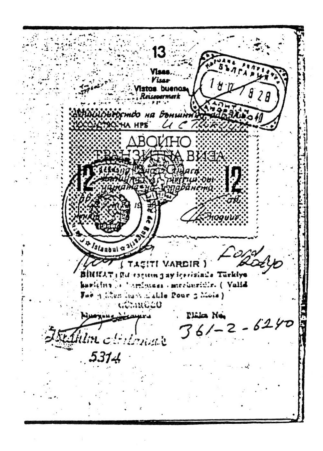

SUPREME COURT OF THE UNITED STATES
OFFICE OF THE CLERK
WASHINGTON. D. C. 20543

October 19, 1981

Mr. Garry Davis
3603 Ordway Street, N.W.
Washington, D.C. 20016

Re: Garry Davis
v. District Director, Immigration and
Naturalization Service
No. 81-427

Dear Mr. Davis:

The Court today entered the following order in the above entitled
case:

The petition for a writ of certiorari is denied.

Very truly yours,

Alexander L. Stevas

Alexander L/ Stevas, Clerk

SUPREME COURT INDEX—1981-82 TERM

TABLE OF CASES

and

CASE STATUS REPORT

Volume 50, Nos. 1-13

July 7, 1981 – October 6, 1981

Davis v. District Director, Immigration and Naturalization Service, 81-427

81-427   filed (8/28/81) 50:3157

ALIENS AND CITIZENSHIP

No. 81-427. Davis v. District Director Immigration and Naturalization Service.

Ruling below (CADC, 3/31/81, unpublished):

Federal district court decision that native born American who, in conformity with 8 USC 1481 (a)(5), unambiguously and voluntarily renounced his citizenship may not retain rights to enter and remain in U.S. without visa, is affirmed.

Aliens and Citizenship

81-427

Native born American's renunciation of citizenship — Subsequent return to U.S. as permanent home.

Ruling below (CADC, 3/31/81, unpublished):

Federal district court decision that native born American who, in conformity with 8 USC 1481 (a)(5), unambiguously and voluntarily renounced his citizenship may not retain rights to enter and remain in U.S. without visa, is affirmed.

Questions presented: (1) Is 8 USC 1182(a)(20) applicable to native born American who expatriated himself in accordance with 8 USC 1481 (a)(5), thus becoming stateless, who does not acquire another nationality and subsequently returns to U.S. claiming it as his permanent home? (2) Was 8 USC 1481(a)(5), resulting in statelessness, intent of Congress and, if so, is such expatriation constitutional? (3) Is enabling statute of 8 USC 1481(a)(20) validly constructed and, if not, can U.S. citizen legally expatriate himself according to its construction? (4) Can Ninth Amendment be construed as sanctioning individual to exercise his right to claim citizenship transcending that of U.S. in accordance with concept of multiple citizenship enshrined in Tenth Amendment?

III. Petition for Rehearing (Dec. 22, 1981)

No. 81-427

IN THE

SUPREME COURT of the UNITED STATES

OCTOBER TERM, 1981

GARRY DAVIS,

Petitioner

v.

DISTRICT DIRECTOR
IMMIGRATION AND NATURALIZATION
SERVICE

Respondent

On Petition for Writ of Certiorari to the
United States Court of Appeals for the
District of Columiba

PETITION FOR REHEARING

Garry Davis
Petitioner
Pro Se

Address of Petitioner:
3606 Ordway Street, N.W.
Washington, D.C. 20016
(202) 364-0871

TABLE OF CONTENTS

TABLE OF AUTHORITIES

OTHER

GROUNDS FOR PETITION FOR REHEARING:

This petition for rehearing is intended to clarify arguments advanced in original petition for certiorari. *Hickman v. Taylor*, 327 U.S. 808, 328 U.S. 876, 329 U.S. 495; *Brinkerhoff-Faris Trust Co. v. Hill*, 280 U.S. 604, 550, 281.[1]

The underlying issue herein under review is that of ultimate sovereignty which the nation claims but which claim, in terms of world war, is both anachronistic and suicidal versus the sovereignty of an individual world citizen exercising inalienable human rights, representative of and speaking for all humankind.[2]

Petitioner respectfully submits that the instant case offers unique features permitting the Court to affirm its historic mandate, "Equal Justice Under Law", as well as its given constitutional prerogative as envisioned by the framers when confronted with an executive impotent to make peace by sanctioning once again the inalienable rights of the people, justly and democratically exercised by your petitioner.[3]

1/ "Any constitutional society commits itself to certain values, and the United States by the original Constitution and the Bill of Rights is consciously dedicated to individual liberty, integrity, and equality, an open society, and the rule of law. Of these values the Supreme Court is the ultimate guardian and trustee."
   Modern Constitutional Law, Chester J. Antieau, Vol. 1 V (1969) The Lawyers Co-Operative Publishing Co.

2/ "...a reverence for our great Creator, principles of humanity, and the dictates of conscience, must convince all those who reflect upon the subject that government was instituted to promote the welfare of mankind and ought to be adminstered for the attainment of that end."
   Thomas Jefferson, *Declaration of the Causes and Necessity of Taking Up Arms*, Continental Congress, 1775

   "...the very esssence of the charter (Charter of the Tribunal, Nuremberg) is that individuals have international duties which transcend the national obligations of obedience imposed by the individual state. He who violates the laws of war can not obtain immunity while acting in pursuance of the authority of the state if the state in authorizing action moves outside its competence under international law."
   The Charter and Judgment of the Nuremberg Tribunal, 1949 (See Office of United States Chief of Counsel of Prosecution of Axis Criminality, Nazi Conspiracy and Aggression, Opinion and Judgment, Government Printing Office, 1947)

   "Any method of maintaining international peace today must eventually fail if it is not grounded on Justice under Law and the protection of the Individual under due process of law."
   World Habeus Corpus, Luis Kutner, 1968, p. 73

3/ "Let it be stated again that the generation that gave us the Articles of Confederation and the Constitution believed solidly in the doctrine of natural rights. They understood that the purpose of government was to protect men in their basic, natural rights, and they were sure that they could hold their own state governments to this end."
   Modern Constitutional Law, Chester J. Antieau, p. 676

   "International Law is more than a scholarly collection of abstract and immutable principles. It is an outgrowth of treaties and agreements between nations of accepted customs. Yet every custom has its origin in some single act, and every agreement has to be initiated by the action of some state. Unless we are prepared to abandon every principle of growth for international law, we cannot deny that our own day has the right to initiate customs and to conclude agreements that will themselves become sources of a newer and strengthened international law..."
   Mr. Justic Robert H. Jackson, Chief Prosecutor at the Nuremberg war crime trials, 1945; J.S.C.

1

The concept of expatriation when linked to statelessness as argued in the previous petition (p. 11) exposes a basic dichotomy in national law revealed by petitioner's alleged renunciation of nationality. That dichotomy posits the inalienable sovereignty of the individual, the primary source of national — as well as local and state — law itself against the national sovereignty as an exclusive political fiction.[4]

The instant case dramatically focuses juridical attention on this dichotomy in a novel interpretation of the Ninth Amendment and is germane to the issue of war itself which petitioner seeks to clarify below.

It would be absurd to argue that the exclusive character of the nation was absolute and eternal. Such an argument would be a denial of the evolution of law itself from which resulted the United States Constitution — as all national constitutions — in the first place.[5]

The absence of a world government to which the petitioner could refer his prime civic commitment as a countervailing force to world war obliged him to divest himself of the national exlusive character which per se violated the principle of a planetary citizenship alone capable of coping with the global problems facing him.[6]

4/ "Since under the express terms of the Constitution, there is no one political sovereign — other than the ill-formed notion of 'popular sovereignty', which are taken seriously only as slogans but not as descriptions of reality — the theoretical problem of sovereignty in the United States has not yet been fully resolved."
    Presidential Power In A Nutshell, Arthur S. Miller, West Publishing Co., 1977

5/ "A Constitution designed to endure for the ages to come must perforce bend with the winds of social change."
    Ibid, p. 67
"Each generation writes its own constitution, just as each generation writes its own history."
    Ibid, p. 67
"Constitutional law in essence is politics writ large; and government is always relative to circumstances."
    Ibid, p. 67
The only intention of the Founding Fathers worth serious attention today is that they left the tasks of goverance to the good sense and wisdom of succeeding generations of Americans."
    Ibid, p. 66

"Government can be safely acknowledged a temporal blessing because, in terms of the power it wields, there is nothing inherent in it. Government is not an end in itself but a means to an end. Its authority is the free and revocable grant of the men who have promised conditionally to submit to it. Its organs, however ancient and august, are instruments that free men have built and free men can alter or even abolish."
    Earl Warren, C.J., S.C.

6/ The United Nations Secretary-General, in his Supplementary Report to the General Assembly of 24 October 1946 stated that "In the interests of peace, and in order to protect mankind against future wars, it will be of decisive significance to have the principles which were implied in the Nuremberg trials (II. Jurisdiction and General Principles, Article 6(a)(b) and (c) which defines 'crimes coming within the jurisdiction of the Tribunal for which there shall be individual responsibility'), and according to which the German war criminals were sentenced, made a permanent part of the body of international laws as quickly as possible. From now on the instigators of new wars must know that there exists both law and punishment for their crimes. Here we have a high inspiration to go forward and begin the task of working toward a revitalized system of international law."
    On 15 November 1946, the U.S. delegation introduced a proposal to the U.N. "...to initiate studies and make recommendations for the purpose of encouraging the progressive development of international law and its codification..." and reaffirmed"...the principle of international law recognized by the Charter of the Nuremberg Tribunal and the judgment of the tribunal."
    U.N. General Assembly Resolution 488 48(v) 1950, "Nuremberg Trials", entered the principles to international law.
    The right to assume individual civic responsibility in a given community is the essence of course of the democratic principle and the true meaning of sovereignty. This has been subsequently confirmed by Arts. 1,2,3,6,7,15(2),18,19 and 29 of the *Universal Declaration of Human Rights*

2

Petitioner suggests that the implicit and historic advantage of the United States Constitution is contained in its provision for acts of individual sovereignty via the 9th and 10th amendments in situation arising from circumstances distinct from those which resulted in the Constitution originally.[7]

Not to recognize this constitutional advantage would be to deny the essential universality of the Constitution itself as well as the innate and inalienable sovereignty of the people. ("The theory of our political system is that the ultimate sovereignty is in the people from whom springs all legitimate authority." McLean, J. in *Spooner v. McConnell*, 1. McLean, 347.)

With respect to the framer's commitment to the amendment of "enumerated rights," (9th), petitioner respectfully suggests that the Court address the question: As citizenship itself is defined within the parameters of a civic code, are not the rights "retained by the people" natural or human rights existing outside the purview of that code, in this case the U.S. Constitution itself? (*Vanhorne v. Dorrance*, 1795, CC Pa., 2 Dall 304, 310 1 L Ed 391, 394, F Cas No. 16857: "The Supreme Court in 1793 said there were 'natural, inherent and inalienable rights of man..'")

Pertinent to this question, would not this reasoning be supported by the framers themselves who, bound civically by their separate state constitutions, nevertheless exercised sovereign rights outside those then exclusive legal frameworks in order to formulate, then codify in a document a new sovereignty which was innate and inalienable in the people themselves, distinct from that of the several states[8], that of the United States of America?

7/ "The Government of the United States can claim no powers which are not granted it by the Constitution; and the powers actually granted must be such as are expressly given or given by necessary implication."
Per Marshall, C.J., *Martin v. Hunter's Lesse*, 1 Wheat. 326, (from Virginia Ct.) (1816)

"Mr. Justice Douglas' use of the ninth amendment carries a greater potential. Under his theory, the ninth amendment might be utilized to expand the concept of privacy or, perhaps, to guarantee other basic rights." (Emerson)
Nine Justices In Search of a Doctrine, 64 Mich. L. Rev. 219, 227 (1965) (See *Palmer v. Thompson*, 403 U.S. 217, 233-39 (1971) (Douglas, J. dissenting). (See B. Patterson, *The Forgotten Ninth Amendment*, (1955); Dunbar, *James Madison and the Ninth Amendment*, 42 Va. L. Rev. 627 (1956); Kelley, *The Uncertain Renaissance of the Ninth Amendment*, 33 U. Chi. L. Rev. 814 (1966); Kelsey, *The Ninth Amendment of The Federal Constitution*, 11 Ind. L.J. 309 (1936); Kutner, *The Neglected Ninth Amendment: The "Other Rights" Retained by the People*, 51 Marq. L. Rev. 121 (1967); Paust, *Human Rights and the Ninth Amendment: A New Form of Guarantee*, 60 Cornell L. Rev. 231 (1975); Ringold, *The History of the Enactment of the Ninth Amendment and Its Recent Development*, 8 Tulsa L.J. 1 (1972); Rogge, *Unenumerated Rights*, 47 Calif. L. Rev. 787 (1959)

8/ "At the time the Articles of Confederation were adopted the overwhelming majority of Americans accepted the doctrine of natural rights. All men possessed certain basic, fundamental rights which government could not deny. Government was organized to protect and safeguard these rights. It was the unspoken assumption in the Continental Congress that no state could ever justifiably deny to its own citizens their natural rights. It was unthinable that the possessors of political power needed the protection of the Articles of Confederation against their *temporary trustees of governance*..." (Emphasis added.)
Modern Constitutional Law, Chester J. Antieau, Vol. 1, v. (1969) p. 673

3

Pursuing this strictly constructionist line of argument, petitioner further inquires of the Court by what right this new and inclusive government was founded if civic rights were circumscribed only by the existing state codes? Is not the answer self-evident — affirmed by the 9th and 10th amendments — that the people retained rights *not* codified and indeed uncodifiable by such codes, the major one being the right to choose a new *political* identity for the protection of those very rights?

This Court of course cannot determine further that the founding fathers, in maintaining the sovereignty of the people via both the 9th and 10th amendments, were condoning anarchy in recognizing rights beyond the Constitution's limits. For it would then be denying due process per se. Yet when the violations of human rights are perpetrated by the national government itself — as in the instant case and in myriad others throughout the world — as a person with legal standing before this High Court, petitioner has the right and duty to inquire by what legal process can such inalienable rights be protected? The question is not only germane to his personal situation, as described in the petition for certiorari, but to a host of global issues of which war — legitimized by the very nation-state system — is the central one.[9]

The paradox seems insoluble unless we admit to higher laws therefore uncodified by the nation, to which the people could refer. In their judicial recognition of the limitations of the Constitution and retained powers of the people, the courts have referred obliquely to these laws:

> "The powers the people have given to the general government are named in the Constitution, and all not there named, either expressly or by implication are reserved to the people *and can be exercised only by them, or upon further* grant from them." (Emphasis added). *U.S. v. Williams*, N.Y. 1904, 2 S.C. 119, 194 U.S. 295, 48 L Ed. 979.

Such common laws, protecting fundamental human rights, existing outside and independent of national constitutional law, could only be worldly in character. They need not however be inconsistent with national or local law. The relationship of the several states to the federal union is not irrelevant here:

> "The general government and the states, although both exist within the same territorial limits, are separate and distinct sovereignties, acting separately and independently of each other, within their respective spheres." *Buffington v. Day*, Mass. 1871, 78 U.S. 124, 11Wall. 124, 20 L Ed. 122.

This Court cannot but determine that these natural/human rights require legal protection since it itself is the juridical inheritor of the very constitutive process

---

9/ "Material progress in total destructive explosive weapons has yielded the conclusion that the right to individual security is the pre-requisite of all other human rights and freedoms. Collective individual security can be protected only under the Rule of Law and in the mainstream of Due Process of Law."
World Habeus Corpus, Luis Kutner, 1962, p. 71

"As long as there are sovereign nations possessing great power, war is inevitable. There is no salvation for civilization, or even the human race, other than the creation of a world government."
Albert Einstein, Letter to World Federalists, Stockholm Congress, 1949

4

by which such protection was, until the advent of total war, afforded. But, in that petitioner's natural/human rights are not only not protected by the United States sovereignty but indeed menaced by it — in the sense that the U.S. government has no legislative or judicial control over the actions of any other sovereign state, its so-called foreign policy therefore being essentially reactive, i.e. defensive — petitioner's right to life, liberty and the pursuit of happiness, to name those inalienable rights enshrined in the Declaration of Indepedence, are unsecured.

This Court's grant of certiorari will not only confirm the mandate of the 9th and 10th amendments but will, at last, uphold the very constitutive process as the sine qua non of world peace.

In other words, a world citizenship unprohibited and undenied by the U.S. Constitution — as the state constitutions neither prohibited nor denied a national constitution — both recognizing and protecting inalienable human rights could be confirmed by this Court as not only the rightful political expression of popular sovereignty implied in both the 9th and 10th amendments, but the direct and substantive challenge to war-making itself at a moment when such judicial insight is desperately needed by a world of ready-to-explode nation-states. Today's very headlines starkly underline this imperative need.

Contrarily, a denial of certiorari may be interpreted as confirming the infamous and contemptible dictum *inter armes silent leges* which has dominated the Court's history from its inception.[10]

To illustrate this charge, petitioner cites Justice Marshall's observation in 1803 that

> "By the constitution of the United States the President is vested with certain important political powers in the exercise of which he is to use his own discretion...and whatever opinion may be entertained at the manner in which executive discretion may be used, still there exists, and can exist, no power to control that discretion."[11]

How may the citizen view this "monarchial" power in view of Justice Samuel Miller's opinion in *U.S. v. Lee*, 106 U.S. 196, 220, 1882, that

> "No man is so high that he is above the law. All...officers are creatures of the law and are bound to it "?

It is clear that the Constitution both defines the parameters of legitimacy while yet conferring on the President arbitrary powers in his capacity as Head of State — totally vitiating the concept and exercise of civic rights — placing him thereby "outside" those parameters.

10/ "The judicial attitude is more than abstention; it verges at times upon courts being an arm of the executive when violence, foreign or domestic, erupts."
   Presidential Power In A Nutshell, Arthur S. Miller, p. 163. (See also, *A Mason*, Harlan Fiske Stone., Pillar of the Law, 1958)

11/ "It requires no special prescience to forecast that should a thermonuclear war erupt the President and his subordinates will do whatever they think is necessary to maximize the national interest, without regard to the Constitution, the Congress or the Courts."
   Cf. E. Corwin, *Total War and the Constitution*, 1946; C. Rossiter, *Constitutional Dictatorship*, 1948

5

"In times of declared war," according to Arthur S.Miller, (*Presidential Power In A Nutshell*, p. 169), "particularly in the 20th century when wars have become planetary in extent, the President acts as a 'constitutional dictator'. There is a tacit understanding that nothing — literally nothing — will be permitted to block *winning the war*. What is necessary, as determined by the executive, is done. Legal niceties are given little attention. National survival is the ultimate issue." (Emphasis added.)

In short, "Judicial control of presidential action is next to nonexistent." (Ibid., p. 30)

Yet, war to be legitimate, must be winnable.

"The war powers of Congress and the President are only those to be derived from the Constitution...the primary application of a war power is that it shall be an effective power to wage war *successfully*." (Emphasis added.) *Lichter v. U.S.*, 334 U.S. 742, 782, 1948 per Burton, J.

Also, the war-making power must be accompanied by its opposite: peace-making power:

"The authority to make war of necessity implied the power to make peace, or the war must be perpetual..." *Ware v. Hylton*, 3 Dall, 231 per Chase, J. (See also *Penhallow v. Doane's Adm'r.*, 3 Dall 91, remarks of Tredell, J.)

Yet, the U.S. President declared on October 21, 1981:

"In a nuclear war, all mankind would lose." (New York Times, Oct. 22, 1981)

This statement only confirms overwhelming evidence since 1945 of the totality of modern war, both conventional and nuclear.

If indeed war is no longer winnable and its "end" is total annihilation, it can no longer be considered legitimate.

The history of the discretionary powers of the U.S. President as Head of State is, of course, not at issue in the instant case. Nonetheless, in his claim to recognition by this Court as a world citizen following Judge Thomas Flannery's oblique recognition (See Memorandum and Opinion, District Court, p. 11), petitioner cannot but challenge incidentally such arbitrary power as a fundamental contradiction of the constitutional process itself.

As Arthur Miller rightly contends, "...the United States has one Constitution for peacetime and another for wartime." (*Presidential Power In A Nutshell*, p. 184.) (See *Prize Cases*, 67 U.S. 635, 1863, Grier, J.; also *Martin v. Mott*, 12 Wheat. (25 U.S.) p. 19)

As determined by the lower courts' decisions in agreement with the INS's determinations as to the petitioner's status plus this Court's denial to date of certiorari, he is likewise "outside" those parameters as is the U.S. President. For as a person enjoying natural/human rights, does he not also enjoy "discretionary power" to represent his own sovereignty along with that of humankind per se? And is not this Court's denial of certiorari tacit confirmation of that "discretionary power" which cannot but be inherent in the exercise of inalienable rights.?

It goes without saying that, in the event of a nuclear war, when the nation is destroyed, as the U.S. President has advised us, this Court will likewise cease to exist. In the face of this ultimate threat to the nation, does not this Court have an imperative judicial obligation to utilize whatever powers it possesses constitutionally to avert such a catastrophe? Or else the aspirations and sacrifices of the original framers and their descendants would have been in vain.

Your petitioner, in standing before the bar of world public opinion for over thirty years as a world citizen, is evidently not alone in his quest for a peaceful world through just law.

No less distinguished a jurist than former Chief Justice Earl Warren stated in 1954:

> "In these troubled times, the hope for a peaceful world is of a world based on law as distinct from a world based on authority..."

Then former Justice William O. Douglas reminded us in 1958:

> "More and more people are coming to realize that peace is the product of law and order; that law is essential if the force of arms is not to rule the world."

The present Chief Justice, in greeting the assembled jurists from over 100 nations at the 1975 World Peace Through Law Conference in Washington, stated, in part:

> "We agree that man was meant to be free and that a state should be the agent and servant of its people, not the master...We agree that the proceedings of justice and the search for peace are among the highest aspirations of human beings...We know that justice is indivisible; it recognizes no boundaries; it is not confined in concepts of geography or jurisdiction; it is not limited in terms of language, creed, or political doctrines. It belongs to all who are now alive and to all those unborn who will follow us." (See Appendix for additional statements from Heads of State)

7

CONCLUSIONS

Wherefore, in this universal spirit of "Equal Justice Under Law", which is a global rallying-cry for beleagured humanity itself, Petitioner respectfully requests that this Court grant this Petition for Rehearing.

Respectfully submitted,

Garry Davis
Petitioner Pro Se

3606 Ordway Street, N.W.
Washington, D.C. 20016

December 22, 1981

CERTIFICATE OF GOOD FAITH

Petitioner hereby certifies that the foregoing Petition for Rehearing, was submitted in good faith and not for purpose of delay.

(signature)

Garry Davis
Petitioner-Pro Se
3606 Ordway St., N.W.
Washington, D.C. 20016
(202) 364-0871

Subscribed and sworn to before me

this _22nd_ day of December, 1981

at Washington, D.C.

(signature)

Notary Public

My Commission Expires February 14, 1985

CERTIFICATE OF SERVICE

I HEREBY CERTIFY that three copies of the foregoing Petition for Rehearing were mailed by regular mail or delivered to JAMES P. MORRIS, Attorney, General Litigation and Legal Advice Section, Criminal Division, and ERIC A. FISHER, Attorney, Department of Justice, Criminal Division, Washington, D.C. 20530.

Garry Davis
Petitioner-Pro Se

3606 Ordway Street, N.W.
Washington, D.C. 20016

December, 1981

January 25, 1982

Mr. Garry Davis
3606 Ordway Street, N.W.
Washington, DC 20016

Re: Garry Davis,
     v. District Director,Immigration and
     Naturalization Service
     No. 81-427

Dear Mr. Davis:

The Court today entered the following order in the above entitled
case:

The petition for rehearing is denied.

Very truly yours,

Alexander L. Stevas

Alexander L/ Stevas. Clerk

NEWS RELEASE February 1, 1982

SUPREME COURT REFUSAL TO CONSIDER WORLD CITIZEN GARRY DAVIS' CASE VS. THE INS POSES PROBLEM FOR U.S. GOVERNMENT: DEPORT HIM, DETAIN HIM OR FORGET HIM?

WASHINGTON, D.C. — The case of Garry Davis, which began actually when he stepped off the Pan Am plane at Dulles Airport on May 13, 1977, versus the U.S. Immigration and Naturalization Service is seemingly closed. Or is it?

Legally, Davis is still stepping off that plane. On January 22, 1982, the Supreme Court denied Davis' last appeal for a hearing after having refused to grant him certiorari on October 9, 1981 to review lower court rulings.

The Court's decision in effect confirms these rulings that the 60-year-old American-born Davis is an "excludable alien" as well as a "stateless person." Now the INS has to legitimately exclude him.

But to where?

Unlike the Cubans, Haitians, Iranians, Ethiopians, Mexicans, Russians and numerous other nationalities now living legally or illegally in the United States, Davis, a U.S. bomber pilot in World War II, has no other country to which he can be "returned."

In his petition for certiorari, he challenged both the law allowing expatriation and the law excluding him from his native land. He claimed as well that the ninth amendment of the U.S. Constitution protected his inalienable rights to claim a new political identity in the face of an imminent world war between natrion-states.

Then, in his Petition for Rehearing, Davis challenged the U.S. president's discretionary powers which, he claims, can lead to world war, positing the discretionary powers of the citizen to "make peace" by raising the level of civic commitment to the global level.

Ironically, he heads a District of Columbia-based corporation, the World Service Authority, which issues the very passport the INS refuses to recognize to individuals throughout the world who either have no national documents and cannot obtain them or whose national papers are either invalid and cannot be renewed.

The WSA was founded in 1954 as the administration agency of the world government declared by Davis on September 4, 1953 from Ellsworth, Maine. To date, over 250,000 WSA documents have been issued, mostly to refugees and stateless persons. They have been recognized on a case-by-case basis by over 60 nations according to WSA records. These include, incredibly enough, the United States.

"I have claimed for over thirty years," Davis said, "that the nation-state system was incapable of solving global problems. President Reagan, in his State of the Union message, clearly confirmed this position. He had no plan for world peace claiming only that military strength insures peace, a total denial of his own role as chief executor of the national law. He even referred to George Washington who, as the nation's first president, symbolized the triumph of law over anarchy. Then Reagan's so-called new federalism is a backward step without a new federalism extending to the world community itself. National dictators fear above all the loss of their power-base, the nation-state.

"In 1787, the founding fathers also proposed a 'new federalism' of which President Reagan is the latest presidential inheritor. But, ironically, Reagan has no plans for a world federation to protect the several nations and the world's people. We, the world's people, must therefore take our destiny in our own hands."

The World Government of World Citizens has registered over 100,000 citizens and has issued the world passport to Afghanistan refugees in Pakistan, Iran, Turkey and elsewhere, Eritreans in Saudi Arabia, Burmese, Vietnamese and other Southeast Asian refugees in Thailand, Malaysia and Indonesia, African refugees in the Sudan, Somalia, Botswana, Kenya, Nigeria, Ghana, etc., seamen with invalid national passports, and the tens of thousands of others who, for one reason or another, have problems with national travel documents.

Since Davis has no other country to which he can be deported, the INS must either detain him permanently or...do nothing. In that case, Davis will have in effect won his right to remain in the United States indefinitely. The only question remains, what is his status?

According to the law, he is not yet legally admitted. Therefore, he is not legally here. Now the Supreme Court, which permitted him to petition it, therefore, obviously considered him a person before the law, has contrarily denied him a legal status in the United States. Or, indeed, is its decision a tacit confirmation that Davis' "inalienable rights" can only be exercised by him as he claims and will neither be prohibited nor denied by the high court?

The second question concerns his right to travel. The INS will obviously not deny his right to leave the United States. But what happens when he returns? He still will be deportable according to the law. Will the INS then detain him permanently or, as it has done since May 17, 1977, will it consider him a "free agent" continually getting off the plane but physically able to come and go as he pleases?

If so, the World Citizen will have proved his case.

V
The U.S. Supreme Court and World Citizenship
A Postscript

The U.S. Supreme Court, on October 19, 1981 and January 25, 1982 respectively, denied both my petition for certiorari and Petition for Rehearing to be considered a legal world citizen in the United States.

The decision has proved my thesis that my right to identify myself as a world citizen is indeed legal.

How do I arrive at that seemingly extraordinary conclusion? First of all, since January 25, 1982, when the final court decision was published, the lower courts' decision—that I am an "excludable alien" as well as "stateless"— prevail according to U.S. law. This in turn obliges the Immigration and Naturalization Service to "exclude" me from U.S. soil.

In that the same INS contends that I am "stateless" and therefore unexcludable, it has failed to obey that U.S. law at this present writing. (Other "excludable aliens", Haitians, Afghans, etc. remain in U.S. jails.)

This conclusion, that the U.S. code was inoperable in my case, was part of my argument to the Supreme Court.

What then is my **legal** status in the United States? In default of U.S. law assigning me a legitimate one, it can only be that which I myself claim.

Secondly, in both petitions, I claimed that the Ninth Amendment—"The rights enumerated in the Constitution do not deny or disparage other rights retained by the people"—sanctions the exercise of the **inalienable** right to claim a new and **higher** political allegiance along with the existing ones.

That is precisely what the Founding Fathers did. Why "founding"? Why "fathers"? The very two words connote a newly created entity.

In denying my petitions, the high court in effect denied its jurisdiction in determining the nature of those rights "retained by the people" in that such rights, being inalienable, are thus **anterior** to the formulation of the Constitution itself and the founding of the Court.

Thirdly, the Supreme Court upheld the long-standing principle that expatriation is a **human right** regardless of the consequences of statelessness.

That means, incidently, that any Haitian, Ethiopian, Eritrean, Iraqian, Iranian, Mexican, Ghanian, Nigerian, Russian, Israeli, Burmese, Vietnamese, etc. who arrives on U.S. shores by whatever route or means can **unilaterally** renounce his or her nationality—a registered letter is sufficient—return all state documents and the U.S. law must in turn respect that human right.

In fact, this right is actually spelled out in the *Universal Declaration of Human Rights,* Art. 15(2): *"Everyone has the right to a nationality and every-one has the right to* **change his nationality.***"*

If we have the right to "change" our nationality, obviously we have the right

to choose our own government.

That is one of the inalienable rights implied in the Ninth Amendment. The 1981 Human Rights Report of the U.S. State Department, confirms this revolutionary notion categorically: *"individuals do not owe their humanity to the community, as earlier philosophies often argued; the community owes its whole* **legitimacy to the individuals,** *whose existence is prior to it."* (Emphasis added) (p. 3, col. 2)

Now comes the political bombshell. If the expatriate—or the national citizen—willfully chooses World Government as the object of his/her sovereign global allegiance **as many are today doing in lieu of any other government to represent them at this highest and newest civic level,** they have thus **legalized themselves** in a revolutionary yet non-violent and democratic way and in perfect conformity with both U.S. historical precedent and constitutional law!

Now is the time once again to test my theory in the field of world action.

CHAPTER 12

FROM DULLES TO NARITA TO SEATTLE...ON A WORLD PASSPORT

The elderly clerk at the Northwest Orient counter at Dulles Airport looked amiable enough. I had arrived at 8 a.m. on April 28, 1984 half an hour before a scheduled take-off to Tokyo, tightly planned to avoid scrutiny of my passport to see if I had a visa for Japan. But, to my disappointment departure was 9:30, the check-line was empty and the clerk would certainly have ample time to check me and my papers out thoroughly.

Three days before, the Japanese Counsul in Washington had unfortunately refused to visa my World Passport. He was being transferred to another post, he had informed me stiffly, and too busy packing to listen.

If I could just manage to get aboard the plane, I reasoned, I would take my chances with Immigration at Tokyo Airport. Surely my telegram to Emperor Hirohito congratulating him on his 83rd birthday and spelling out my peace mission would impress them. Then there were the written invitations, one from the Japan Congress Against A & H Bombs, another from Professor Hanaka, vice-chancellor of the International Association of Educators for World Peace, who taught education at Hirosaki University. If that didn't work, there were the official letters of recognition from Togo, Zambia, Upper Volta, Mauritania, Ecuador and the Yemen Arab Republic as well as the hundreds of photostats of entry, residence and exit visas from over 80 other nations all affixed on a passport issued by the embryonic world government.

My ticket was a round-trip with the return open. That was good. It would reassure the clerk. Then I had a few trivial questions to divert his attention.

"I called several days ago to say I was a vegetarian. Would you be good enough to check if the order got through?"

"Will I be able to keep this seat after Chicago?"

"Yes, non-smoking...and a window seat, if you please."

"What is the weather like in Tokyo this time of year?"

"I understand we will be arriving on Hirohito's birthday. Is that correct?"

He never did ask me for my passport and the non-existent visa. With boarding pass safely in hand, I passed happily to the waiting room.

I had issued a release that day explaining my reasons:

"My trip is part pilgrimage, part election campaign," it read. " As a former B-17 bomber pilot who helped wipe out German cities, I feel a kinship with the citizens of the only two cities whose destruction symbolize today a potential global nuclear holocaust. That dreadful heritage must give rise to a worldwide crusade for peace through law. I will ask the citizens of Hiroshima and Nagaski, as well as other Japanese citizens, to register as World Citizens, and to exercise a world franchise sanctioned by the *Universal Declaration of Human Rights* by voting for me as world president."

"No national candidate for public office" I concluded, "has a program for world peace. I am the only real world peace candidate."

The problem of re-entry to the U.S. had been covered by a letter of April 28 to Ronald Reagan whom I had informed of my intention to leave for Japan that day and return on June 1st via Chicago.

"I will be travelling with a World Service Authority passport," I wrote the President, "derived from Article 13(2) of the *Universal Declaration of Human Rights*...I expect full cooperation and approval for my entry from the Executive Office in that you have publicly endorsed both the concept and practice of world citizenship for all Americans."

This was my first trip outside the United States since I laid my World Passport down at the Immigration desk at Dulles Airport on May 13, 1977. It had taken almost five years to exhaust all the US legal remedies. All the court decisions had upheld the INS's original claim that I was an "excludable alien." But then INS didn't deport me. Thus I had been in a legal vacuum since May, 1977, neither in the United States legally nor outside physically.

When I embarked for Japan, therefore, from Dulles Airport on April 28, 1984, I was not leaving the United States since I had not yet legally entered. I was what I claimed to be, a legitimate world citizen. When I returned from Japan, that legitimacy would be tested directly at a US frontier.

Section II

We arrived at the Narita Airport outside Tokyo at 3:30 p.m., Sunday, April 29, the flight almost over the North Pole taking only 9 hours.

The Immigration inspector at the control booth took a quick look at my passport, picked up a phone, spoke rapidly, then motioned me to follow him, another inspector sliding into his vacated seat. We went to an interrogation room where another inspector asked me politely. "Where you get this passport?"

"It's issued by our government."

"Your government? Ah so. And what government is that?"

"The World Government of World Citizens. It says so on page 36."

"But this not national government?"

"No, it's a government based on human rights."

Mentioning human rights to an immigration offical is like holding a cross before Dracula.

"Why you come to Japan?" he asked angrily.

"First, I have been invited to speak on world peace through law, and secondly, I am on a pilgrimage."

"You peacenik?"

"No, I am a world citizen. Also, I am a candidate for world president. You see, your constitution is the only one in the world which renounces war. So I want to begin my campaign at Nagasaki at the Peace Park. Also, I have honorary World Passports for the mayors of Nagasaki and Hiroshima." I took them out and showed him. He looked them over eagerly.

"But why you get no visa for Japan?"

I explained what had happened at the Japanese Embassy in Washington. "I even gave the Consul this booklet containing photocopies of visas from seventy countries," I told him. "But still he wouldn't give me a visa. So, since my plane was leaving Saturday and my schedule is very tight — I have to be back in the United States for a conference in Washington on June 10th — I decided to seek entry here at the airport which, of course, is controlled by the Ministry of the Interior rather than the Ministry of the Exterior."

I showed him my telex to Emperor Hirohito, a letter from Washington, D.C. Mayor Marion Barry wishing me well on the trip, a press package containing a Yomieri Shimbun — Japan's and the world's largest newspaper — story on the World Passport and then, at his insistence, my credit cards. He took the lot and photocopied everything including the credit cards.

"You cannot enter Japan," he said curtly, handing me back my papers. "You no have valid passport and no visa."

"But this is the only passport I can get," I told him. "I am stateless and this passport represents my inalienable right to travel on my home planet. After all, Japan is a member of the United Nations. According to the Charter, all Member-States are obliged to respect and observe fundamental human rights. Your refusal to let me into Japan is a violation of the right to travel."

"We have strict regulations," he replied. "No one allowed into Japan without national passport and Japanese visa. No exceptions."

I picked up the Japan Times I had bought in the International Section, where on the front page was a story of the Dalai Lama coming to Japan that day.

"Tell me, what kind of passport does the Dalai Lama possess?" I asked him. "He is as stateless as I am. He is living in North India but doesn't hold an Indian passport as he is not an Indian citizen. Besides, many of his Tibetan monks, ever since they were expelled from Tibet by the Chinese, have been issued the World Service Authority Passport you are now refusing. Both I and the Dalai Lama are working for world peace. Are you going to allow him into Japan and not me?"

He seemed confused. "I not know what Dalai Lama have. He different from you. He religious man, you political man,. He go to Buddhist monastery but you want go to Nagasaki."

"But your own constitution has renounced war." I opened a folder and pointed to Article 9 of the Showa Constitution: "See, 'The belligerency of the state will not be recognized.' I have been living this doctrine ever since 1948," I told him. "But it is not enough just to renounce war."

He became formal. "You have right to appeal decision of Immigration to Minister of Justice. Do you wish to appeal?"

"Yes, of course."

The papers were prepared. One was headed "Ministry of Justice, Japanese Government, Narita Immigration Office." It read: "Your application for landing is pending. Therefore, it is requested that you stay at the Airport Rest House and that you do not leave the hotel without prior permission from this office. If you fail to comply with the foregoing requirements, you may be charged for illegal landing and may be deported from Japan." It was signed by the Immigration Inspector.

Section III

The Narita Rest House was next to the terminal building. When signing the register, under "Nationality," I wrote "World Citizen." No one behind the desk paid the slightest attention.

Monday, April 30, was a national holiday. The whole week is called "Golden Week" with holidays Wednesday and Friday as well. From my room telephone I tried to contact the International Secretary of the Japan Congress Against A and H Bombs as well as Professor Hanaka at the Hirosaki University but to no avail. The next best strategy was to inform as much of the press as possible of my plight. The wire services, Associated Press, Reuters, DPA, AFP and the Kyodo News Service took the story and wanted to be kept up-to-date of any developments.

The next day at 6:30 p.m., the Northwest Orient airport manager informed me by telephone my appeal had been denied. I would be sent back to San Francisco on Northwest Orient departing 8:30 that night...at their expense.

Four Northwest personnel came for me at 7. We came to the front desk to return my key. As I turned to leave, the manager said, "Here is your bill, Mr. Davis."

"What bill?"

"The bill for your two nights plus meals. It comes to $177."

"Oh, I see." I was awed at their hutzpah. This deserved a counter-attack, global style. I reached into my inside coat pocket for my wallet. The manager was smiling, the Northwest personnel waiting patiently. I took out a roll of World Dollar bills in ten dollar denominations and proceeded to count out 18 of them.

"No, no, Mr. Davis," the manager exclaimed, "that not money. We accept only US dollars or Yen. You have credit card, yes? We take credit card too."

"Listen, I didn't ask to be in your hotel in the first place. I am detained here, and, incidentally, wasting valuable time. Does a prisoner pay for his detention? Secondly, take a look at your register. I signed in as a world citizen. You accepted me as such. Now when I pay in world money, you don't accept me anymore? Sorry, but if you want to be paid, that's what you'll have to accept."

"We cannot accept this...this paper," he replied disdainfully. "This not backed by anything..."

"I tell you it's money so I am prepared to negotiate it for any national currency you want. But you have to accept it first, then trust me. I'll give you the address of our World Government Treasury Department in Washington, D.C. Send it there and you'll receive a money order by mail for the amount minus one percent for the transfer. Of course you have another alternative. You can pick up that telephone there and call the local police. Tell them I have refused to pay my bill and charge me with defrauding an innkeeper. I will be happy to defend myself before a court of law in Tokyo."

"No, no, you cannot enter Japan," he exclaimed. "You being flown out tonight."

"Then how in hell do you have the audacity to claim I owe you money?" I replied. "You knew I was in the custody of Northwest Orient and under the threat of deportation if I left this hotel. So first you accept a prisoner and then you dare present me with a bill. I ought to sue you for defrauding a world citizen."

The Northwest Orient personnel, realizing I would not pay in US dollars nor use my credit cards, took the bill from the counter and asked me to move along. We arrived at the international section where the individual runways go to the planes. I sat down.

"I would like to see the pilot of the plane I am supposed to be flying on," I told the Northwest manager.

"He is aboard plane. Come, you must go to plane now." It was 8:15.

"I refuse to go any farther until I see the captain."

"But why you want to see captain?"

"Because you want to put me aboard a commercial airplane, not a prison ship. The captain is the only law on that ship once it takes off. I want to tell him my conditions for being aboard."

"**Your** conditions?"

"That's right. And I suggest that you do not undertake the responsibility for the captain in this case."

227

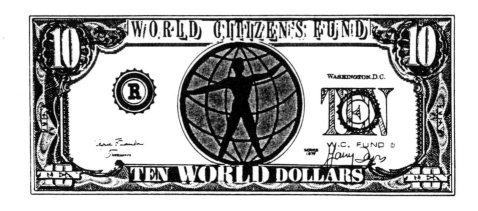

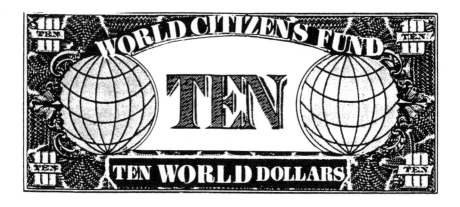

Money For A World Citizen

"An Immigration official stepped in. "Do you refuse to go aboard the plane?"

"I don't refuse anything," I told him. "But before I go aboard, I want an understanding with the captain as to what I consider my rights on his ship."

He motioned to his Immigration colleagues. They closed in and proceeded to pick me up bodily. A minute later, I was dumped at the feet of the captain who was standing inside the ship's door. I got up, straightened out my coat and tie and turned to him.

"You have a prisoner aboard your ship, captain. You saw me being carried on. I am obviously not a paying passenger. Therefore, I am obliged to inform you, in these circumstances, I cannot assume any responsibility for my conduct while aboard. In other words, I do not accept your authority."

He turned away in apparent confusion at this unwanted mini-insurrection. "Yes, of course," he said innocuously. I thought to myself, he's not going to buy it. No doubt the Northwest Orient manager had told him I was a nice old gentlemen, a reasonable man who, once aboard, would give him no trouble. After all, a man dedicated to world peace would not cause a small war in a crowded plane.

I turned to the passengers seated directly in front of me. "I have an announce-ment to make," I began in a loud voice. "I am a prisoner aboard this airplane. You saw me being literally carried on by Japanese Immigration officials. This is a gross injustice. You are entitled to a peaceful, pleasant trip to the United States..."

At this point the captain said to the bewildered, embarrassed and impotent Japanese Immigration officials, "Get him off. He's not flying on my plane."

Section IV

The manager of the Narita Rest House stared at me as if I were a ghost when I walked in accompanied by two young Northwest Orient clerks.

"My key, please?" I asked him with a smile. He looked at the NWO clerks in utter disbelief. They shrugged. He gave me the key to my former room and I went upstairs to shower and prepare for dinner.

The next morning, two guards were posted outside my door. They were large-ly ceremonial since, when I left the room for breakfast, they remained glued in place obviously having been given instructions only to "guard the room." The morning was spent in informing the press of the previous night's aborted depor-tation. Tiring of the food at the hotel, I walked to the terminal at noon, bought an International Herald Tribune, had lunch and returned at 3. Apparently no one had missed me. The two guards were still posted in the hallway zealously guar-ding my room. That neither of them acknowledged my presence as I came and went was a little disconcerting.

Around 6 p.m., the hotel management, now somewhat awed by my continuing presence, informed me I was again to be put aboard the 8:30 Northwest Orient plane for San Francisco. This time I decided not to cooperate, starting from my hotel room. And to complicate their task of arbitrary deportation, I would employ the penultimate tactic of non-violence: I would be naked when they came for me. (The ultimate tactic is a hunger strike to the death.)

I confess, however, that I lacked the courage to carry out this tactic fully, so when the two Northwest Orient clerks arrived with the manager, Mr. Ling, at 7:30 that evening, I was sitting on my bed with only jockey shorts on. They were appalled and embarrassed, totally unprepared psychologically or emotionally to dress a 62-year-old man who had sound arguments as to why he should be admitted into their country and strong objections to the injustice of his being refused entry just because of an arbitrary bureaucratic ruling.

At their pleadings for me to get dressed, I replied pleasantly that I would speak to the captain by telephone in order to save us all a lot of trouble.

"Do you want us to call the police?" Mr. Ling asked ominously.

"Again you threaten me with violence," I told him. "Is that all you people can think of? You talk of politeness. But are there no reasonable men here? Given my reasons for coming to Japan, given your experience in World War II, given the Reagan administration's attempt to force your government to raise the so-called defense budget — I understand Caspar Weinburger is due to arrive tomorrow to try to convince Mr. Nakasone of just that — in fact, given the very passport I travel with which represents the world community of which you are a major part, I should think you would welcome me with open arms rather than reject me in this highly insulting, aggressive and cowardly manner."

"But we are merely employees doing our jobs," Mr. Ling replied lamely.

"Oh, so your job as civilians is to threaten a non-national with violence? To assault him against his will? Are you the flunkies of the Immigration Service who don't want to do their own dirty work? Then they should pay you and not Northwest Orient. After last night's experience don't you realize that you cannot deport me against my will, that no captain will accept me or anyone for that matter who will not assume responsibility for his actions aboard ship?"

"Then let us take you to the pilot," Mr. Ling pleaded. "He decide. Come, be gentlemen. Get dressed. We are gentlemen. We only do our job."

"I'm doing my job too." I said wearily. "If the deportation order is unjust, I cannot collude with it. How else can I protest except by not cooperating? That is non-violence. If I go willingly, I am colluding with injustice. I understand your dilemma. But the Japanese government put you in the middle, not I . You are doing their work, patsies for Immigration. A commercial airline can only take paying passengers. You have no ticket for me."

"Oh yes, there is ticket," Mr. Ling said brightly.

"Who paid for it?"

"We did," he replied happily.

"Then it's yours, not mine, and you are forcing me onto a plane against my will. Any free, reasonable man must protest such treatment."

The walkie-talkie was fairly screeching by now. It was 8:15. After listening to the latest desperate protestations against the delay, Mr. Ling angrily gave an order to his two clerks. Startled into action, they found socks and pants and began forcing them onto my feet and legs. There is a point where resistance becomes violence in such confrontations. I was not prepared to push the opposition that far at this point.

Socks, pants, and shoes on, with a suit jacket draped over my bare shoulders, I was picked off the bed, still by the Northwest Orient personnel, carried down the hall, onto the elevator, through the hotel lobby and onto the van. Once at the terminal, a wheelchair was waiting on the sidewalk onto which I was unceremoniously hauled and wheeled away hurriedly through the almost deserted terminal to the waiting plane, accompanied by at least ten Immigration officials and a dozen airport policemen.

The wheelchair was halted directly at the plane's entrance. I remained in it. The same strong-armed clerks were therefore obliged once again to pick me up bodily and carry me the three steps onto the plane. No captain awaited me, however. He had been sequestered in the first-class cocktail lounge to which one ascended by a narrow spiral staircase. It is doubtful that a person of generous girth could make his or her way up that staircase. But surely three persons, one being carried by two, were an impossibility.

I had worked on my declaration to the other passengers during the day and was eager to see the effect.

"Ladies and gentlemen, you are witnessing an act of modern piracy. As you note, I have no wish to fly on this aircraft. I am doing all I can to prevent it." One of the clerks tried to muzzle me with a blanket. I shook it off. "But you too have the right to protest this wanton kidnapping and at your expense. If you agree that I not fly with you, make your protest now both to the captain and to Northwest Orient personnel both of whom are colluding with this injustice..."

A voice from the inner reaches of the cocktail lounge thundered to us struggling below. "I've heard enough! Get him off my plane, pronto!"

I shrugged off my captors and with as much dignity as I could muster, considering my almost bare condition, walked off the plane. The Immigration chief practically threw me back into the vacant wheelchair.

"Tomorrow you go into cell!" he bellowed.

"What is the charge?" I returned mildly. He didn't reply. The plane door closed behind us as I was wheeled up the winding corridor. No one spoke. Frustration, anger, disbelief marked the Japanese faces surrounding me. Outside the terminal the van was waiting. The two NWO clerks who had toiled so to get me to the plane accompanied me silently to the hotel. When we walked in once again, the manager took one look at me, clapped his hand to his forehead and scurried into his office. The bellboys laughed uproariously.

That's a curious thing, I thought. Here I am once again in the hotel, unguarded, no instructions and threatened with jail the next day. Besides, for the first time, NWO had kept my luggage and all my papers at the terminal. It was clear this was my last night of freedom, I had better make the most of it.

At 4 a.m., I got up, dressed, walked down the back stairway, crept under the security office window where a light showed and was out on the street. I walked briskly down the road away from the terminal, the early morning cold seeping through my thin shirt. Sleepy guards were spaced at various entry points to side roads. I paid them no attention as I almost jogged by. Far ahead, a huge gate closed off the road with a tiny guard post at the left side. Can this airport be closed, I wondered. Then I remembered the controversy, the thousands of farmers and students trying to prevent it opening because of the noise over farmland. As I was about 50 yards from the gate, a truck drove up, a guard opened it and the truck drove through. Before he closed it, I shouted, "Hey, wait a minute. I want to go through." Another guard stepped out of the guard house with a sub-machine gun in his hands. Before he could say anything. I asked "What time does the airport open?"

"Six."

"Can I go through now?" I asked smiling.

"Where you stay?"

"Narita Rest House."

"Where your passport?"

I motioned smiling. "It's back at the Rest House."

The other guard had already closed the gate but halfway opened it. The two guards stood debating what to do with me. I motioned as if I were smoking. "Need cigarettes. Is that Shell station open?" They still hesitated. I touched the guard's shoulder. "Don't worry pal, I'll be right back," I said, and walked out the half-open gate. I heard it close slowly behind me as I sauntered on.

At the red light 300 meters further on, I crossed to a Hilton Hotel. A taxi was coming to the opposite traffic light. I hailed it. "Tokyo," I said on getting in. "Narita station?" he asked. "Yes."

I arrived at Narita train station at 5:40, bought a ticket for the Ginza and sat down to sweat out the next 20 minutes. The gate guards would not blow the whistle, I thought, and they would probably be relieved at 6. If Immigration didn't come for me until 8, I had two hours head start.

At the famous shopping area, the Ginza, I waited around for a coffee shop to open. At 9:30 I called Christine Chapman, correspondent for the International Herald Tribune, to whom I had spoken the day before. She agreed to meet me at 11:00 at the Foreigner's Press Club for an interview and lunch. She suggested I stay that evening at the International House of Japan, which I did.

The next morning, the story of my escape from Narita appeared in the Yomieri Shimbun and the Japan Times. Against my better judgment, after researching the anti-nuclear movements in Japan at the library of the Foreigner's Press Club and sending a telex back to my office in Washington, I went to the main offices of the Yomieri Shimbun for a substantive interview rather than the flash story.

The editors seemed amazed to see me. After being introduced all around, I was taken to a small room where for over an hour I answered questions about my mission to Japan, whom I knew, how the world citizenship movement began, what could the people of Japan contribute to the problem of world peace, etc. But the two young reporters seemed to be doing more listening than writing. I gave them an "Open Letter to the Japanese People" I had composed that morning:

> While you debate Article 9 – Renunciation of War – of your Constitution, the nations of the world, especially the USA and USSR, continure to prepare for World War III.
>
> Renunciation of war without world laws, is like renouncing hunger with no food to eat.
>
> Your Constitution claims that you aspire 'to an international peace based on justice and order. . .' Order means laws and their institutions; legislative, executive and judicial.
>
> Therefore , if you legally renounce war, then you as legally advocate world public order.
>
> And as your Constitution also claims that you, the people, are sovereign, then you have the right to claim the only citizenship which can now protect your Japanese citizenship: that of the world itself.
>
> That is the message I bring to Japan. I claimed world citizenship over 35 years ago. I come to Japan as a declared candidate for world public office, I travel with a World Passport. Your government has refused me entry. . .
>
> So while you debate Article 9 of your Constitution, A World Citizen, who renounced war in 1948, is refused entry to your country. . .
>
> The Dalai Lama is now visiting Japan. He is as stateless as I am. His mission is world peace, as mine is. The passport on which I travel has been issued to many of his Buddhist monks throughout the world. And yet, while he is graciously received by your government, I am today threatened with imprisonment for trying to enter Japan with a message of world peace through law.
>
> Therefore I appeal to you as the sovereigns of this great country. While I must continue to remain in seclusion, I seek your help in rever-

sing this unjust decision of your Minister of Justice, this in the name of justice, of world peace, of your own Emperor, and of all the citizens of the world who, like you, desire a peaceful planet.

During the interview the telephone rang. One of the reporters answered it, glancing at me several times during the conversation. "I'd better get out of here fast," I thought. When the one who had answered the telephone advised me to return to Narita Airport and give myself up, I knew I had blown it.

I arose, gathering my things. We went to the elevators. They insisted on accompanying me down to the lobby. Were they being polite or making sure I exited by the front door? There were already three prize fighter-looking types loitering in the lobby. There was no use asking the way to the back exit.

Section VII

Half a block away I was quietly surrounded by four young men with hard eyes, one of whom flashed an Immigration badge.

"How did you guys find me?" I asked.

"We staked out this whole area where the newspapers are," he replied as we piled into the black sedan which had pulled up.

At the Tokyo Immigration headquarters, I was told I would be returned to Narita International Airport. Well, so they're going to try to deport me again, I mused. Or did Northwest Orient have other plans for me?

We stopped off at the International House so I could pick up my toilet articles and pay the bill.

We arrived at the airport gates at 8:45 p.m. Control was airtight. We drove past the terminal and entered an almost hidden road leading downwards under the building. "What Immigration headquarters doesn't have its cellblock," I thought grimly, "hidden away from public view?"

I was escorted into an Immigration office where ten men or so in uniform were lounging around. The interrogation began. I was being charged with entering Japan illegally, which "crime" carried a prison sentence of 30 days. Did I have the right to counsel? No. Could I defend myself. No. The charge comes from the Ministry of Justice. There would be no trial and therefore no defense. Just the charge, the conviction and the sentence: 30 days. Neat. They didn't say where the 30 days would be served, "inside" or "outside" Japan.

"This is arbitrary detention without due process," I told the interrogating officer, "A violation of article 9 of the *Universal Declaration of Human Rights*. As Japan is a member of the United Nations and as all member-states are bound by the Charter under article 56 to observe and respect fundamental human rights, I protest this procedure."

No reaction.

234

"Also, if I am detained, I will sue the government for a writ of habeus corpus."
Polite stares. I tried to explain what habeus corpus meant.

It was no use. The officer could have been the Buddha himself for all the earthly reaction he had. One last try, I thought. "I am a stateless person. I have no nationality. Besides, the United States government has determined that I am an excludable alien. In other words, I cannot re-enter the United States."

"Why you come to Japan?" He must not have read the file.

I went briefly through the catalogue of reasons adding that I did not recognize the validity of the refusal to enter Japan in that my passport was perfectly valid and being used by over 200,000 individuals.

After all this was noted in extraordinarily few Japanese characters, I was passed on to another official who merely slid into the vacated seat of the first.

"I am deciding Immigration official," he said proudly, "after proper investigation just concluded." He waited for that astounding fact to sink in. "My decision is, you are refused to enter Japan."

"No kidding?"

"What is kidding?"

One of the men at the table said something to him in Japanese. He gave me a withering look.

"You have right to appeal my decision to higher officer even than me. Do you wish to appeal?"

"Let's go," I replied. The "higher officer" just happened to be standing by, about two feet to his right. He was also about ten years older. He took the vacated chair in front of me. At least there were no transportation costs, I thought, and no delay between trials. The efficiency of the procedure could be an object lesson to courts throughout the world.

"I explain procedure," he began. "You give me additional information you want for Japanese government. We write all down. Then appeal goes to Minister of Justice for final decision. You understand?"

"Yes," I replied, thinking to myself, "and then you deport me." Well, might as well get everything into the record first.

"In my over thirty-five years experience as a stateless person, I have been subjected many times to the crime of ommission, that is, of not possessing what various Immigration authorities of different nations consider a valid passport or identity paper. Twenty-nine times I have been imprisoned for this crime. Now I face the dilemma once more. But also my experience tells me the laws concerning passports are as flexible as they are arbitrary. In other words, other factors enter the picture which can determine the outcome of whether a person is granted or not granted entry. For instance, the purpose of his trip, the length of his stay, his sponsorship in the country, his available means and his possibilities of leaving, such as having a round-trip ticket. All these factors were relevant here. I was invited, my stay is less than a month, I have money to live on, I have a return ticket. The only point of disagreement is in the so-called validity of my passport and not even the fact that I have not been issued a Japanese visa. But the passport properly identifies me. It represents my right of freedom to travel. It derives from an article in the *Universal Declaration of Human Rights*. And it has been recognized by many national governments. Furthermore, these decisions about passports are not subject to democratic control but are made by ministries and then called laws."

A rapid translation began. Everything I said was again miraculously transcribed in two lines of Japanese characters.

I had already emptied my pockets, my money had been counted and enveloped, papers dumped into my black bag, belt and shoe laces off, and with a friendly shove, I found myself once again encaged in a 14 by 6 foot space.

I awoke at 7. Breakfast came at 8: Fish, chopped cabbage, two pieces of buttered white bread, tomato juice and a tiny cup of jasmine tea. I told the guard I was a vegetarian. He asked me what I ate. "Rice, grains, vegetables, miso, tofu, fruits, seaweed and nuts." He said, "OK, I see."

When lunch came, it was two pieces of white bread, a sort of egg batter fried around white bread, tomato juice, chopped cabbage and a cup of jasmine tea. This menu is enough to drive me back to the U.S., I thought to myself.

Section VIII

They came for me at 4 p.m., the usual Immigration and Northwest Orient gang. We walked out onto the ramp where a huge 747 stood, a special bus parked alongside it which could be cranked up to be level with the plane's door. I began to smell a rat. I looked around me, but a bevy of Immigration officials closed in to prevent any escape. They marched me to the bus. Inside stood two heavy-built men, obviously Americans.

"Hello Garry," one of them said pleasantly as I walked in. "Looks like we're going to be riding together."

"Is that so? Where are you guys from?"

"Seattle."

"Do you mean Northwest flew you out here to strong-arm me back to the States?"

"Well, I wouldn't exactly put it that way. Let's just say we're here to see that you don't get into any more trouble."

I looked from one to the other. Two private security guards from a Seattle security firm, the Flight Terminal Security Co., had been hired by Northwest Orient Airways, flown to Tokyo, and ordered to "accompany" me back to Seattle. What was the legality involved? By what right could Northwest Orient return me to the United States without first questioning me as to where I might want to go? What were my rights? Was I merely an object to be thrown about at the carrier's will? I knew this was the lot of millions.

236

They sensed my question. "Now please don't be giving us no trouble," the other cop-for-hire pleaded. "We're just following our orders."

The bus backed up to the plane. A platform at the rear slowly elevated to the height of the door.

"Let's go, Mr. Davis," the first guard said. The other guard moved behind me. A TV camera was filming us from below. A dozen Immigration officials and Northwest Orient personnel watched as I was pushed into the plane. It was empty. I was moved to the rear section and the rear row. Now I understood the strategy. The entire rear section would remain empty except for me and my two guards! Clever, but costly. I was shoved, always gently but firmly, to the center of the back row. The two private guards sat on either side of me.

After an hour's wait, passengers began to be onloaded. They were seated first in the forward section, then in the middle section. Stewards and stewardesses blocked the aisle leading to our section. In desperation, I stood up and began in a loud voice to explain my situation. The two guards were horrified, trying to pull me down. "Please, Mr. Davis, be nice. Please, no trouble."

"I am a prisoner aboard this ship, not a paying passenger," I practically shouted. "I am guarded by these two hired guns. This isn't a prison ship. It's a commercial airliner. You have the right to a peaceful, uneventful trip . . ."

"If you continue, Mr. Davis, I will have to tranquillize you," one of the guards said.

I looked at him in amazement. Then loudly, "I have just been threatened by one of the guards who said that he would tranquillize me."

"Oh my God!" he exclaimed.

"This is an injustice, an outrage," I continued. "I will continue until I have no more voice. Please inform the captain you do not wish to ride in this plane as long as a prisoner is aboard . . ."

It was no use. No one paid any attention. They were over 50 feet away and blocked by the flight personnel. Besides, most were Japanese, probably couldn't understand English anyway. But more important, the captain was safely up in the cockpit obviously in total agreement with my plight and willing to collude with Northwest's piracy.

Section IX

We arrived at Seattle International Airport at 9:30 a.m., May 7. The passengers disembarked. Five minutes later, six men came aboard and strode purposefully down the aisle toward me.

"All right, Mr. Davis, come along," one of them said brusquely as if I were the culprit and they were the aggrieved party.

"Who are you, please?"

"I am the Northwest Orient airport manager. Now, if you please."

237

"Let me explain certain facts," I told him grimly. "First, I have been put aboard this plane unwillingly. Northwest Orient therefore has been party to a literal shanghaiing. Secondly, I have no legal right to be in the United States. Thirdly, I have no desire to be in the United States at this time."

"But you have to deplane. This flight is going on to Philadelphia."

"So let it."

"But Seattle is the gateway. You have to see Immigration."

"Why?"

"Why? Because...because Immigration has to decide whether you can enter the United States."

"Immigration has already decided that question. The answer is no."

"But you must deplane! You can't remain aboard. It's against regulations."

"You should have thought of that when your co-workers in Tokyo accepted me aboard this plane. That, according to me, was also against regulations."

"Do you want us to call the police?"

"Why are Northwest Orient personnel always asking me if I want them to call the police? You people collude with injustice, and then when I don't go along, you ask me whether I want the police to help you out. Are you suggesting that the police will collude with your piracy?"

He spoke into his walkie-talkie. "He refuses to deplane. Send the police." Five minutes later, a black policeman came sauntering up the aisle.

"Okay mister, let's go," he said to me.

"Why?"

"Because I say so. Now move!"

"One moment. What is the U.S. code which allows you to order a stateless person off an international carrier at an international airport?"

His eyes narrowed. "Just get your things together and come with me."

When I didn't move, he added, "I've been requested by Northwest."

"Yes, I am aware of that. But as a police officer, you are subject to the legal codes and not the arbitrary wishes of a private carrier. All I am asking is the specific code which pemits you to board a carrier and force a person off."

"I'll give you the code after we get to Immigration. Now, will you come off?"

"Do you refuse to give me the code now, or is it that you don't know it?"

"I told you, I'll get it for you later. Now, let's go, mister."

"You mean you don't really know whether there is a law or not authorizing you to order me off this plane?"

"I didn't say that, but I'm not going to stand here arguing with you. If you don't get moving, I'll move you."

"Are you threatening me with violence?"

"I'm threatening you with..." He stopped at the looks of the NWO management. He became conciliatory as if I were a madman who had to be humored.

"Now mister, I don't want no trouble and I'm sure you don't either. Let's just go into the lounge and talk this over, shall we?"

"May I know your name, please?"

"Bankston."

"And your number?"

"008." ·

I noted them and turned to the Northwest manager. "May I have your name please?"

"Nysox. Mr. Nysox. 'N' 'Y' 'S' 'O' 'X'." His voice dripped with venom.

"You are a witness, Mr. Nysox, that the police officer would not or could not give me the U.S. code authorizing this forced action."

The mini-drama completed, I rose and walked up the corridor, off the ship and to the Immigration section. It was crowded with Filipinos, Japanese, Mexicans, Central Americans and others, all with visa or other entry problems. One pot-bellied Immigration officer was attempting to cope with them while another was snapping pictures of would-be entrants.

"May I see your passport please?" The blonde, good-looking INS officer asked me after I had been seated for five minutes.

"Why, are you going to stamp it?"

She gave a nervous laugh. "No, I just want to see it."

"There really is no need, is there? I'm not a U.S. citizen, nor an immigrant, nor a transient, nor a visitor. So I can't enter the United States, can I?"

"Oh yes you can," she said brightly. "As a parolee."

I was shocked. In its desperation, Immigration was dragging out a phony status it tried to impose on me on Januaury 11, 1957 when I arrived from Skipholt Airport on a KLM Flying Dutchman.

"Where did you get that information?" I asked her.

"That's what we were told," she replied vaguely.

"You'd better check that again. There's been five years of court decisions since all confirming that I'm an excludable alien. Two are from the Supreme Court."

She seemed confused. "But you never left the United States."

"Wrong, I was never in the United States in the first place so there was no question of leaving it. The INS wouldn't let me in in 1977, so how can it let me in now?"

She stared at me. "I have to make a phone call," she said abruptly, returning to her office.

The hours passed. I waited, bored. Once, as she passed by, I motioned her over, taking out the World Passport with the Togo and Upper Volta visas on it. She looked through it without comment or questions. I then handed her the brochure with the photocopied entry visas. When she came to the U.S. visa issued in the Consulate at Buenos Aires with the INS admittance stamp at Miami Airport, she stared, her mouth open. Suddenly, she slammed the booklet closed, handed it back to me and stomped off. It was the last I saw of her.

At 5:30 p.m. I was taken to a nearby hotel by a Northwest official and two private security guards dressed to kill, literally. Before leaving the airport, another INS official, Ms. Yee, had informed me I would be interviewed by INS Monday when they had my file from Washington.

In my room, I picked up the phone to call the Associated Press. The guard ran over and grabbed the phone from my hand.

"No phone calls, Mr. Davis."

The instructions given to the armed guards by Mr. Nysox were that I was not to leave my room, I could have no visitors and no telephone calls. I informed him that I could not be held incommunicado, that it was a violation of the first amendment of the U.S. Constitution.

"Being held incommunicado while under detention is against the law. So you've been instructed to break the law. And you're the one wearing the uniform and the badge. Did you know that in the Brooklyn Detention Facility in New York where there are anywhere from 300 to 400 detainees, there are two floors of pay telephones? And in most prison cells, there are pay telephones now." I reached for the phone again.

"Please, Mr. Davis, let's call Mr. Nysox first. I don't want to get my ass in a sling."

We got the Northwest Orient supervisor on the phone. I explained the law to him. "I will pay for my calls," I told him, suspecting that was really the main issue. "In that case, you can make outside calls, Mr. Davis."

Section X

At 8 a.m. Monday morning, I was "delivered" to the Northwest Orient supervisor at the airport and from there taxied to the Federal Building with my guard Emmanuel who had developed a rough faith that maybe I was not a security risk after all, but on the contrary could not "escape" without risking my entire claim that neither could I re-enter the United States nor did I want to.

We were directed to the 6th floor, a detaining officer's office.

"This here is Mr. Davis," Emmanuel told the man at the desk.

"I'd like to know why I am here," I asked him.

"Why are you here? I'll be goddamned if I know why you're here." Emmanuel handed him the transfer paper from Northwest Orient, He looked it over.

"You're here because you tried to enter the United States illegally. That's why."

"Really? Is that really what the paper says?" I asked angrily. This was unbelievable. "For your information, I even refused to get off the damn plane. Northwest had to call the local police. Does that sound like I tried to enter illegally? The statement is an outright lie. The truth is that Northwest put me aboard the plane illegally in Tokyo..."

Another officer came in. "Just make out the exclusion papers," he told the man behind the desk. "Come with me, Mr. Davis." We went to the first floor to a small office where another officer sat at a typewriter.

"I'm Mr. Dow, detaining officer. Do you mind if I ask you a few questions, Mr. Davis?"

"Yes I do, Mr. Dow. I resent even being here. I told the first Immigration officer I saw at the airport that I have no intention of entering the United States at this time. And I have been under house arrest ever since I arrived. What the hell is going on?"

"Then you refuse to answer my questions?"

"Categorically."

He tore the paper out of the typewriter and inserted another, then started typing furiously.

I was returned to the first office on the sixth floor.

"Do you have the air fare to go back to Tokyo, Mr. Davis?"

"I have the fare but I'm certainly not going to pay for a passage when I was forced to come from Tokyo. That's Northwest's responsibility to get me back where it picked me up."

"In that case, you have to have a hearing. The judge has to declare you inadmissable."

"But I never said I wanted to come into the United States in the first place."

"But where did you embark from?"

"What does that have to do with it?"

"Everything. If Northwest brought you into Japan, it's responsible for getting you back here if Japan doesn't accept you."

" Well, though I left physically from Washington, D.C., since I was never legally admitted into the U.S. in the first place, I never left from here. So they couldn't legally bring me back."

He scratched his head. "That's too much for me. Anyway, that's the way it is. Now, please come with me."

We went into the next room where a burly Japanese-American told me brusquely to "empty your pockets."

"What for?"

"No one goes into one of my cells with anything in his pockets."

"Cell? But why am I going into a cell?"

"That's where you're going to wait for your hearing. What do you think we're running here, a hotel? Now, empty your pockets." As an afterthought, he growled, "And then I'm going to search you."

"But I'm not interested in coming into the United States in the first place, don't you understand? I was brought here, and I should not be treated like a common criminal."

"Listen, Davis, like I said, no one goes into my cells with anything in his pockets. And that goes for pencils and pens, too. They could be a weapon. You could stab a fellow prisoner."

I couldn't help laughing. "Stab a fellow prisoner! Brother, have you got the wrong number!"

"Come on, I haven't got all day."

I started pulling things out of my pocket. The man sitting at the table took my wallet, emptied it, and started counting out the Japanese yen.

"How much is this worth?"

"What do you care. Just note it. I want it all back."

He gave me a dirty look. Then the credit cards came out: two VISA cards, Diner's Club, American Express, Choice. The Japanese-American started calling out the numbers. The first man came back into the office.

"Let's get rid of this guy."

"O.K., put the stuff back into your pocket. You'll have your hearing today."

Section XI

After pocketing my various papers, money, cards and change, I was escorted to the bull-pen where about fifteen others waited for a hearing. There were two Nigerians, five or six Mexicans, some Guatamalans, a few others from South America, one fierce-looking chap from El Salvador, and a young German who had just turned himself in because he couldn't find a job in Washington state, was broke, had lost his German passport and had a leather tanning job waiting for him in Stuttgart.

One of the Nigerians was finishing his course of studies as an architect when his visa ran out. A young exuberant Mexican was being deported because his estranged wife, jealous because he was living with another girl with whom he had fathered two children, had informed INS she no longer sponsored him in the U.S.

"I will be back in six days," he informed me, smiling broadly. "Then I pay sixty dollar, get a divorce and get married with my girl friend."

When I entered the large cell-block, everyone gathered around me asking what I was doing there. I immediately felt the old comradeship of prison buddies – all equalized by the iron bars surrounding us. An immigration jail is special, however, because it is a microcosm of humanity, a pot pourri world community, united in its "crime" of ommission, of being "outside" the system and its victim, caught "between" nations, in the very anarchy which divides them, yet living, breathing proof of its falseness, its fictional character. I was right at home.

I showed them the world passport and the other WSA documents. At first they didn't understand. They looked at them skeptically, as if they didn't really exist.

"These are for us, all of us," I told them. "They are based on our rights as humans."

"You mean, we can get them too?" asked a swarthy Guatamalan.

"But who issues them?" a Mexican asked.

"Our own government, the World Government of World Citizens. You are all world citizens but you must claim it. Then you give yourself a legal status above these national officials. You see, they don't recognize human beings, but they do recognize documents. That's their trip."

Then what are you doing here with us?" the Salvadorian asked cagily.

"I am deliberately confronting national governmants with my world passport. The Japanese government recognized it by declaring it not valid. In other words, they had to first recognize its existence then take a stand on it. Well, they denied its validity and that makes them look foolish because it's based on the human right of freedom to travel which they have already agreed to as members of the United Nations."

I distributed my card. "Does the WSA passport cost anything?" the El Salvadorian asked.

"Yes, of course. There is an issuing fee. We are neither rich nor philanthropists. We provide a popular service. It is $40 for an eight year passport and $25 for a three year passport."

Section XII

The cell door clanged open and my name was called. At the office, a form was handed to me.

"Please sign at the bottom," I was told.

The form was entitled "NOTICE TO APPLICANT FOR ADMISSION DETAINED FOR HEARING BEFORE IMMIGRATION JUDGE."

It read:

"To Garry Davis   May 7, 1984

PLEASE TAKE NOTICE THAT you do not appear to me to be clearly and beyond a doubt entitled to enter the United States as you may come within the exclusion provisions of Section 212(a) 20 & 26 of the Immigration and Nationality Act, as amended, in that **you are an immigrant applying for admission to the United States** and you are not in possession of a valid unexpired immigrant visa, border crossing card or re-entry permit. You also are not in possession of a vaild unexpired non-immigrant visa. Therefore you are detained under the provisions of Section 235(b) of the Immigration and Nationality Act, as amended, for a hearing before a (sic) Immigration judge to determine whether or not you are entitled to enter the United States or whether you shall be excluded and deported. During such hearing you will have the right to be represented by counsel and to have a friend or relative present. AT THE HEARING BEFORE THE

IMMIGRATION JUDGE YOU MUST ESTABLISH THAT YOU ARE ADMISSIBLE TO THE UNITED STATES UNDER ALL PROVISIONS OF THE UNITED STATES IMMIGRATION LAWS."

(Emphasis added.)

It was signed by "Byron P. Dow."

I stared at it. Was there no limit to the duplicity? And the outright stupidity? So this was the paper Mr. Dow was so energetically typing? No wonder he pounded the machine so unmercifully!

"Whoa, wait a minute! This statement is an outright lie! A fraud! I never applied for admission to the United States as an immigrant. And you want me to sign this?"

"All you have to do is explain it to the hearing officer."

"But why should I have to explain an outright lie to the hearing officer at all when it is Immigration which tells the lie? I mean, by what right do you people deliberately falsify a document being presented to an Immigration judge and then have the gall to ask me to sign it first?"

He ignored my question. "It's O.K if you don't sign. But it'll go into your record as being uncooperative."

"Oh, for God's sake! And what about the record of Mr. Dow who wrote it when I told him exactly the opposite? Did he cooperate with me? Will it state on his record that he made a deliberate false statement?"

"Let's go, Davis. Back to the cell."

Later, after a "vegetarian" lunch of cold rice and a lettuce and tomato salad, I was told I would have my hearing at 1:30. But at 1:30 when the cell door opened, three smiling and seemingly chastened INS officers came to fetch me.

"Do you mind talking to the press, Mr. Davis?" one of them asked.

So that was it. Now I was a celebrity. The press had "legalized" me.

"No, not at all."

"We'll have it in the hearing room."

Two TV camera crews were setting up when we arrived plus four journalists including John Wiley of the Associated Press with whom I had been on the phone several times.

The press conference lasted almost a half-hour. The hearing judge kept poking his head in the door asking plaintively "How long will this go on? I want my hearing room back." I distributed my original release, "A World Citizen Goes To Tokyo," the statement announcing my candidacy for world president, and the "Open Letter To The Japanese People." The television interview opened with the question, "Mr. Davis, why not go by the rules?"

"There are no rules where I'm operating," I replied, "that is, no real laws. I am between nation-states where there is only anarchy. All the decisions are arbitrary from the heads of state on down. And that's why world citizenship is necessary. We insist on agreed-upon rule or, in other words, world law and its institutions. That is the price of world peace."

After the conference, an INS officer informed me that there would be no hearing that day, that my file hadn't arrived yet from Washington, D.C. yet. I would be returned to a hotel in Northwest Orient's custody, i.e. under 24 hour guard.

Section XIII

Two hours later, I and my faithful guard corps were checked into the Hyatt Regency Motor Lodge near the airport to await Immigration's further pleasure. The hotel personnel, seeing me always with my private guard, no doubt considerd me a top banana in some underworld activity. When I asked for typewriting and photocopying facilities, the alacrity with which they were furnished free of charge went beyond mere innkeeper hospitality. It was only on Friday when a bill was presented for telephone calls which included those made by my guards to their office that they discovered the truth. I insisted the calls be separated on the bill! My secretary in Washington tried to contact me that Friday along with local press people and was informed that I was "persona non grata." No calls.

The "definitive" hearing was scheduled for Monday, May 14 so Immigration took charge of me over the weekend by locking me up at the Renton City Jail.

Section XIV

The hearing officer, Newton P. Jones, entered the room sharply at 10 p.m., shortly after the government attorney, David Hopkins and I had been seated. I was sorry to observe that no press attended. This hearing was the culmination of seven years of legal tests to prove my original thesis of May 25, 1948 that the individual possessed inalienable, therefore legitimate rights to choose his or her political allegiance and that that choice had to be recognized by the existing legal institutions.

American history books overlook the banal fact that the entire personnel of the United States government in 1787 totalled 53 people, all amateurs! It is told that Alexander Hamilton, President Washington's Secretary of the Treasury, complained of the lack of a secretary! Remember, everything was written in longhand, no word processors! Congress only met three months out of the year, and each state retained its militia for two years and its currrency for longer. In other words, the central government was a good (or bad) joke to much of the American population at the outset.

Today's test was the first since May, 1977, when the U.S Justice Department claimed I was excludable from the country of my birth where, again, the Immigration and Naturalization Service, at the lowest level, the frontier, was obliged to determine whether I could remain in, not enter, the United States as a "world citizen."

The "bottom-of-the-line" issue was sovereignty.

If the government still claimed I was an "excludable alien subject to deportation" yet did nothing to deport me, it was implicitly recognizing my innate sovereignty as a human being. That in turn was a tacit recognition of my claim to the status of world citizenship as an inalienable right. My sovereignty in turn denied the "absolute" sovereignty of the United States of America!

Section XV

Judge Newton Jones after calling the hearing to order, read into the record my name, birthplace, and birthdate. He then quoted excerpts from the court record of the 1st Court of Appeals giving my history of renunciation of nationality and subsequent events including those of May 13, 1977 at Dulles Airport.

"You may have counsel, Mr. Davis," he informed me kindly.

"Your honor, I don't need counsel because I have no defense. I have just been handed a notice by Mr. Hopkins asserting that I am an applicant to enter the United States. It is signed by a Mr. Bryon Dow. But I informed Mr. Dow that I am not an applicant to enter the United States. Therefore the official immigration form is fraudulent. In fact, Mr. Jones, this hearing itself is totally irrelevant in that I am an excludable alien, a status determined by the INS itself in 1977 and confirmed by seven court decisions including those of the Supreme Court."

Mr. Hopkins interjected, looking through his papers. "According to my records, Your Honor, Mr. Davis is indeed an excludable alien with no right to enter the United States."

"I agree fully," I added.

The judge looked non-plussed. "But. . .I have to make a determination. You're in my jurisdiction."

"I'm in your jurisdiction because I was forced into your jurisdiction," I told him. "I'm not here of my own free will. I was shanghaid out of Tokyo by Northwest Orient."

"But the Japanese government wouldn't accept you," he said.

"Are you basing your determination on what another nation does or doesn't do?" I asked. "I was under the impression that the United States of America and Japan were two separate sovereign governments."

"They are," he replied testily, "but if the Japanese government didn't accept you, that is, if you didn't legally enter onto foreign soil, then, according to U.S. law, let's see, Kaplan vs. Todd, you never left the United States."

"I beg to disagree, Mr. Jones. Both the Japanese government and the United States government refused me admittance. That's a matter of court record. So

246

how can you maintain that I never left the United States when I was never admitted into the United States in the first place?"

He leaned back in his chair. "It is quite a dilemma. I don't see . . ."

"I think it is quite clear," Mr. Hopkins said. "Mr. Davis is inadmissible, period. The Justice Department has always maintained that position. It has been upheld by the civil courts. And Mr. Davis himself agrees."

"That's right, inadmissible under the law," I agreed. "So I repeat, this hearing is actually irrelevant. Both parties agree. What is the need for a hearing?"

The judge looked grim. What to do if there is no confrontation, if both parties agree to what he must oppose? My test case was being proven: National law stopped at national frontiers. Human law or inalienable rights were global. In my case, United States law was about to be denied by a U.S. judge himself faced with an individual exercising his inalienable right to travel.

If he declared me inadmissible, legally, the INS would be obliged to turn me over to Northwest Orient which would then be obliged to fly me back to Japan. On the other hand, if he declared me admissible, since I was no longer a national citizen nor an immigrant nor a visitor, he would be implicitly recognizing my claim as a world citizen.

The judge picked up a paper from his desk. "I will now read into the record the text of a telex received today from Immigration and Naturalization Service in Washington, D.C. Quote: 'The file on Mr. Garry Davis has been lost.' Unquote."

I stared at him. My file has been lost? A file which goes back to 1950! Which must be about ten meters long! Part of which is now printed in various legal texts including those of the Supreme Court! I didn't believe it. I knew the D.C. INS office was hopelessly inefficient with files in cartons stacked up to the ceiling. We had dozens of letter in our office from individuals living in the U.S.A. complaining of years of delay in their cases with the INS. No, inefficiency is one thing, but this sounded like a cover-up. Or a cop-out.

(My mind raced through an unlikely scenario.) When the D.C. Immigration office received the request for my file from the Seattle office, it turned the news over to the State Department where it wafted quickly up to Secretary of State Schultz's desk.

He, knowing Caspar Weinberger was closeted with Prime Minister Nakasone plotting to raise the Japanese military budget above the 1% allowed by the Constitution, in turn brought the fact of my ill-timed presence to the next morning's cabinet meeting.

President Reagan then recalled that he had received a letter recently from me to the effect that I would be returning on June 2nd and not May 5th and via Chicago and not Seattle.

"Well, Mr. President," Schultz explained, "he's here now. The Japs wouldn't let him in, and Immigration wants to know what to do about it."

Everybody thought for a while. Then the president said, "I've got the solution.

247

We'll simply lose his file. That way, Immigration takes the rap, they can blame it on the cuts and Davis can't go anywhere but home."

"Brilliant! Genius!" everyone said.

"One question," Schultz asked. "What is his status in the United States?"

"He's a fellow actor," replied the President. "That's good enough for me." End of scenario.

Section XVI

"Here is my determination," said Judge Jones doggedly. After recounting for a good ten minutes the past facts, he concluded, "and so, I hereby determine that you never left the United States and that you are in the same legal status now that you were on April 28, 1984. Case closed."

Eh voila!

It was now a part of the permanent record. On May 14, 1984, at an official hearing in Seattle, Washington, thirty-six years to the day I sailed to Europe to renounce my nationality and declare my world citizenship, a U.S. Immigration judge rendered a decision which in effect sanctioned my legitimate status of world citizenship, at least in so far as the United States of America was concerned!

When he claimed that I never left the United States, he was also claiming that I was legally in the United States. Yet, according to the same INS, I had never been admitted to the United States, so I could not have left it. Then the "same legal status" was that of "excludable alien subject to deportation," which meant, inadmissible, therefore, move out, on the next plane to Tokyo.

But no, the INS simply didn't obey His Honor—just like it hadn't all those other times. The case was "closed." Now, thank heavens, the file was "lost." Whew! INS dropped the handcuffs, gave me a lift to the airport and waved me goodbye. Get lost, Davis, and good luck. And please don't come back again from abroad via Seattle!

I had left the country of my birth as a World Citizen and returned as a World Citizen.

The implications were far-reaching.

But there was another implication, perhaps as important from a legal point of view though less obvious.

If I were excluded from the constitutional jurisdiction of the United States yet left physically "free" in the United States, though I would not enjoy either national civic rights or duties, still I would be subject to "international law" as defined by the Nuremberg Principles.

These principles, which became part of international law by a General Assembly resolution in 1950, explicitly state that "any person who commits an act which constitutes a crime under international law is responsible therefore and liable to punishment." (Principle I). Secondly, "crimes against peace, war crimes and crimes

248

against humanity are punishable as crimes under international law." (Principle VI). And thirdly, "complicity in the comission of these crimes is itself a crime under international law." (Principle VII).

As to the responsibility of the national citizen acting on orders from his or her government, Principle V states that "the fact that a person acted pursuant to orders from his Government or of a superior does not relieve him from responsibility under international law, provided a moral choice was in fact possible to him."

The U.S. president, along with every other United States citizen, is equally subject to international law as defined by the Nuremberg Principles. But, when he acts as head of state vis-a-vis other states, his discretionary powers protect him from civic restraints imposed on the national citizenry he otherwise represents. Thus like me, in his capacity as head of state, he is bound only by international law.

On this legal plane, I am eye-balling Ronald Wilson Reagan.

The difference is that he is pointing a nuclear gun at me which, if it goes off, will end my physical existence on this planet along with, no doubt, that of my fellow humans.

In real terms, therefore, he is threatening my life and if the threat becomes an act, I would be unable to take any legal action.

That he also would not be indictable, being dead also, would be irrelevant.

But do I have any legal remedies in the face of that moral threat?

According to the Nuremberg Principles, absolutely!

But a seminal question still pertains in jurisprudence: is the individual really a subject of international law? We will examine this question more closely in the next chapter.

CHAPTER 13

IS THE INDIVIDUAL A SUBJECT OF INTERNATIONAL LAW?

"Everything has changed except our way of thinking."
Albert Einstein

This paper will examine a seminal legal question the answer to which can lead either to a final world war or finally, world peace.

Sixteen thousand megatons of destructive force is today available to the nuclear powers. Only three megatons were used during the entire six years of World War II. Only two hundred and fifty megatons is enough firepower to destroy all the large and medium-sized cities in the entire world

Each single human being on planet earth has a nuclear "gun" pointed directly at him or her.

But, in that "nuclear" for all practical purposes means "total," that same "gun" is pointed directly at humanity itself.

The relationship therefore between the individual and humanity, in the latter half of the 20th century, has become dynamic, immediate, one-to-one, and what is even more revolutionary, organic.

For sheer survival, it now demands legitimate recognition and institutionalization.

The question therefore whether the individual is a subject of international law is crucial to the question of survival itself. For the nuclear "gun" is controlled and condoned by the so-called sovereign nationstate, each of which maintains the legal right to wage war with other states. We will examine briefly the paradox this presents both to the states themselves and to you and me as two of the (world's) people.

Another way of asking the title question is: Do you and I have the inalienable right to live on planet earth? If so, is that right legitimate?

"We, The People," Human Rights & International Law

The Preamble of the United Nations Charter, in its opening statement of purpose, claims that "We, the Peoples of the United Nations determined. . .to reaffirm faith in fundamental human rights. . .and. . .to establish conditions under which justice and respect for. . .other sources of international law can be maintained. . .have resolved to combine our efforts to accomplish these aims."

Chapter I, Article 1, defining further the UN's purposes and principles, once again in para. 1 reaffirms the principle of "international law" with regard to "adjustment of settlement of international disputes or situations which might lead to a breach of the peace. . ." In para. 3 of the same article, again the "promotion and encouraging respect for human rights and fundamental freedoms for all" is enjoined in order "to achieve international co-operation. . ."

The General Assembly, according to Article 13(1), "shall initiate studies and make recommendations for the purpose of. . .(a). . .encouraging the progressive development of international law and its codification. . ." and (b). . ."assisting in the realization of human rights and fundamental freedoms for all. . ."

Chapter IX, Art. 55 is even more explicit concerning the UN's obligation to human rights:

> "With a view to the creation of conditions of stability and well-being which are necessary for peaceful and friendly relations among nations based on respect for the principle of equal rights and self-determination of peoples, the United Nations shall promote. . .(c) **universal respect for, and observance of, human rights and fundamental freedoms for all without distinction as to race, sex, language, or religion.**" (Emphasis added.)

Then Art. 56 pledges "All Members. . .to take joint and separate action in cooperation with the Organization for the achievement of the purposes set forth in Article 55."

The Charter of the United Nations was signed on 26 June 1945, in San Francisco and came into force on 24 October 1945 therefore binding the 50 original nation-states and all subsequent "Member-States" to this successor to the League of Nations.

On December 6. 1949, the U.N. General Assembly unanimously endorsed Resolution 375(IV), "Declaration on Rights and Duties of States." Art. 14, stated that "Every State has the duty to conduct its relations with other States in accordance with international law and with the principles that the sovereignty of each State is subject to the supremacy of international law."

The Universal Declaration Of Human Rights

On December 10, 1948, after two years of research by leading experts on human rights as the "Human Rights Commission," the **Universal Declaration of Human Rights** was proclaimed by the General Assembly as "a common standard of achievement for all peoples and all nations..."

Herein the principle of law was raised implicitly to a global status in both the Preamble, and Articles 15(2), 21(3) and 28 respectively: "Whereas...it is essential if man is not to be compelled to have recourse, as a last resort, to rebellion against tyranny and oppression that human rights should be protected by a regime of law...." "No one shall be arbitrarily deprived of his nationality nor denied the right to change his nationality." (Here the human right of both expatriation and choice of political allegiance is confirmed globally) "The will of the people shall be the basis of the authority of government..." (The ultimate sovereign on planet earth, humanity, is here implied as being the sanction, if its will is duly express-ed, for the authority of a world government.) "Everyone is entitled to a social and international order in which the rights and freedoms set forth in this Declaration can be fully realized."

U.N. Admits Its Impotence To Act On Human Rights Violations

In direct contrast, however, to these affirmations of human rights and interna-tional law, at its first session in January, 1947, the Commission on Human Rights established a Sub-Committee on the Handling of Communications which later concluded in its first report (E/CN.4/14/Rev.2), para. 3, that "The Commission has no power to take any action in regard to any complaint regarding human rights." This subsequently became Resolution 75(V) and though subject to review and increasing concern in succeeding years by the Economic and Social Council – a reaffirmation of Res. 75(V) became Resolution 728F (XXVIII) of 30 July 1959 of the ECOSO C – remains unmodified to date.

The question naturally supposes, if human rights are to be protected by "inter-national law," and if the Member-States of the United Nations are bound by their signatures to the UN Charter to that international law, yet the United Nations itself admits its impotence to deal with human rights violations, what body, if any, determines, executes and enforces international law to which the human in question can refer?

Let us first examine briefly the nation-state vis-a-vis human rights to gain fur-ther insight both of the main perpetrators of human rights violations and the pro-tection or lack of it for fundamental human rights.

Human Rights And National Constitutions

Since the proclamation of the French "Declaration des Droits et du Citoyen" in 1789 and the ratification of the U.S. Bill of Rights in the same year, the juxtaposition of human rights and national constitutions has enjoyed an uncertain and often hazardous alliance.

The exigencies of "national security" on the whole, have, in the final analysis, always prevailed over human rights issues. Art. 2 of the United States Constitution, for example, defining the powers of the chief executive provide a telling commentary on the dilemma of human rights within the national legal framework. The discretionary powers conferred on the U.S. president effectively separate him from all civic responsibility and accountability when speaking and acting as head of state.

Myriad examples from President Lincoln's abolition of habeus corpus prior to the Civil War, Franklin Roosevelt's Lend-Lease program, Truman's unilateral decision to bomb Hiroshima and Nagasaki thereby unleashing the nuclear arms race, Kennedy's "Bay of Pigs" fiasco, Johnson's Tonkin Bay deception, Nixon's undeclared war in Cambodia, Carter's aborted attempt to rescue the U.S. hostages in Iran, to Reagan's deployment and redeployment of Marines in Lebanon and CIA-supported insurgents against the Nicaraguan government, etc., decisions in which the U.S. electorate had and have no part, illustrate vividly and often disastrously "the imperial presidency."

The Supreme Court's Traditional Silence

The U.S. Supreme Court has traditionally refused to curb the executive when he is acting as head of state. The doctrine therefore "Inter armes, silent legis," has dominated the U.S. Supreme Court since its founding. That is, in national concerns involving other nations, the High Court inclines totally to the executive branch even to declarations of war. "The judicial attitude is more than abstention," wrote Arthur S. Miller, in **Presidential Power In A Nutshell** (West Publishing Co., 1977, p. 163). ". . . it verges at times upon courts being an arm of the executive when violence, foreign or domestic erupts." "In times of declared war, particularly in the 20th century when wars have become planetary in extent, the President acts as a 'constitutional dictator'. . . . There is a tacit understanding that nothing—literally nothing—will be permitted to block winning the war. What is necessary, as determined by the executive is done. Legal niceties are given little attention. National survival is the ultimate issue." (Ibid, p. 169) The U.S. Supreme Court's judicial silence on international issues aptly illustrates the impotency of national law to implement fundamental human rights which, by definition, require the protection of "a regime of (world) law."

Yet since the UDHR's proclamation by the UN General Assembly, with some irony, 18 Member-States have incorporated it directly in their national Constitutions, some in the Preamble, others in the body directly. (Ref. 48 Revue Internationale de Droit Penal, Nos 3 & 4, at 211, 1977).

"We, The People" in National Constitutions Are Sovereign

Virtually all national constitutions refer to "the people" as either sovereign or the mandating authority for the constitution itself.

To cite a few examples, the 1947 Japanese "Showa" constitution begins traditionally with "We, the Japanese people..." and Chapter III, Art 13, claims that "...Their right to life, liberty and the pursuit of happiness shall, to the extent it does not interfere with public welfare, be the supreme consideration in legislation and public affairs." Further implicitly confirming these individual human and inalienable rights, Article 9 states unequivocally that "...The right of belligerency of the state will not be recognized."

The 1971 Bulgarian constitution likewise begins with "We, the citizens of the People's Republic of Bulgaria..." The 1974 "Instrument of Government" of Sweden states in Chapter 1, "The Basic Principles of the Constitution," Art. 1, that "All public power in Sweden emanates from the people." Likewise Article 1(1) of the 1967 Brazilian constitution affirms that "All power emanates from the people and is exercised in their name." The Greek constitution of 1975 in Article 1(2) claims that "Popular sovereignty is the foundation of government" and that (3) "All powers are derived from the People and exist for the People and the Nation..."

The "Basic Rights" of the 1949 West German constitution in Article 1(1) refers to "The dignity of man" as "inviolable." "To respect and protect it shall be the duty of all state authority." Para. 2 then allies this human dignity with the protection of rights as follows: "The German people therefore acknowledge inviolable and inalienable human rights as the basis of every community, of peace and justice in the world."

The "Fundamental Principles" of the 1978 Portugese constitution under Article 3(1), "Sovereignty and legality," states, with equal firmness, "Sovereignty, one and indivisible, rests with the people, who shall exercise it in accordance with the forms laid down in the Constitution."

The Preamble to the French constitution of 1958 boldly asserts that "The French people hereby solemnly proclaims its attachment to the Rights of Man..." and in Title I, "On Sovereignty," para. 4, affirms that "Its principle is government of the people, by the people and for the people."

A comprehensive study of national constitutions reveals this fundamental similarity, that, without exception, they derive from "the people" and at least in theory are designed only to serve the sovereign people.

Anomaly: Human Rights Versus National Security

The inclusion of inalienable human rights or the UDHR itself, however, in a national constitution presents the anomoly of positing the latter's exclusivity with the former's inclusivity. In other words, national law, being relative to a given state, therefore limited despite its implied claim of absolutism (not to mention eternity), fails to meet the challenge of universality implicit in the protection of "universal" human rights. It is thus that all national constitutions contain the caveat of "national security," or "public order," as conditions nullifying human rights' guarantees of legal protection.

Patrick Henry's remark in 1787 that "The U.S. Constitution squints toward monarchy," and latter-day charges by eminent American constitutional lawyers of "the imperial presidency" underline this duality enjoyed by all national constitutions and therefore heads of state when human rights collide with so-called national security, the 20th century catch-all for their repression or outright violation, always with disastrous consequences for the citizenry.

Human Rights and International Due Process

Dean Acheson observed: "Law simply does not deal with...questions of ultimate power—power that comes close to the sources of sovereignty.... No law can destroy the state creating the law. **The survival of states is not a matter of law**." (Emphasis added

And herein lies the human and humanity's dilemma.

For if the only source of law is the state, then "world" or "international" law is a chimera.

Why then does the United Nations, an association of sovereign states, refer continually to "international law" if indeed law stops at national frontiers? Further, we are obliged to ask, from what did states themselves originally derive since they were not always in legal existence? The answer becomes increasingly obvious as we backtrack historically to ever smaller human groups. Finally we arrive by sheer logic and necessity to the subject of law itself, the individual human and find, ironically, that he/she is likewise the object, that is, the promoter, the evaluator, and perenniel evolver. *"Government can be safely acknowledged a temporal blessing, because in terms of the power it wields, there is nothing inherent in it. Government is not an end in itself but a means to an end. Its authority is the free and revocable grant of the men who have promised conditionally to submit to it. Its organ, however ancient and august, are instruments that free men have built and free men can alter or even abolish."*

Chief Justice Earl Warren, US Supreme Court

National Attempts at World Peace Fail

Since 1899, international gatherings of national delegates have been trying to reach beyond their state frontiers to achieve peace amongst themselves. The latest effort is of course the United Nations. But since the states retain at all costs their claim to absolute sovereignty thereby neither recognizing the sovereign human nor the ultimate sovereignty, humanity, their efforts cannot but be vain and illusory.

The 35 national wars raging today as well as the preparation for a final nuclear holocaust bear out this excruciating denial of reality.

The First International Penal Code

The classic example of the national impotence to create the conditions of peace are the Nuremberg Principles formulated by the International Law Commission of Jurists, and incorporated into "international law" by a 1950 Resolution—488 48(v) 1950—of the UN General Assembly. These Principles explicitly state that "any person who commits an act which constitutes a crime under international law is responsible therefor and liable to punishment."

Principle I states that "crimes against peace, war crimes and crimes against humanity are punishable as crimes under international law." Principle VI states that "complicity in the commission of these crimes is itself a crime under international law." Principle IV states that "the fact that a person acted in pursuant to orders from his Government or of a superior does not relieve him from responsibility under international law, provided a moral choice was in fact possible to him."

Principle VI states that "Complicity in the commission of these crimes is itself a crime under international law."

"Crimes against peace" were defined as

"1) Planning, preparation, initiation or waging of a war
of aggression or a war in violation or international
treaties, agreements or assurances;
2) Participation in a common plan or conspiracy for the
accomplishment of any of the acts mentioned under (1)."

Here was a legal paradox. "International treaties, agreements or assurances" are the province of diplomacy totally outside popular control. How then can the national citizen be a party to violations of international treaties if he was not a party to the agreement? Yet the Nuremburg Principles applies only to individuals "under international law."

It can be argued with telling logic that, based on the powers conferred on them by national constitutions as well as exigencies of the anarchic condition between states, the only national citizens enjoying an "international law" status are the very heads of state exercising discretionary powers **beyond** the internal civic network. And if this position is correct, then most if not all present-day heads of state are war criminals under the terms of these Principles for, with notable exceptions such as Switzerland, Grenada and the Seychelles, all are either "planning, preparing, initiating or waging war," one of the principal exports of the modern state.

On the other hand, as shown above, if the people are sovereign and individuals enjoy inalienable sovereign rights, as most if not all states claim in their very constitutions, even those asserting dictatorial powers, then the Nuremburg Principles confer on them international civic character thus rendering them responsible for the above crimes.

The Unique 9th Amendment

The U.S. Constitution, in the 9th Amendment, uniquely and with total confidence in democracy – no doubt Tom Paine's influence - refers to rights "retained by the people" without in fact enumerating them. As inalienable rights are by definition anterior to government itself and incidentally the courts, the U.S. Supreme Court, by virtue of this amendment, has no jurisdiction over rights "retained by the people" and further, defined by them.

"The Constitution of the state and the nation recognize unenumerated rights of natural endowment."

Colorado Anti-Discrimination Comm. v. Case, 1902
380, p. 2d 34, 151 Colo. 230

The legal and historic implications of this amendment for the American people faced with international anarchy leading inevitably to a nuclear holocaust, are profound and awesomely challenging.

In a writ for certiorari submitted to the Supreme Court, October Term, 1981 by the author, the challenge was summed up as follows: *"By elementary reasoning, if the people are sovereign, as inferred in both the Ninth and Tenth amendments, then they are sovereign not as 'Americans' or national citizens but as humans. It follows that the world's people, i.e., humankind, as such represents the ultimate and largest sovereignty of which the 'American' people are a part. As the national public order derived from the sovereignty of the people residing within the national community, so it must follow that a world public order can and must derive from the world's people residing in the world community. Then any social order which excludes the recognition of humankind itself as the ultimate sovereignty denies at the same time the essential sovereignty of the people from which it itself derived. Thus a national constitution can neither deny, inhibit or in any way limit the sovereignty of humankind itself."*

(Note 30, Petition for Writ of Certiorari to the United States Court of Appeals, No. 81-427, October Term 1981, U.S. Supreme Court: Garry Davis v. District Director, Immigration and Naturalization Service.)

257

Natural Law vs. World Law

And so we arrive inevitably at natural law.*"Let it be stated again that the generation that gave us the Articles of Confederation and the Constitution believed solidly in the doctrine of natural rights. They understood that the purpose of government was to protect men in their basic, natural rights, and they were sure that they could hold their own state governments to this end."*
Modern Constitutional Law, Chester J. Antieau, Vol. IV, (1969) p. 676, The Lawyers Co-Operative Publishing Co.

Given the physical and social interdependency of the world community, like the silkworm in the cocoon developing into a butterfly through the process of metamorphosis, as single individuals we extend our innate and inalienable sovereignty throughout the natural world we inhabit thereby dynamically relating ourselves as humans to our world in toto.

This inexorable process follows, as exposed by the late Marshall McCluhan in "The Medium Is The Message", lines of technical communication which in turn enables social and then political intercourse.

Jurisprudence Breakthrough

Herein lies the crucial point and together with the recognition of humanity's sovereignty, inalienable human rights and the Nuremburg Principles represents a major breakthrough in jurisprudence. Protection by law against war become global means eliminating the war-making prerogative **of all states** just as they eliminated war-making between the communities they grouped. This historical process in turn involves the establishment of a sovereign world government responsive to democratic control.

The Cause of War

"Wars between groups of men forming social units," wrote Emery Reves in *Anatomy of Peace* in 1945, "always take place when these units—tribes, dynasties, churches, cities, nations—exercise unrestricted sovereign power. Wars between these social units cease the moment sovereign power is transferred from them to a larger or higher unit."

The precursor of the Nuclear Age tried to awaken us to the new shocking truth: the price of world peace was nationalism:

"As long as there are sovereign states possessing great power, war is inevitable. There is no salvation for civilization, or even the human race, other than the creation of a world government."
Albert Einstein, Letter to World Federalists, Stockholm Congress, 1949

Thus the new "international citizen," recognized implicitly by international law by virtue of the above-mentioned instruments , is, ipso facto—in the absence of international government—both empowered and compelled by the necessity of sheer survival to form such a government as the sovereign human person directly concerned.

Mryes McDougal, in *Human Rights and World Public Order*, (Yale University Press, 1980, p. 178), moreover minces no words as to the legitimacy of the individual in this historic task: *"The notion that states are the only appropriate 'subjects' of international law is belied by all the contemporary facts. . .about participation in the global processes of effective power and authoritative decision. This notion, unknown to the founding fathers and deriving from certain parochial misconceptions of the late nineteenth century, lingers on to impede the protection of human rights merely because it sometimes serves the power purposes of the state elites. . .Historically, the greatest difficulty concerning participation in the world constitutive process has been this exaggeration of the role of the nation-state as the principal subject of international law. Because of the overwhelming emphasis of the 'sovereignty' of nation-states, there has been a great reluctance to recognize other participants in world social process as in fact active subjects of international law."*

Responsible citizenship, therefore, under international law, is that citizenship which, in englobing human rights by transnational yet sovereign institutions, can ensure survival by outlawing war as a tool of "foreign policy" between states.

"Any method of maintaining international peace today must eventually fail if it is not grounded on Justice under Law and the protection of the individual under due process of law."

World Habeus Corpus, Luis Kutner, 1968, p. 73

If Humanity is to Survive, the Answers Must Be Affirmative

The answer therefore to the title question of whether the individual is a subject of international law must be answered in the affirmative if both the human race and the individual are to survive. For survival in the nuclear age enjoins the categorical imperative of a "world public order" or world government and government itself, we have seen, derives always from the sovereign people.

Tom Paine, the lightening rod of the three major revolutions of the 18th century, clarifies this overlooked yet revolutionary process: *"It has been thought a considerable advance towards establishing the principle of freedom to say that government is a compact between those who govern and those who are governed; but this cannot be true, because it is putting the effect before the cause; for as men must have existed before government existed, there once was a time when government did not exist, and consequently there could originally exist no gover-*

259

nors to form such a compact with. The fact therefore must be that the individuals themselves, each in his own personal and sovereign right, entered into a compact with each other to produce a government. . ."

On the other hand, if states alone are international law subjects, then humankind is doomed to extinction through a final test of "strength" via nuclear arms between equally sovereign states.

As positive law itself, however, reflects and follows natural law, as members, one and all, of the human "global village," born of a human womb, we arrive finally at the concept and actuality of a positive world citizenship transcending national citizenship as the sine qua non of world peace, human freedom and general as well as individual wellbeing and happiness.

CHAPTER 14

WORLD GOVERNMENT OR WORLD WAR?
by Garry Davis
EDUCATION FOR SURVIVAL
International Association of Educators for World Peace
Georgetown University
November 25, 1982

May I express my pleasure at having the opportunity of addressing this important conference.

Its theme, **Education for Survival**, bespeaks the total crisis facing our human race on planet earth. Total crisis calls for total solutions no matter how disagreeable these may appear for some. The time for theory about world peace is past. Bombs are ready to fall on our collective heads. Economic collapse is imminent. Millions starve daily, Pollution, including radio-active, encroaches on our very bio-system. Bold and global action is required.

I consider my purpose here then to address squarely our common crisis as well as to propose a workable solution already in operation.

In sum, I intend to advance four propositions:

1. The cause of war is a state of anarchy between exclusive sovereign social units.

2. The sovereignty of these social units depends in turn on the exclusive allegiance given them by single human beings possessing, whether they know it or not, inalienable rights to choose their own political identity.

3. As one sovereign human being, owing no allegiance to any nation-state, I claim, as now do many others, to be a citizen of a global government as legitimate, if not more so, than any and all nation-states.

4. The evolution of this global government is the **sine qua non** of world peace.

Specifically, given the totality of war between sovereign nation-states, I maintain that exclusive nationality, being the civic condition which perpetuates anarchy between nations, is not only immoral and irrational but illegitimate; and

261

secondly, both world citizenship and world government are not only practical realities but possess their own legitimacy and are the only method to achieve world peace.

To better illustrate the first point, in the nation-state world, no matter how you may regard each other personally or organizationally, every one in this room is designated an "alien" by billions of his or her fellow humans. That is, as exclusive nation citizens, every human outside your particular nation is labeled "alien" by your own nation. Furthermore, many of you are also labeled "enemy" by many millions more no matter what other contacts you have or what your religious beliefs are.

Now, like you, I have several labels. If you are a United States citizens, for instance, I am for you an "excludable alien." I am also "stateless." These labels are the result of Justice Department and judicial determinations in the civil courts.

If you are a citizen of another nation, I am simply an "alien." If, on the other hand, you are a refugee or a stateless person, I am a fellow human legally outside the civic paradigms of the nation-state as you.

But there is another legal label for those who are already declared world citizens and registered with our global government. For you, I am legally your fellow world citizen. More of this process later.

Now the nations to which most of you belong claim that war is legitimate and their sovereign right, each and every one. Though half-hearted attempts have been made by national delegates since the Kellogg-Briand Pact of 1928 to outlaw war, none have obviously been successful.

The first question we must then ask it, are delegates of nation-states capable of eliminating war between them? Another way of asking the same question: can sovereign nations in deadly competition with each other give up that one quality which justifies that sovereignty: the right to wage war or in its own euphemistic terms, "defend" itself?

Obviously, the essential condition for the elimination of war-making between equally sovereign units would be to deprive those units of that so-called legitimate right. And here is the Catch-22. The answer as to whether they can do it themselves is evidenced by the 128 wars since 1900 with today's superpowers deadlocked in a suicidal arms race.

Emery Reves in "Anatomy of Peace" wrote in 1945:

> *"The real cause of war has always been the same. They have occurred with a mathematical regularity of a natural law at clearly determined moments as a result of clearly definable conditions. 1. Wars between groups of men forming social units always take place when these units – tribes, dynasties, churches, cities, nations – exercise unrestricted sovereign power. 2. Wars between social units cease the moment sovereign power is transferred from them to a larger or higher unit. . . In other words, wars always cease*

when a higher unit establishes its own sovereignty, absorbing the
sovereignty of the conflicting smaller units."

Applying that formula to the nation-state system, an outside or higher sovereignty would be required in order to outlaw war between equally sovereign social and political units. In virtual confirmation of this largely unrealized fact, the Secretary-General of the United Nations, Dr. Perez de Cuellar claimed yesterday that though all U.N. members have signed the Charter, they "have conveniently forgotten that it binds them to settle their disputes through negotiation."

Reves, writing while the San Francisco Charter was being designed, reminds us that "Throughout the entire history of all known civilizations, only one method has ever succeeded in creating a social order within which men had security from murder, larceny, cheating and other crimes, and had freedom to think, to speak and to worship. That method is law.

"In short, peace among men and a civilized society – which
are one and the same thing – is imaginable only within a legal order
equipped with institutions to give effect to principles and norms in
the form of law, with adequate power to apply those laws and to
enforce them with equal vigor against all who violate them."

Now, thirty-eight years, 75 wars later and some 4 trillion dollars spent on armaments, we know the truth of that statement.

But if nations cannot eliminate war amongst them and it requires a higher authority, the question remains, from what source can this higher authority derive?

Here is the first mental and emotional barrier to overcome.

Does it involve you and me?

My friends, if world war involves you and me, then conversely world peace must involve you and me...and intimately.

And that is the bullet we must bite if we are serious about world peace. However, if I am to be involved in this process of establishing an outside or higher sovereignty, it is irrelevant that I call myself a monotheist or a human being, a father, a world educator for peace or even a peacemaker. Nor should I be concerned that you are or are not any or all of these or that you call yourself Christian, Jew, Moslem, Buddhist, Quaker, black or white, male or female, father or mother. Because what alone is relevant in this context is your and my legal participation in war-making or your and my legal participation in peace-making.

To arrive at this realization may not be easy for most of us because it means a reexamination of the loyalties which now bind us. We fear to lose them. Better the devil we know than the devil we don't. However, as I began, total crisis implies total solution. Nothing less will suffice than total commitment to world law.

The obfuscation surrounding the question of peace comes from all directions: moral, social, economic, biological, educational; still, when it is a question of the sheer survival of the species, the bottom of the line is the legal right either to wage war or to make peace.

If this is true, then, as I indicated, the problem of peace is neither moral, educational, social, biological or technical but legal. If you doubt this, let us examine its premise more closely.

Legally, we are living in a geocentric world of nation-states. We look upon economic, social and political problems as "national" problems. No matter in which country we live, the center of our political universe is our own nation. In our outlook, the immovable point around which all the other nations, all the problems and events outside our nation, the rest of the world, supposedly revolve, is – our nation. Unfortunately, our attachment to our particular nation is not only legal but pervasively emotional.

But when nations deal with other nations, the individual citizen is forgotten. The civic communication is cut between individual and head of state. He speaks for the "nation" itself not for individual citizens. You have no input to such decisions supposedly taken in your name.

Yet such is the duality of the nation that even though it claims to be the legitimate representative of its people, a closer examination will reveal that it has relinquished its legitimate right to wage war both by its own laws and by binding international common law.

I will give only three examples as proof though there are myriad more. Though the first declaration of illegitimacy of war-making and even war-preparing was the Kellogg-Briand Pact of 1928, it was the Nuremberg Decisions formulated in 1945 to try the Nazi leaders which actually defined an international penal code.

These principles explicitly state that "any person who commits an act which constitutes a crime under international law is responsible therefor and liable to punishment." (Principle I); secondly, that "crimes against peace, war crimes and crimes against humanity are punishable as crimes under international law." (Principle VI); and thirdly, that "complicity in the commission of these crimes is itself a crime under international law." (Principle VII).

As to the responsibility of the national citizen acting on orders from his government, Principle V states that "the fact that a person acted pursuant to orders from his Government or of a superior does not relieve him from responsibility under international law, provided a moral choice was in fact possible to him."

The United Nations General Assembly accepted the Nuremberg Principles in 1950 as part of international law. We have to conclude therefore – with the International Commission of Jurists – that "the Principles of Nuremberg are today fully accepted as a part of international law."

These Principles constitute the first international penal code which superceded national obligations.

But what are "crimes against peace?" They are defined as

"1. Planning, preparation, initiation or waging of a war of aggression or a war in violation of international treaties, agreements or assurances;

2. Participation in a common plan or conspiracy for the accomplishment of

264

any of the acts mentioned under (1).

But, you will ask, aren't these all acts of sovereign nations, especially violating international treaties, agreements and as surances? Isn't that the game of diplomacy totally outside popular control? Then how can the Nuremberg Principles hold the individual citizen responsible? Well, there is one citizen who possesses the legitimate right to speak of the state. That is the president or prime minister or secretary-general of the controlling party. And if the Nuremberg Principles applies only to state leaders, then with minor exceptions, all are war criminals for all are either "Planning, preparing, initiating, or waging a war of aggression" though such inhuman activities are always couched in the sacred name of "national defense."

Nonetheless, the Nuremberg Principles, in spite of no enforcement process, at least in princple, declare war outlawed.

The second proof of the illegitimacy of war, this time pertaining directly to the nation itself begins with the 1947 Showa Constitution of Japan, Chapter 11 entitled, "Renunciation of War."

Article 9 states, *"Aspiring sincerely to an international peace based on justice and order, the Japanese people forever renounce war as a sovereign right of the nation and the threat or use of force as a means of settling international disputes. In order to accomplish the aim of the preceding paragraph, land, sea and air forces, as well as other war potential, will never be maintained.* **The right of belligerency of the state will not be recognized."**

The extraordinary and precedent-shattering implications of Article 9 is that the concept of state sovereignty no longer has any validity.

After a trial of 30 months beginning on May 3, 1946 in Tokyo, the International Military Tribunal for the Far East gave down the "Tokyo Judgment." It pronounced sentence on 25 accused war criminals. Part of the Judgment dealt with the alleged right of self-defense of a nation. It stated: *"The right of self-defense involves the right of the State threatened with impending attack to judge for itself in the first instance whether it is justified in resorting to force. Under the most liberal interpretations of the Kellogg-Briand Pact, the right of self-defense does not confer upon the State resorting to war the authority to make a final determination upon the justification for its actions."*

The implications of this judgment have largely been ignored by both the succeeding national leaders and the general public. It confirmed and universalized the concept of Article 9 in two ways. First, it introduced into the concept of command responsibility an arbitrary element of chance which effectively denied the state the right to impose such a risk on any individual. Second, by a radical interpretation of the Kellogg-Briand Pact of 1928 which condemned "recourse to war for the solution of international controversies. . ." and renounced it "as an instrument of national policy. . .", the judgment removes the sovereign right of self-defense.

The renunciation of the right of belligerency contained within A-9 was therefore given international legal standing by the Tokyo Judgment.

My last example of the illegitimacy of war-making by nations is contained in the *Universal Declaration of Human Rights*. Certain nations argue that the Declaration is not law. Yet eighteen nations today have incorporated it into their own constitutions. Many more refer to it in the Preamble. But the crucial fact about human rights is not their universality but their legitimacy. Consider firstly that war-making is a function of sovereignty. Yet all national constitutions without exception claim to derive from the sovereign people. In other words, the exercise of fundamental human rights in the first place gave rise to all national constitutions. It follows that the legitimacy of human rights themselves is categorical.

Then by elementary reasoning, if the people are sovereign and innately legitimate, as stated in all constitutions and reaffirmed in such documents as the U.S. Bill of Rights, particularly in the 9th and 10th amendments, then we are sovereign and legitimate not as "Americans," "Indian," "Soviets," "French," or "Nigerians," but as humans.

It follows that the world's people, that is, humankind as such, is the ultimate and largest sovereignty on planet earth.

This humankind, of which each of us is a dynamic part, is innately and inalienably legitimate and in contra-distinction to that of the so-called sovereign state. Otherwise, human rights themselves are not legitimate.

The United Nations Charter, in Article 56, obliges each Member-State to "observe and respect fundamental human rights" as a very condition for its membership. In so conforming, it negates its own sovereign character.

The *Universal Declaration of Human Rights* is explicit concerning our sovereign rights. Article 1 states that

> *"Everyone is born free and equal in dignity and rights. They are endowed with reason and conscience and should act towards one another in a spirit of brotherhood."*

For the protection of our fundamental rights, Article 28 states that

> *"Everyone is entitled to a social and international order in which the rights and freedoms set forth in this declaration can be fully realized."*

We have at last arrived at the genesis of world government by first exposing that exclusive sovereignty is no longer legitimate and secondly that human sovereignty in terms of fundamental human rights is legitimate.

Thomas Paine has some illuminating thoughts on how government begins:

> *"It has been thought a considerable advance towards establishing the principle of freedom to say that government is a compact between those who govern and those who are governed; but this cannot be true, because it is putting the effect before the cause; for as men must have existed before governments existed, there once*

was a time when government did not exist, and consequently there could originally exist no governors to form such a compact with. The fact therefore must be that the individuals themselves, each in his own personal and sovereign right, entered into a compact with each other to produce a government."

This "entering into a compact" is the social actualization of our innate and inalienable legitimacy.

Therefore, world peace, as a result of a new global compact with fellow humans which legitimizes each partner in the partnership — a veritable horizontal network of sovereign individuals — and in turn the aggregate the "citizenry" or "people" which creates the new institution of government, no longer appears idealistic or utopian but eminently realisable in the here and now since it depends essentially on the sovereign will and **discretionary** decision of each individual concerned.

To conclude, for world government to come into being, humans must first identify themselves legally **beyond** the national paradigms. This is no feat since simply to recognize oneself as human is already to transcend the nation-state. But human law is evidently not exclusive national law. Therefore, each individual must identify himself or herself as a world citizen. **This then becomes the first social communication or compact essential to the evolution of world government.** But I must warn you, while to sign this Pledge of Allegiance to World Government is a perfectly legal act and the exercise of your inalienable right, it is also a revolutionary act. For it means that you are declaring your own sovereignty as against that of the state. You are taking your destiny into your own hands and declaring your worldly independence and freedom. You are crossing the razor's edge from the theory of world peace to its reality in microcosm.

E. B. White has written:

"World government is an appalling prospect. Many people have not comprehended it or distinguished it from world organization. Many others, who have comprehended it, find it preposterous or unattainable in a turbulent and illiterate world where nations and economics conflict daily in many ways. Certainly the world is not ready for government on a planetary scale. In our opinion, it will never be ready. The test is whether the people will chance it anyway like children who hear the familiar cry, 'Coming, ready or not!' "

Educators for world peace, I enjoin you to educate by your world peace-making action. . . .ready or not.

CHAPTER 15

BUT ARE THEY PEACE ORGANIZATIONS?

The 1983 *Yearbook of International Organizations* (Brussels) lists over 1,000 organizations supposedly devoted to the establishment of world peace.

The *World Government of World Citizens*, however, is not listed. The directors of the yearbook rejected it on the basis that it was not a "non-governmental organization" but "governmental" therefore inadmissible. Being "for" world peace is OK for listing; claiming world peace is not. No organization actually "representing" world peace could be listed in a directory "for" world peace. For such an organization would necessarily be sovereign, i.e., **be** the solution, not be seeking it in the future. So long as there is no world peace, there will be "peace organizations."

Being honest and being "for" honesty is, in philosophical terms, the difference between ontological and teleological reasoning. "Ontological" simply means, "pertaining to the science or doctrine of being" whereas "teleological" pertains to the "science or doctrine treating of the end or design for which things were created." Jesus Christ, for example, enjoined his followers to "Be perfect as Your Father in heaven is perfect." This is ontological. His priests, however, say, "You can't be perfect since you are already sinners. So you have to be 'saved' through God's grace." The emphasis here is on the end result always sometime "up ahead" in never-never land. Teleological.

Organizations "for" world peace are teleological. (The only ontological "organization" where world peace would be the result is a world government.) They would, of course, be out of business if world peace ever arrived. The War Resisters International, for instance, would cease to exist when wars ceased. To justify WRI's existence, war is therefore necessary in order for it to be resisted. Consequently, the WRI has no program for the elimination of war itself. It does not promote world law or world citizenship. It does not promote world government. Moreover, many members of the WRI who are, for the most part, Christian pacifists, confess, in political terms, to an anarchist position. The same per-

268

tains for most Christian pacifist organizations such as the Fellowship of Reconciliation, a highly respected organization "for" world peace.

On my desk is a petition of the FOR addressed "To the President of the United States and Members of Congress. . . . To Save Our Endangered Human Species," which I am asked to sign. With all due respect, if putting your name on a petition would save the human species, I question that it is in any great danger. An enemy threatened into submission by pieces of paper covered with signatures of totally uncommited individuals is a paper tiger indeed.

The truly commited, let's face it, do not sign petitions. They "sign" their minds, their hearts, their fortunes, their blood. Petitions are at best, public opinion polls; at worst, a sop to idealism by the timid, and yes, the ignorant. In 1938, the British public presented a petition for "peace" of over one million signatures to its government. Hitler was only convinced the British wouldn't oppose his march into Czechoslovakia. A petition not only will not remove the danger, but will confuse the public both as to its cause and therefore its solution. It's a portent of impotence.

The FOR petition claims that "It is time to defend ourselves against militarism and against war and poverty, and their dehumanizing effects upon ourselves and the rest of the world." So far, so good. Then, "The cost of weapons, other military equipment and military training is the largest item in the United States Federal tax budget." And further, the US government "has used our taxes to accumulate a stockpile of nuclear weapons with a minimum firepower of 580,000 Hiroshima bombs—enough to destroy every major city in the world."

The facts are indisputable and always horrifying. We are properly afraid, angered and rebellious.

Having stated its desire to save the human race and having pointed out the alleged causes of its possible demise, the FOR makes its pitch: "Therefore we call upon our government to begin to disarm at once without waiting for other nations, and to announce its disarmament intention to the world, and to publish a disarmament schedule in which other countries are challenged to join. We further call upon our government to lead a national effort to change our present war economy to a peace economy so that disarmament can occur within the framework of peaceful changeover, increased employment, economic stability, and so that we can look forward to a richer future based on the satisfaction of human needs, the protection of fundamental human rights, the growth of human values, and the preservation of the Earth itself."

My first observation is that the writer speaks only as a national citizen. What happened to his (or her) Christianity? What happened to his/her human status? If it is the world to be saved, mustn't those who want to save it first recognize it? And then speak for it? Represent it? As world citizens first? How can you save the world as only a national citizen? And where is the historical insight even *as an American*? Thomas Jefferson didn't try to "save" his fellow Virginians by only addressing himself to Virgina's House of Burgesses, nor did Ben Franklin cajole the Pennsylvania legislature to disarm its militia unilaterally on the frontier facing New Jersey.

Their appeal was to the whole endangered population of disunited America which included their fellow Virginians and Pennsylvanians.

And it was a political appeal.

The political ignorance as to the cause of conflict between sovereign nations is shockingly evident here. As Emery Reves pointed out, "Equally sovereign entities, expanding into the same territory, either unite of fight."

In brief, sovereign entities can only disarm *if* government is established **over them** outlawing war itself between them, thereby removing the basic *cause* of conflict.

Every benefit mentioned in the FOR petition could occur *only after* general and universal disarmament, i.e., after the establishment of a world government.

I have no doubt the writers of this petition sincerely desire to eliminate war and poverty. They simply don't know how to do either.

"Prayers will not make a mango fall."

Such well-intentioned initiatives—which are the standard for many so-called peace organizations—are in reality worse than doing nothing since an illusion is created of "doing something for peace," a pretension to commitment—"I signed a peace petition today so I can sleep well tonight"—an appeal to pseudo-idealism dissipating energy and spreading confusion.

On my desk are the brochures of the *Freeze Movement, Women Strike for Peace, The World Peace Through Law Center, World Jurist, The Task Force Against Nuclear Pollution, SANE, World Action, Clergy and Laity concerned, The Friend's Committee on National Legislation, The National Committee for the Peace Ballot, The World Constitutional Convention and People's World Parliament Association, Peacemakers, Planetary Citizens, The World Citizen's Assembly, The World Federalists, The Planetary Initiative, The Campaign for World Government,* and innumerable others.

Not one accepts *a priori* the fact of world law. Not one confronts and challenges exclusive national citizenship with an inclusive world citizenship. Not one invokes its readers to add world citizenship and its corollary, world government, NOW to their already existent civic duties and rights. They are all teleological in conception and program.

The political equivalent of "Be perfect. . ." is "Be a world citizen directly allied with a world government!"

Yet all the good-willed members of these organizations would swear up and down they are "for peace."

Therefore, they will never achieve it.

A conference entitled "International Conference on Peace and Human Rights" took place August 25-26, 1979 at Campobello Island , New Brunswick, sponsored by the Los Angeles industrialist/philanthropist Armand Hammer. Representatives from 21 countries gathered, including two former Nobel Peace Laureates, Lord Phillip Noel-Baker and Sean MacBride.

In a keynote speech during the second day of the conference, Senator Jennings Randolph (D-W.Va.) told the delegates bluntly that "Those who seek universal peace and human rights hold in their hands the hope of the world (and) the fate of civilization."

Then Dr. Louis P. Bloomfield, chief of "global issues" in the National Security Council, accepted a gold medal (for peace) for then president Jimmy Carter. In a message, Carter thanked the delegates in accepting "this honor not as a personal tribute, but as an affirmation of our effort to support the brave and decent people everywhere who struggle for human dignity, often against daunting odds."

President Carter was debating at the time whether to raise the military budget to $125 billion instead of $115 billion. (He requested $142 billion in 1980).

A motion to recognize the right of individuals to refuse military service if that service is construed to be a threat to peace was roundly defeated. A proposal that individuals be affirmed the right to join with others, irrespective of frontiers, nationalities and zones of conflict, to oppose military preparation "beyond strict requirements of defense" was omitted from the conference's official communique issued August 26, 1979 as "too controversial."

While Lord Noel-Baker decried the fact that expenditures on armaments had tripled during the past 20 years and that $445 billion was spent on armaments in the world in 1978, he did not propose a world government, nor world law, nor world citizenship nor did he affirm his own collusion in the armament process as an exclusive British citizen.

The conferees plaintively called for "the establishment of effective procedures and machinery to deal with violations of man's right to peace." These "leaders," many paid by their respective governments each month, did not state, however, that "effective procedures and machinery" for peace is simply government itself. And when so-called peace leaders "call for" global remedies, just whom are they calling to? Other national politicians? U.N. delegates? Religious leaders? Multinational corporation presidents? The man in the moon? Or maybe, just maybe, you and me? Certainly they exclude themselves from the process since they continually ask others to do the job.

The final communique of the Campobello conference was a classical parody of a craven cop-out totally and shamefully vitiating the original theme: "We *propose* (to others) that all agreements *aimed at* disarmament or arms limitations (especially the 2nd SALT talks) *should be* followed by a *declaration of intent* committing *participating countries* to *promote* education for peace and disarmament *with a view to* the implementation of the right to peace as a basic human right." Count 'em: seven caveats *before they get to the purpose of their conference: peace as a basic human right.*

"Peace is a basic human right" would have been sufficient.

Note no mention of world law, world citizenship or world government.

Dr. Hammer called his conference a "great step forward" in the "quest for peace and human rights" but cautioned obliquely that SALT II "must be ratified" by the U.S. Congress "to make recent disarmament proposals become a reality."

At the risk of appearing disrespectful, in the name of an already sceptical yet eternally hopeful public, I condemn such blatant nonsense as base treason to reason and morality.

A "successful" peace conference would be one where all the participants personally pledged their immediate and prime allegiance to World Government.

Emery Reves minced no words about what came first in the search for world peace:

> *"The San Francisco League [United Nations] is not a first step toward a universal order. To change from a treaty basis to law is one step, one operation, and it is impossible to break it into parts or fractions. The decision has to be made and the operation carried out at one time. There is no first step toward world government. World Government is the first step."*
>
> *Anatomy of Peace*, 1945, p. 87

While peace-making is obviously a political process, "peace" organizations, at least in the United States, dilute or vitiate their effectiveness, indeed their very purpose, by acquiring a tax-exempt status from the Internal Revenue Service permitting a tax write-off for contributions. Such an exemption, however, places them outside the area of effective political action since they must convince the IRS of their strictly educational nature as well as their non-profit operation. The irony of seeking from the very national powers you wish to deprive of sovereignty to wage war the privilege of collecting money for "educational purposes" so that "revolution" can take place, indicates an abysmal lack of commitment and betrayal of the very qualities required to lead such a revolution. "Cast your whole vote," wrote Thoreau in 1780.

> *"It is a mysterious characteristic of human nature," wrote Emery Reves in Anatomy of Peace, "That we are prepared to spend anything, to sacrifice anything, to give up all we have and are when we wage war and that we are never prepared to take more than an 'initial step,' more than a 'first beginning,' and adopt more than 'minimum measures' when we seek to organize peace. When will our religions, our poets and our national leaders give up the lie that death is more heroic than life?"*

Our world house is on fire and our leading thinkers are either proposing an educational campaign on why fire burns or pleading with the arsonists to mend their ways!

To criticize the Nuclear Freeze Movement is to risk at the least a verbal lynching. The well-known personalities and organizations "for" a nuclear freeze reads like the Who's Who of liberal America: Joan Baez, Hans Bethe, Helen Caldicott, Harvey Cox, Bishop James Crumley, Richard Falk, Bernard Feld, Friends of the Earth, Roger Fisher, Theodore Hesburgh, George Kistiakowsky, Mario Cuomo, the National Assembly of Women Religious, the National Association of Social Workers, the National Conference of Black Mayors, the National Council of Churches, Linus Pauling, Archbishop John R. Quinn, Rabbi Alexander Schindler, Union of American Hebrew Congregations, Victor Weisskoph, the YWCA of USA and tens of thousands, if not millions of others, not to mention the dozens of Senators and Congresspersons who have voted for it.

Both Randall Forsberg, who drafted the original paper, "The Call to Halt the Nuclear Arms Race," and Randall Kehler, the National Coordinator vs. the Freeze Movement have admitted to me that they are "for" world government "eventually." "But we have to do something now to prevent nuclear war," they told me. "World government is an ultimate solution and who knows how many years off? We are six minutes away from target and cannot wait for a world government to begin functioning. Nuclear war must be prevented NOW." So goes the argument.

Before exposing the irrationality of this argument, note two major points. The first is that war itself is not to be eliminated by the freeze movement, just nuclear war. Conventional war is apparently OK. In other words, nuclear freezers admit implicitly they have no answer for the elimination of war as such. The second is that "freeze" connotes paralysis brought about by a condition of unreasoned fear. Thus, the Freeze Movement represents an emotional response to a latter-day *political* impasse: an anarchic condition between roughly 160 equally sovereign nations in a totally interdependent world. Both points indicate a total disregard (or ignorance) of the conditions which alone result in peace.

This disregard is nakedly exposed in the issue of verification. Who or what would verify a "bilateral freeze" between the USA and the Soviet Union? (Never mind France, Great Britain, China, Israel, South Africa, Pakistan, Libya etc., etc. who already or some day will possess nuclear bombs.)

The Nuclear Freeze advocates don't say. Here the political naivete shows. They simply don't know. There's nobody "out there" beyond the nations. Only potential war, some multinationals interested only in short-term profit, and satellites whirling around and around photographing everything.

And it is those satellites that subconsciously substitute for a world government created by world citizens; but nuclear freeze advocates won't even admit that. Why? Because they still think "nation-centrically" and not globally. Or wholistically. Or ontologically. It is "We, the Americans" and "They, the Soviets."

Randall Kehler writes in the Freeze Newsletter of January, 1983:

"It (our overall national strategy) is to bring enough citizen pressure to bear upon our elected representatives in Washington in Congress and the Administration—to force our government to do everything in its power to bring about an immediate, mutual, and *verifiable* Freeze on the nuclear arms race." (Emphasis added.)

Nuclear "war," however, is no longer war but total holocaust. There is no "we" or "they" for nuclear power, Reagan & Chernenko to the contrary notwithstanding. Neither "Americans" nor "Soviets" will die in a nuclear holocaust. The human race will perish. The crisis is total. ABSOLUTE. The solution to it must be consistent. NOTHING LESS WILL RESOLVE IT. Good-will and good intentions allied with fear alone are a deadly combination. A dynamic political linkage with humanity itself then—which is anyway a given, morally, socially and biologically —is an outgoing, rational *act* which at once exposes the relativistic nature of both the United States and the Soviet Union caught in a mutual and suicidal dilemma.

"Nuclear Freeze," let's face it squarely, is a chimera. It can't "work" because it's a mass hysteria movement of terrified if well-meaning people who haven't done their political homework or are afraid to face the truth of their own global sovereignty.

Besides, it's historically and shamefully "un-American." The Founding Fathers did not "freeze" the state militias on the frontiers in mortal terror of each other. They recognized that a *political* problem required a political solution and, despite the tremendous odds, crafted a new and higher civic order to replace the anarchy which threatened to destroy them.

World Peacemakers, a highly respected if numerically small organization headquartered in Washington, D.C., is presided over by Richard Barnet, founder and fellow of the Institute of Policy Studies, a former official in the U.S. State Department, the Arms Control and Disarmament Agency and a consultant to the Department of Defense. He served in the United States Army as a specialist in international law.

Mr. Barnet's credentials, it would seem, would eminently qualify him to speak with authority on the why and how of world peace. Let us see.

In *World Peacemaker's* "World Peace Paper No. 1," we are not disappointed by Mr. Barnet, its author, as to whether we are safe and sound behind our separate nation's frontiers:

> *"Statesmen, politicians, economists, indeed most anyone who thinks about public policy, realizes the nation-state cannot solve the fundamental political and economic problems facing humanity. No matter how many missiles a great nation amasses, it cannot defend its people. The Pentagon cannot defend the people of the United States if, despite the near certainty of its own destruction, the Soviet Union should decide to attack. The Soviet Union cannot defend its vast territory either. . . ."*

Unlike the FOR, the Campobello Island "peace" delegates and the "Nuclear Freeze" advocates, Barnet has at least fingered the enemy: the nation-state. And why is the nation-state, so full of promise in the 19th century, and still maintaining a stranglehold on the minds and hearts of millions of humans, no longer to be considered the political object of our highest allegiance?

"The reality of interconnectedness," continues Barnet, "is forcing us to think beyond the religion of nationalism and to work toward political structures that are obedient to the biblical injunction that humanity is one."

In considering nationalism a creed, Barnet scores the entire diplomatic scene as mythical and an illusion. This thought joins our own in acknowledging the reality of common world laws. Barnet, however, does not cross the "razor's edge" between theory and practice as his teleological phrase "to work toward" indicates. In other words, neither *he* nor *World Peacemakers* is going to *create* "political structures" based on humanity's oneness now, leaving that task to a vague future and unnamed individuals. In spite of his own timidity, however, he is firm indeed about their need:

"The end of colonialism, the new awareness that vital resources of the globe are limited, and the realization that the political and economic problems of the United States (and every other country) cannot be solved except in the context of global solutions, are transforming the dream of world community into a political imperative."

Then follows a brilliant analysis of the idiocy of the arms race "which now threatens to destory the possibility of world community. Indeed, it threatens all life on this planet."

Mr. Barnet thus presents us with a total crisis situation, the classical opener of literally all so-called peace organization's literature. Convince the reader of impending Armageddon at the outset and the "peace" plan follows, selling itself. In brief, lay on the fear and guilt, and "confession" in the form of a $25 check will inevitably result. Well, 2% of the mailing anyway.

But what's this? To meet the ultimate, i.e., world crisis, Barnet claims that

"Until there is a national movement dedicated to looking behind the myths of national security, of which most Americans are unwitting prisoners, there will be no end to the escalation of the arms race."

That's it. Total regression. After citing humanity's total crisis, Barnet himself exposes his own captivity to the "religion of nationalism" he condemned earlier. He does not consider himself yet a world citizen. His orientation is to work not even through the nation-state system as such but only his own nation. *World Peacemakers* "presents the urgent need and possibilities for the United States to take bold action to stop the arms race..."

The real enemy is not the nation-state system itself but our ignorance as to what causes war and our blind allegiance to it.

To Dr. Barnet, and all those sincere, well-intentioned "peace-makers" who still think "nation-centrically," I recommend the striking words of world patriot Thomas Paine, who mid-wifed the birth of the United States 200 years ago.

> *"Every age and generation must be free to act for itself in all cases as the ages and generations which preceded it. The vanity and presumption of governing beyond the grave is the most ridiculous and insulting of tyrannies. . . The circumstances of the world are continually changing and the opinions of men also change. And as government is for the living and not the dead, it is the living only that has any right in it. That which may be thought right and found convenient in one age may be thought wrong and found inconvenient in another. . ."*

What is the blind spot which permits righteous and good-willed men and women to cry for world peace and reject world law?

Is not war fought by nations. . .against each other? Then how can "national viewpoints" not only intrude but continue to dominate such conferences, such movements, such "peace" organizations?

So long as the nationalistic "we-and-they" syndrome prevails in organizations for peace, there will be no peace. Contrarily, there will be wars and rumours of wars.

WHO OWNS THE WORLD?
©1983

by

Garry Davis

"The fact is that now — for the first time in the history of man for the last ten years, all the political theories and all the concepts of political functions — in any other than secondary roles as housekeeping organizations — are completely obsolete. All of them were developed on the you-or-me basis. This whole realization that mankind can and may be comprehensively successful is startling.

Buckminster Fuller, *Utopia or Oblivion*

CHAPTER 16

WHO OWNS THE WORLD?

In recognizing the human race as a viable species, a drastic revision in economic thinking is imposed. Referring to humankind as a fact deserving immediate attention, as do myriad organizations from the United Nations through UNESCO to religious, social, labor, and educational, implies global or total thinking to cure economic as well as other ills.

Nataraja Guru, in a remarkable essay on economics[1], wrote, "There is no textbook on world economics, though economics as a science — if it is really a science — should necessarily be most directly concerned with the happiness of humanity as a whole. Instead, economists visualize a world consisting of differently-colored Hitlerish patches of territories from within which each man is thinking hard economically so as to defeat his neighbor."

This conception of wholesale human welfare is even more explicitly spelled out by Buckminster Fuller when he writes:

"It is scientifically clear that we have the ability to make all of humanity physically successful. Industrialization itself relates to the resources of the entire earth, the entire universe. The industrial system is a comprehensive system and if reversingly fractionated will fail." [2]

Historical Analysis

The religious world view of former centuries endowed governments of the Western world and the political state system as it exists today with a quasi-divine character. The principle of "supreme authority," monopolized by the church and the monarchical system, was refashioned by the 18th and 19th century revolutions to serve as the moral basis of nation-state sovereignty.

World War I effectively eliminated the last remnants of the monarchical state which embodied the notion of divinity through the king and queen. What remained and remains is the "sovereign" state, each one a surrogate "world-state" of "absolute" power over the particular parcel of the plantary soil, wherein political democracy briefly flowered in exclusive nations only to flounder as the new "modern" institutions slowly bankrupt themselves in inter-national wars.

Fuller writes that "The world's people and their politicians think erroneously in terms of sovereign states with colonial empires... Today's world people think naively that politicans have always run things. They never have and they never will. Politicians were only the pirates' visible stooges."[3]

278

The colonial empires, he claims, where never the product of the ambitions of the people of any nation. The British Empire was built on the greed of the great pirate's admirals and captains. It was the stock market crash of 1929 which eliminated the pirate's power, due principally to the breaking away of science from economic monopoly and mechanism which developed far beyond the financial capabilities of the old pirates to cope with. "Only nations and groups of nations could now cope with the magnitude of capital undertaking."[4]

Accelerated means of communication coupled with crisis survival conditions triggered by the '29 crash, precipitating ten years later World War II, leads Fuller to conclude that "...because of the dawning awareness that the weaponry phase and its quarter-century lag can be eliminated, the second half of the tool-invention revolution is to be identified as the consciously undertaken continuance of the accelerated doing-more-with-less *by world society as world society.* (Emphasis added.)[5]

Nation-State System An Anachronism

Thus it seems fairly obvious that a major if not the major problem in translating the *theory* of the human species as an economic reality into realisable fact is the necessity to reject *a priori* the notion of the absolute exclusive sovereignty, i.e., supreme authority, of the nation-state and its now anachronistic and suicidal system.

Economic analysts from hard-line socialists to monopolist capitalists and all grades in between operating from *within* the nationalistic framework stop far short of the obvious and vital relationship between global politics and global economics. While analyzing today's deteriorating economic situation as "crisis-ridden," with its soaring inflation, exorbitant interest rates, stagnating industrial productivity, ballooning national deficits[6], wobbling and absurd "floating exchange rates," rising unemployment, shortages of critical materials and parts, exponential increase in bankruptcies in both business and nations themselves[7], and monstrous, futile and suicidal armament budgets in the midst of agonizing human misery and need, they myoptically reject a world *political* government as "impractical," "utopian," or simply "irrelevant."

The World Revolution

During the first half of the century, little awareness percolated through either the public or official consciousness of "the greatest revolution in history:"

> "It is not surprising that man, burdened with obsolete 'knowledge' – his spontaneous reflexing conditioned only by past experience, and as yet unable to realize himself as already a world man – fails to comprehend and cope logically with the birth of Universe Man."[8]

Yet the dynamic relationship between economic failure and political failure is becoming highly visible even to those who still hold political power. National candidates for political office must address themselves, albeit somewhat mystically, to global economic problems speaking grandly and inconsistently of an "interdependent world economic order." Their very political framework, however, precludes realistic legislation capable of regulating such an "order" which could not exist in the first place without such legislative apparatus.

"National governments are inadequate when it comes to dealing with the planet's necessities, and we may legitimately wonder whether the importance of nation-states isn't greatly exaggerated and whether politicians deserve star status." [9]

"Established" economists, pretending to be experts in the dismal science, with rare exceptions, are beyond redemption, holding fast to antiquated and obtuse, even whimsical ideas, partial, grounded in scarcity, and basically unmindful of either political or moral realities. [10]

Yet, while hopelessly divided as to solutions, most economists are by now agreed, if only by sheer necessity, that world recession has reached a crisis stage where draconian and wholesale measures are necessary if total collapse is to be averted.

No less an expert than Lenin spelled out the consequences of unbridled inflation's consequences to citizens: [11]

"By a continuous process of inflation, governments can confiscate, secretly and unobserved, an important part of the wealth of their citizens. And as the inflation proceeds and the real value of the currency fluctuates wildly from month to month, all permanent relations between debtors and creditors, which form the ultimate foundation of capitalism, become so utterly disorganized as to be almost meaningless."

National "Security" vs Global Affluence

As national economics are increasingly linked with "national security" and yet the inevitable outcome of a total arms race between them is war, let us start from the opposite polarity: general and total disarmament strictly for an economic viewpoint.

"World military expenditures since 1960 reached the $3 trillion mark ($3,000,000,000,000) in 1975." [12] Then from 1975 to 1981, one-third the period, world military spending rose another $3 trillion. "National security" today costs the citizens of all states between 8 and 9% of the world's gross national product. Five nations, however, contribute 75% of the monstrous sum for sheer destruction: the U.S.A., the USSR, Great Britain, France and West Germany, the first two making up 60%.

The relationship between total disarmament and raised standards of living was indisputably established by a 1962 report [13] entitled "The Economic and Social Consequence of Disarmament," prepared by 25 leading economists from both socialist and free enterprise countries and commissioned by the Economic and Social Council of the United Nations.

"The present level of military expenditures not only represents a grave political danger but also imposes a heavy economic and social burden on most countries. It absorbes a large volume of human and material resources of all kinds which could be used to increase economic and social welfare throughout the world – both in the industrialized countries which at the present time incur the bulk of the world's military expenditures and in the less developed areas."
(Introduction, Part I, p. 14)

The unanimous agreement "that the diversion to peaceful purposes of resources not absorbed by military expenditures can and should be of benefit to all countries and lead to improvements in the social and economic conditions for all mankind" led former U.N. Secretary-General U Thant, in transmitting the study to Member-States for comment, to state that "The most fundamental way in which disarmament affects economic life is through the liberation of the resources devoted to military use and their re-employment for peaceful purposes."

In that year, roughly $120 billion spent on armaments was at least two-thirds of the entire national income of all the developing countries, close to the value of the world's annual exports of all commodities, and corresponded to about one-half of the total resources set aside each year for gross capital formation throughout the world.

However, no decrease in military spending is envisaged by the Super-Powers themselves in the foreseeable future despite the common recognition of former as well as present leaders of both the U.S.A. and the Soviet Union of the absolute necessity for total disarmament if the human race is to survive.[14]

In its response to the 1962 Report, the U.S. delegation noted:

"The motivating force behind the efforts of the United States to achieve general and complete disarmament is to save present and future generations from the scourge of war, and to attain for them more certain and beneficent security. This basis and vital objective completely overshadows any economic calculations of gain or loss connected with disarmament." [15]

The Soviet delegation, in perfect geo-dialectical harmony, echoed:

"The Soviet Union has resolutely and consistently championed the cause of disarmament. In our time, military technology has made collosal progress. States have stockpiled, and still are stockpiling, such vast quantities of nuclear and thermonuclear weapons, together with the means of delivering them to any point on the earth's surface, that this abnormal situation, if allowed to continue, will in itself constitute a mortal danger to peace and to the survival of entire countries and peoples... The world, therefore, is faced with a choice between two alternatives – either a monstrous thermo-nuclear war or disarmament." [16]

We have the right to conclude that both the United States and the Soviet union are *unilaterally* opposed to the arms race, both politically and economically. Further, neither sees any major problem in converting from a war to a peacetime economy.[17]

The Multinationals

The economic clout generated by the "multis" is too well-documented to bear repeating here. Suffice it to say that the annual sales volume of General Motors alone — around $65 billion in 1982 — was greater than the gross national product of 130 developing states. In terms of the 100 world's largest economic units of 1980, GM rates 23rd. Thirty-nine of the hundred were multinational corporations![18]

Operating in many countries with diverse currencies, and subject to floating exchange rates, multinational corporate management can and does manipulate resources, accounting, revenue and even government — as the recent ITT-Chilean episode revealed — and for one purpose alone: to maximize short-term profit.

In its present "dinosaurean" state of development, the corporate "state" represents the most deadly and widespread exploitive tool ever devised, not only to protect the wealth of the few but to circumvent government control which has proven too narrow a base for modern technology.

National legislators, such as U.S. Senator Gary Hart (D. Colo.) have asked the obvious questions: Has concentrated economic power now extended its reach so far that no government can control it? And more to the point, does the scale of world trade necessitate giant conglomerates which their home government cannot afford to defy? The late Emmanuel Celler, U.S. congressional representative, in consideration of ITT's "extraordinary jumble" of companies, questioned "whether the good Lord has given anybody the prowess and the expertise, the ingenuity, to be able to control all these operations..." And Senator Estes Kefauver, as far back as the forties, in introducing the Celler-Kefauver Act to strengthen a controversial section of the Clayton Act, stated bluntly, "The people are losing the power to direct their own economic welfare."

Ralph Nader, along with consumer movements in other countries, attempts to instill in the popular consciousness that we, as consumers, are also part of the fundamental economic equation *and* the most important part. In his introduction to "America, Inc." by Morton Mintz he writes of the "sovereignty of the consumer" as the ulimate countervailing force to concentration of corporate power.

> *"Irresponsibility toward public interests becomes institutionalized whenever the making of decisions is so estranged from any accountability for their discernible consequences... The modern corporation is the engine of the world's largest production machine. If it is to be more than a mindless, parochial juggernaut, the hands of diverse values and trusteeships for future generations must be exerted on the steering wheel. There should no longer be victims without representation. In any just legal sys-*

tem a victim would have the right to decide with others the be-havior of the perpetrator and his recompense."[19]

Nader claims that the "corporate involvement pervades every interstice of our society. Companies are deep in the dossier-credit, city, building, drug, medical, computer intelligence, military and education, health and military-theater contracting... and with these engagements come the parochial value system and insulation of the corporate structure."[20]

A United Nations' report of August 12, 1973, stated that "The questions at issue is whether a set of institutions and devices can be worked out which will guide the multinational corporations' exercise of power and introduce some form of accountability to the international community into their activities." The report, while acknowleging that MNCs "are depicted in some quarters as key instruments for maximizing world welfare..." yet are seen in other quarters "as dangerous agents of imperialism," inadvertently admits the UN's own impotence as a global authority able to control the MNCs by concluding that "...Unlike national companies, they were not subject to control and regulations by a single authority which can aim at ensnaring a maximum degree of harmony between their operations and the public interest."

We may conclude with Anthony Sampson that "...The sovereignty of the multinational corporation has emerged...in its independence of government, in its self-contained organization and trade, in its private diplomacy and communications, in its avoidance of taxes, and in the security of the company record."[21]

Who Owns Them?

The underlying and largely ignored question concerning corporate accountability is: Who owns the corporations? In other words, where do the profits go?

Despite all the nonsense about people's capitalism and the millions of orphans, widows and wounded war veterans living off a share of America's capitalist pie, corporate profits go only to the stockholders and America's stockholders are mostly upper middle-class to rich. About 5.2% of America's adult population owns 66% of the privately-held shares of the nation's corporations.[22] The owner percentages in other countries are far less.

The Individual vs. the Multinational

How then can the multinationals be brought to accountability? Further, how can the "sovereign" consumer benefit from the phenomenon of the MNCs as the dominant economic factor of our century, given the two worlds of "haves" and "have-nots," that is, owners of corporate equity and non-owners of corporate equity?

Louis Kelso tells us in *Two-Factor Theory* that "Any society wishing to be free must structure its economic institutions so as to widely diffuse economic power while keeping it in the hands of individuals."[23]

The United Nations, in its Universal Declaration of Human Rights (UDHR), proclaimed by the General Assembly on December 10, 1948, defines the goal of global economics likewise in individual terms:

> *"Everyone has the right to a standard of living for the health and well being of himself and his family including food, clothing, medical care, housing, social services and the right to security against unemployment, sickness, disability, widowhood, old age or lack of livelihood in circumstances beyond his control."* [24]

With regard to the ownership of property, the same Declaration reaffirms George Mason's third "inalienable right" enshrined in the Virginia Declaration of Independence of 1775 and for sectarian motives unfortunately omitted from that of 1776 of the Continental Congress: the right to private property. Article 17 states:

> *"Everyone has the right to own property alone as well as in association with others."*
>
> *"No one shall be arbitrarily deprived of his property."*

The definition and ownership or non-ownership of "property" would seem to be at the heart of the entire question of economics, whether worldly or local. Until we analyze this controversial word more closely in the light of today's technological society, any discussion of economics remains sterile.

What Is Property?

What exactly is "property" in terms of economic theory? Is it a home, a car, a TV set, jewelry, clothes? Or is it a set of rights one has with respect to things owned? Karl Marx wrote that "The theory of the Communists may be summed up in a single sentence: Abolition of private property in the means of production." In *Das Capital*, he defines property as "an institution essential to controlling income distribution patterns." [25]

If a few individuals own and control industrial capital and the majority of workers own little or no capital, according to Norman Kurland[26], "...income patterns will become grossly distorted and lead necessarily to the abandonment of the orderly processes of supply and demand, and eventually to a breakdown of the property system itself."

In a paper delivered to the Eastern Economics Association of Hartford, Connecticut, April 15, 1977, Kurland minced no words as to property's meaning:

> *"Many people erroneously equate property with material objects, such as land, structures, machines, tools, things. In law, however, property is not the thing owned but rather a set of rights, powers and privileges that an individual enjoys in his relationship to things. It is the social 'link' between a particular human being and the social levers of power to choose and use particular things to meet one's needs. And property says who can share its profits. Since power [i.e., the means to influence change] exists in society whether or not particular individuals own property, those who are concerned about the corruptibility*

of concentrated power should be reminded of Daniel Webster's eloquent statement: "Power naturally and inevitably follows the ownership of property."'

The Homestead Act

In early America, the Homestead Act, under the genius of Abraham Lincoln, made it possible for men born without capital, by their courage and efforts, to acquire real property, i.e., capital. But when the land frontier ran out, the possibility of realizing this historic dream seemed to run out with it. The world was no longer primarily an agricultural world, but an industrial one, and the yearning of the average man for a "piece of the action" could only be satisfied within the context of industrial "land," i.e., capital tools.

No National Ownership Strategy

Despite the overwhelming importance of corporate-owned capital as a production input and means of income, however, no industrialized nation has every adopted a democratic "ownership strategy," i.e., an institutional means of assuring popular private ownership of productive capital comparable to the now outdated Homestead Act. During the 130 years since its passage, the world experienced an enormous expansion of production capital formation, but contrary to preindustrial efforts to diffuse capital ownership — at least in the United States — national economic policies and institutions have permitted massive amounts of productive capital to become owned by a small minority.

The consequences are paradoxical and appalling:

• a small minority earns income far in excess of their capacity and desire for consumption;

• A majority have unmet consumption desires and inadequate purchasing power.

• Yet we have unused and potential physical capacity and technical know-how to fulfil unmet consumption if only we had sufficient widespread purchasing power.

Outmoded Methods

The present inability of our national economies to achieve broad private ownership of productive capital and to significantly raise everyone's income, is largely the result of outmoded private capital investment financing methods — the financing of new capital formation exclusively out of the accumulated financial savings of individuals and/or their narrowly-owned corporations. The consequences of this method of financing is to bring massive amounts of capital into existence without creating new owners. This conventional capital financing method virtually guarantees that all new capital formation will be owned by an existing minority of wealth-owning citizens.

The method further weakens an already weak market mechanism — still the most democratic yardstick for measuring economic value — since it limits purchasing power for the propertyless many. Lastly, it frustrates the economic growth necessary to permit the economy to be able physically to produce general affluence, the only humane and rational goal for a democratic, post-industrial economy.

Big Brother

As a counterforce to concentrated, economic power in corporations owned by only a handful of the total population, we have turned ironically to "big government" to protect the propertyless many. Once again, this development has demonstrated that power is linked to property. In a society where political and economic power is combined in the hands of a monolithic, elitist government, whether acting "in the name of the proletariat" or for "democracy," the future of individual freedom is dim indeed.

To rely on government bailouts from corporate oppression is tantamount to seeking judicial redress from the accomplice to the swindler who robs us in the first place. In this regard, Nader reminds us that "...there has emerged a fundamental change in our political economy. The arms-length relationship which must characterize any democratic government in its dealing with special interest groups has been replaced, and not just by ad hoc wheeling and dealing, which has been observed by generations ..." but by ..." the institutionalized fusion of corporate desires with public bureaucracy — where the national security is synonomous with the state of Lockheed and Litton, where career roles are interchangeable along the industry-to-government-to-industry shuttle, where corporate risks and losses become taxpayer obligation."[27]

And what is the major labor unions' reaction to this cosy, corporate/government incestuous relationship? "For this most part," Nader writes, "the large unions do not object to this situation, having become modest copartners, seeking derivative benefits from the government."[28]

Thus linked to big business including private banking interests as well as labor, national economic policy legislation of income in direct relationship to productive output makes no commitment to fostering widespread ownership of capital.

Full Employment A Panacea?

Economists as well as politicans like to promote "full employment" as a panacea for economic recovery. But full employment, without simultaneous redistribution of all the wealth or income produced by capital to the non-capital owning employed, will never provide the fully-employed with sufficient purchasing power to buy all the goods and services produced.

286

Furthermore, as an economic goal, full employment is deficient if the function of the economy is to provide general affluence instead of universal busywork and equalized poverty.

In plain fact, full employment in itself is a socially hazardous goal. It aspires to restore through political expedients the pre-industrial state of toil that science, engineering, technology and modern management are pledged to overcome. Thus national political leadership finds its prestige contingent upon the success of an unnatural policy against which the most rational forces of the economy are aligned, a policy which it cannot enforce except at the cost of the demoralization and ultimately the destruction of the economy's productive sector.

Every Man A Producer

In the uncomplicated pre-industrial world, every man not an invalid knew he was an economic producer, that he possessed in his own mind and body the power to produce wealth. Productive power was his as a gift of nature. He knew he was needed, and the knowledge gave him both dignity and self-assurance.

Industrial man has lost that primal security. For while capital instruments are needed "extensions of man," as Marshall MacLuhan has pointed out, in the economic sense, they are extensions only of the man who owns them, and who, as a consequence of ownership, is entitled to receive the wealth his "extension" produces.

In a world where capital instruments are owned by the few, technology enhances the productive power of the few.

Thus, under today's "wage systems," where most people own little or no productive wealth, the great majority of men are robbed of their productive power by technological advance. They are deprived of their economic virility. This loss has disastrous social effects, especially on the family unit, first organism of social life.

Leaders of national society do not yet recognize their obligation, by deliberate social policy, to enable every man legitimately to acquire private ownership of viable holdings of productive capital, restoring thereby and indeed enhancing the productive power he has lost, or stands to lose, as technology shifts more and more the burden of production from men to machines.[29]

> *"We are, therefore, required by justice to do more than abolish chattel slavery. We are required to organize the economy in such a way that every man or family can use his or its property to participate in the production of wealth in a way that earns a living for that man or that family."* [30]

The Human Right To Property

One of the new principles of economic justic in one physical world is that when wealth is produced primarily by non-human capital instruments, men must have the right to acquire viable amounts of capital as a supplement to their labor power. Thus economic opportunity in an industrial economy is not merely the opportunity to work, but the opportunity to own capital, and to acquire capital without having to invade the property of others, or to cut down on one's already inadequate consumption.

"The harnessed energy, production, distribution, communication tools, and techno-scientific literacy thus inadvertently established– all of which can produce peace-supporting– is the wealth."[31]

Results of National Policies

Today's short-sighted and absurd national economic policies are in no small way contributing factors of:
- continued concentration of capital ownership;
- perpetuated class and group conflict and violence;
- rising crime against property;
- rising cost of living and uncontrollable inflationary forces;
- mounting tax rates and imminent taxpayer's rebellion worldwide;
- widespread alienation among the young, the working "class," minority groups, and the disadvantaged from the leaders of government, business and other basic institutions;
- resistance and fear among workers to new technology;
- self-defeating and harmful demands of organized labor for increased income through wages rather than through ownership of industry;
- loss of traditional autonomy of local government, business and the academic community because of the growing dependency on Big Government for economic survival;
- historically high interest rates;
- inability to plan rationally our economic growth and produce a more livable and humane environment;
- the "privileged class" mentality that says only a elitist few can take full advantage of leisure;
- failure to exploit fully the technological potential for improving the material lives of the general public.

In Summation

1) Individual liberties and a democratic form of government cannot exist unless every person has the means to become a "have" rather than a "have-not;"

2) The nation-state, as an institution of economic legitimacy, has been overtaken by industry and technology in general and by rise of the multinational conglomerates in particular;

3) The multinational corporation, while effectively producing goods and services in quantities sufficient for the general needs of the public, has no countervailing equitable distributive philosophy or system whereby the worker can benefit

directly from ownership of the corporate assets of the world's productive instruments.

4) The elimination of armaments from the national economic scene will result in the raising of living standards worldwide with social, cultural and spiritual benefits beyond measure;

5) A world government, representing the *sine qua non* not only of economic survival but of survival itself, is the goal of the 20th century; the alternative is possible extinction;

6) Neither doctrinaire Communism nor monopolistic Capitalism can encompass both the material as well as the spiritual needs of humankind as a species and as free individuals;

7) A distributive economy based on democratic ownership of the means of production emphasizing affuence while retaining contingent values of freedom, equality and justice, must be incorporated into the present-day situation without disruption.

The Global Mandate

The ownership of the world of tools and their institutional instruments of income-distribution, in other words, must now be considered globally "by world society as world society," translated by right into individual ownership of income-producing property by the sovereign individual, i.e., the world citizen.

Therefore, economically speaking, the World Citizen claims by right ownership of a share of the new industrial, wealth-producing frontier which, according to Buckminster Fuller, "can support all of the multiplying humanity at higher standards of living than anyone has ever experienced or dreamed."

To claim world citizenship is to claim partnership with the planet earth, "homeship" with the world community as such and therefore possession of one's rightful domicile and all it contains. Just as no human can claim to have chosen his parents or place of birth, so no one can rationally justify exclusive ownership of resources needed by one and all. The atmosphere, the oceans, the soil, the water, the sun even, are common to the human species as such as to each and every individual human.

We must first assert that global citizenship, however, in order to acknowledge that ownership as our rightful heritiage. No one will hand it to us. The claim of exclusive national citizenship perpetuates the philosophy of economic scarcity as defined by Malthus and later fortified by Darwin's survival-only-of-the-fittest. World citizenship, on the contrary, is the corollary of earth ownership as it is of human survival since, unless the individual human, who is the microcosm not only of the earth but of the cosmos itself, assumes ownership of his world, false ownership, i.e., exploitative, unjust, monopolistic, elitist, will soon destroy the earth itself and all humans thereon as it is already doing at an accelerated rate.

World Ownership

The new formula then for economic democracy and freedom for one and all becomes:

World Citizen = World Owner

No national leader would or indeed could oppose a global institution functioning with the sovereign support of declared world citizens, the raison d'etre of which was precisely to eliminate the necessity of armaments amongst states to the mutual economic, social and spiritual benefit of the entire human community.

The very nature of the common crisis facing humankind, as well as each individual is obviously beyond the mandated power of any national leader or group of national leaders to resolve. Former U.N. Secretary-General Dr. Kurt Waldheim, in addressing the opening session of the 29th General Assembly said that the world's problems "were beyond the control of any group of nation." He warned that "profound economic and social problems are threatening the world with a crisis of extraordinary dimensions."

Willy Brandt's introduction to the Brandt Commission's 1980 update on the global economy reconfirmed this dire warning:

> *"The world's prospects have deteriorated rapidly; not only for improved relations between industrialized and developing countries, but for the outlook of the world economy as a whole... Further decline is likely to cause the disintegration of societies and create conditions of anarchy."*

World citizenship as a dynamic concept and ownership of the earth have not so far been linked except in theory by such writers as Buckminster Fuller.[33] The reason is simple. Till now, no single global and sovereign organization existed which could translate theoretical ownership of the earth into practical ownership for the individual world citizen and humankind. Nations, caught in their dualistic, archaic, duel-to-the-death, oppose by definition world citizen ownership of the earth. Either nations are sovereign or humanity is. Either world law is valid or exclusive national law...but not both together.

The multinationals in their turn, with their pitifully few owners, are making a near-approach to total ownership, but with the built-in, self-defeating defects of specialization, maximizing short-term profit philosophy plus nationalistic political orientation. Even should they combine into one monolithic world corporation — as Art Buchwald, tongue-in-cheek, prophesied for the United States — the inevitable result would be violent world revolution between the billions of have-nots and the 5% or less haves, owners of the Total Corporation.

"Earth, Inc." is only valid if economic justice reigns as the guiding philosophy.

So if we refer back to Nataraja Guru's definition of economics as being concerned primarily with the happiness of humankind as a whole as well as each individual as its microcosm, and if we consider the two factors involved in the production of wealth, that is, capital and labor, it becomes clear that only through direct participation in the profits of the entire industrial machinery of the world, i.e., the capital assets, can everyone achieve affluence, or put negatively, eliminate disaffluence or poverty.

Mutual Affluence System

A global "mutual affluence system' therefore may be said to be the economic philosophy of the embryonic World Government.

Its fundamental tenet is expressed in the geo-dialectical formula: "One for all and all for one."

As such, it is the logical extension of the fundamental human rights expressed by such documents as the *Universal Declaration of Human Rights.*

It correctly revises both Marxist and capitalist theories to provide the "synthesis" — necessarily divorced from the vitiating nation-state system — whereby Man's true nature is fully realized: spiritual, social, biological.

Capital Formation Process Defective

If everyone is to have a chance to own his share of capital, then the current process whereby most newly formed capital automatically flows into the hands of the upper 5 to 10 per cent of families who already own all the existing capital is defective. Ways must be devised to allow the acquisition of newly-formed capital to be acquired by the remaining 90% of families.

The single laborer, lacking capital, credit or effective political power as a consumer, is virtually helpless to pull himself up by his own economic bootstaps. True, he may organize into unions but only as a worker, neither as a consumer nor, more reasonably, as a potential owner. There is as yet no labor union advocating more purchasing power through capital ownership for less work. On the contrary, workers organize irrationally for higher wages and full employment thereby fueling the inflationary fire.

He already has the necessary potential power, however, if he combines his single identity/forces: consumer, worker, citizen, tax-payer with investor, i.e., owner. In other words, to counter-balance the now-monopolistic corporation, he must be allowed to share its profits as an "insider" or investor. The existence and growth of mutual funds and money market funds are highly instructive arguments for the creation of a worker/consumer global mutual fund to share a "piece of the world action." The details of the organization of such a mutual fund must be worked out and then made part of an overall economic strategy of the aggregate of world citizens of the World Government.

The Missing Link

Vital to any consideration of global economics is the one element which can make a "mutual influence system" actually work: world money, the "lubricant" without which no plan however just can be effected practically. While economists avoid the subject like the plague, I must try to demystify the word "money" since ostensibly this is the "name of the game."

What exactly is money? There is a subtle mystery here. Is it only, as Webster defines it, "metal as gold, silver or copper, coined or stamped, and issued as a medium of exchange"? Or "wealth reckoned in terms of money"? Or "any form or denomination of coin or paper lawfully current as money"? Or "Anything customarily used as a medium of exchange or measure of value, as sheep, wampum, gold dust, etc."?

Obviously, without exchange value, the coin or paper is not "money." But exchange value is not limited to single transactions; it is public and general. Enter the conceptual side of money: trust. Without trust or confidence in its exchange value in the market-place, the "medium" itself, be it shark's teeth, clay disks, or gold bullion, would be of ornamental value only or objects to hold paper in place.

The subject of money is disposed of by the United States Consitution with extreme brevity.

"Article I, Section 8, Clause 5: The Congress shall have the power to coin money, regulate the value thereof and of foreign coins."

The fundamental definition of money is here taken for granted! And for good reason since trust as a pyschological and emotional value cannot be legislated. And that leads to a startling fact: There is no legal definition for money!

Implicit in "medium of exchange" is the confidence that he who accepts a dollar bill, a kroner, franc, mark, ruble, rupee, yen or cedi can pass it on to another and receive commensurate value. A dollar bill, however, may circulate all week buying bread, light bulbs, toothpaste, and paying the rent but on Friday, at the bank, when the teller informs the last unfortunate holder that the bill is "no good," it suddenly loses its exchange value, its trust side. In other words, people's trust made it "work" despite its forgery. A Mickey Mouse certificate would also have worked if it had trust as a "medium of exchange."

The essence of money is therefore trust.

National money, historically, is as provisional as sea-shells, sperm-whale teeth, round stones with holes, mud tablets and even gold dust. While the actual or material side of national money still exists, its conceptual or trust side is fast disintegrating.[34]

If nations, as exclusive political and economic units, by definition don't trust one another, how can confidence exist for their respective monies? In Emery Reves words:

"What we usually call world economics, international trade, has little if anything to do with economics or trade. They are, in fact economic warfare, trade warfare. The dominating motive of all economic activity outside existing national barriers is not trade, is not production, is not consumption, is not even profit, but a determination to strengthen by all means the economic power of the nation-state." [35]

The "game" of money exchange is itself big business, a whole breed of men in exchange offices throughout the world parasitically engaged daily in reaping the benefits of this institutionalized distrust at the expense of the world public.

Central bankers, speculators, special departments of multinationals, in fact, anyone who understands there is a profit to be made from monetary distrust is in reality ripping off the public which naively considers money only as Webster did, a "medium of exchange."

The game aspect of money was brilliantly exposed by Adam Smith (a pseudonym) in "The Money Game," a biting satire of the daily play of the New York Stock Exchange: "The irony is that this is a money game and money is the way we keep score." As to the vital element of trust, Smith writes, "Markets only work when they believe, and this confidence is based on the idea that men can manage their affairs rationally."[36]

National citizens, today, more than ever, are being made aware by inflation that their particular national currency is literally unstable, no longer able to serve their economic interests as a constant thus valid means of exchange. The U.S. citizen in particular suffered as much a psychological as economic shock in the '70s by two dollar devaluations in less than three years due principally to massive national deficits and dollar drains to pay for foreign wars.[37]

The reestablishment of confidence in money in terms of public service as a medium of exchange for goods and services and not as a means of exploitation of the poor by the rich, can come about only on a global scale. For only globally can problems of exchange of goods, equitable distribution of wealth-producing capital and the elimination of the have-nots be accomplished.

"American corporations are outwardly bound. Their evolution is, however, the evolutionary prototype for all of society. All of humanity are soon to become worldians."[38]

Contrary to what timid and inwardly-looking economists and finance ministers, not to mention the whole clique of central bankers and money changers admit, this implies — as it did in 1787 for the separate states of the newly-formed United States of America — the total relinquishment of money issuance and control by sovereign-states. Conversely it means global and sovereign institutions designed to serve the citizens of the world in their entirety and to protect their individual rights.

The multinational corporations, no doubt inadvertently, are moving inexorably in this imperative direction:

"National profiles are hard to distinguish in many cases because multinationals shy away from being identified with any one country; most are proud of the fact their subsidiaries are indigenous everywhere... The trend is toward increasingly global structures and decision-making, and toward allocating corporate resources on a world scale."[39]

As I have pointed out, world man and world ownership are indissolubly linked. World money, both conceptually and actually, is thus the indispensable — and heretofore missing — ingredient for the two to be joined and begin working.

Who Issues Money?

The key question remains, who or what can issue world money? The history of the contending forces at work in money issuance in the United States is highly illustrative. Contrary to the provisions of the U.S. Consitution which gives power to Congress alone to "coin money, regulate the value thereof, and of foreign coin," according to those who considered money as a profit-making commodity and method for gaining control of labor by capital, mostly London bankers at the time, the issuing institute must be in private hands.

Those who considered money — as did most of the founding fathers, notably George Washington, Thomas Jefferson and Benjamin Franklin — as only a medium of exchange for goods and services, that is, real wealth, at the service of the people, know that it had to be authorized and issued by representative public institutions, under public control since it was and is the general as much as the individual welfare which must be considered by any democratic government.

During America's development in the 18th and 19th centuries, the running battle between private banking interests and public spokesmen was bitter and often deadly. In Oliver Cushing Dwinnel's words:

"There is little doubt but that the financial monopolists have brought about the wars when their control of the issuance of money was threatened. It was not a coincidence that the Revolutionary War took place after the British Empire was unable, after many years of effort to control the Colonies by controlling their money; and it was not a coincidence that the War of 1812 was prosecuted against us after Congress refused to renew the bank charter. Much of the stock had been bought by England. It is pretty obvious from our history that the financial hierarchy of the world will go to war if necessary to gain control of money issuance, and they will do so to renew control, and to maintain control, regardless of how many wars it may take."

Abraham Lincoln, Economist

The importance of government control of money issuance was endorsed by the great emancipator, Abraham Lincoln, who believed that the spending power of the government and the buying power of the consumer could and should be created and issued by the state free from interests, discounts and other charges imposed as a profit of the private money system. Lincoln's monetary program offered the means of paying debts and current expenses of government without profit to the bankers and without disaster to the taxpayer. As Gerald McGreer records:

"Quite naturally the bankers opposed Lincoln's 'National Currency Program,' for under it he proposed to take away from the bankers the privilege of issuing an effective substitute for money. The bankers' plan for controlling money was for the government... to farm out its power to issue money to the bankers. Having thus lost its power to issue money, the government would be reduced to the position of a

perpetual borrower at interest from a private monopoly which secured its power to issue a SUBSTITUTE FOR MONEY FOR THE GOVERNMENT."[41]

The issue, then as now, was vital to economic well-being, the fundamental question being: Shall government be subordinate to moneypower with money changers ruling democracy, or shall democracy rule the money changes? Lincoln knew that it was upon the determination of the primal issue in favor of democracy that the progress, prosperity and peace of humanity depended.

In a Congressional Report to the 76th Congress of 1862 written by Robert L. Owens, then chairman of the Committee on Banking and Currency, was a summary of Lincoln's monetary views, as relevant today in the global context as they were then in the national:

"1. Money is the creature of law and the creation of the original issue of money should be maintained as an exclusive monopoly of...Government.

"2. Money possesses no value to the State other than given it by circulation.

"3. Capital has its proper place and is entitled every protection. The wages of men should be recognized in the structure of and in the social order as more important than the wages of money. (In this vital recognition of the primacy of men's 'wages' over money's 'wages', i.e., interest, Lincoln was laying the groundwork for ownership of capital by labor in which 'wages' were derived both from labor and wealth-producing capital instruments. Author's note.)

"4. No duty is more imperative on the Government than the duty it owes to the people to furnish them with a sound and uniform currency...so that labor will be protected from a vicious currency (controllable by private interests).

"5. The available supply of gold and silver being wholly inadequate to permit the issuance of coins of intrinsic value or paper currency convertible into coin in the volume required to serve the needs of the people, some other base for the issuance of currency must be developed. And some other means than that of convertibility of paper currency or any other substitute for money of intrinsic value that may come into use.

"6. The monetary needs of increasing numbers of people advancing toward higher standards of living can be served by the issuing of National Currency and Credit through the operation of a National Banking System. The circulation of a medium of exchange issued and backed by the Government can be properly regulated...Government has the power to regulate the currency and credit of the Nation.

"7. Government should stand behind its currency and credit and the bank deposits of the Nations. No individual should suffer a loss of money through depreciated inflated currency or bank bankruptcy.

"8. Government, possessing the power to create and issue currency and credit as money, and enjoying the right to withdraw both currency and credit from circulation by taxation and otherwise, need not and should not borrow capital at interests as a means of financing governmental work and public enterprise.

"9. The Government should create, issue and circulate all the currency and credit need to satisfy the spending power of the Government and the buying power of the consumer.

"10. The privilege of creating and issuing money is not only the supreme prerogative of Government, but it is the Government's greatest creative opportunity.

"11. By the adoption of these principles, the long-felt need for an uniform medium of exchange will be satisfied. The tax-payers will be saved immense sums of interest, discounts and exchanges. The financing of all public enterprises... the maintenance of stable government and ordered process, and the conduct of the Treasury will become matters of practical administration.

"12. Money will cease to become the master and become the servant of humanity. Democracy will rise superior to the money power. "

In his introduction[42], Owens summed up the underlying concept of trust in Lincoln's monetary views:

"The plan is founded on benevolence, justice and righteousness. It is based on reason, on thoroughly well-established facts, and on sound precedents that cannot be disputed by intelligent men of good will and honest purpose... The plan is Constitutional... The Supreme Court of the United States has justified (it) on its opinion in the Legal Tender Cases. It is based on the exclusive right of the Government to create money and on the explicit duty 'to regulate the value thereof.' (The Plan) points the way by which the Government, representing all the people, shall prevent either inflation (which is indefensible expansion of credit or money or the corresponding undue and indefensible contraction of credit: deflation, through which people have suffered... The Plan proposes to end the suffering of one-third of the American people because of undeserved poverty."

This remarkable and superbly relevant testament could be considered the forerunner to modern economic democracy and finance. Oliver Dwinnel rightly concludes that "As Washington is the symbol of the political democracy of the coming world of his day, so Lincoln foreshadowed the economic and financial democracy of the world to be."

Gold

This brings us to the question of gold as a worldly "medium of exchange." Does it fulfil the exacting requirements?

According to Stuart Chase, "The international monetary problem will not be solved when the U.S. achieves a strong domestic economy with full employment. International trade is bound to expand in a shrinking world, but, as the New York Times has pointed out, 'any further expansion in the business that nations, and their citizens, do with each other would be limited by the newly-minted gold that enters the world's money system each year.' It isn't enough." The search is on, he adds, "for a new invention to make it enough, and to take the place of gold in international exchanges."[43]

There are many who think that a dynamic relationship exists between gold and one world economics. Was General de Gaulle correct in his famous press conference at the Palais Elysee in 1965 in announcing the monetary exchange

296

standard between nations was no longer effective and that a "true gold standard" was essential? "We consider it necessary," he stated regally, "that international trade should rest, as before the two world wars, on an indisputable monetary basis having the mark of no particular country. What basis? Indeed there can be no other criterion, no other standard than gold. Yes, gold, which never changes, which can be shaped into ingots, bars, coins, which has no nationality and which is eternally accepted as an alternative fiduciary value par excellence."

The economic "warfare" between nations was never better illustrated than by this unilateral declaration of de Gaulle who then led a "run" on the gold in Fort Knox by Western European nations. This led inexorably to President Nixon's "unilateral" decision in August, 1971, when U.S. gold reserves had fallen from a record $24 billion in 1947 to $10 billion (due to concurrent deficits throughout the Vietnam War years), to declare that dollars would no longer be exchanged for gold. This in turn left billions of unwanted and unredeemable "Eurodollars" in central banks throughout Europe. Nixon's act, "to save the dollar" was as much directed against "friendly" as against "enemy" nations.

The hold gold retains on the public is more emotional than logical. "Apart from its aesthetic appeal." writes Timothy Green, "gold has no instrinsic value. It is hard to imagine being cast up on a desert island with anything more useless than a bar of gold."

Lord Keynes referred to gold as "that barbaric relic," while others have sung paeans of praise for its beauty, its indestructibility, its scarcity and its almost mystical appeal as a symbol of power. Ancient alchemists sought the "elixir of immortal life" by extracting the oligo-elements of gold for concocting the god-like ambrosia. Astrologers link gold with the sun and the nervous and circulatory system in a mystical triumvirate. Again, these are fascinating sidelights to gold's history and may serve to explain in part the tenacity with which it is considered of high value. But from a strictly economic viewpoint, it lacks vital factors to serve as a basis of a one world system.

To answer the "gold bugs" definitely as to why gold cannot adquately serve as a basis for a one world currency, we must again appreciate, in Arthur Kitson's words, that "The entire financial factor presents itself from two distinct and entirely opposite and conflicting standpoints. The one is the bankers as 'moneylenders;' the other, the producers. To the banker, money represents itself as a valuable commodity from which he must draw dividends in the shape of interest...For this reason the banking interests have waged unceasing warfare against State Banking and what they term 'cheap money expedients.' Moreover, the histories of cheap currency expedients have mostly been written by bankers, their employees, or hired professors, who have invariably presented the subject from this interested class' point of view. It is for this reason that so much importance has been attached to gold for currency purposes. Its scarcity, its dearness, gives weight to the demand for high interest charges. On the other hand, the producer regards money more from the standpoint of its utility — his interest requires the cheapest form available — consistent with its ability to perform its work."[44]

World Money

A true world currency, relating itself directly to world consumer needs vis-a-vis world production of goods and services, is not a commodity in itself like shoes, chewing-gum or computers, but a "a medium of exchange," a convenience at the service strictly of the producer and consumer, made one by the aforementioned new right of world ownership for world man and woman.

World Economy = World Accounting System

Carried to its logical conclusion, "world money" becomes a simplified book-keeping system which, according to Buckminster Fuller, "must be converted from agricultural metabolics to an eternal world-around accounting which includes all generations to come, and which is consistent with the cosmic accounting of an eternally regenerative physical universal system. The accounting system would include a redefinition of wealth with the scarcity model of economics to be made obsolete by the magnitude of man's participation in the irreversible amplification of the inventory of information, i.e., know-how."[45]

World or cosmic accounting then "assumes omnivalidity" which, translated into individual terms means the right to ownership of the means to wealth. While humans today, conditioned by the archaic "earning the right to live," scarcity-oriented ethic, still compete, ergo fight each other, as do states, for bare sustenance, World Citizen Fuller reminds us that:

> *"The Universe is not operating on a basis in which the Star sun opines ignorantly that it can no longer afford to let Earth have the energy to keep life going because it hasn't paid its last bill."*

The sun does not have to make a profit. And just as the world moral view is synergistic, that is, wealth-producing[46], so an economic overview radically reverses the failure-prone Malthusian and Darwinian theories to support a totally successful and totally human economy. In Buckminster Fuller's words:

> *"Ephemerization, a product of the metaphysical conservation being more effective and coherent than physical entropy, is the number one economic surprise of world man. Up to ten years ago, all world economists counseled the world political leaders that there never had been and never would be enough vital sustenance to support more than a very few... The invisible, inexorable evolution will soon convert all nationally and subnationally identified humanity into worldians, universally coordinate, individual 'people.' The inexorable trending to one-world citizenship is ignorantly and expeditiously opposed by the sovereign nations' self-perpetuating proclivities."* [47]

International "Money" of States

In order to bring inter-national economic programs more in line with global needs, in March, 1967, the International Monetary Fund, an outgrowth of the

298

Bretton Woods Agreements of 1944, following a meeting of the "Group of Ten," finance ministers and central bank governors of the ten most developed nations, announced a new "reserve asset," i.e., inter-national "currency" to supplement gold — which accounted for a mere 30 per cent of the monetary reserves of the membership of the IMF dollars, sterling and existing IMF credits. These were the "Special Drawing Rights" (SDRs) which started out as a unit of credit based on the then official value of gold, $42.22 per Troy ounce. Once issued, however, they could not be reconverted into gold.

In other words, the States, through the IMF, created a new "legal tender" in order to increase liquidity *between States*. There was, and is, of course no single sovereign governmental authority sanctioning that creation. The concept is not new. Lord Keynes had proposed his "bancor," along with gold, would be the international reserves available to all States on a long-term, low interest basis, and, as with the SDRs, gold could buy "bancors," but "bancors" could not be reconverted into gold. Thus would be created a phony "paper" gold.

Some economists consider it excellent that nations "are acting together" because together they are bigger than the speculator or the businessmen hedging against currency problems. Adam Smith saw the SDRs however as "only a device which gives more time to resolve the problem."[48] "These problems," he claims, "are universal. They arise because governments are now held responsible for the welfare of the people...What this means is that if governments have a choice between attempting full employment and defending their economies, they will nearly always pick jobs over the worth of the currency. Currencies do not vote...the Full Employment Act (of the U.S.) spells this out. The government is commited to full employment and if it must pump money into the economy to achieve this, and if there isn't enough money, it creates the money. Long-range inflation is the policy, articulated or not, of every country in the world."[49]

Timothy Green tells us that "so far, the SDRs represent a very small part of reserves, but their very existence is a significant step along the road that is gradually by-passing gold as a monetary metal."[50]

Of particular interest to world citizens in this monetary creation by States is the precedent which is pregnant with implications. I note in passing that the existence of SDRs has in no way relieved the individual of the inflationary crisis facing him presently since they are only a supplement to the entire State-oriented economy and not a true step toward a one world economy.

Neither gold nor "paper gold" can serve as a viable, permanent monetary base for a world market as such. It can at best be considered a stop-gap measure in lieu of a true world legal.

> *"After all, if the mines are running out of gold, the problem of finding an alternative is all the more acute."* [51]

Super-analysts like Dr. Harry Schultz, Harry Browne, James Dines and Louis Rukeyser propose an economy based on gold and a "new political system" though they fail to go the full way to world government. On the other hand, world government advocates sidestep the delicate question of world economics which requires a spelling-out in down-to-earth monetary terms how we get from here to there without blowing everything apart. Vague theory won't do. "Prayers will not make a mango fall."

In all fairness to the "gold bugs," they realistically assess the international muddle as it is with no holds barred. Dr. Schultz bluntly states that "My job is not to idealize on what the world should be like. Those who think we've already evolved enough to do without gold discipline...will sink while singing their individual national anthems...My job is rather to offer a lead toward real patriotism, i.e., to humanity and to yourself & your family (not to a gov't. or nation). My job is to tell it like it is and show how to survive."[52]

We can only applaud and affirm patriotism to humanity and oneself at one and the same time which is the essence of world citizenship along with revealing the know-how of survival. What concerns us more directly, however, is not survival of the privileged few because, apart from considerations of simple justice and humanity, living on an island of plenty surrounded by a sea of misery is hardly conductive to happiness, economic or otherwise.

Only through survival of the Total Species can any single member of the human species survive in any manner resembling a human condition. The late Justice Wm. O. Douglas wrote prophetically, " The liberty of one man will hereafter be closely linked with the hunger of another. The world economy is more and more the testing ground for every man's freedom."[53]

Who or What Can Issue World Money?

Guru Nataraja's Memorandum on World Government gives the clue as to how world money can come about. "It would not be impossible for the World Government to have its own credit and currency the world over, and planned on some rational human basis."[54]

Travelers going abroad are urgently advised to convert their ready cash into traveler's checks which if lost are easily replaced. The largest bank in the work, BankAmerica, advertises its traveler's checks as "world money". Being backed by a negotiable currency, they are literally "mediums of exchange" for goods and services worldwide.

The extrapolation of this already recognized public service to a true global medium of exchange as envisaged by Lincoln is far simpler than generally realized requiring only the proper institutional framework for its immediate functioning.

Just as the SDRs are "legal tender" between nations, sanctioned by international "law," i.e., the Washington Agreement of March, 1968, and thus could be considered an "international money," so the **Mondo**, sanctioned by World Government, may be considered "legal tender" between world citizens "outside" the jurisdiction of national frontiers — as is gold — who seek a sound, global, real currency with which to do business and exchange needed goods and services. The **Mondo** will be initially an inter-world citizen money, legal, logical and functional. Whereas the SDRs only complement the economic warfare practised between nations and do not meet our needs, the **Mondo**, possessing immediate intrinsic value as a global medium of exchange, backed by today's "negotiable" currency and emitted by a legally-founded bank will supply the missing liquidity to lubricate the **Mutual Affluence System.**

Besides being a peace currency, further considerations will convince the public of the **Mondo's** value. As national currency preserves pockets of wealth for those who already possess far in excess for personal luxury, maintaining a system of economic serfdom for the rest of the populace, as exacting and degrading a condition as any of our ancestors faced under a despotic monarchy, the **Mondo** will be a general affluence currency, freeing us of our economic servitude, unattached to monopoly, "...founded on benevolence, justice and righeousness." In short, it will be the first truly human rights currency.[55]

The Duties of Economic Democracy

The right to economic democracy implies duties as well. Ownership of a piece of industry means owning equity or corporate shares in that industry. While it is no doubt true that we exercise "economic democracy" with our money as a consumer at the marketplace, that is not the whole story. It is an indirect "vote," not a controlling one. A true economic vote would be one linked directly to the entire productive apparatus just as a political vote relates to the entire governmental apparatus guaranteed by constitutional right.

If therefore we are all economic "citizens," what is the total economic framework in which we can exercise our "vote" for determining our personal and general economic well-being?

It must obviously be allied with the entire productive apparatus, not governmental. In brief, it must be as an *economic world citizen* with an across-the-multinational-corporation-board vote!

To illustrate, a share in one multinational corporation owned by a worker of that corporation is already an international economic vote by definition. If that same worker buys one share of other multinational corporations, he increases his international voting power horizonatally in direct proportion to the number of corporations he buys into. This is the principle of the mutual fund, an across-the-corporate-board portfolio.

Now if he manages to buy a share in all the multinational corporations, his voting power in each is compounded by his ownership strategy which now includes all. But he is not only an international economic citizen. He is also an international economic legislator! His one vote permits him to introduce actual resolutions at the yearly general assembly of stockholders.[56]

Since his one vote permits him to propose policy changes in each corportion, should he introduce in each and every general assembly the same resolution, i.e., his economic "ticket," the very accumulative effect would reinforce the voting power of each separate introduction.

The Economic World "Ticket"

If the "ticket" were designed to upgrade his ownership stake as a worker — along with his fellow workers — by means of the widely-accepted *Employee*

Stock Ownership Plan (ESOP), boards of directors, not to mention fellow shareholders, would quickly appreciate what real economic democratic power meant. The strike for higher wages would quickly be seen for what it was: an obsolete strategy for perpetuating the status quo inequality between owners of capital equity and the work-serf in the name of "justice." "Big labor" management must collude in this work-serf versus capital owners conflict otherwise it would lose its power hold over the individual worker.

A worker owning a share or shares in the corporation for which he works is already a potential world owner. No doubt he presently disregards totally his voting rights — as do most shareholders — turning his proxy back to management for their disposal as *they* see it. Viewed objectively, he thus deserves the economic rip-off of which he is the perpetual victim.

Shares Equal Votes Also

Although the United States vaunts itself as the most enlightened nation in the world as regards its economic philosophy, economic voting is not taught in schools or even universities. Perhaps the best kept secret among the financial elite is that "Shares represent ownership votes, i.e., control." But since no political party or labor union unites share owners in a common ownership front against elitist, monopolistic ownership — the Communists and Socialists have captured in the public mind the notion of capital ownership by the "people" (read "State capitalism") — single individual or even groups, such as religious bodies, cultural, educational, social or other organizations, are concerned mainly with their corporate investments as saleable capital, in other words, a commodity or as a producer of dividends, but not as a democratic economic voting right.

Second "Plank": World Public Order

Let us carry our worker/owner analogy a step farther. Realizing that his multinational ownership shares are highly vulnerable in an anarchic political world, in order to protect his stake — which now crosses the economic "frontiers" between the multi's — he must introduce into his economic "ticket" the notion of overall political protection as a corporate policy. Not to seek such political protection in a world of over 170 nation-states would be in effect to deny his new global economic civic status. Indeed, the continuance of an anarchic political world in an interdependent economic industrial world where the right of ownership beyond national frontiers by the national citizen is increasingly apparent and exercised, is the guarantor of its eventual destruction. Common-sense alone dictates the protection of our productive tools providing our well-being.[57]

No organization yet exists, however, to which our worker/owner can address his proxy which would represent him in the global manner described. A "World Citizens' Investors Corporation" — a global, democratically "elected" economic congress — designed so as to feed-back profits to the individual like the mutual funds is yet to be created though shareholders, especially those in certain religious institutions are becoming aware that economic ownership, however, minor, of a multinational giant, connotes civic responsibility of a new order.[58]

General Citizenry Property Rights

The extrapolation of the ESOP to include the general citizenry in ownership of the expanding industrial "pie," thereby expanding affluence, is already theoretically developed in Kelsonian economics.[59] Various tentative proposals for direct civic ownership of the Washington, D.C. metro system, certain public utilities, the telephone company, certain bankrupt railroads, even such giants as the Chrysler Corporation have been developed by Kelso experts such as Norman Kurland.[60]

World Citizen "Labor" Union

The second economic prong necessary to complete the mechanism picture of creating personal affluence is the creation of a new-type "labor" union having as its goals 1) increased purchasing power through ownership of capital equity by workers, and 2) increased reliance on modern science-design technology to decrease the toil side of "work" in order to decrease the actual work-time. This "labor" union would support the work ethic only so far as it included the machine work as an integral part of the worker's share. In other words, just as a journeyman or even a garage mechanic owns his own tools, so an industrial worker would "own" his own tools in the form of income-producing shares in the company for which he works.

Such a "world citizen's labor union," like the multinationals themselves, would cross national frontiers thus equalizing the now unequal power of the multi's to bypass labor pressure in one country by switching production, resources and even whole plants to another.

The debate rages among statesmen, lawyers, jurists, and laymen around the question: Is there a body of international law, institutions, procedures and precedents which can appropriately be described as the "law" of human rights? We have dealt with the poltical side of this question in other chapters. But who is debating the question of the economic "law of human rights? What labor union is representing the economic rights spelled out in the Universal Declaration of Human Rights?

Article 17: [*1*] *"Everyone has the right to own property alone as well as in association with others.*

[*2*] *No one shall be arbitrarily deprived of his property.."*

Article 23: [*1*] *"Everyone has the right to work, to free choice of employment, to just and favourable conditions of work and to protection against unemployment."*

[*2*] *"Everyone, without any discrimination, has the right to equal pay for equal work."*

303

[3] "Everyone who works has the right to just and favourable remuneration ensuring for himself and his family an existence worthy of human dignity, and supplemented, if necessary, by other means of social protection."

Article 24: *"Everyone has the right to rest and leisure, including reasonable limitations of working hours and periodic holidays with pay."*

Are Labor Unions Thinking "Global"?

Under the rubrique, "Multinational Business Enterprises," the 1970-71 Yearbook of the Union of International Associations referred briefly to "the union point of view on industrial and commercial concentration."

"A special August 1970 issue of the economic and social Bulletin of the International Confederation of Free Trade Unions was entitled: 'The International Free Trade Union Movement and Multinational Corporations.' It contains a report by Mr. Herbert Maier who, whilst acknowledging that the unions are not unaware of the positive aspects of the multinational corporations (improvement of employment and income levels, potential benefits arising from the application of new technologies, the help provided in developing and increasing both home and export markets, and speeding up the industrialization of developing countries), expressed a whole set of reservations, fears and demands which would be too long to mention here. He considered it fundamentally necessary to draw up a **code of behavior** to govern multinational company operations applicable both to the industrialized nations and to the developing countries. . ."

Eleven years later, in the July-August, 1982 edition of *Economic Notes*, editor Dr. Joseph Harris, Executive Director of the Labor Research Association, in an article entitled "Multinationals and U.S. Workers" writes "...in the era of multinational corporations, the closet cooperation between the various industrial unions in each country — and with unions in other countries where the multinationals have spread their tentacles— has become the **necessary next step** for the trade union movement." (Emphasis added.) In other words, to date, trade unions are still struggling to achieve a truly global viewpoint and thus unity. Where a "confederation" of trade unions remains the ultimate in cooperation between workers — which, in plain language, means "equally sovereign" national trade unions, a sort of trade union United Nations, no "code of behavior" necessary to govern multinational company operations can be devised or implemented.[61]

Human economic rights can only be spoken for by representatives acting in the name of all concerned, individually and wholly.

"A qualitative change that will enhance trade union effectiveness is coordinated union bargaining on a global scale with the MNCs on all matters relating to employment, wages and conditions." [62]

Who Can Represent the "Worker of the World"?

The worker/owner of the world, as an economic World Citizen, can only be represented by a global organization transcending national boundaries. This fundamental right of global association is sanctioned by **Article 20**, Universal Declaration of Human Rights:

"Everyone has the right to freedom of peaceful assembly and association."

A world-wide trade union is likewise sanctioned by **Article 23(4)** of the same declaration:

"Everyone has the right to form and to join trade unions for the protection of his interests."

Is the Mutual Affluence System Realizable?

Therefore the major elements required to evolve a "mutual affluence system" (MAS) worldwide are:

1. A legitimate world bank under the aegis of the World Government;

2. A global currency based on the conception of money as a "medium of exchange" between producers and consumers having no intrinsic value in itself, i.e., monetary world citizenship divorced essentially from monopolistic nation-state system;

3. A democratically-organized and controlled investment corporation of, for and by world citizens whereby they may cooperate and individually profit on the basis of economic justice (equity) in the purchase of approved securities of industries throughout the world; popular ownership of voting equity will lead inevitably to its legitimate protection on a global scale;

4. A world citizen labor union based on increased purchasing power through employee stock ownership plans with progressive decrease in the work/week due to full utilization of design-science, automation, ephemerization, robotics, and ecologically-sound energy sources;

5. A world institute of economic justice staffed by wholistic-thinking economists 1) to educate the world citizenry to the new global ownership philosophy and strategies, 2) to educate national and world leaders to the "new look" in affluent economic thinking as opposed to obsolete scarcity-economic thinking, and 3) to educate multinational management and personnel as to the economic, social, technical, ecological and moral advantages of adopting the new economic philosophy and strategies.

Discerning readers will note there is no single element here incapable of practical realization. Indeed, the seeds of all have been sown many years ago and are already breaking ground.

Certain national, enlightened trade unions, for instance, are becoming sympathetic to ESOPs for their own members in the realization that the collision course between "big labor" and "big management", which encompasses government as well as industry, can and must be avoided at all costs. (The experience of Solidarity in Poland and industry-wide labor strikes in so-called capitalist countries leads to similar results in sheer economic terms, though not in political.)

Furthermore, both management and labor, given the totality of nuclear war, are beginning to assess their responsibility to a world public order to guarantee peace. Former president of IBM Thomas Watson's call for "World Peace Through World Trade" was a forerunner of multinational corporate recognition that war is a no-growth business, a truth which unfortunately has yet to penetrate the board rooms of many of Fortune's 500.

Labor representatives likewise, such as Ernest DeMaio, World Federation of Trade Unions representative to the United Nations, see the dead-end of the nationalistic arms race, no matter how lucrative to certain industries in the short-term:

> *"The military cost of bolstering deteriorating spheres of vital interests are counter-productive and can be maintained only by further reducing the living standards at home. Nor can this trend be reversed by military adventures abroad."* [63]

The President of the United Electrical Workers of Canada, Dick Barry, in citing the conservatism of the national leaders of the major American labor unions, notably the AFL-CIO, as regard global responsibilities, writes that *"In a climate where the peace question is coming increasingly to the forefront, we should be taking the lead to see to it that it gets discussed in our local unions."*[64]

The **Mutual Affluence System** eliminates the need for nationalization, the chimera of old-line socialism, by implementing ownership directly to those concerned, the individual and his or her family.

As to the **World Government**, it already exists in the legitimate pledges of individuals throughout the world to the status of world citizen. Indeed, if human rights themselves are legitimate, then the human right to choose one's global political status is likewise legitimate.

> *"Everyone is entitled to a social and international order so that the rights and freedoms set forth in this Declaration can be fully realized."*

Article 28, UDHR

In sum, extending globally, there is no reason why, given our electronic, computerized, technically-advanced world that this individual ownership principle coupled with the dynamic fact of a political recognition of our species cannot transform the world in which we live to that promised land of general abundance and world peace with freedom in order to maintain the age-old thrust toward higher intellectual, cultural and spiritual worlds which have been revealed to us throughout the ages by the sages and poets.

Who owns the world?

The citizens thereof.

But we must claim it or there will be no one and nothing to claim.

****

NOTES AND REFERENCES

1. *Values Magazine* Vol. 4, No. 2, Gurukula Press, Varkala, India.
2. Buckminster Fuller, *Utopia or Oblivion*, (The Overlook Press, 1969), p. 242.
3. Ibid, p. 276.
4. Ibid, p. 277.
5. Ibid, p. 176.
6. A 1982 study by the National Taxpayer's Union reveals that the U.S. Government is saddled with a "Taxpayer's Liability Index" (TLI) of over $11.6 trillion, a hidden burden of approximately $145,000 on each taxpayer. According to the report, there are now only an estimated 80 million real taxpayers left in the U.S. This TLI includes the public debit of $1,050 trillion, accounts payable, $167 billion, undelivered orders, $487 billion, long term contracts, $21 billion, loan and credit guarantees, $360 billion, insurance commitments, $2,227 billion, and annuity or pension programs, $7,281 billion. Interests payments alone on the "official" Federal debt of 1980 cost taxpayers an estimated $57 million, six times the Federal interest costs in 1960 and $14 billion more than the total Federal budget in 1950.
7. Third-world nation debt is now over $500 billion, up from roughly $100 billion a decade ago. Over 60% of that debt is owed to Western banks. Mexico is 60 billion in debt, Brazil, $87 billion, and Poland, $26 billion. With regard to African nations according to the Christian Science Monitor (February 3, 1983, p. 13), "What is significant about Africa's foreign indebtedness is not its size, but the rapidity of its growth — from under $20 billion in 1975 to almost $45 billion in 1979 (reflecting the impact of the rise in oil prices), to $56 billion in 1981, and $66 billion in 1982." "The debt problem threatens to overwhelm the world economic system..." (Christian Science Monitor, January 25, editorial.)
9. Axel Madsen, *Private Power*, (Wm. Morrow & Co., NY, 1980), p. 11.
10. In a January 31, 1983 *U.S. News & World Report* article, "How To Get The Country Moving Again," six Nobel Prize economists, Milton Friedman, Paul Samuelson, George Stigler, Lawrence Klein, Kenneth Arrow and James Tobin expose their grasp of fundamental economic realities by ignoring: 1) the gross inequality of ownership of wealth-producing machines not only in the United States but in all other countries; 2) the dynamic relationship between war economy, i.e., the nation-state, and today's global recession; 3) the interdependence of all national economies implying that economic solutions must be wholistic or global to be realistic; 4) the imperative need for a world political order as concomitant to a world economic order.
11. J.M. Keynes, *The Economic Consequences of the Peace*, 1923.
12. Stockholm International Peace Research Institute Yearbook, 1979, MIT Press.
13. U.N. Publications, Sales No., 62.IX.1 (E/3593/Rev.1).
14. Leonid Brezhnev on October 20, 1983 stated that "Only he who has decided to commit suicide can start a nuclear war." President Ronald Reagan on October 21, 1983 stated that "In a nuclear war, all mankind would lose."
15. Introduction, Reply of the U.S. Gov't., p. 235.
16. Reply of the Government of the U.S.S.R., p. 194.
17. Stuart Chase interviewed Michael Bohr, a high official of Gosplan, the central planning agency of the Soviet Union, in Moscow in 1961. In his book *Money To Grow On*, p. 146, he recalls the following conversations:"'What are you going to do about the transfer from bombs to butter; won't that bring economic disruption and unemployment?' The reply was, 'Not too much. We have the transition pretty well planned. Besides, we've been through it before... In 1959 we reduced the armed forces by two million, principally personnel for land armies and ships, now obsolete. Because of previous planning...we had no great trouble relocating the enlisted men...Placing the officers, however, gave us a good deal of trouble; they only knew how to do one thing...'"
18. "Sixty firms control the capitalist system," *Der Spiegel* headlined a three-part inquiry into global enterprise in 1974. By 1985, the Organization for Economic Cooperation and Development (OECD) estimates, some 300 companies will produce more than half the world's goods and services, but already in 1967, *Fortune* magazine could say that the inner core of capitalizm consisted of 60 enterprises, controlled by less than 1,000 individuals." Axel Madsen, *Private Power* (Wm. Morrow & Co., NY 1980), p. 40.
19. Morton Mintz, *America, Inc.*, (Dial Press, 1971), p. 12 & 18.
19a. Ibid, p. 15.
20. *Multi-national Corporations & World Development*.
21. Anthony Sampson, *The Sovereign-state of ITT* (Viking Press, NY 1975), p. 302.
22. M. Blume, S. Franklin, D. Wion, *The Distribution of Financial Assets*, 1973 Conference on Wealth Distribution, People's Policy Center, Wash., D.C. Also, *Broadening the Ownership of New Capital: ESOP & Other Alternatives*, Staff study, Congress of the United States, June 17, 1976, p. 13.

23. Louis O. Kelso & Patricia Hetter, *Two-Factor Theory* (Vintage Books, NYC, 1967), p. 11. "The heart of an economic system is its principle of distribution. Real wealth is goods and services; its production takes place in the physical world under natural laws that are everywhere the same. Regardless of an economy's political structure, production problems must be solved pragmatically through science, engineering, technology, mangement and skills of labor. Out of the production process, however, arises wealth or income, and distribution of this wealth or income involves problems of a different order. There is a political dimension to distribution as well as a physical one; its character is derived from the economy's principle of distribution." p. 12.

24. Article 25(1).

25. Karl Marx & Friedrich Engels, *The Communist Manifesto*, 1843.

26. Director, Center for Economic & Social Justice, Arlington, VA.

27. Ralph Nader, *The Monopoly Makers*, (Grossman, NY, 1973), p. x.

28. Ibid, p. x.

29. The duplicity of national leaders was exposed by President Ronald Reagan in his January 25 State of the Union message wherein, with over 10 million unemployed in the U.S., he made no mention of the gross inequality of United States' ownership patterns whereas in a letter of June 12, 1981 to Delaware Governor Pierre du Pont IV, on the occasion of that state's General Assembly adoption of House Bill 31 making it the policy of the state to encourage broadening the base of capital ownership among the citizens, Reagan wrote that "I have long believed that the widespread distribution of private property ownership is essential to the preservation of individual liberty, to the strength of our competitive free enterprise economy and to our republican form of government."

30. Louis O. Kelso & Mortimer Adler, *Capitalist Manifesto*, (Random House, 1958), p. 79.

31. Ibid, Note 2.

32. Ibid, p. 158.

33. "Essence of the world's working will be to make every man able to become a world citizen and be able to enjoy the whole earth, going wherever he wants at any time, able to take care of all needs of all his forward days without any interference with any other man and never at the cost of another man's freedom and advantage." *Utopia or Oblivion.* p. 158.

34. "The war on (U.S.) inflation is not being won. Inflation at the fiscal level is simply being transferred from dollar inflation to interest rate inflation. This new inflation is clearly measured by ominous increases in budget deficits and national debt." ("Washington Wonderland", Sid Taylor, *Dollars & Sense*, Vol. 13, No. 6, National Taxpayers Union.)

35. Emery Reves, *Anatomy of Peace*, (Random House, Inc. 1945), p. 14.

36. Adam Smith, *The Money Game*, (Dell, 1967), p. 20.

37. The U.S. military expenditures jumped from $44 billion in 1960 to $81 billion in 1970.

38. Ibid, Note 2, p. 262.

39. Axel Madsen, *Private Power*, (Wm. Morrow & Co., 1980), p. 26.

40. Oliver Cushing Dwinnel, *The Story of Our Money*, (Meador Publishing Co., Boston, 1946), p. 88 (Note).

41. Gerald G. McGreer, *Conquest of Poverty*, (The Garden City Press, Gardenvale, Quebec, Canada), p. 174.

42. Congressional Report (Senate), Document No. 23, 76th Congress, 1st Session "The National Economy and Banking System of the United States." p. 80.

43. Stuart Chase, *Money To Grow On*, (Harper & Row, 1964), p. 79.

44. Arthur Kitson, *Trade Fallacies*, (P.S. King & Son, Ltd., Orchard House, London), p. 25.

45. Ibid, Note 2.

46. Sages express this notion as the law of fulfilment: "To he who has, it shall be given, etc." while modern-day psychologists call it the "Law of Expectations."

47. Ibid, Note 2, p. 302.

48. Ibid, Note 36.

49. See Note 34.

50. Timothy Green, *The World of Gold*, (Walker & Co., NY, 1968).

51. Ibid. Note 50, p. 217. "Even then, the SDRs will be introduced cautiously and will not provide enough liquidity to keep up with the expansion of world trade", Ibid, p. 216.

52. *International Harry Schultz Letter*, (July, 1975).

53. In 1974, the world's hungry totalled 740 million, according to President Carter's Commission on World Hunger, headed by Sol Linovitz. Three years later, after good world harvests, the hungry totalled 800 million. "The principal cause of world hunger," the Commission reported, "is not the occasional disaster that captures world attention, but the enduring condition of subhuman poverty that afflicts as many as 1 in 5 members of the human family." According to Linovitz, "While recent international events have

heightened concern for national security, we as a people (USA) must understand that the U.S. and other developed countries can never be secure in a world of widespread hunger and intensive poverty."

54. Nataraja Guru, *Memorandum on World Government*, Section V, part 2.

55. "In the words of United States Senator Charles Mathias, as quoted in today's Monitor, 'The dilemma we face is not just an economic one, but also one of general confidence in our financial system." Editorial (Christian Science Monitor) January 24, 1983.

56. In 1975, only 370 shareholder proposals were submitted to the SEC of which half eventually appeared in the proxy statement. Ref.: International Human Rights and Practice, ABA, 1978.

57. "With the firm's (Lockheed Aircraft) resources spread out all over the world and the firm's threats and opportunities similarly dispersed, the managers have seen themselves as exposed and vulnerable. As they see it, the sovereign-states can apply force with little or no restraint. With impunity, they can break previous commitments, raise taxes, cancel patents, nationalize properties, and expropriate assets." Raymond Vernon, Director, Harvard Center for International Affairs, Cambridge, Massachusetts.

58. Such as: The Religious Order for Corporate Responsibility, New York, NY.

59. Ibid, Note 23.

60. Ref.: Center for Economic & Social Justice, P.O.B. 40849 Wash., D.C. 20016

61. "Theoretically, labor should have no difficulty countering the challenge of global enterprise. In reality, however, unions are stuck in neutral, benevolent monopolies too chauvinistic and too parochial to accommodate to modern economics. Although their early leaders called upon workers to unite, unions pay only lip service to the brotherhood of the laboring masses when it comes to risking jobs to support workers in other lands. In thinking, structure and goals, they are rooted in the last century." Axel Madsen, *Private Power*, p. 181.

62. Ernest De Maio, *Taming The Multinationals*, Economic Notes, July-August, 1982, p.4.

63. Ibid, p. 4.

64. Ibid, p. 6.

CHAPTER 17

WHO OWNS SPACE?

Whereas in the 18th century, discretionary powers of heads of state enabled them to address other, distant nations—separated by great time and distance barriers as compared to today—with a single voice, necessary to trade, communications and even limited security, today such powers render them, including President Reagan, virtual dictators.

In this respect, the U.S. president and the Chairman of the Supreme Soviet are identical.

But unlike other eras when such extraordinary and even extra-legal powers did not risk the extinction of the race itself, our present time, literally nuclear-triggered, principally by the two super-powers, can permit no margin of error in the use of the unilateral power by single heads of state, no matter how large and seemingly powerful.

Neither Mr. Reagan nor Mr. Chernenko pretend to nor can speak for the human race itself. Yet it is the human race today, along with each human, which is being held hostage to their collective nuclear threats.

Both Mr. Reagan and Mr. Chernenko legally assume control over the destinies of their respective nations and people. But such an assumption, given the nature of the relative power they both wield, and the nature of the problem their people face, is patently irrational.

Given the nature of today's weapons, the assumption is suicidal.

Furthermore, it reveals a fundamental ignorance of the wisdom-science known in Western philosophical terms as dialectics and in Eastern as Brahma Vidya (sanskrit). The branch of dialectics dealing with human events is known as geo-dialectics. In the geo-dialecticasl equation, USA = USSR, as the tension at each end of a stretched rubber band is equal and opposite.

United States unilateral "power," being interdependent and bi-polar to its counterpart, the USSR, is illusory, and vice versa. In short, the so-called power of Mr. Reagan and Mr. Cherneko is relative to each other and moreover *dependent on*

310

each other. Witness the "foreign policies" of each being totally negative: "anti-Communism;" anti-capitalism" or "anti-imperialism," (read "anti-USSR nation," "anti-USA nation") whereas the problem facing them both and the common people are total or global, the major one being world war itself, ironically legitimized by the very nation-state system, a carryover from the age of the sailing ship and the speed of the horse.

This dichotomy leads to statements and policies which only exacerbate the apparent duality and inevitably lead to the holocaust they both seek, at least theoretically, to prevent. A "launch-on-warning" national policy is a prime example of such two-dimensional thinking.

In simplistic terms, the supposedly "foreign" policies of the USA and the USSR depend exclusively on each other. Take one away and the other would collapse. The action-reaction syndrome is easily and almost daily exposed by any amateur historian, discerning newspaper readers and now by deeply concerned high school and even grammar school students.

Mr. Reagan fails to recognize this obvious bi-polarity or at least it is never mentioned in his public remarks and certainly not in his advocacy of a "strong national defense."

For example, on March 8, 1983, in his address before the National Association of Evangelicals, in positing the "cold war" as a "struggle between "right and wrong," "good and evil," where the United States is "right" and "good" while the Soviet Union is "wrong" and "evil," he totally ignored the co-partnership of the two nations in maintaining an anarchic state between them. That he recognized such a state exists, however, was implicitly revealed in his June 17, 1982 address before the United Nations' General Assembly wherein he called for a "rule of law" over the Member-States. His national policies before and since, totally contradict that recognition.

Then in the same address of March 8, 1983, he justly equated righteousness and goodness with the deity. But since the deity, being the Supreme Law which is, by simple definition, universal or in earthly terms, worldly, he cannot but accept then that these virtues have nothing to do with the political fiction called the national state. On the contrary, the very exclusiveness of the sovereign nation denies that universality. Thus, in the U.S. president's terms, it, the nation, must be "evil," and "wrong."

Since his entire foreign policy is sustained by a condition of anarchy between nations—despite the twaddle about "international law"—he obviously supports evil, wrong or immorality. Chairman Chernenko likewise supports the same evil, wrong or immorality. So must every head of state who does not actively advocate world law and its sovereign institutions.

Furthermore, his reference to Jesus Christ as supporting America's "cause" reveals a distorted if not totally wrong view of both Christ's mission and America's "cause." Christ's mission was obviously global and humane (and anti-state) amply expressed in biblical writings and eye-witness accounts of his actions. His "Lord's Prayer" aptly defines his mission: "Thy will be done on earth as it is in heaven." His allusion to the sword the night of his betrayal was an example of pure dialectical reasoning. Neither the American nor the Soviet people want to "die by the (nuclear) sword," yet that is precisely the way both leaders oblige them to live.

As to America's "cause," if there be any, it is to help fulfil the doctrine of representative government on a global basis. Otherwise, the very universal principles enunciated by the founding fathers and enshrined in the opening words of the Declaration of Independence and the Constitution will have been betrayed.

Then, the U.S. president's March 21, 1983 address proposing a so-called space defense against the threat of a Soviet nuclear attacks reveals starkly not only the impotence of national power when applied to a universal medium but again an abysmal and perhaps mortal ignorance of dialectical reasoning.

While the technical and economic absurdities of his proposal are being exposed elsewhere by specialists in these fields, here I will deal only with the fundamental irrationality and then illegality or lawlessness of his proposition.

The supposed intellectual basis of the proposal, if one could dignify it with a thought process, can only rest on the assumption that the United States "owns" the space surrounding our home planet. Otherwise, it could not place "defensive" missiles in space at will. To state this is to expose its irrationality. For if true, each and every nation, being equal in sovereignty, including Seychelles, Nauru and Lesotho, could make the same claim, including, of course, the Soviet Union, the U.S.A.'s geo-dialectical counterpart or "twin."

But space, by definition, is vertical to nations and humans living on the planet. Indeed, it is literally about 80 miles from every human. It "mirrors" the entire planet and human society. It reveals stunningly and starkly our common home. In brief, it forces us to face reality, the reality that the atmosphere is common, the soil is common, the water is common, the energy is common, the earth itself is common to all humans, not to mention the myriad other species who live here with us.

It exposes, by contrast, our politically parochial and tunnel vision, as Emery Reves wrote in *Anatomy of Peace*, as "nation-centric."

National law is, in geometric terms, horizontal, that is, it deals with relationships between humans on earth as well as relationship with other nations on earth (international law). It cannot deal with space as such, which is vertical to earth itself. The best proof is that should extra-terrestrials land on earth, national law could not define their status, prosecute them for entering illegally or legally prevent their leaving. Indeed, national law cannot even cope with the seas, the atmosphere, or the status of "stateless persons" such as the author.

Likewise, when Cosmonauts and Astronauts take off vertically, they pass no immigration or customs, no national frontiers and carry no national passports—

what an absurdity! Upon their return, they break no national laws of entry. (It would be amusing as well as instructive if a Soviet manned satellite landed one day in a Kansas cornfield or the Columbia landed in a plowed field near Minsk.) Therefore, "legally," they leave and return to earth as humans, not as national citizens. Some of them have had interesting wholistic and no doubt embarrassing statements to make upon their return to earth.

Law concerning human relations in space, by definition, must obviously be global agreed to by all the citizens of the world.

As President Reagan continues to advocate the monopolization of space, he cannot escape the obvious relevant legal questions: How high does national law extend? By what constitutional right? Does he consider that his discretionary powers arrogate to him a legal right to pollute our common space with national conflicts he cannot resolve on earth? Does he not recognize such a policy as not only treason to humankind and to each human but fundamentally illegitimate? Or does he claim that the constitution framers meant for a U.S. president to claim legitimacy over the very space blanket surrounding the entire planet? For that is the program he is advocating as U.S. president.

If it were not for the dignity of his office and the obvious affront to the American people, one could claim clinically that the man occupying the White House is as insane as his would-be assassin, John Hinckley, for while he owes his present mandate to a constitutional process, his "Space Wars" scenario is a reliance on destruction so massive as to threaten the entire human race whereas the pitiful Hinckley only tried to eliminate one person.

To consider that two latter-day political fictions, one barely 200 years old, the other a mere 62 years old, can monopolize or "militarize" space around the entire planet is to suspend, or better, deny the accumulated moral and wisdom heritage of over 3,000 years.

The human venture into space, in fact, already raises our civic status to the planetary level, a status this writer claimed over thirty years ago (emulating Socrates and Erasmus) and which even Reagan claimed both for himself and the American people in his U.N. speech of June 17, 1982. Yet he continues to ignore the required wholesale approach to world peace in his simplistic and illusory advocacy of "security through strength" for the United States alone.

Fortunately, his and Chairman Chernenko's two-dimensional view of the world is being increasingly exposed as inherently irrational (if not criminal) and inadequate to the safety and well-being of the American and Soviet peoples as to our human race itself. That is why serious men and women from all walks of life not only question their policies but are awakening in vast numbers to the reality of one world and the imminent danger it faces.

The bottom of the line is, as Jonathan Schell brought out startlingly in *Fate of the Earth*, the term of the exclusive nation-state has run its historic course. Humanity's survival depends on human, i.e., global institutions of, by and for the people of the world.

Ronald Reagan's responsibility to that survival is exceedingly heavy at this fateful moment, as is Konstantin Chernenko's. They will both have much to answer for if they fail to understand and act accordingly.

CHAPTER 18

WILL REAGAN ENDORSE WORLD GOVERNMENT AT U.N.?

It's not as if the U.S. President isn't informed. As Governor of California, he joined the World Federalists during Alan Cranston's presidency of that organization.

Then on July 15, 1980, during the campaign, we wrote the candidate that "If you are elected President of the United States, without the institution of a political world order, you must remain powerless to bring about the changes to which you are commiting your present efforts before the U.S. electorate.."

"A national president, within the framework of an exclusive constitution," the letter continued, "cannot obviously extend the very constitutional mandate binding him.."

The candidate replied on September 5, 1980 thanking us for the information, ending with "I will study it carefully and am most grateful for your thoughtfulness."

Our next letter to the candidate of September 24, 1980 pointed out that ". . . Peace in the world can only result. . . when war is eliminated *between* nation-states . . ." and that "As any legislator or public official knows, peace is the result of law, not raw strength. . ."

John McClaughry, a Reagan Senior Policy Advisor, replied on October 8, 1980 that "You raise some vital issues which candidates should address." He continued that "I believe Governor Reagan would agree with you that 'peace in the world can only result when war is eliminated between nation states'. . ."

Then on January 19, 1981, the day before Ronald Reagan took his oath of office, we personally delivered the following letter (excerpted) to Blair House where he and Mrs. Reagan were staying:

"As you are about to take office as the next President of the United States, please accept my wishes for a successful and above all, peaceful term of national office. . .

"In my letters to you of July 15, 1980 and September 24, 1980, I reiterated the theme that world peace is every human being's business and could only be effectuated by the outlawing of war between nation-states. This due process of

315

law, I insisted, was beyond the legitimate framework of the nation-states themselves just as the nation is a separate and enlarged legal framework distinct from both states and/or local jurisdictions.

"This is to inform you then that the Government which represents us in matters pertaining to inclusive or global concerns – such as international war, for instance – is the World Government of World Citizens, declared September 4, 1953 at Ellsworth, Maine.

"Each and every individual who pledges his/her allegiance to this world government does so in the full knowledge that he/she is exercising a fundamental human right of direct representation in the community of his/her interests, i.e., the world community.

"To that end, your administration – as all like national administrations – will be duly informed of those U.S. nationals who so extend their allegiance to our Government so that, in so far as the 'foreign' policy of your administration is concerned, they will henceforth be represented by the World Government of World Citizens and not by that strictly national policy . . ."

The President did not reply to this letter. Neither did he reply to our letter of November 1, 1981 after both he and Brezhnev declared respectively that "In a nuclear war, all mankind would lose," and "Only he who has decided to commit suicide can start a nuclear war." In this letter our pointed out the illegitimacy of a war which was not "winnable."

"We, the world's people," the letter stated in part, "have an acceptance, finally, from the leaders of the two nations most heavily engaged in the so-called nuclear arms race that, once started, a nuclear war would not only prove unwinnable for either side, but would be virtual suicide for the human race. Thus, an original premise of war as a legitimate facet of national policy, i.e., that it was winnable, is admitted by you and the Soviet Chairman as invalid in the case of nuclear war. I note further that the power to wage war itself has been declared illegitimate by both the Nuremburg Decisions and the International Military Tribunal for the Far East as well as the United Nations Charter, Article 1, and the Universal Declaration of Human Rights . . ."

We enclosed our petition for certiorari to the Supreme Court which makes the legitimate case for world citizenship utilizing principally the Ninth Amendment. ". . . you will note my claim, among others," we added, "that the Ninth Amendment to the U.S. Constitution implicitly sanctions an extension of citizenship to the global level without which national citizenship itself becomes – as both you and Chairman Brezhnev tacitly agreed – a collective suicide pact."

So President Ronald Reagan cannot plead innocence as to what are the requirements for world peace. Neither can he deny the 250,000 odd fellow world citizens' claims to our worldly government, publicly declared and wilfully chosen as the object of our highest allegiance, which transcends national frontiers by definition and defines a new social contract.

The U.N. podium is perhaps the most ironic spot from which to advocate a world government. But the U.S. President has chosen it deliberately and we will be listening for his words of wisdom...and world peace.

World renowned violinist and traveler Yehudi Menuhin [right], receives an honorary World Passport from World Service Authority president Garry Davis following a benefit concert at the Kennedy Center, Washington, D.C. A WSA World Passport holder since 1954, Menuhin was given the honorary passport in recognition of promoting freedom of travel everywhere.

CHAPTER 19

OVERCOMING THE BARRIERS TO
TRANSNATIONAL CIVIC IDENTITY
by Garry Davis
(Presented to the 2nd Annual Meeting of the
INTERNATIONAL SOCIETY OF POLITICAL PSYCHOLOGY
May 26, 1979, Washington, D.C.)

INTRODUCTION

As the human race stands inside the threshold of the last quarter of the 20th century, it finds itself paradoxically on the brink of calamity while at the same time physically capable of realizing the promises of the Millenium.

The stark and now permanent interdependence of human civilization in terms of economics, ecology, politics, and general human fulfillment as forced upon us by a number of factors including population growth and the technological compression of space and acceleration of time has, in reality, if not in public awareness, become the issue underlying all other social issues.

For the first time in human history, the problems of the planet in toto have become the problems of the individual; conversely, the problems of only one individual could become the problem of the planet. In a world where the push of one button by a national figure or a terrorist could trigger the end of civilization as we know it, world peace has become, in reality, the concern of each individual.

But world peace will depend upon a profound psychological and political transformation for its achievement; thus we search for an understanding of and a method for achieving that transformation permitting us to examine and overcome the barriers that stand in its way.

It is the conclusion of the author after more than 30 years' experience in dealing with this issue that the transformation required involves far more than religious passivity, "born again" nationalism or organizations that are merely "for peace." Rather, it requires a wholistic rethinking of the entire relationship between the individual, the world community, and power institutions, and the achievement of

318

a new, transnational civic status involving both subjective and objective components.

This paper, then, will describe the gaps between individuals across national frontiers and individuals vis-a-vis the world community itself. It will examine the causes for the persistence of these gaps, drawing out along the way the conceptual and psychological implications of transnational civic identity and the barriers that cause us continually to bypass that identity in our search for solutions to global problems. Finally the paper will describe how a recent phenomenon called the World Government of World Citizens has tried and is trying to implement the concept and overcome the barriers.

We conclude that the gaps between individuals and between the individual and the world community can be bridged, but only by a profound orientation of our fundamental human sovereignty.

The Gaps

When we think of a gap, we think of two sides with no bridge between them, two sides of an equation with the "equals" sign missing.

For example, two humans face each other, each speaking a different language. The result: a language gap, no verbal communication.

Two humans face each other on opposite sides of their respective national frontiers. Here is the classic political gap. The result: national defense against the "foreignor." The economic gap is obvious. The result is social unrest and eventual revolt.

In human terms, a gap means that the parties on opposite sides of the human equation are identified with elements that exclude one another. Despite their shared human identity and environment, relative difference have evolved which separate as well as oppose them, seemingly with no possibility of reconciliation. Violent conflicts are thus almost inevitable in such situations.

The gaps between individuals within the world community, in certain essential ways, have never been greater than they are today.

Economically, the scale ranges from starvation to individual billionaires and defense bureaucracies that spend every 1.5 years enough money ($600 billion) to provide the entire world population with adequate sanitation—a feat that would eliminate the deaths of over 9 million people per year, according to figures from the World Health Organization.

In language and education we see a world where, excepting Mandarin Chinese, no language is spoken by more than 10% of the world's population. Yet almost no official effort is being made to create or choose a common second language so that any member of the human race could, upon desire or necessity, communicate with any other member. Instead, students spend years trying to learn a difficult "foreign" ethnic language, governments spend millions on promoting their respective languages abroad, and the United Nations spends over $100 million per year translating itself into six "official" languages.

Language is one of humanity's most precious possessions, yet national languages, while preserving cultural values, also contribute to international disunity. Linking the individual and the world community together is already possible in terms of communication technology, but despite its enormous potentials for education and the process of democracy, this possibility lies undeveloped because of nationalism and the language gap.

The Political/Legal Gap

The political/legal gap consists chiefly of one simple fact: neither the individual human nor the world community has yet been fully legalized or politically represented.

Put another way, there does not currently exist a sovereign political or legal framework with which the individual can directly interact on a transnational civic basis. The history of national governmental peace initiatives from the 1899 First Hague Conference to establish a permanent court of arbitration to settle international disputes all the way through the creation of the United Nations in 1945 shows a steady denial by national officials of the necessity of considering the individual as a subject of international or world law, insisting instead on the "sovereign equality of peace-loving states" as the basis for the process of peace.

Yet this lack of standing in international law leaves the individual without a legal remedy against a criminal action committed by people serving in a foreign national government. If a government official detonates a nuclear bomb, the fallout may damage citizens in another country. Yet there is no court that will accept their suit for damages and an injunction, even though the factual situation is in every physical and human way analogous to an actionable offense under common law. The anomoly is carried to absurdity by the court established by the nation-states themselves, the International Court of Justice at the Hague. In this so-called court, the offending party may not only ignore any findings or decisions the court may make, but also can refuse to be a litigant.

Likewise, the individual has no direct political remedy against the offensive policies of foreign national governments. There exists, for example, no world parliament to which the individual or the world community can turn for legislative relief. No electoral machinery exists as yet whereby the concerned individual could run as a world candidate on an anti-nuclear or even anti-war platform.

The international political gap between individuals of separate countries has its corollary within nations as well, where even as national citizens we are virtually excluded from the making of "foreign policy." Our leaders speak and act in the name of the state itself in the world of states, using the citizen in effect as objects of fear or threats to the outside world. Democracy has no part in this process. Instead, the citizen is reduced to an appendage of the state machine. Taking to the streets is his only recourse left for influencing his leaders, at least until the next election.

The psychological implication of all this is that because we lack effective legal and political remedies against the criminal actions of persons in national governments – either abroad or at home – both the individual and humanity as a whole are rendered insignificant and impotent. Each of us in effect finds himself in the psychologically crippling position of having no effective control over his fate or environment as constituted and determined by the foreign policies of crisis-ridden nation-states, which foreign policies nonetheless have vital implications for our immediate wellbeing and future.

In summary, the input for each of us as individuals is direct, personal, and global in its origin, yet our responses are limited to being indirect, impersonal, and merely national (at best). In effect we live in a perpetual engine of frustration. Lacking a transnational civic status, we thus turn the problems in upon ourselves as sublimal tensions which we then try to avoid through pleasure, fantasy, escapism, or by confining our interests to more limited spheres wherein the sense of relative influence, power and being can be maintained. When it comes to the subject of world peace, we manifest apathy, avoidance, or hostility, thus perpetuating the inherently conflictive political system which robbed us of our power and sense of purpose to begin with.

Why Do The Gaps Persist?

To describe the historical causes of all the gaps is a task beyond the scope of this paper obviously. The factors that contribute to their persistence and intensity, however, need to be examined.

As factors intensifying the effects of the gaps we might first mention population growth, now at over 2% per year with a population of 4.7 billion. Should present trends continue, the world community will have 8 billion by the year 2000. Thus, should the current gaps continue, they will be compounded by the increased number of people involved.

Secondly, the speed of travel has increased 1000-fold in less than 100 years. The horse was the fastest mode of transportation until 1839, when the railroad came on the scene. In 1907 the car made its appearance, and in 1917, the warplane, going over 200 mph. From there technology took us to the intercontinental ballistic missile, travelling thousands of miles per hour and thus eliminating distance as an element of national security.

Thirdly, communications have become almost instantaneous, travelling at the speed of light. Information has exploded also in quantity as fundamental revolutions have occurred in all branches of science. Yet here again we should observe that much of our current information simply reinforces the separate sides of the gap equation. As a result, without the organizing principle of transnational civic identity, it degenerates in effect into mere "social noise" rather than enlightening, clear signals, into overload rather than in-depth understanding.

Many other factors, above all thc cxponcntial growth of the destructiveness of weapons, have contributed to bringing the world together in physical ways that render the gaps within the world community far more obstrusive and far more potentially dangerous than ever before.

Why then do the gaps persist?

In addition to the social and emotional components of the cycle of decreasing individual sovereignty and importance noted previously, there is, of course, the component of ignorance of alternative approaches to the problem. But even ignorance by itself does not suffice to explain why the gaps have persisted, because we can ask, "Why does ignorance itself persist in the face of the tremendous stresses involved, which ordinarily should lead us to seek innovations to relieve those stresses?"

The ignorance and lack of interest in alternative approaches to peace persist because, as we recall, a gap connotes opposition and the barrier to overcoming that opposition is that the parties involved are identifying with elements that preclude linkage or truly shared identity. These are not only intellectual but often emotional elements that are much more powerful than the mere intellectual fact of overall unity.

We think of politicians as dealing in the realm of action. Yet because they identify themselves in ways that polarize the field of action into exclusive territories, they preclude unitive actions that are necessary to maintain the quality of that holistic field. Thus in focusing on "God and country," they become blind to the possibility of "God and planet." Conversely, religions, which should make us think of wisdom and wholeness, by trying to claim for themselves the stamp of exclusive divine origin or approval, short-circuit the application of the universalist ethical principles that in fact lie embedded in their teachings.

We wind up with politicians who cannot truly act and religionists who miss the point of their whole teaching.

For world peace to occur, these two elements, the elements of action and the elements of wisdom must somehow reunite within the individual to produce the new transational civic stratus and institutions that our situation calls for.

Bridging The Gaps — A Case History Of The World Government of World Citizens

> *"As nations are torn apart and restructured, as TNCs and other new actors move onto the global scene, as instabilities and the threats of war erupt, we shall be called upon to invent wholly new political forms or "containers" to bring a semblance of order to the world – a world in which the nation-state has become for many purposes, a dangerous anachronism."*
>
> *The Third Wave*, Alvin Toffler

Simply to describe why the gaps persists is unfortunately not automatically to overcome them. To do that, we must opt out of being one side of the conflict equation. We must beging dealing with each other as human beings *on a universal basis.*

This process starts by realizing that by definition all humans have, at least in terms of physical and mental processes, a shared identity. In political terms, this is called "citizenship." Citizenship as used here implies an additional shared social content, the conscious linking of the individual to the group whole and of the individual to other individuals under a common framework of law and justice. It implies qualities of responsibility, impartiality, creativity and concern for oneself as well as for others.

In relation to the political gaps described earlier, we recognize that the qualities embodied in citizenship are the keys to bridging them. The mandate for a world citizenship is generated by the necessity by each and all individuals to eliminate the political gaps for the sake of sheer survival in the nuclear age.

In addition, the physical limitations laid down by the environment and the biosphere have become an absolute mandate for world citizenship and its government if we wish to avoid disastrous penalties.

Granted that now we have some idea of what transnational civic identity, or world citizenship, implies, psychologically speaking, and of where we want to go with the concept in terms of world institutions. Granted also that we have not been totally "psyched out" of our individual sovereignty by the nation-state system and that we have therefore the motivation to "begin walking" as world citizens. The question now becomes, how do we begin to move our legs, so to speak. The rest of this paper, as a case history of the World Government of World Citizens, will try to sketch out an answer.

We note first that throughout history, men of vision, courage and good-will have attempted to bring peace through law to warring factions. From the *Decalogue* of Moses through the *Magna Carta,* the *Declaration of the Rights of Man and the Citizen* of 1789, the *Declaration of Independence,* The U.S. *Bill of Rights,* the *Atlantic Charter* and the *Universal Declaration of Human Rights,* deeply concerned men and women have sought to resolve conflicts by right based on individual sovereignty rather than the might of exclusive social units.

This vision of peace, from the earliest days, contained global aspirations, Plato's "Republic," the perenniel "City of God," one of the meanings of Zion, Christ's universal command that "Thy will be done on earth as it is in heaven," to present-day declarations of "one world" and "world order" from statesmen and ordinary citizens alike, certify a deep drive, almost a categorical imperative, to consider peace as indivisible, total, or simply human.

The sovereign individual is then, we claim, the starting point for genuine peace. Now, despite the individual's lack of standing in most areas of international law, we find an implicit recognition of the individual's universal standing contained, with regard to war-making, in the Nuremberg Principles of 1945, under which the individual per se becomes subject to an international penal code defining war crimes as well as crimes against humanity, one of which is "preparing for. . .war." The Nuremberg Principles are part of international law.

With this point in mind, I must transpose from the general to the particular, and at the risk of appearing immodest, speak about my own actions.

Exactly 31 years ago yesterday, I renounced my exclusive allegiance and national identification as a United States citizen and claimed for myself the status of world citizenship.

I was opting out of the criminal framework forced upon me by the nation-state system, a framework that involved me personally under the Nuremberg Principles in complicity for the preparation of war or the threat of war. I was projecting myself as a sovereign human being into the global arena, which was as yet uncodified by law and thus ungoverned.

Admittedly, the act was one of desperation. But the psychological and emotional affinities of family, education, ethnic pride, love of profession, of social linkages, were subordinated to a fear of a third world war and a deep sense of personal commitment to world peace.

The legitimacy of this exercise of individual sovereignty was subsequently sanctioned by Article 15(2) of the *Universal Declaration of Human Rights,* which states in part: "Everyone has the right to change his nationality."

Unwittingly and somewhat unconsiously, I became over the next several years a "human tool" for a new type of world-level framework, hitherto lacking in all peace efforts.

Through a series of adventures involving the government of France and the United Natisons in Paris, the idea of world citizenship spread. Many others began joining in self identification as world citizens. From 1948 to 1953, a grass-roots movement evolved with little central cohesion or direction. Each declared world citizen was recognizing his or her sovereign right to choose a new political identity. In 1949, a world citizen registry was organized in Paris. Identification tools were issued called "World Citizen Identity Cards." Upwards of 750,000 individuals from over 100 countries registered and received such ID cards. It was the beginning of a *de facto* world political constituency.

On September 4, 1953, a new "tool" to complement the individual's affirmation of world citizenship was brought into being; a government of world citizens, if only in microcosm, was declared from the city hall of Ellsworth, Maine. As presumptuous as this act and undertaking may appear, it was entirely consistent in its response to the circumstances of nation-state anarchy to which I was subject personally as a stateless world citizen.

This world-level governmental framework, which was the missing link in previous peace efforts by both national leaders and citizens alike, is implicitly sanctioned by two articles of the *Universal Declaration of Human Rights.* Article 21 (3) states: *"The will of the people shall be the basis of the authority of government..."* Article 28 states: *"Everyone has the right to a social and international order in which the rights and freedoms set forth in this Declaration can be fully realized."*

Now that declared world citizens had their own fictional government, a third organizational tool was developed in 1954 to cope with the growing administrative tasks of the new government. The need, often desperate, for a travel document for world citizens and refugees – documents often impossible to obtain for one reason or another from national governments – gave rise to a new kind of passport, a passport not based on the restrictive powers of the nation-state but on the human right to travel as outlined by Article 13(2) of the UDHR, which states: *"Everyone has the right to leave any country, including his own, and to return to his country."*

The new administrative agency of the World Government of World Citizens was called the World Service Authority and opened its first offices in New York in January, 1954.

There was opposition as well as recognition of the new passport from various nation-states. The full story is told in my book *My Country Is The World.*

Suffice it to say, the conceptual basis of the World Government of World Citizens itself helps to overcome the psychological barriers imposed by the polarized, dualistic nation-state system simply by fully exposing that duality, in other words, by exposing the entire nation-state system as involving repression and lack of democracy, despite ideological appearances to the contrary; that is, vis-a-vis the nation-state's foreign policy functions and prerogatives we are not free citizens but subjects, and no nation-state, especially the super-powers, is prepared to relinquish control over its citizens in regard to these functions. This area of agreement between states, even those otherwise considered enemies, is clearly exposed by the World Government of World Citizens.

The World Service Authority puts alternatives to national identity documents within easy reach. Not only World Service Authority passports, but also World Government ID cards and birth certificates certify as to this new allegiance professed by the individual sovereign human. No act of becoming officially stateless or renouncing national citizenship is required to be a citizen of World Government, since what we are renouncing is not borders per se but allegiance to the exclusivity and absolute sovereignty of the national state. For the refugee, who has been cast outside the nation-state framework entirely, the World Government of World Citizens represents a global political asylum.

As a first test of the first world passport, I myself travelled to India in 1956 at the invitation of Guru Nataraja of Travancore. I felt my totally Western orientation was inadequate to understand the deeper psychological insights of the world citizen concept. The dualities of the nation-state were obvious enough: the outward anarchy vis-a-vis the internal order and law; the appointed diplomatic world vis-a-vis the elected legislative bodies, the civic commitment to internal peace vis-a-vis the soldier's commitment to external war. But what were the modalities of world unity? What was unity itself grounded on from a wisdom context? Nataraja Guru claimed he knew the answers. I went to sit at his feet.

From the visit came the beginnings of a new science "geo-dialectics" or as the guru has written: "...the method of clearly recognizing the two counterparts which belong together in any given situation or problem to be eased or resolved in human affairs."

In summary, we offer an idealistic yet empirical world government based on human rights as a counterpart to present nationalistic politics with its built-in gap syndrome. The registered world citizen has bridged the political/legal gap. He or she has become the veritable human equals sign between the two opposing sides. He/she has effectively neutralized the illusion of conflict

Since I am addressing a largely American audience, I want to refer to a clear mandate to this transnational civic identity incorporated in the very U.S. Constitution. It is the 9th and 10th amendments which refer sovereign decision-making power back "to the people," should the Constitution itself fail to delegate power for a particular problem.

For the European citizen, the upcoming election for a European parliament, while still essentially nationalistic, is indicative of the political trend towards globalism. Indeed, if an elected European parliament can come into being out of thin air, as it were, why not a peoples' world parliament? It but takes the candidates, the electors, and the election. The need is already apparent.

The World Government of World Citizens allows the individual to put his foot, so to speak, on solid, new ground, supported morally, politically and ecologically. It is a sovereign framework in which he can function up to his ethical and dynamic potential as a human being while at the same time learning to bridge all the other inherited gaps which heretofore have "psyched him out" into a state of confusion and isolation.

Finally, this clear signal of world unity personified by the world citizen will penetrate the public conscience in direct proportion to the loss of credibility of the present nation-state system to its own citizenry. Once the dynamic link between the individual consciousness and the transnational civic identity is made, that individual wakes up to the incredible fact that the world is *his* world and that he, not the mythical state, is sovereign.

At this point, the universal elements of religious teachings and democratic political and legal theories converge, bringing about a wholistic way of thinking about oneself and the world in which the individual becomes in a profound sense psychologically transformed and reoriented as a fuller human being. From the arena of our present chaos and conflictive loyalties, humankind and the sovereign human will wake up to what I am firmly convinced to be the fact, namely, that the reason national governments haven't been able to solve our human problems is that the exclusive national governments *are* the human problem.

Having awakened and taken action, having put national sovereignty into its proper perspective, we can then emerge into our rightful heritage of world peace, well-being and freedom.

"Alone in space, alone in its life-supporting systems, powered by inconceivable energies, mediating them to us through the most delicate adjustments, wayward, unlikely, unpredictable, but nourishing, enlivening, and enriching in the largest degree – is this not a precious home for all of us earthlings? Is it not worth our love? Does it not deserve all the inventiveness and courage and generosity of which we are capable to preserve it from degradation and destruction and, by doing so, to secure our own survival?"
Barbara Ward/Rene Dubois, *Only One Earth*

CHAPTER 20

NATIONALISM & RELIGION

"Thy Will be done on earth as it is in heaven."

The Lord's Prayer

All religious leaders have taught the unity of humankind and its oneness with the Creator of the universe.

Where is the equivalent of the prophets of old who roared their indignation and wrath against the forces of disunity and destruction to which in their blindness the people clung and proferred their allegiance? And more to the point, what is the latter-day equivalent of those ancient forces which sought to divide and then destroy?

In short, where are the religious leaders who condemn nationalism as the most insidious and powerful enemy of humankind and those principles of unity and universality underlying its very existence?

Nationalism demands the absolute allegiance of its subjects. A "national citizen" is actually a misnomer since a citizen is one "who owes allegiance to a government, and is entitled to protection from it." "Citizen" further implies that the government to which he/she owes allegiance enjoys its authority on the basis of the consent of the governed, whereas a "subject" is controlled arbitrarily by a personal sovereign or a power elite totally outside his/her control.

What nation-state today can protect its own "citizens" against World War III? National "peace-keeping machinery" is simply more armies. According to the International Institute for Strategic Studies "the political-military system that has more or less kept global order since World War II is breaking down and nothing is in sight to replace it." Dr. Christoph Bertram, its director, at a September, 1976 conference of 200 scholars, government officials and military experts, stated bluntly that "a new era is beginning (when) many of the old rules of the world game are no longer workable but that nobody has yet figured out the new rules."

"The big powers still have overwhelming force, but they can no longer use it to keep the rest of the world in line. Some of the developing countries are gain-

ing awesome military strength, but their conflicting interests have yet to be absorbed into a new system able to work out frictions peacefully."

The "hot line" between Francois Mitterand and Konstantin Chernenko underlines the impotence of Mr. Reagan, Mr. Kohl, Margaret Thatcher, Verwoed, Mubarek, Hassad, Khomeini, Gandhi, et al protecting their "citizens" from nuclear holocaust accidentally triggered off by either France or the Soviet Union.

In terms of the anarchy dominating the world community, national "citizenship" therefore is an illusion. If you claim such of a particular nation, disabuse yourself in the recognition that "your" nation is literally helpless to guarantee you the first human right, that of life itself. Indeed your religious convictions are without a doubt more in keeping with real citizenship than your present legal status.

Baha'u'llah, the prophet of the Baha'i faith, stated boldly that "The world is one country and mankind its citizens." Yet he himself admonished his followers to obey all constituted authority. A few religious cults, like the Seventh Day Adventists, prohibit their followers to fight in national armies but they do not advocate world citizenship and world government nor do they take a stand on national allegiance itself. Indeed there is no religion extant which takes a stand on the question of national allegiance as being diametrically opposed to the teachings of their particular saviors, prophets or masters.

Here is the collosal and monstrous blind spot on the part of present-day religious leaders who know full well, and preach so well, that you cannot serve two masters. "Christian" generals proudly talk of wiping out millions of humans, innocent and "guilty" alike in either a first or second nuclear strike. The spectacle of Moslems killing Christians, Protestants killing Catholics, Jews killing Moslems and vice versa, and even Baha'i's, whose very founder became stateless and was exiled from his native home, entering national armies or paying war taxes with no sense of contradiction, blatantly betrays their avowed religious convictions and mocks their very founders whom they pretend in pious servility to worship and serve in their daily life.

The silence of religious leaders on the burning issue of exclusive national loyalty to the violent nation-state is a sickening commentary on the dominance of nationalism over true religious belief. How do religious leaders equate not only the actions of their followers but their own commitment to nationalism with their professed faith? How can the Pope preach love and divine justice to Catholics throughout the world community yet not invoke them to become citizens of that community in order to *practice* their faith? How can Jewish leaders, professing to the sacred mission of Sinai, not only not give concrete evidence of the monotheistic concept by professing a worldly citizenship, but contrarily retreat into the archaic and feudalistic notion that "homeland" and "nation-state" are one? How can Moslem leaders, whose prophet Mohammed proclaimed the universality of the human race in the full recognition of those prophets who proceeded him, and who likewise admit the oneness of the Deity, cling abjectly to the nations

329

which deny and contradict that very unity?

How can anyone with any religious convictions not recognize the frightful dichotomy imposed on us by the modern nation-state with its monstrous armament budgets, its diabolical yet absurd spy systems, its insidious creeping bureaucracy and its denial of freedom, moral, intellectual, social and cultural throughout the world in the sacred name of "national security"? Every precept of religion enjoins us to help our fellow men. The very notion of nationalism denies that generous act as it claims everyone outside its frontiers as "aliens," "foreignors," "strangers," unlike us, therefore inferior, and in the final analysis, threats to our existence and unworthy to live.

How did such a blind spot develop? The nation itself controls our educational institutions. No school has a course on world citizenship. No university has a chair on statelessness. Civic rights courses do not extend beyond national frontiers. International law deals with "law" between states for the most part. National political parties unite in a common "foreign policy." Wisdom teachers all travel with national passports. The Vatican itself is a sovereign state with its ambassadors accredited to all other states.

Moreover, innumerable individuals call themselves world citizens today, yet totally dissociate that claim from their allegiance to their own nation-state. They fail to realize that the former claim must take priority over the latter in positive legal form. But this reversal of primary allegiance would immediately confront them with a like claim imposed on them by their particular nation-state. Love of humanity and God is no match for love of their nation.

The truth is that nationalism has to a large degreee replaced religion or has become synonymous with it, to be more accurate.

Jews, Christians, Moslems, etc. slaughter each other indiscrimately not in the name of their religious beliefs which are grounded in monotheism, but in the name of the nation to which they "belong." Good and just men and women watch in frustrated, agonized and bitter silence. But why are they silent? Do they not realize that religion and nationalism do not mix, that the political equivalent of true religion is worldism, that a new common denominator combining both religious principles and political idealism is vital to survival?

The forces of division are well-entrenched, fortified by over 300 years of evolution, supported by language barriers, cultural traditions, ethnic personalities, customs and symbols which are designed to separate fellow humans, dignified by courts, laws and legislative bodies.

Happily, however, the young are not so blinded as their elders. While the nation is losing its legitimacy along with institutionalized religion, young people everywhere are straining their eyes outward, both morally and physically to perceive the vastness in which they live, to understand the cosmos which binds them one to another and one to the cosmos itself, which unites them with Nature whose laws transcend nationalism rendering it archaic and ridiculous.

330

Thoreau wrote that you can educate either the citizen or the man but not both.

The true world citizen is that man or woman dynamically related to his/her fellow person and to all humankind, thereby expressing the age-old unity and universality taught and exemplified by our prophets and saviors from time immemorial.

World citizenship is the true "religion" of the 20th century.

Dear World Citizen:

As one holding one of your World Passports bearing a number prior to the very first one, I have been related to the Principle of World Citizenship that you represent in your person as its Co-ordinator. As a contemplative samnyasin of India I have no pro-gramme of action at all in the political, social or economic sense, but I am deeply interested in you and what you represent. Whether considered silly, childish or sophomoric by others who claim to be sane or mature in their ways of thought or behaviour, I can see no flaw in the attitude that you adopt. The Kingdom of God for which all good Christians pray is in principle not different from the idea of a World Government. Someone has to stand for a good principle for the sake of Humanity and you happen to be chosen by dint of circumstances which were not artifically created by you with other motives. The Constitution of the United States itself began with two or three sitting around a table before it was recog-nized. This does not show that those who started it were acting illegally or against human interests. I do not attach any import-ance to the form or protest you make and in fact the flimsier the issue the better it is to set off the purity of the cause and its motive. You have been brave in courting imprisonment many times in many parts of the world when you could have lived in comfort like all other respectable looking people that one meets in the suburban trains and buses of all big cities. Because you have chosen the harder way of sacrifice I send you all support from a humble human being at a far corner of the world can give you. May the blessing of the Absolute be with you!

Nataraja Guru

Gurukula, Fernhill
Nilgiris, South India   Sept. 25. 1960

CHAPTER 21

A Lover of Humanity
(In commemorating Nataraja Guru's 100th birthday)
August, 1983

While strolling amongst the stately trees at Ooty (Ootacamond, the Nilgiris, India) with Nataraja Guru one day in the Spring of 1956, he said, "To be a lover of humanity, one must first acknowledge its existence. This is difficult for most people to do. It means giving up many false notions."

We continued walking in silence. The immense calm of the forest, with the sun's rays scarcely penetrating their foliage, the wonderfully mild climate and his homely yet strangely impersonal kindness soothed me greatly after the hurly-burly of America and Europe.

"Lover of humanity?" It was the first time I had heard that phrase. It had a strange ring. How could one love all humanity? Wasn't love a strictly personal emotion one felt toward another individual, or to one's family, or to a sport or a favorite food, in other words, to someone or something with which one identified personally? How could you identify personally with humanity as such? How could one even grasp the reality of humanity in order to "love" it? True, I had read much science-fiction in my teens. "Humanity" was often pitted against alien races in distant galaxies or far-off star systems. Invariably "home" planet was "Mother Earth," and I came to regard this notion as natural, even banal, as most self-evident facts are. My "travels" in space and even time thanks to Isaac Asimov, Arthur Clarke, Jr. and Ted Sturgeons allowed me to "leave home" mentally and emotionally and to return not without theoretical appreciation. But to accept the reality, the existence of humanity, as the guru demanded of its "lovers," required a dimensional leap in sheer comprehension, almost an acceptance on faith bypassing one's already acceptance of lesser groupings such as family, nation and even corporation. Yet was not the extension more than logical, more than reasonable? Did not all lesser groupings by definition derive from "common" humanity? To love the part therefore without loving the whole was to be ignorant of its very source.

As I was pondering these thoughts, the Guru stopped and looked at me, his head slightly cocked.

"I think," he started slowly in that deliberate way of his, "you are a true lover of humanity." I stared at him, my feelings mixed. "Love" and "humanity" were not yet a pair in my mind. Love was personal and humanity an abstraction. Yet somehow, I sensed the rightness of allying them, even the necessity. I was strangely pleased if not fully comprehending the significance. Now, more than a quarter of a century later, I am beginning to understand just what it means to be a "lover of humanity." And to what commitments such an individual is enjoined.

Narayana Guru and Nataraja Guru, as indeed all "proper" gurus, identified directly with humanity as they identified with humanity's creator. The two were recognized as corollaries, as inseparable as the individual with his/her creator. Just as all gurus refer "backwards" to their own teacher, so they acknowledge former masters or sages as proponents or examples of this dynamic relationship.

Thus, the human microcosm and macrocosm became in their persons dynamic bi-polarities – to use the language of dialectics – to be taken always and inevitably together.

When contemplating the precious dialectics of this mystical yet ever-generating union flowing inexorably through time, the guru once told me that he could not repress a sense of ecstasy coursing through him.

Through the years, in my work as a world citizen, I have found few fellow "lovers of humanity." Many acknowledge humanity's existence and proclaim its right to survive and prevail, but that is not the same as loving it. To love is to be willing to die for one's love. There are millions willing to die for their country or maybe their religion, though that is less evident. Nationalism is the 20th century religion, the latter-day "Golden Calf" around which humans gather in worship and love. But die for humanity? For planet earth. Who or what is threatening it? We are not being attacked from outer space . . . yet. And though the insect world seems to be deadly and hardy enough to outsurvive the human race, still we are holding our own it appears.

Yet the threat to humanity itself has become increasingly apparent since 1945. Just as humanity has not only endangered other species on its home planet but forever eliminated them in its crude and thoughtless expansion, so it is today endangering itself by itself by its ignorance of its essential unity.

When Nataraja Guru was teaching at the International School in Geneva in the late 1940's, he used to listen to the daily broadcasts of the United Nations' debates. It soon became apparent to him, he said, that what was missing was a representative of humanity itself at the UN. Among all those state delegates, no one "loved" humanity enough to place humanity's interests above those of his particular nation.

Then later, when I met him for the first time on the S.S. America in 1950 going from Europe to the United States, he told me that renouncing U.S. nationality was equivalent to an Indian taking a vow of Sannyasin, both being required for a direct affiliation with humanity's wisdom heritage. My claim to world citizenship, he added, was nothing more or less than a manifestation of wisdom-seeking. I immediately rebelled against this ludicrous notion that I was seeking wisdom rather than a political solution to the nation-state's dilemma of war-making.

"If you are a true wisdom-seeker," he said, sensing my rejection, "you will have to test my claim to be a guru or wisdom teacher. How else can you find out whether it is valid or not? On the other hand, if wisdom does not interest you, you will simply dismiss my claim as phony and run away."

As I was in the "wilderness" of intellectual and emotional depression at that precise moment, secretly I would perhaps have listened to the devil himself if he had promised to teach me wisdom. Besides I had enough confidence in my own value structure and intelligence to be able to discern a true teacher from a phony. Inconsistencies would eventually reveal themselves, I told myself, besides the obvious fact that the deeds and words of a real wisdom teacher had to equate unlike the ivory-tower intellectual's aversion to action.

The fulfilling lesson I have learned since then is that the maturing of wisdom in one goes side by side with the capacity to love. It is as if love provides the "crucible" for wisdom to fill. This dynamic relationship between knowledge and love has, to my mind, not been fully realized by many otherwise qualified teachers.

Nataraja Guru's statement that I was a "lover of humanity," came only after I had travelled to India to sit at his feet, as it were, as a wisdom disciple. Though I was at that time only a humble disciple, the mere fact of recognition of his guruhood, therefore the "existence" of Wisdom Itself, confirmed in his mind that my claim to world citizenship and thus membership in Humanity as such, qualified me as its "lover."

The religious world has a major problem with "humanity." Inclusive humanity confronts exclusive religion head-on. What the former affirms by its very existence the latter denies by its partiality. While God is affirmed as sole creator and ultimate Sovereign by religion, His very creation is denied in its entirety. Jesus Christ, for example, it is written, gave two commandments to his followers: Love God and love thy neighbor as thyself. He did not enjoin them to "love humanity." It wasn't until the 19th century that a latter-day prophet, Baha'u'llah, stated boldly that "The world is one country and mankind its citizens." To this revolutionary notion he added, "Let not a man glory in that he loves his country; let him rather glory in this, that he loves his kind."

"Love thy humanity as thyself" is therefore as valid an injunction for the 20th century human as "Love thy neighbor as thyself" was for the 1st century human. But more important, it is the catagorical imperative for both species and personal survival.

In commemorating Nataraja Guru's birthday, we implicitly are recognizing a "lover of humanity." We are therefore acknowledging humanity's existence and in truth our own vital and vitalizing kinship with it as a "being" in itself.

Humanity's "birth" is recent, concurrent with the worldwide communication network, the "gridwork" of over 4,000 satellites supplying virtual instant feedback to its constituent parts. The "baby" is demanding our attention, our resources and...our love. Eventually—and we trust soon, historically speaking—it must become "reasonable," accepting to abide by the Creator's already established rules.

Nataraja Guru, with Narayana Guru preceding him and Guru Nitya following him, as all gurus and saviors before them, manifest these divine rules for the good of all and the general good of our Mother/Father: Humanity Itself.

Nataraja Guru

335

CHAPTER 22

HUMAN RIGHTS AND WORLD CITIZENSHIP
Garry Davis

December 12, 1983 Reception commemorating the 35th anniversary of the signing of the *Universal Declaration of Human Rights,* Washington, D.C.

This occasion has, for me, great historical significance and evokes memories of those momentous events of 1948 when the *Universal Declaration of Human Rights* was first proclaimed in Paris by the United Nations General Assembly.

I too was in Paris at the time. In fact, I actually was obliged to live for seven days on the international territory claimed by that very United Nations.

So this event takes me back to a day in May, 1948 in Paris when I claimed my own political status: that of world citizenship.

It was then I learned two hard realities about human rights. First, they were not only not protected by national law but national law was their principal violator. of human rights.

Of course, as a B-17 bomber pilot during World War II, I myself was an instrument of violation of the basic human right to live in dropping bombs on German, Belgium, and French cities, towns and even villages. I was only obeying national law.

The same national law, but this time, of another nation, was responsible for the death of my brother, a sailor on the S.S. Buck, blown up at Salerno.

But I'll give you a more immediate example. On the same day I claimed to be a world citizen, I walked into the U.S. Embassy in Paris and renounced the exclusivity of nationalism. In other words, I expatriated myself. The right of expatriation was declared by the Congress of 1868 as a "natural and inherent right of all people, indispensable to the enjoyment of life, liberty and the pursuit of happiness."

336

As we all know, the first words of the American Declaration of Independence affirmed that "in the course of human events, it becomes necessary for one people to dissolve the political bands which have connected them with another..."

My renunciation of nationality on May 25, 1948 was my personal declaration of independence.

But when I walked out of the U.S. Embassy that May day without my U.S. passport as a stateless world citizen, and re-entered France, I unwittingly committed a national crime: illegal entry.

Being imprisoned once for the crime of not possessing valid national entry or identity papers is a particularly enlightening experience if you are truly interested in human rights violations. To jail a human, that is, to deny freedom for that alleged crime of omission is an indictment of the nation-state system itself. Yet it is the plight of millions throughout the world today and not only in dictatorships. The Brooklyn Detention Facility is full today with humans without national papers. I know. I was there once.

But being jailed 28 times as I have been for the same reason begins to get monotonous and gives reflection to methods of preventing its reoccurrence.

Therefore, the second hard reality I learned about human rights was that there was no overt world law to protect them, no world government to turn to for appeal of the nations' violation of my or others' human rights, despite such historical documents as the *Universal Declaration of Human Rights,* the *Genocide Convention* and the *Nuremberg Principles.*

Then, in my stateless condition, I also learned of the two opposing views concerning human rights. First, when I was jailed simply for not possessing so-called proper identity papers, I realized that the state considers human rights as grants to be conferred—or not—on the individual. In other words, the nation does not recognize that human rights are inalienable but on the contrary dependent on its recognition. The reason is obvious. If human rights are inalienable, that is, if we possess them because we are human with or without the sanction of government, then the people, you and I, individually as well as collectively, are sovereign. And if the people are sovereign, how then can the state claim its sovereignty as absolute and exclusive?

Then what a government can grant, it can also deny. And we see that denial of fundamental human rights throughout the entire world of nation-states. That modern catch-all is "national security" or "public order." "National security" is a euphemism for war-making; and "public order" is often a cover for dictatorship.

The other view, that human rights are inalienable, as the *Universal Declaration of Human Rights* clearly states in the very first words of the Preamble, and as the *American Declaration of Independence* also affirms, is the historic breakthrough which gave rise to the revolutionary claim that individual human rights are the very foundation of government.

The *Declaration of Independence* first tolled that death-knell of tyranny in its soul-stirring claim that *"all men are created equal"* and *"endowed by their creator with certain inalienable rights"* and further *"that to secure these rights, Governments are instituted among men deriving their just powers from the consent of the governed."*

Article 28 of the UDHR we are gathered here to commemorate reaffirms that shattering claim by stating boldly that, *"Everyone has the right to a social and international order in which the rights set forth in this Declaration can be fully realized."*

The United Nations, which proclaimed the UDHR as a "common standard of achievement for all peoples and all nations" is not that "social and international order," or, in other words, a world government based on the UDHR, but a mere association of equally sovereign states preparing insanely for World War III.

It neither represents the sovereign individual nor sovereign humankind itself. It was not founded to do so nor does it claim to do so.

The World Government of World Citizens I declared in 1953 from the city hall of Ellsworth, Maine is designed to remedy that lack.

Lech Walesa, in accepting the Nobel Peace Prize two days ago, stated that "the road to a brighter future for the world leads to honest reconciliation of conflicting interests and not through hatred and bloodshed." To follow that road, he continued, "means to enhance the moral power of the all-embracing idea of human solidarity."

Today, on this memorable occasion, it is fitting for me, therefore, as a spokesperson for world citizenship, to confirm the latest breakthrough in the history of human rights, as Lech Walesa indicated, implied in the UDHR but not declared explicitly.

The operative word in the term "human rights" is, of course, "human." And to be human is to recognize oneself first and foremost a member of a species called humankind.

Horace Mann, the great educator, said in an address at Antioch College in 1859, "Be ashamed to die until you have won some victory of humanity."

Today, with nuclear holocaust facing our humankind, ironically just entering the Space Age with all its awesome promise, the only victory possible for each one of us to win for humanity is survival itself.

For in that survival, we as individual humans also are saved.

Therefore, the final inalienable right is that of recognizing, then identifying directly, dynamically and legitimately with humanity itself. This is the true meaning of world citizenship, to recognize, to understand, even to love the innate humanity in each one of us and through that recognition, understanding and love, humanity itself.

This is "human solidarity."

In these terms, the exclusive nation-state in the 20th century is not only an anachronism but antithetical to human rights in that it cannot recognize either

338

the sovereign humanity. In personal terms, it is suicidal.

In conclusion, if humanity is to survive, it will do so only by each one of us helping to evolve a just world order based on fundamental human rights.

The mandate is clear. It is already contained in this noble Declaration.

And the choice is ours: Human rights under world law...or Armageddon.

We world citizens have made our choice.

We invite you, in the name of our common humanity, to make yours.

Thank you.

Joan Baez Receives Honorary World Passport from Garry Davis at National Press Club, Washington, D.C.

"We who successfully freed one half of the human race without violence must now undertake with equal devotion, perseverence and intelligence the supreme act of human statesmanship, evolved in the creation of institutions of government on a world scale."
Rosika Schwimmer, July 1948

Message to Women's International Meeting, Seneca Falls, N.Y., celebrating 100 years of struggle for women's rights.

CHAPTER 23

I AM A CANDIDATE FOR WORLD PRESIDENT!
GARRY DAVIS
MARCH ON WASHINGTON MEETING, The Mall
Oct. 22, 1983

I've come here today as a world citizen candidate for public office. Unfortunately the office I seek doesn't exist yet. But for lack of it and the institution it represents, the arms race between nations goes on and we citizens live in deadly fear of a nuclear holocaust.

On the other hand, if it did exist, you would not be marching to Capitol Hill today to ask national lawmakers to make peace or to disarm or to negotiate with their counterparts across the oceans. You and I would be the beneficiaries of a peaceful world where common problems such as hunger, pollution, and human rights violations of every kind could be attacked and solved.

The office for which I am a candidate is world president. The vote I am asking of you is a world vote as a world citizen. If this is a crazy idea, then war is sane for just as sure as you and I are facing each other, World War III is in full preparation, as you well know, by the nation-states to which you give your exclusive national allegiance.

If George Washington in 1786, a year before the Constitution was written, had stood before the Continental Congress and announced his candidacy for president of the United States, at best he might have been declared teched in the head and at worst a traitor to his exclusive Virginian citizenship.

In his inaugural address of January 20, 1965, President Lyndon Johnson said, *"Think of our world as it looks from that rocket that's heading toward Mars. It is like a child's globe, hanging in space, the continents stuck to its side like colored maps. We are all fellow passengers on a dot of earth."*

If tomorrow, earth was invaded by an alien race, E.T.'s from outer space, Chairman Yuri Andropov would pick up that little red telephone by his side and dial 999, Washington, D.C. But the line would be busy. Because President Reagan would be trying to get hold of him at the same time.

The common danger would make them instant neighbors. Instant collaborators. Instant world citizens.

340

I was a B-17 bomber pilot in World War II. I helped wipe out cities in Germany, Belgium and France. We did it with ordinary or conventional bombs. There weren't many Nazi soldiers in those cities, only civilians...like you and me.

Thirty-five years ago, I decided, like Socrates, to declare myself a citizen of our tiny world rather than an exclusive national citizen.

Chief Justice Earl Warren, in the famous case *Perez* v. *Brownell,* wrote, "Citizenship is man's basic right, for it is nothing less than the right to have rights." If Justice Earl Warren was right, then world citizenship was the right to have world rights...such as the right to live peacefully on our home planet.

It didn't quite work out that way. Everytime I came up against a national official they would ask me for national identity papers. When I couldn't produce any, they declared me "illegal." So I would end up in prison. You see, national officials can't recognize the inalienable rights of a world citizen.

This experience over the years convinced me finally that all national politicians were and are in a near-fatal dilemma. Lacking an international sovereign government, with World War III in full preparation, none of them have any program to prevent it.

The reason is self-evident. World War III will be fought between nations and their only power stems from within the nation.

Therefore national politicians pay lip-service to world peace but they never blow the whistle on the cause of war or the exacting conditions for peace.

That's why all national leaders continue to claim the right to fight wars amongst themselves. Even when nuclear bombs exploded over Hiroshima and Nagasaki, they still maintained that war was necessary...to preserve peace.

This was Orwellism at its best.

The latest evidence of this was President Reagan's press conference last Wednesday. In speaking of the Pershing II missiles, he assured us—I quote—"...we're going to deploy, and deploy on schedule." That will convince the Soviet leadership, he said—"to negotiate with us and in good faith." Later, he referred to an Eisenhower letter which claimed that "...we're coming to a stage in weaponry in which there can be no victory as we've always thought of it—no winner or loser in war that can just be the destruction of the people." Now comes the lip-service. "...he said then won't we have the common sense to sit down at a negotiating table and do away with war as a means of settling our disputes?"

It sounds fine but where is the mention of outlawing war between nation-states by a world government? Where is the mention of anarchy between nations as the cause of war?

For five years, between 1948 and 1953, I was a world citizen without a government. During that period, hundreds of thousands of individuals like me also claimed world citizenship beyond their nationality. Henry Ward Beecher wrote in 1887 that "The worst thing in this world, next to anarchy, is government." The Founding Fathers of the United States no doubt were of the same opinion. That's why they delegated powers to the central government sparingly according to the Constitution even adding a Bill of Rights two years later.

On September 4, 1953, in the absence of any government to represent me and my fellow world citizens, that is, existing in a world anarchy, from the City Hall of Ellsworth, Maine, I declared a government for world citizenship and based on common world laws of a moral, social and biological nature.

Thomas Jefferson wrote in 1810 that ". . . a strict observance of the written laws is doubtless one of the high duties of a good citizen, but it is not the highest. The law of necessity, of self-preservation, of saving our country when in danger, are of higher obligation."

This government, we claim, is the new requirement for self-preservation, both individually and globally. It alone speaks for the security of each citizen of the world community and of humanity itself. It is the only government grounded in fundamental human rights. It is the only government with a concrete program for world peace.

Now I am a candidate for president of this government. I would rather run for world umpire or referee since the world public seems more oriented to sports than to politics. A football or baseball or basketball game without referees is unthinkable besides being unplayable. The referees represent the rules of the game and both teams, before coming onto the field, have to agree to abide by those rules or face the referee's whistle and sanctions.

But you will ask, what qualifications have I for being world president? Well, for one, I am a former actor. But unlike President Reagan, I have always played to live audiences whereas his whole training and acting career has been only to the camera. Now as you know, in Hollywood, when you make a mistake, they do a retake. And you do a scene over and over until you get it right. The public never sees the goofs you make. They end up on the cutting room floor. So you become accustomed to retakes and worse, considering your mistakes of no consequence. Then when you go from acting to politics where mistakes cost people's lives, that former training becomes disastrous. On the other hand, when you act before a live audience, you are permitted no retakes.

As for Chairman Andropov, his training and qualifications as head of the KGB is even worse than President Reagan's. Where President Reagan's view of the world is filtered through a Hollywood lens, Yuri Andropov's world view is strained through state absolutism. Both are disqualified for world-class leadership.

Also, the job of world president is for an amateur. It has no precedent so there are no professionals around. I may not be as qualified as the next man or woman, but since no one else but me has sought the job, and it must be filled, I am obliged to stick it out until a better man or woman comes along. Then I am younger than both Reagan and Andropov and have had 35 years experience in dealing with nation-states as such.

My platform is simple: world peace through law based on fundamental human rights. So how do we go about this election? First, I invite you here and throughout the world to declare your inalienable world citizenship. Secondly, register with the only declared world government in our global village. And thirdly, exercise your franchise by voting for me — or indeed any other candidate who declares him or herself — for world office. It's that simple.

Emmanual Kant wrote that, *"When those who do the fighting have the right to choose between war and peace, history will no longer be written in blood."*

We, who do not only do the fighting but the dying, now have that right and we must choose: world citizenship and world law or world war. Not only our own lives, the lives of our loved ones and the lives of our countrymen and women are at stake but the very survival and future of humankind.

Name and address of
Collector of Signatures:

_____

_____

WORLD BALLOT
DISTRIBUTED BY
WORLD SERVICE AUTHORITY
Washington, D.C. 20045

Administrative Agency of
World Government of World Citizens

"The will of the people shall be the basis of the authority of government; this will shall be expressed in periodic and genuine elections which shall be universal and equal suffrage and shall be held by secret vote or by equivalent free voting procedures."
Article 21, Section III — Universal Declaration of Human Rights

As a Citizen of the World, I hereby fulfill my fundamental civic right and duty outlined above by voting for a direct world representative to represent me in matters of common concern for the General Good and the Good for All as defined by the **Universal Declaration of Human Rights.**

I hereby vote for   GARRY DAVIS   to represent me as a Citizen of the World. This world vote is without prejudice to and in no way affects my status, national or otherwise.

No.	Date	Name and Address	City/State	Zip Code
1				
2				
3				
4				
5				
6				
7				
8				
9				
10				

I swear that the above signatures have been given freely by the signers.
Signed:

343

Chapter 24

TO THE CHILDREN OF
THE PESTALOZZI KINDERHOF
WEST GERMANY
(AND EVERYWHERE ELSE)

Have you ever looked up at night and wondered how many stars there are in the sky? I have, lying in the bottom of a canoe floating on a calm lake in the State of Maine, U.S.A.

Today, whirling over our heads are over 7,000 manmade satellites sending information back to earth of all kinds. Barely one hundred years ago, this would have seemed impossible. Today, we accept worldwide communication as an ordinary taken-for-granted fact.

So you could say, this is the age of communication. Global communication. Children all over the world understand this easily. But often adults don't. They still fight over "ownership" of parts of our planet Earth. But the stars look down on us all and see only one human species.

We have made world postage stamps to symbolize the fact of one world. We are world citizens, you see. And even though every one with a modern radio can tune in to world news every day, some people can't write to each other because some nations don't "recognize" other nations. The purpose of the world postage stamps is to pay for a service we provide for these people who are often in the same family. (See Appendix)

As children are innocent of adult's folly and are indeed one throughout the world, we offer you part of the funds coming from the sale of these unique stamps.

Remember, the world is yours too.

God bless you.

Chapter 25

STATEMENT OF GARRY DAVIS
ON PRESENTING HONORARY WORLD PASSPORTS TO
MAYORS HANS-PETER ZUEFLE OF WOLFACH, WEST GERMANY,
and
MARION BARRY, JR. OF WASHINGTON, D.C.
October 5, 1983
World Government Offices, 1012 14th Street, N.W., Washington, D.C. 20005

His Honor Herr Zuefle, His Honor Mr. Barry—represented by Ms. Carter—citizens of Wolfach and of Washington, D.C., honored guests:

Cities, whether large or small, are where most of humanity now lives. The mayors of our cities throughout the world speak and understand the common language of municipal problems and responsibilities.

If ever interdependency had a dynamic meaning, it is to be found in the intrinsic character which all villages, towns, and cities enjoy. This character might be identified as the primal civic equation of "One for all and all for one" to which each and all mayors are legally and socially bound.

Ever since the town of Cahors in France in 1949 adopted the Charter of Mundialization (see Appendix) and declared its site "world territory," an awareness of the interdependency of the world community and the oneness of the human species—exemplified by humanity's sages from time immemorial—has begun to permeate our hearts and minds and has even redirected the lives of many of us.

Herr Hans-Peter Zuefle and Mr. Marion Barry, Jr. represent two cities, Wolfach and Washington, one nestled in the Black Forest with a history of over 900 years; the other, the capital of a latter-day superpower, but of increasingly global outlook and activities. Both share the common planetary soil.

Though they and their citizens are hostage to the nationalistic system where war is still considered an extension of foreign policy, and nations continue their preparation for global suicide, the mayors are bound by oath to uphold civic justice and order. They have no armies at their command, no "foreign policy" to defend. The policemen under their orders represent the principle of right over might, whereas the particular nation in which their separate cities find themselves—despite the dimension of nuclear power—still place might over right in their affairs with other nations.

In this peaceful mission, all mayors are united in a brotherhood and sisterhood of like humans in municipalities throughout the world territory.

345

In the name of the world citizenry and all mundialized towns throughout the world therefore, it is with great pleasure that I present the mayors of these two cities—already united in common danger as well as allied in common purpose to help secure the blessings of world peace through law—with honorary World Passports concretely symbolizing the reality of our global village and the actual oneness of the human family.

This unique passport represents a new, a whole and frontierless world, human and humane, wherein those inalienable rights of life, liberty, well-being and the pursuit of happiness can at last be realized by all citizens of the world.

Chapter 26

WORLD GOVERNMENT, READY OR NOT?
Garry Davis
WORLDVIEW 84
WORLD FUTURE SOCIETY
June 10-14, 1984
Washington Hilton Hotel
Washington, D.C.

The Design-Science Revolution: The Next 50 Years
1301 International Ballroom East
June 11, 1984, 2:00 P.M.

All past revolutions among humans were merely prologues compared to the one facing our race today.

Tom Paine wrote in 1776 that "These are the times which try men's souls."

But 1984 tries more than our souls. It tries not merely our entire being, souls and bodies together, but our dynamic relationship to our total humanity which, likewise faces annihilation.

Two days ago, seven national leaders in London, exposed once again the bankruptcy of the nation-state system. No so-called leader spoke for either humanity or single human beings facing an imminent holocaust. All defended the so-called independence of each nation while at the same time urging cooperation among them.

Buckminster Fuller wrote in his epic book *Utopia or Oblivion* "*The fact is that now–for the first time in the history of man for the last ten years–all the political theories and all the concepts of political functions–in any other than secondary roles as housekeeping organizations–are completely obsolete. All of them were developed on the you-or-me basis.*"

The theme of this congress, Worldview 84, fits perfectly Bucky's totally wholistic conceptual viewpoint. "This whole realization," he concluded, "that mankind can and may be comprehensively successful is startling."

The notion of a world public order or government among thinking people has finally transcended the question of why given its alternative. The primordial question is now how?

The logic might go like this: If you accept the world community as what Marshall MacCluhan called a "global village," and humanity as a true breeding species, then it follows that our species itself domiciled temporarily on planet earth requires simple recognition by thinking individuals.

That recognition immediately impels two further conclusions. The first is that it has not yet developed its overall governing body or, to put it in biological terms, its "brain"; and secondly, that its present so-called governing institutions or the nation-state system not only militates against such global or species governance but must destroy it if left unbridled.

The next speaker will spell out in more detail the reasons for this ambivalence.

Now the contemporary sovereignty of those political fictions called nation-states is directly related to the allegiance given them by individuals.

In other words, they prevail to the exact proportion they are recognized by the sovereign individuals within their geographical limits.

But what if those same individuals, recognizing the greater geographical limits of the planet itself, and the new fact that their own particular nation cannot guarantee them the basic right of life itself, extend that sovereign recognition to the world community and to his or her humanity? What then?

That is the beginning of world governance for it relates the sovereign human being with sovereign humankind just as national governance began when that same individual related himself to the political fiction called the nation.

That is political networking much as the human body "networks" organically by means of a total feedback communication system from cells to brain to cells.

The technological and communication network already exists.

E. B. White, while observing the delegates at the 1945 San Francisco Conference which founded the United Nations, wrote:

> *"Whether we wish it or not, we may soon have to make a clear*
> *choice between the special nation to which we pledge our allegiance*
> *and the broad humanity of which we are born a part."*

Your speaker has adjusted his political allegiance to that already global reality. Thirty-six years ago, on May 25th, I personally divorced myself from the entire nation-state system and pledged my primal allegiance to that "broad humanity," and to its natural government as a world citizen. Put another way, I realized that the national system had divorced me from it from its very inception in that every national leader was impotent to protect or guarantee my fundamental right to live, to be free, and to seek my happiness on my home planet. Their political "network" stopped at national frontiers. Beyond was anarchy.

But there was nothing in any of their national constitutions which denied or prohibited my right to claim a world citizenship. Moreover many of them stated categorically that since the individual was the very source of their power, he or she therefore had the sovereign right to choose his or her political allegiance.

Since that date, hundreds of thousands of my fellow humans have also declared their world citizenship.

So can you.

This exercise of the sovereign right to recognize, then pledge our personal political commitment to humanity and its community is the very price of world peace. All else is irrelevant.

For, if humanity is destroyed by the present nation-state system, then it follows that we, as humans, are also destroyed.

A pledge of allegiance to humanity therefore is a pledge to ourselves.

But how many of you are ready to make such a commitment?

Emery Reves, in *Anatomy of Peace* wrote that "There is no first step to world government. World Government is the first step."

On September 4, 1953, from the City Hall of Ellsworth, Maine, as a declared world citizen of five years standing and with a mandate of over 750,000 fellow citizens, I declared our personal government for that citizenship and called it simply the "World Government."

If this seems ludicrous to you, may I recall two articles in the *Universal Declaration of Human Rights*. The first is Article 21, section 3 which says in part that *"The will of the people shall be the basis of the authority of government. . . ."* Then Article 28 states that *"Everyone has the right to a social and international order in which the rights and freedoms set forth in this Declaration can be fully realized."*

I called for recognition of this miniscule government from both other individuals and from existing government. Many who already considered themselves world citizens responded. They asked for world government I.D. cards, world government passports, world government birth certificates. To satisfy these requests, I founded our own "city hall," albeit a global one. We called it the World Service Authority.

This was in 1954.

Many national governments recognized our first World Passport. Remember, this was six years before the 1951 Convention for Refugees was finally ratified which provided for a refugee passport. So, many people throughout the world were without documents of any sort and suffered much persecution for this "crime" of omission. Our government even has its own world currency now, the World Dollar, negotiable on the basis of one U.S. dollar to one World dollar. It is a world trust and a world peace currency.

The national leaders at London I mentioned before should have proposed a common world currency if indeed they were interested in a real world economic order.

On September 4, 1983, the world government had its first candidate for president. I am seeking the world votes of all registered citizens.

Well, the World Government from 1953 grew in numbers and recognition. Certain individuals, expert in their fields, were approached to head commissions on common concerns. Isaac Asimov became the Coordinator of the government's Space Commission, with Carol Sue Rosin as his Deputy Coordinator. Yehudi Menuhin was appointed Coordinator of the Cultural Commission; Badi Lenz, founder of the World Tree Trust, became Coordinator of the Forestry Commission; Theodore Welles, of Oceanus, the Ocean Commission Coordinator, Michio Kushi, the macrobiotic world leader, Coordinator of the World Health Commission and Guru Nitya Chaitanya Yati, the Coordinator of the World Education Commission.

Two years ago, after meeting Bill Perk here at the World Future Society's congress, I sought Bucky Fuller's agreement to head the government's Design-Science Commission. Indeed, our world government **was** the political design-science tool based on the new science of geo-dialectics, a branch of pure dialectics, the ancient wisdom-science taught by humanity's gurus from time immemorial.

Though Bucky already held a world passport and advocated world citizenship in all his writings and talks, beloved maverick that he was, he declined with thanks to affiliate himself organically with the government even in his own field.

I thus turned to his associate, Bill Perk, asking him to accept this vital post in the embryonic government. He did so with alacrity, enthusiasm, and joy and he will be telling you his own reasons for so doing.

In conclusion, the good news is that a world government grounded in the sovereignty of both the individual and humankind exists and is functioning. We have broken out of the stagnant and suicidal crysallis of the nation-state system and have metamorphasized into new creatures called. . .human beings.

It enjoins your active participation.

E.B. White has written:

> "World government is an appalling prospect. Many people have not comprehended it or distinguished it from world organization. Many others, who have comprehended it, find it preposterous or unattainable in a turbulent and illiterate world where nations and economies conflict daily in many ways. Certainly the world is not ready for government on a planetary scale. In our opinion, it will never be ready. The test is whether the people will chance it anyway like children who hear the familiar cry, 'Coming, ready or not!'"

Friends and fellow world citizens, World Government is here, ready or not!

APPENDIX

EPILOGUE

TO

REPRINT EDITION

OF

MY COUNTRY IS THE WORLD

The story you have just read left off over twenty-four years ago. Today's reader may well wonder: "What happened next? Does World Government still exist? Or was it merely a fiction dreamed up by a modern Don Quixote? And where is World Citizen Davis now? Or is he still a World Citizen? If so, what is he doing about it?"

But more important than all these questions, you might also want to know: "How can I get into the action?"

So the publisher of this reprint edition asked me for an epilogue. Though I have just finished a sequel to this first book entitled *World Government, Ready Or Not!*, I am happy to summarize here essential events since 1958 to assure you of continuity and commitment.

To bring you immediately into the present picture, I write from the Washington, D.C. office of the World Service Authority District III, Inc. located in the Continental Building at 1012 14th Street N.W., 20005, a stone's throw from Ronald Reagan's temporary residence.

Legally however, I am not yet in the United States. But I am getting ahead of my story.

Last month, May, 1984, the WSA issued 1500 World Government documents bringing the total since 1954 to over 250,000. Approximately 22,000 requests arrive per annum from individuals all over the world, including Moscow, Kabul, Teheran, Addis Ababa, Windshoek and Johannesburg, seeking help from national bureaucracy.

In other words, the work continues and grows slowly but inexorably.

The nations also continue and arm inexorably. This year, the international armament tab comes to a shade over $650 billion. Annihilation, it seems, does not come cheap.

As Emery Reves wrote, "The tragic fact...is that we are neither heading nor thinking in a new direction. Those in power have no time and no incentive to think. And those who think have no power whatsoever."

During most of the twenty-four years since finishing *My Country Is The World* I lived in France, in lovely Alsace. My life was more conventional than during the ten years recounted in this book. In 1960, after returning to Europe, I married Esther Peter—see page 84—and we produced a family of three new citizens, Troy, Athena, and Kim. Faced with parental responsibilities, I went enthusiastically to work in a succession of jobs: packer in a machine shop, usher in a theatre, overseas representative for a British paint brush firm, door-to-door salesman for an electric water heater firm, salesman for an airgun for unblocking sanitary pipes, then, in 1965, after opening the first diaper rental laundry in Alsace, acquiring a departmental franchise for an American water treatment firm recently established in France.

To live legally in France, I had to become officially "stateless" with ID card and travel document to match, renewable every two years, issued by *l'Office de Protection pour les Refugies et Apatrides* in Paris. It was based on a United Nations convention on the rights of stateless persons which the French government had ratified.

In 1971, when business conditions deteriorated in France due principally to tight credit policies, small businesses with no capital base to speak of were hard put to remain solvent. With a profit margin base insufficient to cover expenses despite a high volume of sales—over 7 million francs in 5 years starting from scratch—the water treatment business was doomed to failure. I turned in desperation to the importation of the air gun manufactured in England for unblocking pipes I had previously sold. But while I was struggling to remain afloat businesswise to support my growing family, my personal mail was piling up from individuals seeking help in terms of travel documents. Though a number of non-national travel documents already existed such as the one I myself possessed, none represented the fundamental right to travel as outlined by Article 13(2) of the *Universal Declaration of Human Rights*. They were all circumscribed by national restrictions, mainly the requirement of a fixed legal residence, therefore prejudicial. The original World Passport was not. The need for an update was becoming urgent.

A five week postal strike in November, 1971 literally stopped my mail-order business activity. The moment had arrived I knew to re-enter boldly the global political world I had left by reactivating the dormant World Service Authority and updating its passport. Besides my own World Passport was invalid! I had moved the family to the Haut-Rhin from Strasbourg and, after buying a small piece of land in Hesingue near St. Louis, the border town to Basel, Switzerland, had built a house which we called "Chaggara."

The second edition of the World Passport came off the press in January, 1972. It was now in five languages, contained 36 pages with space for a full medical history for the first time in any passport. The first printing—credit for which was extended by a local Mulhouse printer—of 2,000 was quickly exhausted. Many alien residents in Europe, North Africans, Turks and Spanish as well as Asian refugees from Vietnam, China, Cambodia, Burma, etc. plus young people turned on by the "earth passport, man!" and surprisingly enough, a smattering of internationally-minded businessmen who desired a "back-up" travel document with no political liability, became the new possessors of the passport. The "issuing office" was in one corner of our living-room. All national governments had been sent samples through their Paris embassies.

Then, on September 17, 1972, the French government attacked. French security agents, armed with a perquisition order signed by a Juge d'Instruction of the Tribunal de Grande Instance, Mulhouse, seized all available passports from my living-room office, and on June 22, 1973, officially charged me with "swindling," "complicity," and "confusing the public mind." (Meprise dans l'esprit publique.')

Though the first two charges were subsequently dropped after a thorough two year investigation, the trial on the absurd third charge, June 12, 1974, led to my first conviction and made the WSA World Passport subject to seizure and confiscation by all French frontier guards.

The harrassment of an advocate of human rights by a national tribunal—an act which was becoming more common throughout the national world—convinced me and my colleagues that our World Government required its own court, a "World Court of Human Rights " to which an individual could appeal for redress of grievances against national violations of human rights. And so, on June 12, 1974, the trial date at Mulhouse, sanctioned by assembled delegates of World Government, I announced the founding of the empirical World Court of Human Rights. An eminent Chicago attorney, Dr. Luis Kutner, who had flown over for the trial, was appointed as the new court's first Chief Justice. Maitre Jean-Paul Carteron, my French lawyer, was named an Associate Justice. (See Appendix)

After the conviction, the WSA offices were moved to St. Louis. Despite the French court's decision, we continued issuing passports and other World Government documents, including a World Birth Certificate, upon public demand. National governmental recognition was slow in coming at first, but as more people insisted on using the passport, entry and exit visas began to increase. Ecuador, Zambia, Upper Volta and Mauretania gave it their *de jure* recognition.

In December, 1974, we moved our offices to Basel, legally incorporating as a non-profit association under the Swiss Civil Code on January 24, 1975.

On January 25, ironically, I was arrested by the Swiss Foreign Police for illegal entry, brought to trial, convicted and sentenced to 7 days imprisonment. After my week in jail, I was "escorted" to the Swiss-French frontier at Basel-St. Louis and literally left on the line between the two countries.

The French border guards, under strict orders, paid no attention to me as I entered France, identified only by my World Passport, though French law now required its seizure and confiscation.

During 1975, while WSA documents were being issued in increasing numbers from our Basel offices by a growing multi-national staff, I spent a total of 75 days in Swiss jails for "illegal entry." Our documents were in the meantime aiding others to be released from prison and detention and refugee camps in many parts of the world. The irony was not lost on the Swiss press.

Each time I was released from a Swiss prison, Swiss foreign police "escorted" me to the Swiss-French border at Basel-St. Louis. Each time the French border officials ignored my illegal entry into France.

In June, 1975, we designed and printed a third edition of the passport, this time in seven languages, adding Russian, Arabic and Esperanto and dropping Italian, increasing the pages to 42 and incorporating a 6 page section for affiliate identifications.

My second French conviction came in July, 1976, this time from a Paris court, again for the "crime" of presenting to frontier officials at Orly airport on my return trip from the U.S. in April, 1976, a "document purporting to be an official identity paper." Now, for the French judiciary, I was a counterfeiter.

Again I received a three month sentence, suspended for "humanitarian reasons," a recognition of sorts that the World Passport was aiding stateless persons and refugees.

Now rejected by Switzerland—a three year interdiction to enter was served against me by its Justice Department—and facing perpetual prosecution by the French judiciary if I continued to authorize the issuance of WSA documents, on May 25, 1976, I declared the territory on which Chaggara was built "extra-territorial under the sovereign protection of world law."

A third indictment was entered by the Juge d'Instruction of the Tribunal de Grande Instance, Mulhouse, in June, 1976. The same charges of swindling, complicity and "confusing the public mind" were curiously enough, reaffirmed. In the meantime, I returned to the United States in May only with the World Passport to organize a WSA Washington, D.C. office. U.S Immigration, after detaining me for 3 days at the Brooklyn Detention Facility, released me on a $5,000 bond advanced by Mortimer Lipsky, a longtime world government advocate, pending an exclusionary hearing.

The WSA District III, Inc. was filed with the District of Columbia on October 25, 1976. Upon my return to France on November 4, directly after the presidential elections and before the INS exclusion hearing was held, after arriving at Mulhouse, I was served with a restraining order from Juge d'Instruction Ferret forbidding me to authorize the issuance of WSA documents until his inquiry was completed. Failure to comply would result automatically in a contempt of court charge and subsequent imprisonment until the trial.

At his question as to whether or not I agreed to authorize the cessation of passport issuance, I was obliged to remain totally silent. Faced with no reply whatsoever, he had to release me provisionally. I knew my days in France were numbered.

On January 4, 1977, after the holidays, I was ordered to report to the St. Louis gendarmerie "pour l'affaire passeports." That was it. Judge Ferret would jail me until the trial. After good-byes to my family, I reluctantly left France for England, travelling with my stateless document, not to return until and unless all criminal accusations are dropped against me. The trial took place in my absence. This time I was convicted for "counterfeiting" and given a two year sentence. As I write this, a bench warrant exists for my arrest in France, where I will serve the term should I return.

My exodus signaled the end of an era for me. . .and the beginning of a new one. I would be testing my world citizenship against the greatest Caesar of all time, my own renounced United States of America.

Before bringing the test to U.S. Immigration and eventually the U.S. courts, on January 10, 1977, I embarked for the Holy Land, entering Israel with the stateless travel document. After a visit to the Ba'h'ai temple at Haifa, I came to Jerusalem where, on January 17, with Toma Sik, an Israeli World Citizen and WSA agent, I declared the holy sites of the Jewish, Moslem amd Christian religions as "world territory under the sovereign protection of world law."

Trying to leave Israel by the Allenby Bridge to Jordan, I was confronted by both Jordanian and Israeli soldiers united against me. Since neither nation recognized the World Passport, I was literally caught on the neutral line separating the two countries. Obviously, it was the dead center of the Allenby Bridge. The confrontation was "resolved" when I was forced back into Israel by Israeli soldiers on orders from the government in Jerusalem in collusion with the Jordanian authorities.

I returned to London January 24, embarking for the United States January 30, this time purposely entering unheralded with a proper U.S. tourist visa obtained from the Strasbourg U.S. consulate on my stateless travel document.

The Washington D.C. WSA office was beginning to receive dozens of applications daily from U.S. citizens and increasing numbers of resident aliens who recognized the value of a neutral, global travel document.

The British queen's Silver Jubilee Festival of Mind and Body at the Olympia Hall in London was an unusual grouping of esoteric, environmental and world-minded organizations at which the London-based WSA office had an exhibit. While attending the Festival, I helped launch the First World Referendum based on questions of world citizenship, world government and economic democracy. I continued on to Switzerland (the interdiction to enter had been lifted) and in a press conference in Berne, launched the World Referendum in this democratic country.

Returning to London May 7, I embarked once again for the United States, this time landing at Dulles Airport, Washington, D.C. May 13 where I presented my WSA passport to Immigration officials. It indicated my birthplace as "Bar Harbor, Maine", my home address as "1809 19th Street, N.W., Washington, D.C." and my occupation as "World Coordinator and President, World Service Authority District III, Inc."

I was refused entry, classified as an "excludable alien," and detained by Immigration authorities for 11 days before being released "pending deportation."

At an exclusion hearing May 17 before U.S. Judge Bobek, I defended my right to enter the United States on the basis of Article 13(2) of the *Universal Declaration of Human Rights.* "Everyone has the right to leave any country, including his own, and to return to his country."

The attorney for the U.S. Justice Department claimed that, as I had renounced my nationality, was stateless, did not possess a "valid" passport nor an immigrant visa, according to U.S. Immigration law, I could not enter the United States.

The judge concurred and ordered me expelled.

I immediately appealed the decision to the Immigration Court of Appeals and was finally released from detention in the recognizance of my counsel.

On May 24, 1978, the Immigration Court of Appeals upheld Judge Bobek's original decision. But the INS made no move to deport me.

Over a year later, during which the Basel Attorney-General indicted me for "usurping an official function" and closed our Basel office, on July 17, 1979, I filed suit against the District Director of the INS in the 1st Federal District Court petitioning the court for a writ of habeus corpus to enable me to enter the United States legally. The irony of being considered a person before the law able to so file a suit in court for the purpose of being brought before the court as a person before the law escaped the press and the general public.

The court denied my petition December 19, 1979 thereby upholding INS's claim that I was an "excludable alien" and subject to 'immediate deportation."

Once again I appealed in May, 1980, and on March 31, 1981, the United States Court of Appeals, 1st District, upheld the lower court's determination.

I could finally petition the Supreme Court for a writ of certiorari in order to argue the constitutional issues involved. From the beginning I had claimed that both the 9th and 10th amendments to the U.S. Constitution implied an extension of allegiance to a world government. I could as well expose the contradition of the national law which permitted expatriation thereby condoning statelessness while at the same time excluding that stateless person from returning to his homeland. The fact that the INS could not legally deport me in that I was born in the United States rendered the laws of expatriation and of expulsion null and void. Also there was a reasonable doubt that the actual process of expatriation was in fact legal in that it had to be performed "in a foreign state" and "before a consular officer," the latter only functioning in a U.S. Embassy, U.S. "soil."

My petition was duly filed with the Supreme Court on August 28, 1981 and denied on October 19, 1981.

The final legal remedy open to me was a Petition for Rehearing also to the Supreme Court. Since additional and substantive arguments had to be introduced in order for such a petition not to be considered "frivolous," I challenged the discretionary powers of the U.S. president in a nuclear era, maintaining that the only countervailing legal remedy for the citizen was to add a higher level of citizenship in order to protect his inalienable rights. This petition was filed with the Supreme Court on December 22, 1981 and denied January 25, 1982. (See Chapter 11)

In order to test my right to leave my country and to return to it identified only as a citizen of the World Government, I left for Japan on April 28, 1984 from Dulles Airport via Northwest Orient Airways. The Japanese government would not permit my entry claiming the WSA World Passport was not "valid" and forced Northwest Orient to bring me back to Seattle on May 7. An Immigration judge, who read into the record a telex from INS in Washington to the effect that my file "has been lost," declared, in total contradiction to every previous court decision, that since I had "never left the United States," I was in the same legal position then, in other words, an "excludable alien," as I was on April 28th!

I am therefore not yet legally in the United States while still undeportable.

My legal status therefore is determined by the only government which represents me: the World Government of World Citizens.

We have therefore come full circle. In 1948, I renounced my nationality "as a protest to the exclusiveness of the institution of nationalism itself, which encloses all countries today and which has been rendered obsolete by actual world conditions."

In 1953, I "exported" World Government from the United States.

Now, in 1984, World Government has been "imported" into this super-power which presently spends a third of the world's armament budget or about 3% of the world's gross national gross national product.

In the baldest terms, if the World Government is sovereign, then the United States of America (or any other nationstate) is not.

The "collision course" has been inevitable ever since May 25, 1948.

In the meantime, the constituency of our new government grows. On September 4, 1983, on its 30th birthday, I declared my candidacy for world president in accordance with article 21(3) of the Universal Declaration of Human Rights.

Myths are born, some grow to maturity, become powerful, then turn senile as conditions change, and finally die, to become legends, like humans, like civilizations.

The myth of nationalism, with its power of unification in pre-industrial, pre-electronic, pre-nuclear and pre-space 18th and 19th centuries, is giving way in the 20th century to senility and obsolescence. Yet it still claims you, a sovereign human being, at your earthly birth—for without you, it does not exist.

But without us, humanity does not exist either, for, in reality, we and humanity are synonomous.

This is the dynamic truth of this century of overkill, microwave technology, nuclear proliferation, ocean degradation, instantaneous global communication and millenium-messianic-armegeddon religions.

The political corollary of identity with humankind is world citizenship; the institutional identification of world citizenship is world government.

Over 250,000 of your fellow humans have chosen world peace and humans rights over world war and oppression by allying themselves with the emerging World Government, "the only peace game in town."

The numbers at present may be insignificant. Yet if you "add" your human sovereignty to ours, we will prevail.

WORLD COURT OF HUMAN RIGHTS
DECLARATION OF FOUNDING
AND
APPOINTMENT OF DR. LUIS KUTNER AS CHIEF JUSTICE

General Assembly, Delegates of the World Government of World Citizens
June 10, 1972
Novotel, Sausheim, H.R., France

With great pleasure I welcome the delegates on this important occasion. Though our numbers here may be small, we can justifiably claim to represent millions of our fellow citizens throughout the world who have endorsed the cause of world peace through law and citizenship.

Today, twenty-one years after its founding, our world government has faced its first legal test in a national court.

The true significance of this trial lies in its positing an individual claiming his fundamental human rights against the sovereign state claiming its right to deny his rights. Like you, I have chosen a world government to represent my rights. Like you, I have accepted documents issued by this government to identify me. As freedom of travel is a basic right, I have accepted a passport issued by this government based on this right. Others, who also claim world citizenship, have demanded this passport and it has been issued to them.

For this, I am being considered a criminal before French law.

Human rights are being denied throughout our world community by sovereign states. Nowhere can an individual turn for help since all states collude in this denial. Courts set up by these very states merely affirm their exclusive sovereignty which, in the final analysis, perpetuate the crime of violations.

The United Nations' Commission on Human Rights is powerless both to prevent human rights' violations or to consider them when individuals petition it for redress.

The International Court of the Hague treats only cases between sovereign states and only if both parties agree to the litigation.

Today's trial reveals clearly the anomoly between human rights advocacy and practice. For when the individual practices his human rights, already advocated by the sovereign state but which the state considers violating its security, he is condemned before a national criminal court.

My case is by no means unique in itself. Where its uniqueless lies is in the fact that I have represented myself as a world citizen for over a quarter of a century and furthermore allied myself by necessity to a government of my own choosing.

Our need is crystal clear. If in affirming our human rights we contravene national law, we must appeal to a new kind of court, one grounded on the legal defense of such rights. By definition it must be global in character. It must be accessible to all world citizens.

In short, it must be a world court of human rights.

Such a court does not yet exist. Its need is nonetheless real. And since human rights must be protected by a regime of law, as states the Preamble to the *Universal Declaration of Human Rights,* so world law is implicit in a universal human rights declaration.

Therefore, as the acting World Coordinator of World Government and defendant in the present case, acting in the name of world citizens as well as for all those whose human rights have been violated, with the sanction of common world law, I hereby proclaim the existence of the WORLD COURT OF HUMAN RIGHTS as the judiciary arm of the World Government.

To preside over the new court as well as to determine its statute within the principles of the World Government, as its acting World Coordinator, I am privileged and pleased to appoint Dr. Luis Kutner, whose testimony today as well as his commitment to the principle of just world law superbly qualifies him for this high commission, Chief Justice of the new court.

I am honored to present to this distinguished and mandated assembly, Mr. Chief Justice of the World Court of Human Rights, Dr Luis Kutner

Dr. Kutner's Acceptance Speech

I am indeed honored by this appointment which I accept in all humility.

The international community has come to realize that human rights are not an issue to be left solely to the national jurisdiction of individual states. These rights obviously need protection at a higher level within the framework of international law.

If the principle aim of society is to protect individuals in the enjoyment of what Blackstone termed "absolute rights," then it follows that the aim of human laws should serve to promote and guard these rights.

As the World Coordinator rightly pointed out, this morning's trial dramatically exposed the dilemma faced by the sovereign state. While advocating human rights and even proclaiming them as a "common standard of achievement," as does the Preamble to the *Universal Declaration of Human Rights,* it prosecutes blindly—as the spokesman for the French Government so vividly revealed—a stateless person who, to provide a legitimate framework for his own rights, was obliged to found his own government.

I wholly support this action as a logical corollary of the U.N.'s proclamation of the *Universal Declaration of Human Rights.*

If we accept the legitimacy of individual choice in political matters—which is, after all, the essence of democracy—then the legitimacy of a world government chosen by millions of ordinary citizens cannot be in doubt. What began as a declaration of intent on December 10, 1948 has been slowly evolving into a global compact, a set of rules that proscribe and prescribe the behavior of governments toward their citizens.

There exists today a codified body of international human rights laws that include conventions and covenants on genocide, civil and political, economic and social rights, refugees' and women's rights and racial discrimination. The international community is currently working on instruments to prevent torture, to protect the rights of children and to assure the freedom of religion.

While these instruments are not self-enforcing, they do provide means for holding governments accountable. They lead inevitably to this assembly today. We are the citizens concerned. We are the ultimate arbiters of human rights as they are innate and inalienable. Our action today in founding a new court to which the single world citizen can appeal falls within the historical evolution of law itself as an evolving institution.

After all, the standards and norms enumerated and outlined in international human rights instruments have not been imposed on any of the nations that are party to them. They are, instead, obligations that governments, having assumed freely and voluntarily, cannot afford to abrogate or disregard under any pretext.

The World Court of Human Rights, while not operating under any written world constitution, nonetheless can embody a "world bill of rights" which defines guarantees relating to deprivation of life, inhumane treatment, slavery and forced labor, personal liberty, determination of rights, including procedural safeguards in criminal cases, freedom of conscience, expression, peaceable assembly and movement, freedom from discrimination and prohibition against compulsory acquisition of property without adequate compensation.

Indeed the very enunciation and acceptance of these basic human rights implies due process to insure their implementation and punishment to their violators. Such was the premise of the Nuremberg Court. No written world constitution sanctioned the Nuremberg Principles. Yet they were effectively used by the Allies to charge, convict and condemn those accused of the international crimes of war planning, war-making and genocide.

Before this assembly, I pledge my best and most devoted endeavors as Chief Justice of the World Court of Human Rights in the service of the oppressed, the persecuted and the downtrodden. It has been said that the guarantees of personal liberty and impartial justice are the first casualties of a so-called national emergency. Civil courts are too often replaced by military tribunals and the writ of habeus corpus is usually suspended. Inevitably the despicable use of preventive detention replaces constitutional guarantees of personal liberty. The citizenry then is made to live in a perpetual state of emergency. When that happens, the state becomes an end in itself, a mere summation of the individuals within it.

The World Government of World Citizens that you here represent, is the only effective counter-balance to national citizenry becoming national servitude due to suppression of civil liberties in the name of national security and public order.

Now the newly-declared World Court of Human Rights will take its place as a needful addition to provide a legal refuge, a global asylum, as it were, to our fellow citizens everywhere.

I profoundly believe this day's work has the blessings of the Almighty. Thank you.

Linn's STAMP NEWS

ISSN 0161-6234
USPS 314440

$1 U.S.

April 20, 1981   WORLD'S LARGEST WEEKLY STAMP NEWS AND MARKETPLACE   Vol. 54 Issue 2737

'World postage stamps' make debut

By James H. Bruns
Washington Correspondent

A winged globe appears on the 1 mondo world "stamp."

Guy Steele Fairlamb's 50 cendoj design depicts a stylized globe, junk and space capsule.

A pair of "world postage stamps" made their debut March 20 in Washington, D.C.

The "stamps," produced by the World Service Authority, the administrative arm of a Washington-based organization known as the World Government of World Citizens, were issued as part of the 1981 Earth Day celebrations.

The release of the perforated adhesives marked the official inauguration of the WSA's World Government Postal Service.

Garry Davis, founder and coordinator of the organization, said, "At the moment the World Government Postal Service is designed solely to serve individuals in areas where national postal services are not available and where there is a violation of Article 19 of the Universal Declaration of Human Rights."

The impetus for developing such a service came from Hong Kong where a branch of the World Service Authority has been channeling letters to and from the People's Republic of China and Nationalist China since August of 1980.

Thus far over 3,000 letters have been redirected to individuals in those two countries with the help of the WSA using Hong Kong as a terminal point.

Neither of the two Chinas recognizes the postal validity of the other's stamps, so the direct exchange of mail between Taiwan and Mainland China doesn't really exist.

To help break that impasse, the WSA began accepting letters from either country at its Hong Kong office. These would arrive in a cover envelope which the WSA staff would open, affix Hong Kong postage to the preaddressed enclosed letter, and put it into the crown colony's mailstream.

This routing service, which until March was provided free of charge, was becoming rather costly.

"To pay for that and similar services in other parts of the world," stated Davis, "it became necessary to establish a formal method of financing (the operation)."

Davis is the first to admit that his organization's "stamps" don't have any postal validity whatsoever.

"The World Government stamps will have symbolic value only in countries where national postal services recognize the national stamps of the country where the (redirected) mail originated and so deliver them," he said.

This point was echoed by Helmut Kimpel of the organization's Washington headquarters. He emphasized that WSA is not interested in setting up any type of rival post offices anywhere.

The only time it enters the postal picture is when there are two or more postal administrations which won't comply with that section of the Universal Declaration of Human Rights which states in part that:

"Everyone has the right to . . . receive and impart information and ideas through any media and regardless of frontiers."

Even then, he noted, the cost of forwarding all mail is prepaid using the postage stamps of a host postal service.

The only thing the "stamps" of the WSA denote is that a special service has been provided, noted Kimpel. They do not replace any nation's stamps but flank the issues of the nations where the item was redirected.

The "stamps" are available in two denominations — 1 mondo and 50 cendoj (pronounced cendoi).

A spokesman for the WSA said the mondo, which is the equivalent of 1 Swiss franc (or roughly $1.14) is the organization's basic monetary unit.

In Esperanto, an artificial language developed by Dr. Ludwig Zamenhof of Poland earlier in the 20th century, the word "mondo" means "world" or, in this case, "world currency."

The 1c, representing half a mondo, is the rate charged for servicing each half ounce of letter mail by the WSA.

The designs of the two "stamps" were unveiled March 11 by Davis, while a U.S. District Court of Appeals in Washington, D.C., was hearing his long-standing fight to have his status of a world citizen recognized.

He declared himself a world citizen in 1948 when he renounced his U.S. citizenship.

Credit for designing the "stamps" goes to Raymond Whyte of Kennalon, N.J., and Guy Steele Fairlamb of Washington, D.C.

Whyte's design, which appears on the 1m, features a winged globe. The 50c, designed by Fairlamb, depicts a stylized globe, a junk and a space capsule.

Appearing around the edge of both "stamps," in six languages (Arabic, Chinese, English, Esperanto, Russian and Spanish), is the notation, "World Government Post."

The Esperanto version on the 50c (which appears down the right side of the item) was printed incorrectly. The first letter in "Mondregistaro," which translates "World Government," was left off.

This problem was not thought to be significant enough to withhold the 50c nor will a corrected version be printed.

The "stamps" were printed in sheets of 35 each by Sales Niagara of Buffalo, N.Y. In all, 75,000 of each value were produced.

The WSA reported that the "stamps" will be divided somewhat evenly among the organization's eight branch offices located in such places as London, England; Tel Aviv-Jaffa, Israel; and Beirut, Lebanon.

Collectors interested in these items can obtain full sheets of either value directly from the WSA's office, Suite 318, Atlantic Building, 930 F St. NW, Washington, D.C.

The prices per sheet are $39.90 for the 1m and $19.95 for the 50c. There is a $2 handling charge for each order, noted the WSA.

World Government Postal Service

Telephone (202) 638-2662
Telex: 82468 WGOV UR

A department of the
World Service Authority

SUITE 1101 - CONTINENTAL BUILDING
1012 14th STREET, NW
WASHINGTON, D.C. 20005

ORDER / BILLING FORM FOR WORLD GOVERNMENT STAMPS

Date

Dear

In response to your inquiry, following is our price list and order form for the first
World Government stamps:

In response to your order, we are pleased to enclose the items marked below:

____ sheet(s) of the 1 mondo stamp at $39.90 per sheet ....$_____

____ sheet(s) of the 50 cendoj stamp at $19.95 per sheet ....$_____

____ block(s) of 4 mondo stamps at $4.56 per block ....$_____

____ block(s) of 6 mondo stamps at $6.84 per block ....$_____

____ block(s) of 4 cendoj stamps at $2.28 per block ....$_____

____ block(s) of 6 cendoj stamps at $3.42 per block ....$_____

____ First Day Covers (March 21 - Earth Day) with
1 mondo and 1 50 cendoj stamp at $2.00 each ....$_____
(Please check number of cancelled____and/or mint____)

Handling charge for each stamp order ....$ **2.00**

Total for order ═══════

Please make check or money order payable to

WORLD GOVERNMENT POSTAL SERVICE

and send with order to:

WORLD SERVICE AUTHORITY

SUITE 1101 - CONTINENTAL BUILDING
1012 14th STREET, NW
WASHINGTON, D.C. 20005

NOTE: THIS EDITION IS LIMITED TO 5,000 SHEETS OF EACH DENOMINATION.
EACH INDIVIDUAL SHEET IS NUMBERED AND DRY-SEALED WITH THE
WSA DISTRICT III, INC. CORPORATE SEAL

World Government Postal Service

WORLD SERVICE AUTHORITY
DOCUMENTS

World Government of World Citizens

WORLD OFFICE
Suite 1101 - Continental Building
1012 14th Street, NW
Washington, D.C. 20005
USA
Tel: (202) 638-2662
Computer: (202) 638-5614
Telex: 292052 WGOV UR

Global Representation of Registered World Citizens since 1953
Garry Davis, Founder and World Coordinator
Districts:
I Basel II London III Washington, DC IV Bauchi (Nig.)
V(a) Tel Aviv-Jaffa V(b) Ammon VIII Hong Kong IX Colombo

ADMINISTRATION:
WORLD SERVICE
AUTHORITY
Ingrid Dennison
President

JUDICIARY
World Court of Human Rights
Dr. Luis Kutner, Chief Justice
105 W. Adams Street
Chicago, Ill. 60603
(312) 782-1946

COMMISSIONS
(In formation)
Cultural
Yehudi Menuhin, Coordinator
London

Design-Science
Wm. Perk, Coordinator
Carbondale, IL

Forestry
Badi Lenz, Coordinator
Adel-Leeds, U.K.

Ocean
Edward R. Welles, Coordinator
Manset, ME

Space
Issac Asimov, Coordinator
New York, NY

Carol S. Rosin
Deputy Coordinator
Clarksville, MD

World Education
Guru Nitya Chaitanya Yati
Narayana Gurukula
Sirinivasapuram 695145
S. India

WORLD POSTAL SERVICE
Washington, D.C. 20005

Dear Friend;

You are already a World Citizen in fact. By registering* as a citizen of the **WORLD GOVERNMENT OF WORLD CITIZENS** — which does not require giving up your nationality —you are joining a fast-growing sovereign constituency which has committed itself to establishing social, economic and political justice throughout the world in accordance with the fundamental moral codes of all major religions.

As a registered World Citizen, you have the opportunity to help evolve just and democratic **WORLD LAWS,** to be enacted eventually by an elected **WORLD PARLIAMENT,** administered by a **WORLD EXECUTIVE,** controlled by a **WORLD COURT,** and enforced by a **WORLD PEACE FORCE.**

From an economic world viewpoint, the gradual elimination of national armaments and the reconversion from scarcity thinking to abundance can transform our human community from one of increasing physical misery to individual and mutual prosperity. A World Citizen political party is in formation to help power these programs.

The **WORLD GOVERNMENT OF WORLD CITIZENS** in fact is already functioning in representing you and your needs on a global level. We issue **WORLD PASSPORTS, WORLD CITIZEN CARDS, WORLD IDENTITY CARDS, WORLD BIRTH CERTIFICATES, WORLD MARRIAGE CERTIFICATES,** all in seven languages, and an intra-global postal service has begun operations. These represent your *human* rights and are mandated by the Universal Declaration of Human Rights, approved by the General Assembly of the United Nations, 10 December 1948.

WORLD CITIZEN NEWS is the official journal of the WG of WC. Please subscribe. The brochure from the **WORLD SERVICE AUTHORITY** offers world citizenship literature to help you understand your new global commitment. To understand the origins and philosophy of the WG of WC, we urge you to send for the three basic documents: The Ellsworth Declaration, the Memorandum on World Government, and the 1978 Position Paper. My book, *My Country Is The World,* is also available.

The World Citizen Legal Fund is available to registered contributors to help defray their legal expenses in human rights violation cases. (See below).

We are looking forward to working together with you for a peaceful world under the **CREDO OF A WORLD CITIZEN** as stated on the back of this letter.

*See Specimen card
on reverse side

Yours in world service,

Garry Davis
Garry Davis
WGWC World Coordinator

World Government of World Citizens Registration Form

369

CREDO OF A WORLD CITIZEN

A World Citizen is a human being who lives intellectually, morally and physically in the present.

A World Citizen accepts the dynamic fact that the planetary human community is interdependent and whole, that humankind is essentially one.

A World Citizen is a peaceful and peacemaking individual, both in daily life and contacts with others.

As a global person, a World Citizen relates directly to humankind and to all fellow humans spontaneously, generously and openly. Mutual trust is basic to his/her life style.

Politically, a World Citizen accepts a sanctioning institution of representative government, expressing the general and individual sovereign will in order to establish and maintain a system of just and equitable world law with appropriate legislative, judiciary and enforcement bodies.

A World Citizen brings about better understanding and protection of different cultures, ethnic groups and language communities by promoting the use of a neutral international language, such as Esperanto.

A World Citizen makes this world a better place to live in harmoniously by studying and respecting the viewpoints of fellow citizens from anywhere in the world.

PLEDGE OF ALLEGIANCE

I, the undersigned, do hereby, willingly and consciously, declare myself to be a Citizen of the World. As a World Citizen, I pledge my planetary civic commitment to WORLD GOVERNMENT, founded on three universal principles of One Absolute Value, One World, and One Humanity which constitute the basis of World Law. As a World Citizen I acknowledge the WORLD GOVERNMENT as having the right and duty to represent me in all that concerns fundamental human rights and the General Good of human-kind and the Good of All.

As a Citizen of World Government, I affirm my awareness of my inherent responsibilities and rights as a legitimate member of the total world community of all men, women, and children, and will endeavor to fulfill and practice these whenever and wherever the opportunity presents itself.

As a Citizen of World Government, I recognize and re-affirm citizenship loyalties and responsibilities within the communal, state, and/or national groupings consistent with the principles of unity above which constitute now my planetary civic commitment.

Signature of World Citizen

370

WORLD SERVICE AUTHORITY

1012 14th STREET, N.W., WASHINGTON, D.C. 20005

APPLICATION FORM • FORMULAIRE DE DEMANDE
FORMULARIO APLICACION

INSTRUCTIONS: 1. Mark in boxes which documents and postage chosen. **2. Sign ATTESTA-TION OF UNDERSTANDING below.** 3. Fill out form on reverse side in block letters or by typewriter. 4. Have your signature authenicated. 5. Send with photos, bank check, international money order or IRCs to: WSA, Washington, D.C. 20005. **No WSA document will be issued without payment or proof thereof.**

INSTRUCTIONS: 1.Marquer dans les carrés lesquels documents et type poste choisis. 2. **Signer ATTESTATION DE COMPREHESION au-dessous.** 3. Remplir la forme à l'envers complètement en lettres majuscules ou taper à la machine. 4. Fait attester votre signature. 5. Envoyer avec photos, chèque bancaire, mandat international ou CRI à WSA, Washington, D.C. 20005. **Aucun document WSA sera émi sans paiement ou preuve de cela.**

INSTRUCCIONES: 1. Indique lo documentos y el franqueo que desea. 2. **Firme el CER-TIFICADO DE ENTENDIMENTO al fondo.** 3. Llene et Formulario al dorso. Favor de hacerlo a maquina o en letra de molde. 4. Certifique su firma y solicitud. 5. Envie esta solicitud junto a las foto, giro bancario o postal, o Cupones Internaciones de Intercambio a: WSA, Washington. D.C. 20005. **Ningun documento de WSA sera emitido sin pago o certificion del mismo.**

WSA Agent's address and telephone number.
Adresse et numéro de téléphone de l'Agent.
Dirección y teléfono del Agente WSA.

World Pp. No.   World I.C. No.

Send the document(s) to this address
Envoyez le(s) documents á cet adresse
Envíe los documento(s) a esta dirección

World Passport	Passeport Mondial	Pasaporte Mundial	8 years 8 ans 8 anos $40 ☐	3 years 3 ans 3 anos $25 ☐
World Donor Passport	Passeport de Donneur Mondial		Pasaporte Mundial de Donante	12 years 12 anos 12 anos $300 ☐
World Identity Card	Carte d'Identité Mondiale		Tarjeta Mundial de Identidad	$12 ☐
World Birth Certificate	Certificat Mondiale de Naissance		Certificado Mundial de Nacimiento	$12 ☐
Certified Mail (U.S.A. only) Courrier Certifie (que U.S.A.) Correo certificado en USA	☐ US $3		Registered mail anywhere Lettre recommandée partout Correo registrado en otros paises	☐ US $7

ATTESTATION OF UNDERSTANDING

The applicant understands that the World Service Authority can accept no responsibility for the position of any government as regards the WSA passport and or its other identification documents.

Important: Applicants under 16 years of age must have the **Attestation of Understanding** signed by a parent or guardian.

ATTESTATION DE COMPREHENSION

Le demandeur comprend que le World Service Authority ne peut assume de responsabilité quant à la position d'un gouvernement concernant le passeport du WSA ou tout autre pièce d'identité par le même bureau.

Important: Les demandeurs agés de moins de 16 ans doivent avoir l'**Attestation de Comprehension** signée par un parent ou le tuteur légal.

CERTIFICADO DE ENTENDIMIENTO

El aplicante entiende que la WSA no puede aceptar la responsabilidad por la posición de cualquier gobierno en relación con el Pasaporte WSA ó sus documentos de identidad.

Importante: Uno de los padres ó el guardian de los aplicantes menores de 16 años debe firmar el siguiente **Certificado de Entendimiento**.

Signature and date • Signature et date • Firma y fecha

Approximate size of ID photo. Dimension approximative de la photo ID. Tamano approximada de la foto ID.	Submit 4 photos and sign your name on back of each one. Color accepted. Photos are for file, replacement if necessary, and ID card, in addition to passport.
	Veuillez joindre 4 photos et signer votre nom au verso de chacune d'elles. Les photos en couleurs sont acceptées. Elles servent aux archives et la carte d'identité ou passeport, et si besoin remplacement du document.
	Envíe 4 fotografias firmadas en la parte trasera, como en el ejemplo. Se aceptan fotografias a color. Las fotografias son para nuestro archivo, para reemplazo en caso de necesidad, y para la Tarjeta de Identidad, además del Pasaporte.

371

ANSWER EACH ITEM • REPONDRE A CHAQUE ELEMENT • RELLENAR ESTE CUESTIONARIO

Print or type • Tapez ou écrivez en lettres capitales • Escriba a maquina o con letra de molde

Family name • Nom de famille • Apellido

Forename(s) • Prénom(s) • Nombre(s)

Street • Rue • Calle

City & Zip code • Ville & code postal • Ciudad

State Province • Département • Estado

Country • Pays • Nación

Place of birth • Lieu de naissance • Luga de naciemento

Telephone

Telex

Day • Jour Día

Month • Mois Mes

Year • Année Año

M Sex F

Height • Taille Estatura

Color eyes • Couleur yeux Color de lois oios

Special marks • Signes particuliers Caracteristicas especiales

Occupation • Profession • Ocupación

INFORMATION FOR WORLD BIRTH CERTIFICATE • INFORMATIONS POUR LE CERTIFICAT MONDIAL DE NAISSANCE
INFORMACIÓN PARA EL CERTIFICADO MUNDIAL DE NACIMIENTO

Father's name • Nom du père
Nombre del padre

Mother's name • Nom de la mère
Nombre de la madre

I swear that my information
in this form is true and correct.

Je prête serment que les
informations fournies par moi
dans ce formulaire sont correctes.

Juro que esta información
es veridica.

Signature • Firma :

CERTIFICATION OF SIGNATURE, OR PHOTOCOPY OF IDENTITY PAPERS, OR PRINT OF RIGHT INDEX FINGER.
Certification d'authenticité de la signature ou photocopies des papiers d'identité ou l'empreinte digitale de l'index droit.
Certificacion de firma, o fotocopia de documentos de indentidad o impresion digital.

On this _____ day of

_____ , 19____ , before me

came _____ ,
known to me and known by me to be the
person who executed the foregoing application, and he/she thereupon duly acknowledged to me that he/she executed
the same.

En ce _____ jour de

_____ , 19____ , s'est

présenté(e) devant moi _____

_____ , la personne
connue de moi étant l'auteur de la de-
mande actuelle; en foi de quoi il (elle) a
attesté(e) en bonne et due forme s'être co-
formé au règlement.

En este _____ día de

_____ , de 19____ , se

presentó _____ ,
conocido como el cual, quien cumpli-
mentó esta plicación y reconció delante de
mi haberla cumplimentado.

Certifying Official • Agent Officiel • Oficial de Certificaciones

Fingerprint
Empreinte Digitale
Impresion Digital

Seal and signature • Sceau et signature • Sello y firma

WORLD SERVICE
AUTHORITY DIST. III
1012 14th STREET, N.W.
WASHINGTON, D.C.—U.S.A. 20005
Telephone (202) 638-2662
Telex: 292052 WGOV UR

Send me _____ more application forms

Envoyez _____ formulaires d'application supplémentaires

Enviar me _____ solicitudes más

WSA GA 05000 7-83

372

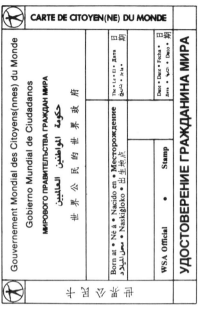

CARTE DE CITOYEN(NE) DU MONDE

Gouvernement Mondial des Citoyens(nnes) du Monde
Gobierno Mundial de Ciudadanos
МИРОВОГО ПРАВИТЕЛЬСТВА ГРАЖДАН МИРА
حكومة المواطنين العالمين
世界公民的世界政府

Born at • Né à • Nacido en • Меsторождение • مسل الميلاد • Naskiĝloko • 出生地点

WSA Official • Stamp

Date • Date • Fecha • Дата • تاريخ • Dato • 日期

УДОСТОВЕРЕНИЕ ГРАЖДАНИНА МИРА

TARJETA DE CIUDADANÍA MUNDIAL

WORLD CITIZEN CARD
MONDCIVITANKARTO

WORLD SERVICE AUTHORITY
CENTRAL REGISTRY | NO.

Name • Nom • Apellido • Фамилия • اللقب • Nomo • 姓名

is a Registered Citizen of the
estas registrite civitano
est enregistré comme citoyen(ne) du
esta inscrito como ciudadano de
зарегистрированный гражданин
مواطن عالمي مسجل • 登记公民

WORLD GOVERNMENT OF WORLD CITIZENS
MONDREGISTRARO DE MONDCIVITANOJ

شهادة ميلاد عالمية

Sex • Sexe • Sexo • Пол • الجنس • Sekso

Year • Année • Año • Год • السنة • Jaro

Day • Jour • Día • День • اليوم • Tago
Month • Mois • Mes • Месяц • الشهر • Monato

Father's name • Nom du père • Nombre del padre • ИМЯ ОТЦА • اسم الأب • Nomo de la patro

Mother's name • Nom de la mère • Nombre de la madre • ИМЯ МАТЕРИ • اسم الأم • Nomo de la patrino

Issued at • Fait a • Expedido en • Выдано в • صدر في • Farita en • 签发地点

Date • Date • Fecha • Дата • تاريخ • Dato • 日期

WSA official-stamp

МИРОВОЕ МЕТРИЧЕСКОЕ СВИДЕТЕЛЬСТВО

CERTIFICADO MUNDIAL DE NACIMIENTO

CERTIFICAT MONDIAL DE NAISSANCE

WORLD BIRTH CERTIFICATE
NASKIĜATESTILO TUTMONDA

WORLD SERVICE AUTHORITY
CENTRAL REGISTRY

Name • Nom • Apellidos • Фамилия • اللقب • Nomo • 姓

Forenames • Prénoms • Nombre • Имя (имена) • الاسم • Antaŭnomoj • 名

Born at • Ne à • Nacido en • Место рождения • مسل الميلاد • Naskiĝloko • 出生地点

World Citizen Card

World Birth Certificate

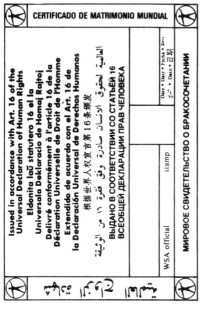

World Marriage Certificate World Identity Card

374

MONDPOLITIKA-AZILO KARTO

WORLD POLITICAL ASYLUM CARD

WORLD SERVICE AUTHORITY
WORLD CITIZENS REGISTRY
WASHINGTON, D.C. U.S.A.

No.

Name • Nom • Apellido • Фамилия • القب • Nomo • 姓名

Born at • Né à • Nacido en •|Месторождение
• محل الميلاد • Naskiĝloko • 出生地点

The • le • H • Дата • رمضان • 出日 • Je la • 生日	Day • Jour • Dia • ДЕНЬ • يوم • Tago • 日	Year • Année • Ano ГОД • السنة • Jaro • 年	Sex • Sexe • Sexo • пол • الجنس • Sekso 性別
	Month • Mois • Mes • МЕСЯЦ • الشهر • Monato • 月		

Eyes • Yeux • 眼睛 Ojos •| Глаза • 颜色 العينان •|Okuloj	Height • Taille • 身高 Statura • Рост • Statur القامة •| الطول •|Staturo	Special marks • Signes particuliers • Signos particulares •|Особые приметы 特征 العلامات المميزة • Specialaj signoj
WSA Official		**Stamp**
Date • Date • Fecha • Дата • تاريخ • Dato • 日期		

ВСЕМИРНОЕ УДОСТОВЕРЕНИЕ ПОЛИТИЧЕСКОГО УБЕЖИЩА

World Political Asylum Card

This card derives from Art. 14, Universal Declaration of Human Rights: "Everyone has the right to seek and to enjoy...asylum from persecution." Report violations to WSA, Wash. DC 20005, USA.

Cette carte se fond sur l'article 14 de la Déclaration Universelle des Droits de l'Homme: "Devant la persecution, toute personne a le droit de chercher et de beneficier de l'asile...." Signaler violations à WSA, Wash. DC 20005, USA.

Esta tarjeta se deriva del Art. 14 de la Declaración Universal de Derechos Humanos: "Todas las personas tienen derecho a pedir y a disfrutar ... de asilo contra persecusión". Las violaciones a esta norma deben notificarse a: WSA, Wash. DC 20005, USA.

Это удостоверение основано на статье 14-ой Всеобщей Декларации Прав Человека: "Каждый человек имеет право искать убежища от преследования ... и пользоваться этим убежищем." О нарушениях этого права следует сообщать по адресу: WSA, DC 20005, USA.

تستند هذه البطاقة الى المادة ١٤ من الاعلان العالمي لحقوق الانسان التي تنص على
ان « لكل انسان الحق في السعى الى اللجوء السياسي والتمتع به اتقاء للاضطهاد »
يرجى تبليغ اى انتهاكات الى هيئة الخدمات الدولية.   WSA, DC 20005, USA.

此证系根据世界人权宣言所颁发的。人权宣言第十四条说： "每个人都有寻求和亨有从迫害避难的权利。有违反事件发生时，请向世界服务组织提出报告。地址是，
WSA, DC 20005, USA.

Ĉi-tiu karto devenis el Artikolo 14 Universala Deklaracio de Homaj Rajtoj: "Ciu rajtas peti kaj recevi ... azilon kontraŭ persekuto." Raportu malobservojn al WSA, Washington, D.C. 20005, USA.

376

These "World Refugee 10 Dollar" bills are receipts for contributions to the World Refugee Fund which issues gratis World Passports to refugees.

ADKINS, N.F.: *Thomas Paine, Common Sense & Other Political Writings,* The Liberal Arts Press, 1953

BERES, Louis Rene: *People, States, and World Order,* F.E. Peacock Publishers, 1981

BROOKLYN LAW SCHOOL: *Symposium on Nuclear Weapons: A Fundamental Challenge,* Brooklyn Journal of International Law, Vol. IX, No. 2, 1983

BROWN, Lester: *World Without Borders,* Vintage Books, 1973

CALDICOTT, Helen: *Nuclear Madness,* Bantam, 1978

CHASE, Stuart: *Money To Grow On,* Harper & Row, 1964

CLARK, Grenville/SOHN, Louis: *World Peace Through World Law,* Harvard University Press, 1971

CORBETT, Percy: *The Growth of World Law,* Princeton University Press, 1971

CLUB OF ROME: *Reshaping the International Order,* Hutchinson, London, 1977

DANIKEN, Erich von: *Chariots Of The Gods,* Bantam, 1969; *Gods From Outer Space,* G.P. Putnam's Sons, 1971

DE MAIO, Ernest: *Taming The Multinationals,* Economic Notes July/Aug., 1982

DWINNEL, Oliver Cushin: *The Story Of Our Money,* Meador, 1946

EFFENDI, Shoghi: *The World Order of Baha'u'llah,* Bahai Publishing Trust, 1938

FALK, R./KIM, S.S./MENDLOVITZ, S.H.: *Toward A Just World Order,* Westview Press, 1982

FENNESSY, R.R.: *Burke, Paine & The Rights of Man,* Martinus Nyholl, The Hague, 1963

FULLER, Buckminster: *Utopia or Oblivion,* The Overlook Press, 1969; *Operating Manual For Planet Earth,* Dutton, 1978, Earth, Inc., Anchor Press, 1973

GLOSSOP, Ronald J.: *Confronting War,* McFarland & Co., 1983

GOMBERT, D./MANDELBAUM, M./GARWIN, R.L./BARTON, J.H.: *Nuclear Weapons and World Politics, Alternatives For The Future,* McGraw-Hill, 1977

GREEN, Timothy: *The World Of Gold,* Walker & Co., 1968

HAMILTON, Alexander/MADISON, James, JAY, John: *The Federalist,* 1788

HAZZARD, Hazel: *The Defeat Of An Ideal,* Little Brown & Co., 1973

HENDERSON, Hazel: *Creating Alternative Futures,* Little Brown & Co., 1973

HIRSCH, F./DOYLE, M./MORSE, E.L.: *Alternatives To Monetary Disorder*, McGraw-Hill, 1977

HOLLINS, Elizabeth Jay: *Peace Is Possible*, Grossman Publications, 1966

HUBBARD, Barbara Marx: *The Hunger Of Eve*, Stackpole Books, 1976

KELSO, Louis/HETTER, Patricia: *Two-Factor Theory*, Vintage Books, 1967

KELSO, Louis/ADLER, Mortimer: *The Capitalist Manifesto*, Random House, 1958

KING, J.C. & R.G.: *Manifesto For Individual Secession Into World Community*, Black Sun Press, Paris, 1948

KITSON, Arthur: *Trade Fallacies*, P.S. King & Son Ltd. London

KUTNER, Luis: *World Habeus Corpus*, Oceana Publishing, 1968; *Due Process of Rebellion*, Bardian House, 1974

LARSON, Arthur: *A Warless World: An Examination of Its Problems and Opportunities*, McGraw-Hill, 1962

LASZLO, Ervin et al: *Goals For Mankind*, E.P. Dutton, 1977

MACDOUGAL, Myres/LASSWELL, Chen: *Human Rights and World Public Order*, Yale University Press, 1980

MACLAINE, Shirley: *Out On A Limb*, Bantam, 1983

MADSEN, Axel: *Private Power*, Wm. Morrow, 1980

MARX, Karl/ENGELS, Friedrich: *The Communist Manifesto*, 1843

MCGREER, Gerald C.: *Conquest of Poverty*, Garden City Press, Canada

MENDLOVITZ, Saul H.: *Legal and Political Problems of World Order*, Institute For World Order, 1975; *On The Creation of a Just World Order*, The Free Press-Macmillan, 1975

MENG, J.J.: *The Constitutional Theories of Thomas Paine*, Review of Politics, VIII, 1946

MILLER, Arthur S.: *Presidential Power In A Nutshell*, West Publishing, 1977

MINTZ, Morton: *America, Inc.*, Dial Press, 1971

MISCHE, Gerald & Patricia: *Toward A Human World Order*, The Free Press, 1975

MORLEY, Felix: *The Power In The People*, D. van Nostrand, 1949

MRYDAL, Alva: *The Game Of Disarmament*, Random House, 1976

NADER, Ralph: *The Monopoly Makers*, Grossman, 1973

NASH, Vernon: *The World Must Be Governed*, Harpers & Brothers, 1949

NATARAJA GURU: *An Integrated Science of the Absolute*, Gurukula Publishing Co., India, 1977; *The Word Of The Guru*, Paico Publishing, India, 1952

NATHAN, Otto/NORDEN, Heinz: *Einstein On Peace*, Simon & Shuster, 1969

PAINE, Thomas: *The Rights of Man*, J.M. Dent & Sons, 1906

PIMNTEL, A. Fonseca: *Democratic World Government and the United Nations,* Escopo Editora, Brazil, 1980

POPE JOHN XXIII: *Pacem In Terris,* Paulist Press

REVEL, Jean-Francois: *Neither Marx Nor Jesus,* Doubleday, 1971

REVES, Emery: *The Anatomy of Peace,* Harpers & Brothers, 1945

RISKIN, Jeremy: *Entropy,* Viking Press, 1980

ROCHE, Douglas, M.P.: *Politicians For Peace,* NC Press Ltd., Canada, 1983

ROOSEVELT, Elliott: *The Conservators,* Arbor House, 1983

ROSIM, Carol Sue/GARFIELD, Charles, *Space Careers,* Quill, 1984

ROSSITER, Clinton: *The Political Thought of the American Revolution,* Harcourt, 1953

SAMPSON, Anthony: *The Sovereign-State of ITT,* Viking Press, 1975

SERVAN-SCHREIBER, J.J.: *The World Challenge,* Simon & Shuster, 1980

SIMONI, Arnold: *Beyond Repair. The Urgent Need for a New World Organization,* Collier McMillan, Canada, 1972

SMITH, Adam: *The Money Game,* Dell, 1967

STAFF STUDY: *Broadening The Ownership of New Capital: ESOP & Other Alternatives,* Congress of the United States, June 17, 1976

THOREAU, Henry David: *Walden and "Civil Disobedience",* New American Library, 1960

TOFFLER, Alvin: *The Third Wave,* Wm. Morrow, 1980

UNITED NATIONS: *The Economic and Social Consequences of Disarmament,* U.N. Publications, Sales No. 62.IX.1 (E/3593/Rev/1), 1962

U.S. BISHOPS: *The Pastoral Letter On War & Peace,* National Documentary Service, 1983

WALDHEIM, Kurt: *Building The Future Order,* Macmillan, 1980

WARD, Barbara/DUBOS, Rene: *Only One Earth,* W.W. Norton, 1972

WARD, Barbara: *Progress For A Small Planet,* George J. McLoed, Canada, 1979

WHITE, E.B.: *The Wild Flag,* Houghton-Mifflin Co., 1943

WILLENS, Harold: *The Trimtab Factor,* Wm. Morrow, 1984

WILLKIE, Wendell: *One World,* Simon & Shuster, 1943

WORLD COUNCIL OF CHURCHES/ROMAN CATHOLIC CHURCH: *Peace and Disarmament,* 1982

WYNNER, Edith/LLOYD, Georgia: *Searchlight On Peace Plans – Choose Your Road To World Government,* Dutton, 1944; reprint, 1949

INDEX

387

Journal de Droit International, 163
Juge d'Instruction, Tribunal de Grande
  Instance, Mulhouse, 354, 356
Justice under law, 208
Jurisdiction & general practice, art. 6, UN
  SG, 117

K

Kabul University, Afghanistan, 103
Kalinova, Mrs., 85, 86
Kandahar, 106, 107
Kant, Emmanuel, 343
Karame, Rachid, Prime Minister of
  Lebanon, 133
Karmal/USSR forces, 106
Karpov, Victor P., 52
Kaplan & Todd, 246
Kaya, Yusuf, 78/86, 89, 92
Khan, Mohammad Ayab, President of
  Pakistan, 136
KGB, 342
Kefauver, Sen. Estes, 282
Kehler, Randall, 273
Kelly, "The Uncertain Renaissance of
  the Ninth Amendment," 210
Kellogg-Briand Pact of 1928, 262, 264,
  265
Kelsey, "The Ninth Amendment of the U.S.
  Constitution," 210
Kelso, Louis, 308
  "Two-Factor Theory," 283
  "The Capitalist Manifesto," 308
Kelsonian economics, 303
Kennedy, John F., 135, 253
Kennedy Airport, 158
Kenyatta, Jomo, President of Kenya, 74, 132
Keynes, J.M., "The Economic Conse-
  quences of the Peace," 307
Keynes, Lord, 297, 299, 307
Khomeini, 329
Kilby, 44
Kitson, Arthur, 297
  "Trade Fallacies," 308
Kittikachoom, T., Prime Minister of
  Thailand, 132
Kirkpatrick, Jeanne, 143
Klein, Lawrence, 307
Kletter vs. Dulles, 161
KLM Flying Dutchman, 239
Kohl, W. German chancellor, 329

Krag, Jens Otto, Prime Minister of
  Denmark, 131
Kuniyuki v. Acheson, 153, 161
Kurland, Norman, 284, 303
Kushi, Michio, 350
Kutner, Luis, Chief Justice, World Court
  of Human Rights, 74-5-6, 89, 92, 207,
  208, 361
  "World Habeus Corpus," 55, 211
  "The Neglected Ninth Amendment," 210

L

Labor (Party), 141
La Guiari, 107
Laos, 119
Lao-Tse, 65
Lasswell, 154, 163, 165, 167
Law
  and space, 312, 313
  authority of, 162
  common, 211
  common world, 57
  common, against killing, 66
  constitutional, 211, 222
  creatures of 212
  due process, 21, 211
  exclusive national, 290
  federal nationality, 179
  French, 360
  human, 247
  international, 77, 118, 162, 165, 168,
  208, 209, 249, 250, 251, 255, 256, 259,
  260, 264, 303
  immigration, 159, 161, 181, 244
  local, 211
  Mauritanian, 184
  natural, 39, 56, 258, 262
  national, 40, 65, 93, 165, 168, 209, 211,
  219, 247, 267, 312, 336
  nationality, 181
  naturalization, 161, 181
  of fulfillment, 308
  of expectations, 308
  of human rights, 303
  on ship, 227
  of war, 208
  over anarchy, 219
  peace through, 224, 225, 324
  positive, 39, 55
  prime, 33

Order Forms

ORDER FORM

Juniper Ledge Publishing company
Post Office Box 381
Sorrento, ME 04677

Please send me the following books by Garry Davis

_____ copies of WORLD GOVERNMENT, READY   @ $14.95
     OR NOT!

_____ copies of MY COUNTRY IS THE WORLD   @ $4.95

Pamphlets
_____ copies of WHO OWNS THE WORLD?   @ $1.00

_____ copies of THE ELLSWORTH DECLARATION   @ $1.00

_____ copies of THE 1978 POSITION PAPER   @ $1.00

_____ copies of WRIT OF CERTIORARI (81-427)   @ $1.00

_____ copies of PETITION FOR REHEARING (81-427)   @ $1.00

_____ copies of the MEMORANDUM ON WORLD   @ $1.00
     GOVERNMENT by Nataraja Guru

I understand that I may return any book for a full refund if not satisfied.

NAME: _____

ADDRESS: _____

_____ ZIP: _____

Shipping: $1 for the first book and 25¢ for each additional book.

_____ I can't wait 3-4 weeks for Book Rate. Here is $2.50 per book for
Air Mail.

A complimentary copy of this book has been presented to all heads of state.

Immigration Director, 183
Immigration and Nationality Act of
1952, 111
Section 235B, 243
Immigration Court of Appeals, 357
Immigration (Japanese), 36
Imperial Presidency, 253
Inalienable right to travel, 247
India, 101
India, Varkala, 307
International Court of the Hague, 77, 162
Individual responsibility, 209
Industrial age, 39
Industrialization, 278
of developing countries, 304
Inflation, 279, 293, 296
elimination of, 141
long range, 299
Inflationary fire, 288, 299
Intensive poverty, 309
Inter Armes, Silent Leges, 212, 253
Interdependent industrial world, 302
Interest payments on federal debt, 307
Interest rates, 279, 288
Intergovernmental on Human Rights,
International
anarchy, 66, 124
authority, 33
government, 259
law, 249, 261
NGO's, 144
order, 31, 266
organizations, 28
orphan, 25
peace, 259, 265
penal code, 264
Red Cross, 102
territory, 117, 336
Paris, 27, 28, 336
trade, 292, 296
trade warfare, 292
International Association of Educators
for World Peace, 223
International Court at the Hague, 361
International Covenant on Civil &
Political Rights, 123
Art. 7, 91
Art. 9, 91
Art. 1, 91
International Conference on Peace &

Human Rights, 270
International Covenant on Human Rights, 122
International Harry Schultz Letter, 308
International Herald Tribune, 229, 232
International human rights and practices, 309
International Law Commission of Jurists,
256, 264
International Military Tribunal, 265, 316
International Monetary Fund, 298
International Registry of World Citizens,
Paris, 119
International Refugee Organization, 112
International section, 225
Iran, 101, 123, 293
Teheran, 105
Iranian hostage crisis, 61
Iraq, 101, 123
Salahudin, 101
Israel, 356
ITT, Chilean episode, 282

J

Jackson, Mr. Justice Robert, 207, 208
Jaffna, 106
Jamaica, Kingston, 102, 123
Japan, 223/7, 230, 234, 246
Anti-nuclear movement, 233
Tokyo, 223, 240/1
Japan Congress Against A & H Bombs,
223, 226
Japan Times, 225
Japanese
army, 178
Government, 231, 255
Immigration, 237
Ministry of Justice, 226, 234, 235
"Showa" 1947 Constitution, 254, 265
Art. 9, 226, 233, 265
Art. 13, 254
Jefferson, Thomas, 72, 138, 156, 166(note),
207, 269, 342
Declaration of the Causes & Necessity of
Taking Up Arms, 294
Jerusalem, 356
Johnson, L.B., 136, 253, 340
Jolly v. INS, 153, 160, 179
Jones, Judge Newton P., 245, 248
Jordan, Hashemite Kingdom of,
Allenby Bridge, 356

388

Order Forms

ORDER FORM

Juniper Ledge Publishing company
Post Office Box 381
Sorrento, ME 04677

Please send me the following books by Garry Davis

_____ copies of WORLD GOVERNMENT, READY   @ $14.95
       OR NOT!

_____ copies of MY COUNTRY IS THE WORLD   @ $4.95

Pamphlets
_____ copies of WHO OWNS THE WORLD?   @ $1.00

_____ copies of THE ELLSWORTH DECLARATION   @ $1.00

_____ copies of THE 1978 POSITION PAPER   @ $1.00

_____ copies of WRIT OF CERTIORARI (81-427)   @ $1.00

_____ copies of PETITION FOR REHEARING (81-427)   @ $1.00

_____ copies of the MEMORANDUM ON WORLD   @ $1.00
       GOVERNMENT by Nataraja Guru

I understand that I may return any book for a full refund if not satisfied.

NAME: _____

ADDRESS: _____

_____ ZIP: _____

Shipping: $1 for the first book and 25¢ for each additional book.

_____ I can't wait 3-4 weeks for Book Rate. Here is $2.50 per book for Air Mail.

A complimentary copy of this book has been presented to all heads of state.